The Theory and Practice of
Personnel Management

By the same author

Hospital Staff Management

Personnel Management in the National Health Service

The Theory and Practice of Personnel Management

Maurice W. Cuming

MA (Wales), FIPM

Seventh Edition

For Eira

Butterworth-Heinemann Ltd
Linacre House, Jordan Hill, Oxford OX2 8DP

PART OF REED INTERNATIONAL BOOKS

OXFORD LONDON BOSTON
MUNICH NEW DELHI SINGAPORE SYDNEY
TOKYO TORONTO WELLINGTON

First published 1968
Reprinted 1970
Second edition 1972
Third edition 1975
Reprinted 1977
Fourth edition 1980
Fifth edition 1985
Sixth edition 1989
Seventh edition 1993

© Maurice W. Cuming 1968, 1972, 1975, 1980, 1985, 1989, 1993

British Library Cataloguing in Publication Data
Cuming, Maurice W.
The theory and practice of personnel management
– 7th rev. ed.
I. Title
658.3

ISBN 0 7506 0713 0

Printed and bound in Great Britain

Contents

Preface

Looking back over the seven editions of this text it seems almost unbelievable that the economic and social climate of the UK has changed so much in the twenty-five years concerned.

I wrote the first chapter of the first edition in 1967 in the context of 'successive governments pursuing a policy of full employment and, apart from regional imbalances, being largely successful in doing so.' Today, in contrast, much of the manpower management carried out nationally, regionally and within individual organizations is undertaken in the context of high levels of unemployment and strenuous efforts to reduce labour costs.

One result is that in many respects the traditional principles of personnel management – justice, recognition of individuals' needs and democratic control methods – have been turned on their heads and harsh economic realities have become the accepted norm. The human relations school of management, fundamental to the style of personnel management advocated in this book, is under tight siege and may have to continue to maintain a low profile until the time when such ideals as appreciation of the dignity of labour and the right to work, and compassion, are restored as marks of civilized behaviour in the workplace and the labour market.

The steady decline of the UK's manufacturing base – in 1983 we became a net importer of manufactured goods for the first time since the Industrial Revolution – new information and production technologies, the government's sponsorship of an ideological shift towards individualism, as well as the very high levels of unemployment mentioned above: all these are factors which are making top managers re-think the models of personnel management appropriate to their organizations.

During the 1990s they will also have to tackle the practical implications of the 'demographic time-bomb'. The problem is simply that in 1983 there were a million young people in the age group 16−19 in the UK, who will not be here in 1993 (a fall of 28 per cent). Although the number of school-leavers will gradually increase from 1995 onwards, by the year 2000 there will still be 14 per cent fewer school-leavers than in 1990. The total size of the workforce will not fall, however, but will rise steadily to just over 28 million by the year 2000. So that success in the labour markets of the immediate future will go to those organizations with the flexibility to unlock talent in their existing workforce and in untapped pools outside.

Maurice Cuming

I

The personnel management function

Definitions

'To obtain and retain employees', or its Anglo-Saxon version – 'To get and keep workers' – is as good a nutshell definition of personnel management as any.

Most people who work in organizations large enough to have specialist personnel officers regard them, in the first place, as the people to whom they applied for their jobs. Their prime task is to *recruit* the number of employees of suitable calibre required to meet their organization's needs. Having got them, they are concerned to keep them happy so that they will want to stay. The personnel officer must see to it that employees are properly *trained* to cope with the demands of their jobs; otherwise they will feel inadequate, become increasingly frustrated, and eventually leave. They will not be happy if their *wages and working conditions* are unsatisfactory: if they feel their pay is unjust, or if hours of work, holidays or the physical environment around them are not what they should be – again they will try to improve on them elsewhere. Disputes that are not settled quickly will upset the delicate balance of *labour relations*. Changes introduced by management without prior consultation to obtain the views of all staff affected will have the same effect. Finally, most industrial communities have now developed a tradition of catering for the *welfare* of employees: helping them in times of need, for example, with sickness benefits and pension schemes, counselling about personal and domestic problems, and providing social facilities for leisure hours.

All these activities together amount to an organization's attempt to maintain a stable labour force and to stimulate the efforts of its members in a positive manner. To expand the 'snap' definition which opened this chapter, then, *personnel management is concerned with obtaining the best possible staff for an organization and, having got them, looking after them so that they will want to stay and give of their best to their jobs.*

There is, of course, a definition that is 'official', in the sense that it is published by the Institute of Personnel Management (IPM). This reads:

> Personnel management is that part of management concerned with people at work, and with their relationships within an enterprise. Its aim is to bring together and to develop into an active organization the men and women who make up an enterprise and, having regard for the well-being of the individual and of working groups, to enable them to make their best contribution to its success. Personnel management is concerned with the human and social implications of change in organizations and methods of working within enterprises, and of economic and social changes in the community.

The scope of personnel management

By no means can all the functions listed below be found in every personnel department up and down the country, but they do cover the range of tasks found in the personnel departments of most large commercial and industrial organizations and in public authorities.

1   Employment

Manpower planning.
Preparation of job descriptions.
Contact with and development of all potential sources of labour supply.
Interviewing applicants for jobs; engaging labour; transfers; promotions; dismissals.
Maintenance of employee records and control statistics.
Application of the organization's terms and conditions of employment; hours of work; overtime.
Grading of employees.
Legislation concerning employment.
Cooperating with employment schemes of the Department of Employment.

2 *Training and education*

Induction and job training of all new entrants; follow-up of their progress.
Provision of instructors and training officers.
Youth Training Scheme.
Development of potential supervisors and managers.
Encouraging further education through the public higher education system and distance learning schemes.
Arranging programmes of visitors for works tours.
Provision of a library.
Meeting legal requirements.
Cooperating with the training schemes of the Training Agency and local Training and Enterprise Councils (TECs).

3 *Wages and salaries*

Maintenance of the organization's wage and salary structure.
Job evaluation – control of differential rates of pay.
Measurements of individual performance – incentives, merit-rating (usually with work study experts).
Running a suggestions scheme.

4 *Industrial relations*

Publishing and interpreting the organization's personnel policy.
Negotiating with trade unions, through a recognized procedure for dealing with workplace grievances.
Providing opportunities for participation and consultation so that all types and grades of employees may join in the management of their organizations.
Publishing a staff magazine; controlling notice boards and information bulletins.
Representing the organization in outside negotiations affecting its staff.

5 *Welfare services and safety*

Employee amenities – canteen, rest rooms, etc.
Superannuation; long-service grants.

Legal aid; counselling about individual personal or domestic
problems.
Assistance with accommodation and transport difficulties.
Provision of social and recreational facilities.
Application of provisions of the Health and Safety at Work Act;
contact with Inspectorate.
Occupational health service – medical examination of employees,
keeping health records, and visiting sick absentees; sickness pro-
visions.
Accident prevention; safety education.

Historical development

The origins of personnel management can be found wherever enlightened employers have tried over the years to improve the lot of their
workers. The activities of such men as the Duke of Bridgewater, Lord
Shaftesbury and Wedgwood are well known; by the mid-nineteenth
century, Courtaulds had something approaching a guaranteed minimum wage scheme for their workers. Robert Owen (1771–1858) is best
remembered for his trade union activities, but he also incurred the
wrath of his business partners by spending some of their profits on
improving the working and living conditions of his labour force at New
Lanark. Perhaps his most enduring memorial, however, are the
principles of management that he pioneered – particularly the right of
all his employees, however low in the hierarchy, to see him personally
on any matter concerning their welfare. This right of access to the
highest authority is still not freely available to industrial workers, 150
years after Robert Owen's insistence upon it in his woollen mills.

Social change developed apace towards the end of the nineteenth
century. The Education Act of 1870 resulted in the growth of a literate
working class, which in turn became much more receptive of the ideas
of trade unions and their activities in improving working conditions.
Religious motives inspired the remarkable social work of employers
like Rowntree and Cadbury, whose own workers benefited directly, of
course.

The emphasis on the provision of welfare facilities grew, marked in
1913 by the formation of the Welfare Workers Association; in 1916 this
became the Central Association of Welfare Workers, in 1924 the
Institute of Industrial Welfare Workers, and after other changes in
name, the Institute of Personnel Management in 1946. A large number
of welfare workers, mainly female, were appointed during the years of
the First World War, particularly in munitions factories. Their
theoretical aim was to try to being closer together the clashing interests

of employers and workers; in practice, their efforts concentrated on making working conditions more congenial, experimenting with fringe benefits, and providing social amenities for leisure hours. Employers split away to form their own organization in 1919: this was the Industrial Welfare Society, which changed its name to the Industrial Society in 1965. Its original aims were to foster the exchange of ideas and information about welfare policies and techniques, but these have long since been broadened to cover the whole field of personnel management.

The *welfare* phase was a period of time, then, when deliberate efforts were made to create the ideal factory, in which the physical environment was perfect in terms of cleanliness, temperature, and lighting, and where worthwhile leisure pursuits were offered to workers in their spare time.

A marked reaction to this sort of paternalism soon developed. Workers always question the unsolicited provision of costly welfare facilities; most of them would prefer to have the money in their weekly pay packets instead. Inevitably, too, paternalism means influencing the private lives of workers: it is wishful thinking for employers to consider their labour force as a family, motivated by the care they show for their welfare. Lavish amenities might attract some types of employees to an organization in the first place, but they will not act as incentives for them to stay; more profound psychological needs must be satisfied to achieve this.

During the 1920s and 1930s Great Britain, in common with most industrial nations, went through long years of economic depression. Inevitably this caused a cutting back of non-essentials in industry, and many welfare departments were closed. The whole climate of economic opinion was negative; by and large, employers adopted a casual approach to labour, hiring and firing almost at will, and accepting no responsibilities towards their employees other than those required by law. For their part, workers feared insecurity so much that they were only too ready to accept whatever jobs and conditions were offered; in such circumstances, trade unions could be nothing else but on the defensive.

Efforts by the Government and progressive employers to overcome the depression led to the emergence of the second main phase in the development of personnel management – the *scientific management* phase. The building of trading estates up and down the country and the expansion of light engineering factories depended largely on their owners' appreciation of the advantages of maintaining stable labour forces. The protagonists of scientific management argued in favour of clearly defined organization structures, each job within them being precisely described. The employees filling these jobs should be carefully selected, given appropriate training, and be provided with an environment conducive to efficient working. Even the economies of high wages, directly influencing labour stability, came to be realized.

These developments were accompanied by research projects controlled by industrial psychologists who aimed to improve selection tests and training methods, and investigated aspects of working conditions, for example, those causing fatigue and boredom. They particularly concerned themselves with worker motivation, seeking to understand people's reasons for working and the factors influencing their morale, in order to devise effective incentives to stimulate them to greater efforts. The result of all this activity was that personnel management became increasingly accepted during the 1930s as being able to offer a positive service to industry and commerce in terms of profitability.

Government recognition came with the Second World War, which brought about the third stage of development – the *industrial relations* phase. During the war, the cry was for continually increased production to meet the demands of the war effort. The emphasis was on cooperation – 'we must all pull together to win': management and trade unions were asked to forget the acrimony of the depression years and combine their energies to win the war. The growth of factory joint consultation, particularly the establishment of joint production committees designed to tap workers' ideas for improving efficiency, was symptomatic of this concept. The Government encouraged the appointment of personnel officers throughout industry, and sponsored crash training programmes for these specialists at universities. A Personnel Management Advisory Service was created, attached to the Ministry of Labour; this, updated, still exists and employers can call on the services of an officer from the Department of Employment's Advisory, Conciliation and Arbitration Service for advice about their staffing problems. Clearly, this demand for cooperation has remained with us: the need to export more to improve the balance of payments and the need to increase productivity to improve standards of living – both are familiar invocations, and both emphasize overcoming the 'them-and-us' mentality in industry. If we all produce more, we will all benefit.

Thus there has been nothing altruistic about the ways in which personnel management has developed. Innovations have tended to be based on the assumption that what is good for the individual is good for the organization as well. Each step forward can be seen as an investment to enhance the contribution, and thus the value, of the labour force, with the ultimate aim of enabling individuals to see that their interests and those of the organization for which they work are the same.

To a large extent, political and economic events have determined the development of personnel management activities since the Second World War. Successive governments in Great Britain pursued a policy of full employment until the mid-1970s, and were largely successful. Anti-inflationary measures, taken to counter worldwide trends of rising prices, then adversely affected this situation with unemployment rising above 2 million in 1981 and touching 3 million in early 1993.

Management's efforts at getting the best return from its labour force led to a fourth phase in the development of personnel management – that of *manpower planning*: on the one hand, trying to deploy the total labour resources available to an organization in the most efficient manner; and, on the other, getting the best from each individual by developing to the full whatever potential he/she has to be trained for bigger and better jobs.

On the national scale this has involved economic planning, with measures to encourage industry to move to those regions with the highest unemployment and to persuade labour to move from contracting to expanding industries. At the level of the individual firm, the concept of manpower planning involves techniques of assessing the suitability of employees in their present jobs and devising training programmes to develop their potential to meet estimated future staff requirements. More and more, too, the participation of the individual is demanded, with encouragement to play a positive part in the staff assessment procedures which determine the pattern of his/her future career; and there is much more concern being shown for immediate improvements in performance, for example by applying the technique of management by objectives.

In recent years there has also been a considerable increase in government 'intervention' across the whole range of personnel management activity, aimed both at securing continuous growth in the country's economy and at developing a greater sense of social justice throughout the nation. There has been decisive, though not always successful, action taken on such matters as improving employment and training facilities, prices and incomes policies, attempts to control industrial relations, better protection for individual workers in employment, improvements in working conditions and accident prevention.

Nothing emerges more clearly from this sketch of the history of personnel management than the increasing emphasis on the word 'management' in the phrase. Much of the work of a personnel department has always been routine in nature, applying established policies and procedures, well understood by the line managers being advised, to solve the sort of staff problems that crop up day by day in any business. Necessary as it is, this type of activity is basically routine or administrative in nature; for example, the provision of personnel records, recruitment services, wage and salary administration, and welfare facilities. But personnel specialists have, in addition, a much more dynamic role to play in the efficient management of their organization. They must be able to advise how present staff and labour resources can be adapted to meet future requirements. To draw a medical analogy, their function should be that of diagnosing the problems inherent in the current situation, and then prescribing the action that must be taken for their organization to move from the here-and-now to its forecasted future position. This function is obviously much more creative than any form of routine administration.

Other, developing roles for the personnel manager can be linked to the significant economic and social upheavals which have swept through the world during the past decade, emphasizing the need for modern managers to act as leaders and for the personnel specialist to be seen as a special agent of change.

Thus within British industrial experience, Sir Peter Parker, former chairman of British Rail:

> The railway strikes of 1982 offer a parable of personnel management: it makes the central point of reality – that there is a constant clash of the long-term with the day-to-day which erupts, distorts and aborts plans and hopes. It is hard to get any movement without friction or if there is no vision of the future. It is hard to deal day-to-day with what is wrong if there is no clear idea of what is right long-term. Change is hard to achieve in any organization in isolation of the social changes going on outside it. I look to personnel management to help managers – and unions – to understand the interdependence of the different culture of the enterprise and of the community.*

Another relevant analysis of the same truth has been made by a former managing director of ICI, John Harvey-Jones:

> The great change in our society, and a long overdue one, is the realization that it is totally impossible to achieve anything in industry without the freely-given collaboration of all people in the organization. Where that mutuality exists, the results have been staggering, e.g., in Japan. Japanese, American and British management is 95 per cent the same – and differs in all important respects. That decisive 5 per cent factor – the 5 per cent mystery – lies in the mutuality of social and industrial purposes. Of all the functions in enterprise, personnel management is most responsible for demystifying that 5 per cent. It is the function charged with special responsibilities to sustain the effectiveness

*Personnel Management, January 1983, page 16.

of human resources corporately, and in parallel to extend every individual's sense of scope at work. To succeed, personnel management must be increasingly involved in the effort to clarify the social policy of enterprise.*

Thus the immediate future of personnel management seems likely to centre around the concept of citizens at work – their expectations to have reasonable access to information and authority, to education and a career open to talent, to being consulted on matters which they feel shape their problems and prospects. Personnel managers will have much to say about how employers diagnose, anticipate and cope with those expectations – recognizing the mutual interdependence of what any citizen looks for on and off the job to make something of him/herself.

The extent to which personnel management has moved into yet another historical phase – that of *human resource management* – is debatable, because some argue that the term is simply a new way of expressing what most good personnel managers have been practising for many years. Certainly the development has been recognized by the IPM, which has subtitled its journal *The Magazine for Human Resource Professionals*.

Human resource management (HRM) should be understood as a total approach to the strategic management of the key human resource (not just employees) which is the responsibility of 'the board', given advice from personnel specialists. In that context, personnel management is concerned both with providing that advice and the services required to implement top management's plans. In practice, of course, this new emphasis placed on the direct responsibility of top management could be very helpful: there may be nothing new in the basic idea of HRM, but over the years it is probably true to say that too little attention has been paid to it in too many organizations.

Accepting that human resources are the most important that an organization has, and that their effective management is essential, the principle underlying HRM is that success is most likely to be achieved if personnel policies and practices clearly and positively contribute to the achievement of corporate objectives and strategic plans. Integration – getting all staff and employees working together with a sense of common purpose – is an important aim of HRM, yet it must be achieved while acknowledging that all organizations are pluralistic societies in which groups of people have different interests.

Undoubtedly one of the main thrusts towards the HRM approach

Ibid.

has been the much-heralded success of Japanese management. This typically centres on the creation of powerful organizational cultures from which are derived shared values between management and workers that emphasize 'mutuality' – a common interest in achieving excellence.

HRM, then, is a strategic approach to the acquisition, motivation, development and management of the organization's human resources. Its programme must be relevant to the organization's circumstances – its purpose, its technology and the methods of working, the environment in which it operates, its dynamics (rate of growth or change), the type of people it employs and its industrial relations situation (presence and strength of trade unions). In particular, the importance of HRM policies and activities fitting the corporate culture is crucial. 'Culture' in this sense embraces a system of shared values (what is important) and beliefs (how things work) which interact with an organization's people, structure and control systems to produce behavioural norms (the way things are done around here).

In turn, strategies must be translated into corporate plans, and a typical human resources plan* might fall under three headings:

1 *People* – improving quality, developing potential.
2 *Performance* – increasing the accountability of managers for results, relating pay more specifically to performance, increasing commitment by better communications and more involvement.
3 *Productivity* – analysing the use of human resources throughout the organization so that planned growth is achieved with lower costs per unit of output.

An excellent practical statement of an HRM policy† is that devised by the strategy group of the Wessex Regional Health Authority:

● Effectively plan and control the size and mix of the workforce to ensure that every employee is fully utilized and able to meet the challenges of work.
● Attract, develop and retain good staff at all levels.
● Encourage understanding of business objectives and the need to improve quality, effectiveness and efficiency.
● Help maintain an informed and motivated workforce.

*'CF Analysis and the Book Club Associates Case Study', Michael Armstrong, *Personnel Management*, August 1987, pages 30–5.
†*Putting People First*, Alex Selkirk, Director of Personnel, Wessex Regional Health Authority.

- Manage staff fairly and with clear respect for each individual employee.
- Make full use of the freedoms now available progressively to extend the scope for flexibility in local determination of pay and other benefits for staff.
- Provide equal opportunities in employment to all staff based purely on their abilities.
- Develop comprehensive and effective education, training and development strategies.

However, the development of HRM is not without controversy. We have seen that the approach emphasizes the common interests of employer and employee in the success of the organization, and hence acts as an important stimulant for commitment. The trouble is that this 'unitary' view is alleged to involve bypassing traditional channels of communication and weakening the position of trade unions. Is this deliberate on management's part? The use of briefing groups, quality circles and new communication techniques ranging from videos to personal chats from top managers – all have the effect of relegating trade unions to the side-lines.

The re-discovered right of managers to manage is being acted up in ways which mean that management gives its version of the world direct to the workforce, unmediated by the trade unions. The aim of management is quite clearly suspected to be that of getting the workforce 'on their side' and subsequently effecting changes in working practice – a long-sought goal in many industries.

Trade unions inevitably see the HRM approach as a threat to traditional collective bargaining and collective problem-solving, and tend to deride it as a means of seeking to secure commitment and flexibility from employees in exchange for relatively high pay and promises of job security (which last until the next re-structuring exercise). Thus while accepting that more stress may sometimes be placed on employee's involvement, consultation and deepening per-ception of economic realities, union leaders charge that all this is programmed on management's terms, with pressure on employees to conform to practices which suit management's objectives: otherwise they face the threat that jobs will be lost and plants close down.

It is often claimed that the HRM approach has a broader vision than the traditional 'personnel and industrial relations' approach, emphasizing such aspects as innovation, flexibility, improvement and change, openness of communications, teamwork, rewards based on results, delegation of authority, total quality, and providing opportunities for individuals to develop their full potential. Fine-sounding concepts – but how realistic all this is in practice, at a time when economic conditions force such cuts in labour costs that hundreds and thousands of employees lose their jobs means that the debate on these points will continue, as they imply unilateral managerial action in pursuit of business strategies, all of which must in future be viewed in the context of a unified Europe. The completion of the internal market, in conjunction with the movement towards monetary union and closer co-ordination of many other aspects of policy, offer the potential for stronger economic performance, more balanced development and closer social cohesion within the community.

It must be acknowledged, however, that continuity of progress in these directions will be challenged in the foreseeable future by the controversy surrounding the European Commission's Social Charter and the extent to which member states may be permitted to retain parts of their traditional systems of personnel management. Opportunities for change, implicit in the founding Treaty of Rome, clearly emerge from the work of the Commission's Action Programme Group. A large number of topics, affecting both individual employment and collective rights are on the agenda for change, including, for example: minimum age for employment, transport for disabled work people, parental leave, child care, overtime hours, new directives on health and safety, freedom of movement of labour between states, control over subcontracts and job creation.

These Social Charter proposals start what may well become a very long process aimed at creating a common European framework of conditions of employment which will take precedence over national systems and rules. Individual employees will possess legally enforceable general rights in detail, subject to interpretation by local courts. Employers will be constrained to fulfil certain basic obligations towards their employees, covering the working environment, safety, employment contracts, and duties to consult, share information and provide opportunities for participation. It might take years to settle all these matters, particularly in view of the intention to preserve some aspects of local systems of social security and employment law. Indeed qualification structures, minimum wage legislation, social welfare provision and collective bargaining procedures will not be harmonized, and differences of national income will be allowed to persist.

Many of these aims may be admirable in concept — but it must be recognized that practical reality within the European market is based on competition, not on the Social Charter. One consequence is that total unemployment figures may continue to rise, even though skill shortages for some specialists may intensify. The internationalization of management may result in conflict rather than tolerance and harmony. Mobility across frontiers may cause difficulties over identity, motivation and commitment. Resistance to the 'new European model' can be anticipated from the great American and Japanese multi-nationals. Again, can a balanced pluralist system of consultation and participation be developed in the face of the trades unions' own crisis of declining membership?

Great pressures may therefore emerge to push individual organizations towards the fuller integration of their human resources policies and practices with their business strategies. Managers of the future, may welcome the collapse of predominantly national models of HRM, at the same time resisting the creation of any new European model. Yet there are already enough examples of successful achievement (Shell, Olivetti, Siemens*) throughout Europe to counter any cynicism. The largest companies realize that they must compete as hard to attract and keep labour as they must in selling their products and services. The high priority issues which they have to address are: standards of and links between education and vocational training: working time patterns; systems of performance incentives; co-ownership and employee involvement; relationships with local conditions and communities; contracting out of services; the introduction of technology; job organization; management of change; mobility; and attracting females and older workers into the labour force.

The successful personnel manager

It is significant, in the context of this detailed account of the function, to acknowledge research done to analyse the component factors of successful personnel management. One such attempt used what the authors admitted to be a crude index of success — that of relating age to grade, so that those personnel managers classed as most successful combined greatest youth with highest rank, while the least successful reflected greatest age with lowest rank ($n = 52$).

The general conclusions of this study, perhaps not surprisingly, suggested that effectiveness within the personnel function is determined by:

(a) The background and experience of personnel staff.
(b) The nature of the personnel role and the tasks performed.
(c) The relative power of the personnel function.

*'Towards a European Approach to Personnel Management' by Keith Thurley; *Personnel Management*, September 1990, page 57.

Individual background   Effectiveness in   Individual
Personnel role   }   role performance   →   career
Power of personnel function   success

Using this model, detailed scrutiny of the careers of personnel staff reveals a 'profile' of the successful personnel manager as possessing these characteristics: graduate; has changed jobs regularly within the organization; reports to someone outside the personnel function; and is a member of the IPM. However, it is recognized that this conclusion is based on rather oblique and subjective measures of effectiveness rather than demonstrable performance in the role.

The cult of excellence, propounded by Peters and Waterman in their seminal work, *In Search of Excellence*, can be applied directly to personnel management through each of the eight homely-sounding precepts which have made their advocacy so famous: viz. keep ahead; practice makes perfect; only connect; simplify, simplify, simplify; stimulate to accumulate; never say die; look after the pennies; and keep the customers happy.

'Keeping ahead' concentrates attention on the crucial need to cope with change – both predicting and being fully prepared to deal with it. Making time to read and think, maintaining contacts with a broad cross-section of other managers, staying attuned to the direction of the business, contingency planning for a range of eventualities, forecasting the possible consequences of actions: all are features of this aspect of success. The thoughtful assessment of industrial relations and employment law will minimize risk or threats to the organization's objectives. Having procedures available to deal with redundancies, disciplinary issues, statutory sick pay problems and renumeration systems are other examples of the concept in practice.

The thrust of 'better value for money' also clearly impacts on personnel management: changes in work organization (greater use of part-timers or contract workers operating from their homes), the review of productivity schemes, harmonization of staff-labour status and 'annual hours' contracts are all steps which can enhance employees' own sense of responsibility and bring about both greater flexibility and simplified management and bargaining.

It is characteristic of successful personnel managers that they are never satisfied: they question conventional ways of doing things and recommend innovations. 'Practice makes perfect' leads to so many new things: recruitment and recent developments in psychological testing, training and the applications of the Youth Training Scheme are two good current examples. Close scrutiny of what best suits an organization and the style of its management requires consistent and continuous effort if communication and consultation with employees are to be improved, and then assiduous follow-up is so often the key to long-lasting success.

'Only connect' – connection between managers of the variety of functions within an organization is vital. Who else needs to know about personnel initiatives? What does the personnel manager need to know about production, marketing, sales, customer relations and financial management? Public affairs, outside the organization but impinging on it, also demand attention.

The cry 'simplify, simplify' applies to all business activity, and hence to personnel management: to statements of policy, to procedures, to the management of time, to ensuring that all individual employees know and understand their particular places within their organization, to convening meetings only to produce results and action.

Fifth, constant stimulation of employees is essential in the cause of progress: two-way communication in full with employees develops that respect and trust on which future success so much depends; i.e. stimulate to accumulate.

'Never say die' in personnel management terms means pursuing what are believed to be high standards of practice, if possible without compromise: particularly, for example, to take initiatives which may call for financial investment when it is very difficult to quantify results. Thus some types of training or efforts to equip redundant employees for new jobs must be accepted as worthwhile acts of faith.

The precept to 'look after the pennies' is another with universal application, and personnel managers must try to ensure the best possible value for money in services rendered throughout the organization. But to cost-consciousness must be added the quality of taking pains to teach and train all other managers in the best policies and practices for dealing with employees within their own units and departments. These are all 'the customers' as far as the personnel manager is concerned – board members, managers and employees alike – and success comes only as the result of perseverance and a consistent approach aimed at keeping them happy.

Theories on organization

Parallel with these developments in the procedures and practices of personnel management have been changes in that branch of management theory concerned with explaining the social organization of industry.

The *classical school*, largely influenced by the principles of scientific management, saw any organization as being firmly directed by one central authority within it, supreme and unquestionable. Organization charts made clear this unity of direction, illustrated the concepts of division of labour and span of control, and defined the lines of command. These followed the military pattern, which also set the tone for a code of employee behaviour based on loyalty and discipline – each individual willingly doing what was expected of him and not doing things which might harm the organization. Management's leadership task was to create conditions that would foster this loyalty among staff; there could be no opposition between management and worker representatives, and both had to pull together to eliminate possible areas of conflict. Since efficiency depended on the clear exercise of qualities of personal leadership, the prerogative of management to manage must be kept intact; for example, the payment of high wages was seen both as a long-term economy and as an indication that negotiations with trade unions were unnecessary. The classical view of loyalty to the authority controlling the organization thus also implied that there should be no interference with its members from any outside body whether trade union, professional association, or government agency.

The *human relations school* saw authority as an attribute requiring acceptance by subordinates, rather than something that they gave up to management. Mayo's research at the Hawthorne Works of the General Electric Company in Chicago had proved that informal leaders emerge in working groups, and that each of these groups is likely to develop its own goals and standards of behaviour which may well be opposed to those of the official organization. Conflict was seen not as a symptom of the technical incompetence of management, but as a weakness in the social skills of individual leaders resulting in breakdowns in communications between management and workers.

Modern *system theory* sees each organization as a complete whole, influenced by its formal and informal structure, external conditions, technological factors, and the individual personalities of its employees. The concept of *role expectations* is a product of this theory – people at work like their relationships with each other to be predictable, otherwise they feel uncomfortable or under strain. Role conflict occurs when an individual is subjected to pressures from different sources and cannot comply with them all; or when the demands of his/her role in one group are not compatible with demands made of him/her in another group. Role ambiguity occurs when people do not fully understand their job nor the expectations that other people have of their role. Both role conflict and role ambiguity cause the individuals affected to feel anxious, which in turn generates stress within the organization, thus making it less effective. Members of working groups cast their fellows and superiors in roles that are prescribed by their own expectations; and there is great pressure, because of the desire for predictability, for these roles to remain stable. Hence the reason why it is so difficult to make social changes, even in times of rapid technological advance.

Joan Woodward* has also proved that the technology of an industry demands certain forms of organization if a business is to be successful. Particular human relations difficulties emerge according to the type of technology concerned. In factories making motor cars, the manufacturing system means that large groups of employees work under conditions of strain and pressure, determined by the speed of the production line, with each supervisor in charge of a large number of workers; in other technologies, for example oil and chemical processing, production arrangements are such that workers are much less harassed and each supervisor has many fewer workers to control. The more leisurely atmosphere in the latter case means that staff problems which arise can be solved more readily. Where the technology is such that change inevitably takes a long time, the chances are better for reaching amicable solutions to the problems usually associated with the introduction of change. Joan Woodward's conclusions clearly show that when creating organization structures, and in trying to stabilize relationships between staff, considerable attention must be paid to the technological demands of the industry or service concerned.

Analysing the historical development of organizational theory led Alan Fox† to plead for management to adopt a frame of reference in the field of labour relations, based on an acceptance of the fact that organizations are composed of individuals and groups with some interests in common but with others in conflict. Managers should stop yearning for teams, families or 'happy ships', and face the reality of workgroups' interests that conflict, quite legitimately, with their own. 'The test of success here is how far management seeks honestly to understand the causes of work-group attitudes and policies, and why they are different from those of management. Failure lies in lacking the patience to find out, in refusing to take seriously the problems of those whose work and life experience is different from one's own, and in dismissing their policies as merely stupid, short-sighted or selfish. There must be recognition that the legitimacy of unions rests not on the misdeeds of (other) managers, but on a socially preferred method of shared decision-making on labour matters. Given that "loyalty" is not an appropriate measure of behaviour in a contractual, impersonal employment relationship, it follows that a man can be aggressive in defence of his or his fellows' rights and still be a valuable employee.

Industrial Organization: Theory and Practice, Joan Woodward (Oxford University Press, 1965).
†'Managerial Ideology and Labour Relations', Alan Fox, *British Journal of Industrial Relations,* November 1966, page 375.

Management's job is that of engineering the highest level of reconciliation among the divergent interests of their divided, pluralistic realm.'

Exhortation has, so far, failed to achieve this state of affairs, and coercion is clearly impractical. What have emerged in recent years, under the guise of productivity bargaining, are attempts to effect structural change through negotiation. Such bargaining illustrates that some aspects of structure which management is seeking to change are positively valued by employees, and they will be strongly defended unless a sufficient *quid pro quo* is offered in exchange.

Justification

How, in this development of theory and practice, have personnel managers emerged as specialists? What peculiar contribution do they make to the efficiency of an organization?

The primary justification, as with any other appointment, must be in terms of business efficiency. The salaries and wages costs of most organizations form a substantial part of total expenditure, in many service industries rising higher than 75 per cent. Capital is also invested in buildings to accommodate these staff and to furnish their rooms; senior staff are provided with assistants and with secretarial and clerical help. The overall concern of personnel management is to make sure that these huge investments are put to the best use.

This cannot be done without regard to fundamental concepts of human relations. Clearly no organization can operate efficiently unless its staff are content with what is offered them as human beings by way of job satisfaction, prospects, and working conditions. The personnel specialist's task is to identify the needs of employees in these areas, recognize what it is about the organization that fulfils these needs or frustrates them, and be able to advise departmental managers on actions that will promote this fulfilment or remove the frustrations. Heads of departments basically have technical responsibilities; the personnel specialist's job is to explain to them reasons for social behaviour which may not be obvious. Why, for example, are decisions that are technically and economically sound sometimes met by seemingly irrational resistance by subordinates? What emotional factors are at play when this sort of thing happens? Offering advice to clarify such situations is a task that demands an expert who has been trained to perceive the ways in which individuals and groups interact within an organization, and who can convey his/her understanding in practical terms to departmental heads who are too preoccupied with their technical activities to have time to consider the social system of the workplace as a whole.

It would clearly be too much to expect personnel managers to practise all the behavioural sciences – psychology, anthropology, sociology, and others – but their training should be such that they can make intelligent use of the conclusions reached by such scientists.

An organizational structure consists of the work necessary to achieve that organization's objectives, divided into job-sized pieces, held together by a network of contacts and procedures between jobs and subunits. In that an organization is a social organism as well as an administrative or operational mechanism, there is inevitably complex interaction between its human and social components and its ability as a structural mechanism to achieve its business or service objectives. The *raison d'être* for personnel management is to help the organization achieve those objectives.

If the human, social and structural characteristics of the organization are so inextricably linked, it follows that personnel managers will not develop the full potential of their function unless they are as proficient in organizational analysis as they are in diagnosing human and social needs.

Advisory role

The role of personnel managers has been tagged as acting as 'the social conscience of an organization', and it is clear that, as such, they are in a position to contribute considerably to the state of its staff morale. But it is important that this contribution is understood as being of an advisory nature: executive decisions must finally be taken by the line managers to whom advice is offered.

'Line' management can perhaps most readily be understood in terms of military organization, which imposes a clear line of command from the most senior officer down to the private soldier. Line managers are held fully accountable for the results achieved and everything else that happens in their departments; they are given orders from above and carry them out, often by passing on instructions to their own subordinates.

The personnel specialist, on the other hand, is a 'staff' or 'functional' manager, offering an expert service of advice to line managers to help them perform their jobs. Other examples are the legal officer, cost accountant, or work study officer – together with the personnel manager, all these specialists advise, assist, and service line managers, but have no direct authority over them or their staff. They work with senior colleagues through ideas, relying mainly on persuasion. Of course, to the extent that the personnel specialist's ideas are useful, timely, and generally acceptable, line managers will come to ask for his/her advice and will take it when given. When such advice is consistently put into effect, there is inevitably some blurring of the distinction between 'executive authority' and 'functional advice', but in such circumstances this is a welcome situation rather than one that should be resisted.

Nevertheless, in the last resort, it must be abundantly clear to everyone working in an organization that final authority rests in the hands of the chief executive. Otherwise personnel managers could well find themselves caught in a dilemma when some issue is raised where they personally feel that the viewpoint of their management colleagues is wrong. Such problems sometimes arise over individual cases of fair treatment, for example where promotion is concerned or hours of work of some employees are changed; personnel managers could well find themselves faced with a clash between the decisions of general management and their own view of the right thing to do.

In fact, difficulties of this nature only occur where executive powers are ascribed to personnel specialists, and when they are put into the position of having to arbitrate between management and employees. This sort of situation simply should not be allowed to develop. The chief executive must retain ultimate control and there should be no blurring of line management's responsibilities by even a partial transfer of executive authority to a specialist adviser; otherwise there is a risk of contradictory policies emerging.

The Commission on Industrial Relations (CIR) fully analysed the role of the personnel specialist in a report* published in 1973, suggesting the following considerations as an aid to the evolution of constructive management relationships. First, both personnel and line managers need the authority to carry out their respective functions. Line managers are necessarily responsible for industrial relations (defined as embracing the broad range of all employment policies) in their particular area of operations; and they need freedom to manage their plant, department or section effectively within agreed policies and with access to specialist advice. Personnel managers should help by supplying expert knowledge and skill and by monitoring the consistent execution of personnel policies and programmes throughout the organization. They need the backing of top management and must establish the authority which comes from giving sound advice.

Constant cross-consultation and collaboration between line and personnel managers make both more effective. Line managers should be involved in formulating personnel policies and plans. 'The personnel manager is an integral part of the management team, and whatever his position in their hierarchy should be consulted and be able to

*CIR Report No. 34, *The Role of Management in Industrial Relations* (HMSO).

influence all decisions where there are human implications.' The relationship between the two is likely to be constructive, however, only if there are clearly defined personnel policies which enable all managers to work towards the same objectives. Ultimately management's responsibility for good personnel practices is collective.

Such a view is readily acceptable as a theoretical concept, but needs to be illustrated by practical examples to achieve full credibility. One such case-study* is that of Watts, Blake, Beame & Co. Ltd, producers of ball and china clay in Devonshire, and employers of 760 operatives, tradespeople, maintenance people, designers, engineers, research staff, salespeople, and managers. The company has developed a philosophy and management style based on involvement and participative principles requiring a high degree of mutual trust and respect for individual abilities, but there is no dilution of management's authority and responsibility to manage the company. Using the well-known definition of management as 'getting work done through people', it follows that line management must have a close and effective relationship with the people they manage. They must be responsible for the employment, training, safety, supervision, and, if necessary, discipline and dismissal, of all employees under their control. In order for this system of employment to function effectively, the company takes great care to train line managers to operate it, and safeguards are built into its personnel policy to ensure that it is administered fairly and equitably overall.

Perhaps the clearest example of the attribution of responsibility for staff management is that of wage and salary negotiations: these are conducted by the managing director and production director, after extensive consultation with divisional managers. Results of negotiations are then immediately communicated to divisional and department managers, who in turn brief all their employees. This is duplicated by shop stewards and employee representatives throughout the company, but nevertheless it is considered important that line management should observe their own direct responsibility for communicating and implementing information.

Such an example is in contrast to the national tendency in recent years for personnel matters and, in particular, wage negotiations to be transferred from line management to personnel departments. This trend has undoubtedly come about as a result of the increase in government industrial relations legislation; yet it is also clear that during this period there has been a deterioration in management–worker relations in many places, and often a failure to introduce the

---

*'Is your personnel department necessary?', Erich Ash, *Industrial Society*, July/August 1979, page 7*f*.

rapid changes in work methods, which are necessary for effective competition and organizational efficiency in the modern world. Personnel departments as such are clearly not to blame for these developments; much more guilty are those line managers at the highest level who have opted out from their most important function, that of managing people. They are especially blameworthy for allowing communication channels to become the province of personnel departments and trade union organizations, so that complaints are now frequently heard from first-line managers that they hear news of changes likely to affect them from their departmental shop stewards.

It is in the context of this practical example that the role of the personnel department clearly emerges in the form of administrative and advisory functions, and not in decision-making. There should never be any question of line managers shunting their *responsibilities for the people they employ* on to a department that is not responsible for the efficiency and profitability of the organization in which they all work.

An interesting personal comment on the relationship between the chief executive of an organization and its personnel management staff was produced by Sir Peter Parker* when he was chairman of British Rail:

1   To keep out of their way until they want me in it – and then to go in there fully.
2   To resist getting into detail too soon: by keeping some distance I am in a better position to offer more objective advice.
3   To show consistency and steadfastness and back them fully when the flack is flying.
4   To show understanding when people behave unpredictably and when logic does not prevail.
5   To present our case powerfully to the outside world.
6   To ensure that, even in the heat of battle, I remind them of the long-term and social demands which must be tackled.

The individual and personnel management

Personnel policies and the techniques of personnel management all imply 'something being done' by an organization to or for its employees. But, if personnel specialists are to carry out a creative role, it must be part of their day-to-day working philosophy to have regard for those employees as individual human beings. They must be able to view the other side of the coin and be aware that everyone working in their organizations may constantly be asking – 'in all the

Personnel Management, January 1983, page 16.

actions taken by my superiors under the guise of personnel management, what are the things that really matter most to me personally?' The answer to this question can perhaps simply be summarized as *knowledge* and *recognition*.

In the first place, an individual needs to know what his/her job is, what the conditions of employment are, and how his/her work fits into the general activity going on in the organization. This seems so obvious as hardly to be worth stating, and yet there is evidence of such an obscurity about job definitions that it is a wonder how some organizations achieve any degree of efficiency at all. Maier and Hoffman's research* into job perception at the University of Michigan showed that of 222 managerial pairs, only eighteen agreed what the junior partner's duties were precisely. Fifteen of the present author's own students, carrying out their first job analysis exercises, each interviewed a hospital employee of supervisory grade. When these analyses were then checked with the supervisors' own bosses, there was not one single case of the subordinate's description of his/her job coinciding with his/her superior's understanding of it.

This whole area of expectation becomes even more confused when senior staff move around. For example, some managers seem unable to delegate authority to their subordinates, while others delegate extensively; when a boss changes from the former type of person to the latter, subordinate staff are sometimes placed in untenable positions, to the extent of feeling that their boss is giving them more work to do simply to make his/her own life easier. All this because no attempt has been made to clarify what is expected of subordinates in the performance of their duties, and what exactly their relationships to each other and with senior and junior staff should be.

Employees, then, have the right to know what their jobs are, what results are expected of them, the standards by which their performance is measured, and what authority they have to take decisions on their own initiative. In turn, this should clarify their relationships with their superiors – for surely, once expectations are clear, most people ask nothing more than to be left to get on with the job. In other words, few people like bosses who continually breathe down their necks – they much prefer them to be unobtrusive, but available to give help when asked.

Furthermore, this may now help to identify the individual's requirements for further training. Managers should know what standards of performance they expect: watching subordinates work day by day will enable them to spot if they are falling short of those standards and try

Superior-Subordinate Communication in Management, Norman R. F. Maier and others (AMA Research Study No. 52; New York, 1961).

to do something, by way of additional training, to close the gap. The vast majority of training should take place in this way on the job; attendances at outside courses are infrequent events, and managers need to show much more courage and integrity in recognizing their personal responsibilities towards subordinates.

Individuals, too, look for recognition. We all like to be told when we are doing well; most of us choose to have our errors or shortcomings pointed out as well, especially if this is accompanied by positive advice about corrective action. The appraisal of staff by their seniors is a controversial subject, however, and its best-known forms are being replaced by the management-by-objectives technique which, in the event, demands the active participation of each individual employee in improving his/her own performance (see Chapter 9). Obviously, recognition must take tangible forms if employees are to be satisfied in the long term, and most individuals are ambitious for promotion and more pay. More frequent informal recognition is also important: on the one hand, a word of praise or the confidence that a boss clearly shows in a subordinate; on the other, the 'rocket' for a mistake. Both have profound effects on the individual's attitude towards his/her boss and hence the organization for which he/she works, and on the status that he/she holds in the eyes of other staff.

Thus all the functions of personnel management must be looked at from the point of view of each individual employee's expectations. This approach helps to show how interdependent they are, for all these expectations must be realized if employees are to achieve efficient and improving results. Turning back to the techniques of personnel management to illustrate this point, an enlightened promotion policy, with an appropriate salary structure linked to it, will be of little use if the initial recruitment procedures are such that poor-calibre people are selected in the first place.

The behavioural sciences

Particularly relevant to the development of personnel management during the past few decades has been the research work carried out by behavioural scientists – sociologists, anthropologists, occupational psychologists, for example – aimed at developing techniques which will enable managers to obtain the best results from their labour forces. If any one common theme has emerged, it is surely that the concern which Alan Fox expressed about reconciling conflict in industry will only be relieved by methods designed to ensure the maximum participation of all employees in resolving the problems which affect them at work.

Historically, the development of the behavioural sciences must be set against the emergence of Western society's way of life. For the dominance of the consumer inevitably means conditioning the labour force to expect mainly economic satisfactions from work; only the higher-status professional groups are allowed to see any real meaning in their work. Admittedly, workers and trade unions are currently demanding more from the working situation than in the past; but although these requests sometimes touch on interesting work and job satisfaction, more commonly they take the form of demands for a greater part in decision-making and participation in management processes.

Against this background, the social organization of the workplace may be analysed as a network of roles determined by the technology of the industry concerned, organizational objects, methods of work control through sanctions, status factors, and communications. As Alan Fox* points out, authority is based on legitimacy, so one of management's main tasks is to get workplace systems accepted as legitimate by their organization's employees. In a democratic setting, management can function successfully only so long as decisions are upheld by shared values on organizational objectives and methods of achieving them. It is this importance of shared values which poses a dilemma in modern industry, for the aspirations of individuals and groups of workers must also be taken into account; pressure is constantly growing from unions for improvements in the rewards and satisfaction which people seek from work, and for greater influence on employers through participation in decision-making.

At the same time, it is also clear that there is no single technique guaranteed to be the panacea for all ills; every organization has its peculiar features and needs, and the multiplicity of available techniques must be examined with those in mind. Nor have the experts yet finalized a 'chicken-and-egg' controversy about some of their more important conclusions. For example, the human relations school insists that the factors involved in motivation (see Chapter 3) are highly significant in determining the structure of relationships within organizations, and hence their efficiency. In simpler words, treating people right has no altruistic purposes: it pays off economically. On the other hand, there is a body of research which supports the opposite view – that the chain of causation is one in which the economic and technical efficiency of an organization determines the pattern of relationships and styles of behaviour revealed by its employees.

In the event, the philosophical question must also be raised – will we ever achieve ultimate truths in management? For instance, in analys-

*A Sociology of Work in Industry, Alan Fox (Collier-Macmillan, 1971).

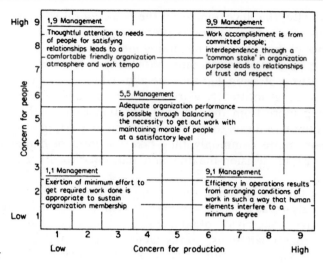

Figure 1

ing styles of management, Douglas McGregor's Theory X and Theory Y (see page 177) carry overtones of general approval for the latter approach. By the same token, the equally famous Blake–Mouton grid* presents a model of managerial commitment and training techniques aimed at developing 9,9 managers who achieve production through mature interpersonal relationships which are integrated with the purposes of the organization (see Figure 1).

Another view came with Reddin's analysis† of managerial styles, in which he discards the concept that any one style is universally desirable. While accepting relationships-orientation and task-orientation as the basic directions of management activity, Reddin argues that flexibility is essential for effectiveness: that is, managers must be prepared to use different styles in different situations. Among all the approaches possible, there is no one general best fit; if the style used is appropriate to the situation, it will be effective; if it is inappropriate, the situation will be handled ineffectively. This has come to be called the contingency theory of leadership.

McGregor's work calls for a rather fuller comment; for in addition to the profound influence which his Theory X and Theory Y proposition has had on management thinking, he developed other basic ideas which collectively assert that long-term progress in staff management will come only with a better understanding of the behavioural sciences. Thus he analysed the standards of performance achieved by an

* *The Managerial Grid*, R. R. Blake and J. S. Mouton (Gulf Publishing Co., 1965).
† *Managerial Effectiveness*, W. J. Reddin (McGraw-Hill, 1970).

individual at work as being a function of the relationships between the personal characteristics of that individual (including his/her knowledge, skills, motivation, and attitudes) and certain aspects of his/her working environment (including the nature of the job, its rewards, and the leadership he/she receives):

$$P = f(I_{abc} \ldots E_{123} \ldots)$$

The relationships among these variables are many and complex; behavioural scientists are concerned with helping managers reach precise and quantitative statements about them. Linked with this, Theory Y postulates that management strategy should be aimed at creating conditions which enable individuals to achieve their own goals best by directing their efforts towards organizational goals. Tactically, this is very demanding of management, who have to agree acceptable performance standards with subordinates, secure commitment to clear targets for improvement, build mutual trust and support, and maintain open communications.

In effect, McGregor's research resulted in a new value system for management. One example is his view on the management of differences, rejecting all the traditional methods of resolving conflict – divide and rule, suppressing disputes, majority voting, and even arbitration – in favour of a strategy of working through differences as a means of achieving innovation, commitment to the decisions reached, and a strengthening of relationships between the members of a working group.

The main problems* to which behavioural scientists have directed their attention have included:

1 Problems of structuring work and authority.
2 Understanding the motivation of people at work, incentives, and job satisfaction.
3 The causes of frustration and conflict in the workplace.
4 The leadership role of managers in optimizing employees' performance.
5 The development of better training techniques.
6 Communications systems.
7 The impact of physical and social environment on employees' health, attitudes, and working efficiency.
8 Methods of introducing changes to effect organizational improvement, especially those involving employee participation.

The Professional Manager, Douglas McGregor (McGraw-Hill, 1967).

In general, the intertwining of the behavioural sciences and personnel management has been concerned with 'tools', concepts and methods of tackling new problems. As regards the former, for example, psychologists have provided tests of specific capacities to help in staff selection; in turn, the results achieved, linked with those of other tests, have helped to develop the theoretical framework of mental ability and skills (thus theory and practice advance step by step). Rewards, especially incentive schemes, and analyses of informal organization* are examples of concepts emerging from personnel practice, while typical of the new problems currently being tackled are those of organizational design and career development.

At the same time, the limitations of known behavioural science techniques must be recognized. Few, if any, purport to apply to a broad canvas; most scientific progress is on a small scale and step by step: so it is with advances in the behavioural sciences. It has also been proved that the best results are likely to be obtained not by importing consultants with prepared packages of ready solutions, but by involving an organization's own representatives and personnel staff in the decisions taken about which behavioural science techniques to use, and in running and monitoring the programme then put into practice. Trade union representatives especially need to be won over, for there is always the fear that any new or unusual approach may exploit their members.

Thus the behavioural and social sciences provide an ideological basis for many of the most recent developments in the practice of personnel management. Psychology has offered many techniques; sociology has investigated organizational design; social psychology has contributed performance assessment and career planning; manpower planning techniques are interdisciplinary.

The new general approach, best known as *organizational development* (OD), has been defined† as – 'The process of planning and implementing changes in an organization through the application of the behavioural sciences with the objective of strengthening human processes and so improving the functioning of the organization in the achievement of its objectives.' Thus planning means making changes in a deliberate manner, and involves applying behavioural science knowledge in the initial diagnosis of problems, planning and executing the necessary changes, and finally evaluating their results. Organizational development in this sense means a continuous process of movement, from a static situation where staff perhaps inherently resist change, to a climate which promotes it so that the organization

*cf. the Donovan Commission Report.
†H. S. Gill and D. R. Tranfield in *Personnel Management*, April 1973.

becomes readily adaptive. If change is seen as a continuing activity in this way, then the organization will be better equipped to survive and grow in a rapidly changing environment.

Typically the OD specialist analyses problems, which may manifest themselves, for example, in delays in production processes and escalation of costs, and recommends practical actions which may require changes in the organization of production, in working methods and in staffing. In such ways the OD contribution is geared to help technically-dominated and high task-centre project personnel to increase their awareness and their ability to manage the interaction and interdependencies between the technical and social systems which make up their projects, and more effectively to manage both the people and the task together.

In the last few years OD work has become closely linked with strategic planning in helping organizations not just to examine their present state, but also to look at their possible future environments, choices about likely goals in these environments, and the capacities and steps needed to be taken to move from the present state towards the possible future states. The link between systems approaches to work design and quality and productivity improvement is another aspect on which many OD practitioners are engaged in various forms. Productivity and quality improvement are increasingly being seen as interconnected with, for example, work design, style of organization, strategy and business objectives. OD means giving clarity to departments' planning – creating a single framework whereby the present organization, its philosophy, objectives, priorities and jobs are recorded, its future intended development set out, and needs identified and costed.

The plan need not be lengthy or complex. It will be an up-to-date record of the structure and senior jobs. It will be a short statement of what the major objectives of each department are, and will provide a checklist for regular appraisal by the departmental management team of the effectiveness of its management processes (e.g. of planning, control, review) and how it develops, affords and rewards its staff.

Its reality will come from the fact that the plan is published, as a record of who is given accountability for any initiative or necessary review, what needs to be discussed with other departments and staff in order to improve organizational effectiveness, and how much that organization costs. It will need to be agreed with the chief executive, shared with colleagues and updated at least annually. This last requirement means that organizational costs must be given a permanent budget heading, with the costs of the organization, skills and motivation of its labour force shown to be a sound and natural investment, which in turn must be positively managed. Provision for management training, for secondments, for redeployment, for pay incentives, for communications with employees, and for management services' help must be assessed in the context of the total remuneration bill for the organization. In these ways are the cost and utilization of manpower put into clear focus and decisions called forth as to how much is worth investing in the development of organizational effectiveness.

Recent OD research* clearly indicates that the prime responsibility for initiating management change in organizations lies with the chief executive, and that the personnel manager has a 'team' role rather than a 'leadership' role in the field of organizational restructuring, typically being given specific responsibility for particular tasks, such as:

1 Strategies for achieving manpower reductions (frequently involving voluntary rather than compulsory redundancy, natural wastage and early retirement).
2 Identifying people capable of filling the vacancies in the new organization.
3 Preparing new job descriptions in conjunction with line managers.
4 Arranging systems for staff transfers, redeployment and filling internal vacancies.
5 Counselling employees about the alternatives available to them.
6 Consultation with trade unions.
7 Preparing briefing programmes for communicating changes to employees.

Further reading

The Manager's Guide to the Behavioural Sciences, Margaret Brown (Industrial Society, Notes for Managers, No. 16, 1980).
Organizational Behaviour, David Buchanan and Andrzej Huczynski (IPM, 1986).
Personnel Management in Britain, Keith Sisson (Blackwell, 1989).
The Role of Management in Industrial Relations, CIR, Report No. 34 (HMSO, 1973).
A Sociology of Work in Industry, Alan Fox (Collier-Macmillan, 1971).

*IPM survey of twenty-eight organizations recently involved in restructuring, Alistair Evans and Alan Cowling, *Personnel Management*, January 1985, pages 14–17.

2

Personnel policy

Principles

The policy of an organization is a clear-cut statement of its aims and objectives, setting out what is to be achieved. Looking at this definition negatively, its significance can perhaps be brought out thus. That policy is *not* the writing of a plan or programme: it is concerned with what is to be done rather than how to do it. *Nor* is policy a summary of what has happened in the past, presented as a report. Above all, policy statements are *not* vague, waffly documents – they must be clear and precise.

Policies are needed for the whole range of an organization's activities, of course: production, financial, marketing, exporting, plant maintenance, and public relations are examples. But the preparation of personnel policies, and their subsequent publication generally or to a limited list of senior staff, seems to arouse much more controversy than the others. Nevertheless, it is generally acknowledged that where policies are not widely known throughout an organization, there is inevitably a reluctance on the part of senior staff to delegate authority. In turn, this means that the confidence of junior managers is not developed in the ways it can be when they are given clear policy statements to guide their daily activities at work. The job of top management is essentially creative in nature and should concentrate on major long-term aspects of the business. But where the use of policies is lacking in the over-centralized manner described above, then this task may become overladen with the heavy burden of having to settle many of the individual grievances and problems that crop up day to day but which, from the point of view of business efficiency, should usually be settled at a much lower level of authority.

To some extent, the personnel policies of any organization will always be determined by factors outside its control – by the nature of the society in which it exists, government action, political pressures, local culture, and business ethics. We in Western civilization observe *Christian ideals*, which have achieved their maximum impact on social service during the twentieth century. The humanitarian content of the Sermon on the Mount is inescapable, and we profess concern about the economic abuses of our affluent society both in our own country and abroad. Of course, even in its limited industrial context, this is an enormous subject, beset with accusations of sharp practice levelled at management and unions alike. Charge and counter-charge are easily made. For example, any victimization on the part of management or strike action by unions can be called un-Christian, because they are aggressive in nature; but the answer that, in an imperfect world, we all have the right to defend our own interests, is shattering in its simplicity.

The political setting of society and industry is another important consideration. A major mystery of the twentieth century has been the way in which poor countries, in gaining independence from colonial rule, chose collectivist models for their economic policies: none have succeeded in any significant way, neither agriculturally nor industrially, nor have they been effective in raising *per capita* incomes fast enough to overcome gloomy demographic prospects. All this despite the glittering examples of free market successes in North America and Western Europe, post-war until about 1973, and the even greater dynamism of that model in some of the Pacific countries since the 1960s.

The latter development started in Japan after the Second World War, based on a constitution which selected the best aspects of British and US experience, achieving an excellent balance between executive and legislature and between central and devolved power. A free press, free trade unions and decentralized control of the police were notable features of a situation in which the state was reconstituted to exist for its citizens, in contrast to Japanese traditions hitherto. A new and healthy individualism, based on loyalty to the concept of the family, was encouraged and, in effect, acted as an antidote to any tendency towards totalitarianism. Also a very stable parliamentary structure – run by a liberal–conservative alliance – gave Japan's economy a consistent free enterprise framework.

The result was a 20-year period of growth which averaged 9.7 per cent per annum – twice the rate of any other industrialized country –

starting with car production, and expanding to embrace a very wide range of consumer goods and, more recently, high technology products. Analysis of the reasons for success indicate not so much a miracle as firm adherence to the application of classical economic theory: a high level of fixed capital formation, but very little of it in non-productive investment; moderate taxation; low defence and government spending; a very high rate of personal saving, efficiently channelled into industry through the banking system; shrewd import of foreign technology under licence; very fast replacement rate of existing plant, made possible by wage restraint, with productivity running ahead of wages; plentiful labour, well-educated and skilled because educational expansion was closely linked to industrial needs and not to social science ideologies. While some measure of protection was provided by the Japanese Government, its chief contribution was to erect a framework of intense internal competition (shades of Adam Smith) and a climate of benevolence towards business.

Furthermore, most Japanese firms supplemented the efforts of unions in looking after their members by enveloping employees in a familial embrace which included housing, meals, medical care, ethical advice, sport and holidays – that is, by successfully providing the sort of collectivized production-propaganda which had failed so badly in Soviet Russia and China – all done on a human scale and in a familial image and, above all, seen to achieve significant improvements in personal levels of consumption.

Growth has been most remarkable in the *entrepôt* economies, with Hong Kong providing the outstanding example. Thanks to pure market economics it raised its *per capita* income to six times that of China, while at the same time absorbing over four million refugees (many times more than the number of Palestinians which the entire Arab world has failed to resettle).

Disillusionment with many forms of collectivism has been a major feature of twentieth century history. Pre-1914 it was rare for the public sector to embrace more than 10 per cent of any country's economy; by the 1970s, however, the state took up to 45 per cent of the GNP. But, whereas at the time of Versailles Treaty, most intelligent people believed that an enlarged state could increase the total sum of human happiness, very few continue to hold that view. The experiment, in many versions, has almost always failed, with the state proving itself in the process to be an insatiable spender, an unrivalled waster and the greatest killer of all time.

By way of contrast, the following table shows how weakly the British economy grew over the 20 years, 1950–70, compared with the EC.

Table 1

	1950 £	*1970 £*
1 GNP *per capita* – UK	940	2170
– EC	477	2557
2 Exports – UK	6.3 billion	19.0 billion
– EC	9.4 billion	91.2 billion
3 Reserves – UK	3.4 billion	3.2 billion
– EC	2.9 billion	31.0 billion

In fact, this position worsened during the 1970s despite Britain joining the Common Market in 1973. Why this chronic weakness?

The causes may in large measure justly be attributed to the development and then abuse of over-weaning trade union power. A sequence of industrial relations legislation and related events may be traced through the twentieth century – the Trade Disputes Act 1906, the Trade Union Act 1913, the repeal of the Trade Disputes Act of 1927 in 1945, special status for trades unions within the nationalized industries, the 1965 Trade Disputes Act, unions' veto of Harold Wilson's 'In Place of Strife' legislation in 1969, the Trade Union and Labour Relations Acts of 1974 and 1976, and the Employment Protection Act of 1975 and 1978 – had the cumulative effect of removing virtually all inhibitions on union power: Lord Denning, Master of the Rolls, commented, 'All legal restraints have been lifted, so that trade unions can now do as they will'.

The result was that excessive union privilege and political power contributed to Britain's growing economic weakness in three ways. First, it promoted restrictive practices, inhibited the growth of productivity, and so discouraged investment. Second, it greatly increased the pressure of wage inflation, especially during the 1970s. Third, trade union social and legislative demands on government had a cumulative tendency to increase the size of public sector spending and the government share of the GNP: by 1975 this had risen to 59.06 per cent, inflation was nearing the 40 per cent mark, and the Government had to call for help from the International Monetary Fund and submit to its dictat. A subsequent change of government resulted in policies of retrenchment, reduced public borrowing, restraint in the public sector, with the economy exposed to the deflationary discipline of market forces. These policies, together with the revenues gained from North Sea oil, served to stabilize the economy and helped to raise productivity to more competitive levels. During the 1980s Britain recovered, albeit very slowly, only to slip into recession in the early 1990s.

Against this background there are certain *principles* which must be observed in formulating the *main personnel policies*. These may be expressed initially in terms of the five main areas of personnel management activity, but they must then be elaborated in the form of a number of *subsidiary policies* under each heading. In turn, associated with all these headings will be certain *rules* and *regulations* to ease the interpretation and application of policy by junior managers who rely on documentary guidance when dealing with particular kinds of problems or when taking decisions in repetitive situations.

The three main principles upon which personnel policies in British industry, commerce and public service are based acknowledge:

1 That all employees should be treated with *justice*, under a 'code of fair play' which means having regard for equity, that no favouritism or antagonism should be shown towards individuals, and that there should be consistency in treatment between all employees and over periods of time.
2 That the *needs* of employees must be *recognized*, particularly their desires for job satisfaction, for knowledge of what is going on within the organization, and for consultation before changes affecting them take place.
3 That a business will function better *democratically* rather than autocratically; success is much more likely if the cooperation of employees is sought in achieving objectives than by trying to coerce them to these ends with the use of authority.

The personnel manager has a direct part to play in ensuring that these principles are applied in practice. To look on them merely as expressions of good intentions is not sufficient; they must be reflected in the policy statements which will be used as guides to decision-taking. This is clearly a much more satisfactory situation than desperately trying to remember, each time a problem crops up, what previous decisions exist by way of precedent.

Main policy statements

Once the principles upon which personnel policies are based have been generally accepted, the next step is to prepare the actual policies for the five main areas of the personnel function. These must be clear-cut and precisely written, so that everyone in the organization knows exactly what are its aims concerning its employees.

Here is an example of a policy statement in each of the main areas, as it might apply to a large company in private industry.

1 Employment policy

To obtain suitably qualified and experienced personnel, and to enable them to derive satisfaction from employment by offering them attractive wages, good working conditions, security, and opportunities for promotion.

2   Training policy

To provide adequate training facilities to enable employees to learn to do their job effectively and to prepare themselves for promotion.

3   Wages and salary policy

To pay wages and salaries that compare favourably with those of other firms locally, within a structure that has due regard for recognized differentials and individual ability.

4   Industrial relations policy

To operate adequate procedures for dealing with all disputes and grievances quickly and to make every effort to improve relations between management and employees through the use of participative methods.

5   Welfare policy

To safeguard the health and safety of all employees, and to provide such welfare and social amenities as are sincerely desired by employees and are mutually beneficial to them and the company.

No matter how precise these main statements are, each covers such a wide area that they must be supplemented by subsidiary policies under more specific headings. To some extent these will inevitably reflect local circumstances and economic pressures; it is likely, for example, that their content will take a more generous form in areas of over-full employment compared with places where labour is plentiful. It is difficult to generalize, therefore, but taking account of the principles and main statements set out above, policies for these subsidiary headings might include the following.

Employment

Examples

(a) *Manpower planning:* The company's recruitment and staff develop-
    ment programmes will be based on forecasts of its future labour

requirements, projected five years ahead, and kept under constant review.
  (b) *Job descriptions:* These will be written for all vacant posts and will be supplied to candidates. Staff charged with filling posts will be given job specifications.
  (c) *Recruitment methods:* The recruitment process will be supervised by personnel department staff who have been fully trained in selection techniques, and who will advise on the methods appropriate to the type and seniority of the job concerned. The IPM professional code of recruitment practice will be observed.

List of other headings

  (d) Staff transfers.
  (e) Promotion policies.
  (f) Termination of employment.
  (g) Redundancy policy.
  (h) Employment of special categories of labour; for example, married women, disabled workers, and the aged.

Note: Policies for these headings are discussed in later chapters.

Training

Examples

  (a) *Induction:* All new employees will be helped to settle in their jobs by receiving instruction in the company's organization, policies, and working practices.
  (b) *Operator:* All employees will be given full training in the skills, methods, and equipment used in their jobs.

List of other headings

  (c) Apprenticeships.
  (d) Staff assessment.
  (e) Foremanship (for potential and experienced supervisors).
  (f) Management development.

Wages and salaries

Examples

  (a) *Basic payments:* These will be made according to national agreements, with local adjustments as negotiated.

(b) *Differentials:* Payment for jobs will take into account such differences as the effort and skill required, the responsibilities involved, and the unpleasantness of working conditions.

List of other headings

(c) Rewarding individual performance.
(d) Job evaluation.
(e) Merit-rating.
(f) Use of financial incentives.
(g) Productivity agreements.

Industrial relations

Examples

(a) *Communications:* All employees of the organization will be kept fully informed of company policies and plans for the future.
(b) *Joint consultation:* No changes concerning working arrangements or conditions will be decided until the views of staff concerned have been obtained.
(c) *Grievances and disputes:* All these will be dealt with by management quickly; they must not be allowed to drag on and thus damage the cooperative spirit established over the years.

List of other headings

(d) Attitude towards membership of trade unions.
(e) Recognition and training of worker representatives.
(f) Negotiating procedure.
(g) Worker participation at board level.

Welfare

Examples

(a) *Occupational health:* It is mutually beneficial to the company and employees to ensure that the physical capacity of all staff matches the requirements of their jobs. Services covering initial and periodic medical examinations, the treatment of accidents and sudden illness of staff, and the prevention of occupational diseases will therefore be provided.

(b) *Safety:* All possible measures, from specialist education to investigation, will be taken to prevent accidents: joint consultation on the subject is essential.
(c) *Personal problems:* All employees may look to their departmental heads, and through them to the personnel department, for help with personal or domestic problems.

List of other headings

(d) Pension plans.
(e) Sickness schemes.
(f) Transport arrangements for employees reaching and leaving work.
(g) Help with accommodation difficulties.
(h) Financial help.
(i) Canteens.
(j) Sports clubs, leisure, and social activities.

These policy statements will need to be further elaborated in some cases by rules and regulations which must be observed by all staff affected. The distinction between these various types of procedure can perhaps best be made clear by the means of an illustration, this time taken from the public sector, concerning salaries and wages.

1 The appropriate *principle* is obviously that of justice – a fair payment for a fair day's work.
2 The *main policy* statement might be: 'to pay salaries and wages according to scales laid down nationally in Whitley Council agreements for all grades of staff and all jobs within those grades'.
3 The *subsidiary policies* will deal with such matters as differentials and incentives, where relevant.
4 An example of a *rule* would be that any increase in salary can only be awarded to individuals if their job is regraded to a higher level.
5 This rule would then be followed by certain *regulations* for putting it into effect. One of these might be that to obtain regradings of their job individuals must submit their case in writing to the Management Committee or Council.

Publishing personnel policies

There has always been controversy among personnel managers about the extent to which policies should be made known throughout an organization. Indeed, some feel that the dangers inherent are so great that the policies should not even be written down – but this all leads to the centralized or personalized view of management activity previously criticized. That there are dangers and problems in theory cannot be denied, but if safeguards are taken against these, then the practical advantages of publishing personnel policies far outweigh the potential snags.

The basic difficulty is that of trying to ensure precise definition of the policies. This is essentially a problem of communications, of overcoming the semantic barrier so that all senior staff share a common understanding of the language used in describing human situations. As individuals, they are, of course, themselves subject to the organization's policies and, human nature being as it is, they may make their own reservations or feel personal resistance in interpreting and applying policy. Personnel managers' advisory work must therefore embrace the conflicts which their line-manager colleagues may feel exist between their own personal objectives and those of the organization.

Other alleged dangers include those of – entering a type of contract with employees from which management could not withdraw, even though circumstances may change considerably; the impossibility of writing policies to cover the whole range of likely staff problems; and the fact that the rigidity of policy statements may restrict management discretion to deal sympathetically with individual cases. In practice, these fears simply prescribe the care that must be taken when writing policy, rather than amounting to a case against its publication at all. The same thoroughness in preparation must be shown as when drawing up any legal document relating to the company's activities. By definition, policy statements indicate the general lines of action; their wording should be flexible enough to cover all possible problems and changing circumstances, and to allow scope for the exercise of judgement on the part of management in interpreting them. In an entirely different field the Wireless and Telegraphy Act 1906 provided an excellent example of flexible policy writing: only four pages long, it required no amendment until 1959, although radio and television were not in use until many years after its original enactment.

Having refuted the theoretical drawbacks in this way, it is abundantly clear that a published statement of personnel policies has many practical benefits. The type of action necessary to achieve the organization's objectives is specified, and thus serves to clarify management thinking on personnel problems. Cooperation and teamwork are encouraged by the fact that decision-making will now be uniform and consistent between departments and over periods of time. Policy statements help in the delegation and decentralization of authority, and consequently they are useful aids when training supervisors and developing managers. As far as staff as a whole are concerned, policies reflect the interest taken in them by employers and show their goodwill. The 'rules of the game' which govern employee behaviour at work are clearly conveyed in this way, too, thus helping in induction and job training. Generally, morale will tend to be high throughout an organization when everyone is aware that any labour relations problems will be tackled in a fair and consistent manner.

In any event, minimum standards of personnel policy are increasingly imposed by legislation: the Employment Protection (Consolidation) Act, the Race Relations Act, and the Equal Pay Act are three examples. Bearing in mind the principles already set out for personnel policies, it ill-behoves professional personnel managers to associate themselves with any of the efforts which, it is alleged, have been made to circumvent various aspects of these statutes because of their potential threat to profits. Personnel managers should, in these circumstances, represent the social conscience of their organizations.

Future enlightenment?

Largely dictated by the increasing challenge of economic conditions, the policies of employers towards their staff have become more and more progressive over the years. The main improvements in the future will be those intended to encourage employees to give of their best in their jobs, by removing the frustrations that affect morale and performance at the moment.

Taking a wider view, personnel policies must always reflect current adjustments to the conflict which inevitably occurs over fundamentals throughout all industry. Peaceful conditions are a prerequisite to efficient performance. Yet, industrial peace is not compatible with the desire of organizations to be autonomous nor with the rights of individuals to pursue their own interests. Policy statements must therefore be made with the goal of securing a balance between peace and autonomy. They must also be concerned with the economic progress of the organization and higher standards of living for its members, overcoming the resistance to improvements which develops if they involve changes that can only be made at a high cost. This is very much the context of today's industrial society, where automation and mechanization increasingly dominate the lives of employees. There are no universal solutions to such problems, but policy can be presented in such a way as to ease the necessary adjustments to changing conditions.

Sociologists see Western civilization moving into a 'post-industrial' state of society, which will have several predictable characteristics. *Per capita* incomes will be high. Employment will become concentrated in the service area: already manufacturing employment in the UK is declining and more than half of the working population is employed in the service sector. Leisure time will be increased as working hours become shorter. Values are likely to change rapidly as regards work, authority, the place of women in the working community, and the power and accountability of large organizations. Growing concern will be shown for the quality of life and the conservation of resources and environments. These are the pressures to which personnel policies must respond if manpower requirements are to be met and if adequate commitment to the overall purposes of an organization is to be ensured.

Much concern is currently expressed over the prospect that human labour in routine work and even in quite complex operations will be superseded by new 'silicon chip technology', with a huge rise in the level of unemployment and a general reversal of the accepted priorities of life – leisure becoming the norm and work the exception. In fact, such a prospect, widely assumed to be inevitable, is based on a false premise – that the existing quantum of production must remain fixed at about its present maximum. If in the near future one person will be able to do the work that previously employed three or five or ten, the real task is surely that of how to make use of the capacity of those displaced so that output may be multiplied and standards of living thus improved. For the moment it seems that large sums of public money are currently being spent on research programmes into the possible uses of leisure, while the more important problems of using the new technology to raise living standards in general remain comparatively neglected.

Increasing concern is being shown for the 'quality of life' in the working situation; this not only affects standards of living and economic security, but extends to an acceptance that individuals have the right to a satisfying job in congenial surroundings, opportunities for the full development of their abilities, and a voice in decisions which affect them. Society also reflects a general concern about the power wielded by large organizations and constantly searches for balancing influences, such as joint consultative machinery, worker members of boards and consumer associations. Authority and conforming to conventions tend to be rejected. Status systems, distinguishing between 'staff' and 'labour', are also disappearing; productivity bargains have given 'staff' conditions to all employees in many organizations, removing such differences as existed in conditions of work, security of employment and fringe benefits. Finally, there is the legislation against discrimination on grounds of colour, creed, and sex.

Britain's membership of the European Community (EC), seen in the general context of the aims of the Treaty of Rome — to harmonize the economic, employment, and social policies of all member countries – has considerable implications for the development of all aspects of personnel management in this country. In fact, the Treaty is quite precise in calling for action on employment matters, vocational training, pay and working conditions, industrial relations, and employees' welfare.

Plans were for all these requirements to be met by 1992, but great problems had to be overcome first: one concerned the Community's budget, i.e. paying for all this and the size of the contributions expected from member states; second, the other European countries are much more used to a legalistic approach than the British are, and our trade unions continue to show great resistance to any domestic attempts to curtail their bargaining freedom through the statute book.

As far as the employment function is concerned, the main provisions concern the free movement of labour between member countries, with EC workers being granted the same working conditions as nationals in each other's territories. Work permits are no longer required, but residence permits will be needed by those staying in Britain for longer than six months. By the same token, workers from this country may seek employment in any of the other EC countries, and will receive treatment equal to their own nationals' as regards employment service facilities in finding suitable jobs, pay and working conditions, trade union rights, vocational training and retraining facilities, social security, and access to housing and property. A Community worker also has the right to be joined by the members of his/her immediate family.

Training policy is covered by the European Social Fund (ESF), created in 1989 to provide financial resources for a wide variety of innovative projects, thus enabling many thousands of people to get jobs and training. (See Chapter 10 for practical links between the ESF and TECs.)

On the wages front, the hope is that continued economic growth, despite current inflation, will perpetuate the levelling upwards to wages and salaries, so that real incomes will go on rising. Cross-frontier joint action by trade unions may be expected to press for parity with the highest existing rates of pay. Equal pay for equal work between men and women is also official EC policy. The harmonization of holiday arrangements will benefit British workers; their European counterparts all have longer periods of annual leave and more public holidays. Holiday bonuses are also common.

The law plays a much greater part in industrial relations in Europe than in Britain – directly affecting trade union and workers' rights, negotiating procedures, consultation and communications processes, redundancy and job security. British unions tend to resist such controls as interfering with their bargaining freedom. The European Company Statute of 1970 has resulted in directives about two-tier management structures, with worker participation on the supervisory board, in all organizations with over 500 employees. The UK is the only West European country where works councils are not mandatory, so 'harmonization' may lead to their wider adoption here; certainly their aims – to promote cooperation, to encourage productivity, and to consider the effects of management decisions on workers – are commendable.

All the points mentioned above are still official EC objectives although, as we move through the 1990s, controversy as to the prospects of their ever being achieved has mounted. A constitutional commission is working on a review of the Treaty of Rome, to try to enable the community to make progess towards economic and political integration; a new 'social dimension' is being discussed whereby the previous emphasis on harmonization in the social field is being replaced by promoting a dialogue between employers and the unions at EC level from which it is hoped that a consensus on economic and social development will emerge. Thus a new accent is being placed on dialogue and flexibility, no longer on regulation via EC legislation and directives.

These changes are under consideration largely in response to the growing awareness of stagnation in the European economy when compared to the economies of the USA, Japan and other emerging Far Eastern states. A lack of dynamism is alleged, and this can only be removed by a programme of action to improve competitiveness: reducing government expenditure, especially on social protection; greater freedom from government controls on industry and commerce; the promotion of small businesses; more flexible labour markets by the removal of excessive regulation; and, at community level, the creation of a free internal market by 1993, eliminating all internal obstacles to trade, thus enabling enterprises to develop and compete on a world scale.

However, at present there is major disagreement between member states about the action necessary to achieve these ends. Some favour the development of more rapid decision-making by the EC by fundamentally altering the Treaty of Rome; others, including the UK, are taking a more pragmatic approach, in particular, favouring only limited restrictions on the existing use of the national veto. With its policy of opposing further government regulation, Britain has indicated an intention to use its veto to block EC draft recommendations on the reduction and reorganization of working time, on part-time work, on temporary work, on parental leave, and on the Vredeling directive (on information and consultation in transnational undertakings).

Accepting, then, that draft directives are not the answer, the new commission sees improved dialogue between the social partners at EC level as the best means of defending and expanding employment, adapting European industry and preserving the basic achievements of the European social model. The problem about this approach lies in the commission's declared objective of concluding 'framework agreements' between the two sides of industry at EC level, reproducing these at the level of member states, and eventually achieving a general European 'collective agreement' between employers and unions on the lines of agreements which already exist in many member states at national level. Employment prospects, total working hours and the introduction of new technologies are central issues for such agreements. Clearly there will continue to be a significant influence from the European continent on the industrial relations scene in the UK. Even if directives are blocked by political action, the process of involvement of employers and unions in EC structures will expose them to new concepts and policies which will be strongly debated and may well lead to modifications in present practice.

Code of professional conduct

The status of any profession depends in large measure on its requirements and methods for entry into membership and on the existence of a code of professional conduct (the latter, in broad terms, is required in connection with that special status symbol in Britain – the granting of a Royal Charter to a professional body). The IPM has published such a code* for personnel managers, not least significant in this statement being the implication that members of the profession are required to observe the provisions of the code and are subject to disciplinary procedures if they fail to do so.

The Code sets out for employers and others the areas of competence that IPM members should possess and the standard of professional conduct that can be expected from them. Competencies include:

(a) *Resourcing:* organizational structure; job analysis; patterns of work; human resource planning; recruitment and selection; equal opportunity; disciplinary, redundancy and termination procedures.

*IPM Code of Professional Conduct, 1987.

(b) *Rewards and benefits:* job evaluation; pay structures; rewarding performance; strategies for employee motivation; contracts; conditions of employment; pensions and benefits.

(c) *Employee relations:* employee involvement and communications; morale and climate at work; employment law; representative structures; relationships with trade unions; negotiation.

(d) *Training and development:* continuous development of all employees; needs analysis; performance review and appraisal; design and implementation of training programmes; career planning; coaching.

(e) *Working environment:* health, safety and welfare; working conditions, internal and external to the organization.

While some personnel practitioners may specialize in one or more of these areas, they are all expected to have a working knowledge of and keep abreast of developments in the others.

The IPM believes that the management of people *must* form part of every manager's job. For their part, personnel practitioners provide professional knowledge, advice and support to their employers on the most effective use of the human resource. Their concern is for the achievement of the goals of the organization as an industrial, commercial or public enterprise and as a social entity. They must have a clear understanding of the economic, financial, political and other factors which affect the success of an organization so that, as members of the management team, they can take an active part in decision making.

The primary responsibility of personnel practitioners is to their employer, though they also have obligations to employees in respect of their working conditions, rewards and development. They are the privileged recipients and guardians of personal information and confidences.

In carrying out their responsibilities, IPM members are expected to adhere to the following principles of behaviour:

1 *Confidentiality:* respect their employer's requirements for the confidentiality of information entrusted to them, including the safeguarding of information about current, past and prospective employees. They will also ensure the privacy and confidentiality of personal information to which they have access or for which they they are responsible, subject to any legal rights of employees in respect of information relating to themselves.

2 *Equal opportunities:* promote non-discriminatory employment practices in line with current legislation.

3 *Fair dealing:* establish and maintain fair, reasonable and equitable standards of treatment of individuals by their employer.

4 *Self development:* continuously update their skills and knowledge in respect of developments and legislation in the personnel field and the impact of technical, economic and social change on people at work.

5 *Development of others:* seek to achieve the fullest possible development of the capabilities of individual employees to meet the present and future requirements of the organization, and encourage others to develop themselves.

6 *Accuracy of advice and guidance:* maintain high standards of accuracy in the advice and information given to employers and employees in the fields for which they are responsible.

7 *Counselling:* be prepared to act in a counselling role to individual employees, pensioners and the dependants of deceased employees in fields where they have competence, and where appropriate refer to other professionals or helping agencies.

8 *Integrity:* at all times act in accordance with this code of conduct and the duties that they owe to employers and employees. Where there is a conflict between those obligations, the practitioner will make a personal decision after considering the options, of which resignation may be one.

9 *Legality:* not act in any way which would knowingly countenance, encourage or assist unlawful conduct by either employers or employees.

10 *Professional conduct:* at all times endeavour to enhance the standing and good name of the profession. Adherence to the IPM's codes of practice* is a prerequisite of this aim.

Further reading

HR vision: managing a quality workforce, Stephen Connock (IPM, 1992).
Personnel Policy: a guide to communicating and implementing personnel policy, Derek Coulthard (Industrial Society, 1990).

---

*See, for example, Recruitment Code, Redundancy Code, Equal Opportunities Code.

3
Motivation

Why people work

Concern with motivation has been apparent since the early work of industrial psychologists and their investigations of the common sense belief that nobody can stimulate anyone else to work unless he/she knows how that person is motivated and to what incentives he/she will respond. What then are the reasons why people work?

Their prime motive is economic, to obtain the resources to meet their physiological needs and support a family, ideally in ever-increasing comfort. Ambition therefore plays a part, in the sense of the desire to get on and acquire more of the good things in life. But ambition is essentially a personal matter and is conditioned to some extent by environment. Thus individuals' job preferences are important – for example, they may prefer a low-paid job where they are left to their own devices, away from the noise and strain of the main production area; or, if they are caught up in a redundancy situation, merely retaining their job may become the height of their ambition. This last point adds security of employment to the list, again an aspect of the economic motive, for security means steady pay over a long period of time.

The second main motive concerns people's social needs, which have wide ramifications. They want to feel that they belong, that they are accepted by their colleagues, and that their work has some importance. This is clearly associated with a desire for companionship, but also has a negative aspect in that they accept work as a social obligation unless they wish to be rejected by the community around them. Burlinghame wrote in the seventeenth century – 'Work is the source of man's most basic satisfactions, it is his social catalyst – the purveyor *par excellence* of his status and prestige among his fellows.'*

This desire for social status is linked with the need for self-realization. The teachings of many psychologists, such as Jung and Adler, centre around the belief that the supreme goal of a person is to fulfil him/herself as a unique individual, according to his/her own innate potential and within the limits of reality. The factors about a job which meet this need are those which challenge people's abilities, stretch them in achieving their aspirations, and place them in a position of responsibility in the eyes of their workmates and the neighbours among whom they live. Self-fulfilment is also dependent in some measure on the degree of specialized training received, which, for example, inspires some people to go on working at their jobs long after it becomes unnecessary in economic terms. Lengthy, meticulous training nurtures the feeling that if a job is worth doing, it is worth doing well. Many types of craftsmen, technicians, and professional people cannot be thinking all the time about the money they are earning, nor for that matter about the good they may be doing mankind; they find it much more satisfactory to concentrate on the work they have been highly trained to do. If, in addition to all this, they can actually be creative, so much the better; but most people in modern civilization are so taken up by the struggle to satisfy their more basic needs that few aspire to this summit of achievement.

Probably the majority of people are most often partially satisfied and partially unsatisfied in all their wants. Even so, it is clear that links forging total motivation form a recognizable hierarchy; those at the base of the pyramid must be satisfied first before those ranged further up can be given much consideration (Figure 2). These facts are important to the personnel manager, for they indicate that as needs become satisfied, they can no longer be taken account of when designing incentives. Sights must then be set higher, and as they rise there must be fuller awareness of employees' reaction against drudgery and routine and their demands instead for jobs which offer interesting work and a chance to get on.

Research into behaviour at work

Industrial psychologists and industrial sociologists have played a great part in the development of personnel management by applying the

*Quoted by J. A. C. Brown, *Social Psychology of Industry* (Penguin, 1984), page 282.

dings of their research work to problems of business administration.
distinguish between them, psychologists are concerned with the behaviour of individuals, while sociologists emphasize group behaviour; both study how people behave, what the relationship is between human behaviour and the working environment, and why people behave as they do. Their ultimate aim may be defined as trying to bring together all knowledge about managing people into one discipline, establishing the universals of the management process, and advocating management tools for general application. Comparing present practice with such an aim highlights the extent to which behavioural sciences are still in their infancy.

The earlier investigators in these fields are criticized today for having looked at isolated factors in the working situation, with little attempt to measure their relationships with other variables in the environment. Practising managers thus often found their results to be academic and of no relevance to their own particular problems.

Not that everyone failed in the challenge to establish 'principles' that would hold true regardless of time and place. The details of Elton Mayo's experiments at Hawthorne have been well documented. In the relay assembly room he proved how closely the production and social functions of management are linked. Dramatic improvements in productivity were effected because the workers involved changed their attitudes towards the organization when their cooperation was asked for and they were thus made to feel important. Their consciousness of being a group with a clear purpose, both as regards production and in helping to solve a management problem, meant that they achieved stability and satisfied their needs for belonging. Mayo even found that the mere fact that research work was being carried out improved

THE MOTIVATION PYRAMID

Figure 2

workers' morale and their relationships with management. Then in the bank wiring room, he demonstrated the realities of group behaviour, with its own leadership, informal organization, social norms, code of conduct, and restrictions on output. He pointed out the futility of trying to break up these groups – management should act positively, planning for group cohesion so that everyone worked towards the same objectives. Later, in the aircraft industry in 1943, he was able to paint a profile of the good supervisor which has influenced foremanship training ever since.

As well as this type of basic research the behavioural scientist carries out applied research on immediate industrial problems or may work as a consultant, advising particular clients and helping them to implement changes. Success in these approaches counts more than anything else in ensuring their acceptability to practising managers, which is so essential if they are to get their continuous cooperation in future research. Research of this nature has resulted in a body of principles about industrial behaviour that influences current personnel management practices enormously. These are:

1 Normally workers desire association with groups where they find security and recognition.
2 Workers' satisfactions are expressed mainly in terms of how they regard their social status in the firm. Such considerations cause far more labour trouble than wage demands.
3 Complaints are not necessarily based on fact – they may be merely symptoms of much more deep-seated disturbances. Giving people the opportunity to talk and air their grievances can boost morale considerably.
4 Management problems of absenteeism, high labour turnover, inefficiency, and poor morale all reduce to the single problem of how to deal with primary group life, for the greatest cohesion can be obtained by building up from small face-to-face groups.
5 The first-line supervisor is more important in determining the morale of a workgroup than any other single factor.
6 The most effective supervisors are 'employee-orientated', being sensitive to their needs and giving priority in their work to motivate them positively.
7 'Flat' organizations with as few levels of authority as possible develop more initiative and greater responsibility in supervisors and managers than the 'tall' type.
8 Clearly defining responsibilities, and granting appropriate authority, reduce misunderstanding and increase efficiency between groups.

9 Similarly, open communications systems throughout an organization reduce the risk of misunderstanding and conflict.
10 Changes in the social environment which affect the people working
in an organization are most accepted when these same people are
allowed to participate in making the relevant decisions.

Putting these principles into practice requires a courageous team of
well-informed managers who have the ability to adapt theoretical
concepts to the peculiar requirements of their own businesses, and to do
so in such a way that production, selling, and financial arrangements
are not disrupted by having to meet the social needs of the organization.

Behavioural scientists will go on providing theories, research findings, analytical concepts and models – all of which are of great value in
the development of a science of management. It is the duty of personnel
specialists to keep abreast of all this activity, to pick out what is useful
to their own work, adapt relevant ideas, and generally integrate the
knowledge gained from behavioural scientists into the practice of
management. Last but not least, they must look ahead and be willing
to promote further research into those areas which are of special
significance to them.

Job satisfaction and frustration

The job of personnel managers has already been described in Chapter
1 as being centred around people's needs while working in the
organization; they must first of all recognize what these needs are and
then identify the ways in which work in that organization promotes or
frustrates their fulfilment. They can then direct their efforts towards
methods of furthering job satisfaction or removing the frustrations.

This is a subject, for once, which is perhaps best tackled with a
negative approach. Satisfaction is clearly in large measure the obverse
of frustration, but the latter reveals easily detected symptoms which
form a ready starting point for management action. Frustration is the
result of tensions arising in a workplace through dissatisfaction with
the jobs concerned, the physical conditions, or the people working
there. It has an obvious link with low morale: if the state of morale is
indicated by people's willingness to work, then their frustration is
shown by an unwillingness to work. The more precise symptoms are:

1 Low level of production or poor quality of service, both reflected by
the number of complaints received from customers.
2 High rates of absenteeism and labour turnover.

3 Bad time-keeping and generally lax discipline.
4 Poor industrial relations, shown by the record of grievances, disputes, and strikes.

Symptoms must have causes, of course, and these can usually be traced to:

1 'Square pegs in round holes' as a result of the placement of people in jobs to which they are not suited.
2 Anxiety, due to inability to perform the job adequately; the ill-matching of people to jobs is often aggravated by not giving them precise job descriptions to clarify what they should be doing, and by lack of training to do the work properly.
3 Ineffectiveness of leadership: supervision too close or lacking; discipline too lax or too harsh; refusal to delegate; delays in reaching decisions; poor communications, particularly regarding changes likely to affect employees; general inability to obtain group cohesion.
4 Lack of recognition of individuals and their capacities to take on more responsible work; this, in turn, is often reflected in the absence of promotion opportunities and in the 'interference' of specialists in what people consider to be their main tasks.
5 Working conditions – employees will accept unpleasant conditions where these are unavoidable, and this will have no deleterious effect on morale; but they will not work willingly if they are conscious that conditions are unnecessarily poor and that management appears to be doing nothing about them.

Providing remedies for these causes is largely the subject-matter of the practice of personnel management which follows in detail in subsequent chapters. First concern must be for the structure of the organization, with all jobs in it precisely defined so that everyone knows his/her responsibilities and sees a clear ladder of promotion between jobs. Second, there must be an enquiry into the quality of supervisors and managers, particularly in those departments that show all the symptoms of low morale. Effective action must then be taken to improve matters, along lines which should be set out in a comprehensive personnel policy statement.

Removing the causes of job frustration will go a long way towards promoting job satisfaction, and there is no need to repeat comments already made. Taking a positive approach to creating satisfaction, however, the overall aim should be to try to get all employees to understand, accept, and identify themselves with the objectives of the organization, thus building up a sense of corporate pride. Proper induction of newcomers; effective communications and presentation of information; joint consultation and encouragement of the techniques of participative management; appraisal of the efforts of individuals and offering them scope for development; and, not least, adequate financial rewards – these are all examples of the detailed steps that would help to achieve this aim.

Possibly the best known research study of motivation is that of Herzberg* et al., who surveyed groups of engineers and accountants. Many similar studies have since been conducted, with different categories of workpeople, their basis an analysis of individuals happy in their work and others who were unhappy.

The following list of motivating factors emerges:

1 Sense of achievement.
2 Recognition of achievements by superiors.
3 Being given responsibility.
4 Times of advancement and promotion.
5 Awareness of prospects for further growth.
6 When work is interesting.

On the other hand, demotivating incidents can be attributed to:

1 Poor features of an organization's policies or administrative procedures.
2 Poor quality of supervision.
3 Difficult relationships between staff.
4 Anxieties about salary, security, or status.
5 The impact of the job on the personal life of the individual concerned.

One important concept emerging from such surveys is that all the motivating factors relate to the content of jobs, while the demotivating factors concern the context in which the jobs are performed. The fact that the former is within the immediate control of superiors clearly indicates that all managers can rightly be expected to have a positive impact in stimulating their staff. That the causes of dissatisfaction lie more outside their control does not, however, mean that they are absolved from the responsibility for removing any frustrating influences: rather, it demands that they work harder at doing so.

*Herzberg, Mausner, and Snyderman, *The Motivation to Work* (New York: Wiley, 1959).

Analysing job satisfaction means looking at the individual's needs at work and the extent to which they are being met. But this must be done realistically, and set against the pressures and restraints which bear on the organization itself and which may prevent it from providing maximum job satisfaction. Thus job satisfaction must be considered in two ways:* first, in terms of the fit between what an organization requires of its employees and what the employees are seeking from the firm; second, in terms of what employees are seeking from the firm and what they are receiving. This may be represented diagrammatically as in Figure 3.

A more generalized approach to studying levels of individuals' satisfaction with their jobs relates to the concept of 'the work ethic', and one significant survey† appears to indicate that British workers

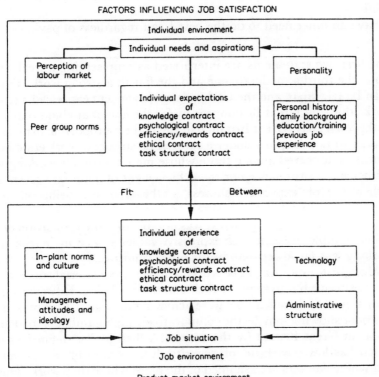

FACTORS INFLUENCING JOB SATISFACTION

Figure 3

---

*'Job Satisfaction: a Method of Analysis', Enid Mumford, *Personnel Review*, Spring 1972.

†'Work and human values: An international report on jobs in the 1980s and 1990s' (Aspen Institute for Humanistic Studies, 1983).

have a weak work ethic compared to many others. The disparity between what they expect from their jobs and what they actually get reveals them to be potentially one of the world's most discontented workforces.

In the survey, workers in six industrialized countries – Great Britain, Israel, Japan, Sweden, the USA and West Germany – were presented with four statements and asked which of these best represented their own feelings about work:

'Work is a business transaction. The more I get paid, the more I do; the less I get paid, the less I do'.
'Working for a living is one of life's unpleasant necessities. I would not work if I did not have to'.
'I find my work interesting but I don't let it interfere with the rest of my life'.
'I have an inner need to do the best I can regardless of pay'.

The first two statements are interpreted as representing a weak work ethic, the third a moderate one and the fourth a strong work ethic.

In Israel, Japan and the USA at least 50 per cent expressed a strong work ethic, but Great Britain was by far the lowest at about only one-sixth; conversely, Great Britain had the highest proportion expressing a weak work ethic, just under a third. The strongest work ethic in all countries appeared among those whose main reason for working was neither mere sustenance nor the achievement of material success but rather that of 'expressive success' – the emphasis being on inner growth (how they felt about it) rather than on external signs of wealth (what they could show for it). It was notable that the proportion of the British sample choosing such expressive values as their main reason for working was far lower than in the other countries.

Most Britons appear to be working to achieve material success, not just to survive but to improve their standard of living. However, fewer than a third of them felt they were achieving their goal. One reason for this poor showing may be the comparatively high number of 'bad jobs' found in Great Britain by the survey. A 'bad job' is defined as one which has low pay, little job security, little chance of advancement, and where workers are ashamed of the place where they work. This is clearly the sort of job least likely to attract commitment.

If this is a true reflection of job satisfaction levels in Great Britain, it makes it particularly important that detailed attention should be paid by employers (personnel managers), unions, employees and government to ensuring that a reasonable proportion of jobholders can potentially regard their work as interesting, challenging or rewarding.

The job itself would have to be improved before a dissatisfied worker is likely to be transformed into a committed one.

Modern behavioural science theory propounds that employees throughout an organization will feel committed to their work if they are offered opportunities for personal development by extending their capacities and responsibilities, backed with positive managerial support and understanding. If work is made more satisfying for individual employees, then an atmosphere can be created which will lead to greater flexibility in introducing necessary changes, which will enable human resources to be used more effectively, and will thus improve productivity.

Effective leadership

A leader is the sort of person who can motivate a group of people to achieve its tasks and maintain team unity throughout the process. This definition has emerged literally after years of debate and research, much of it obscured by misconceptions and half-truths. The original popular assumption was that the desirable qualities of a leader could be listed. Unfortunately, no two authorities ever seemed able to agree precisely on such lists. The problem of this approach is that it ignores the situation in which the leader acts; the village idiot is hardly likely to possess much by way of 'leadership qualities', yet he might very well take over leadership of a group of hikers lost in fog on the local moors. In fact, this example points to the concept which subsequently developed, that leadership is a function of the situation, and that the professional or technical knowledge required in the situation pushes the leader forward. But this again seems to be based on a false assumption, that leadership can be passed from hand to hand within the same group as the occasion demands. In any event, it is undeniable that there is a general area of competence not related to expert knowledge (which the 'qualities investigators' were trying to identify). From the USA then came the 'group' approach: since leadership exists largely to ensure that the common needs of the group are satisfied, then the functions necessary to achieve this can be shared by its members. This idea completely excludes the previous concepts of leadership qualities and professional competence, but its argument in favour of shared responsibility surely wrongly assumes that leadership means the same as authoritarianism.

'Functional leadership' has developed from these earlier analyses, concentrating on what the leader actually does. It too is based on the assumption that the group shares common areas of need:

1 To get certain tasks done, which presumably is the reason why the group was created in the first place; its members will become dissatisfied if the tasks cannot be completed.
2 To be held together as a working team and motivated as such (the need for 'group cohesion').
3 Each individual member of the group has personal needs that must be satisfied through his/her work.

The leader must be constantly aware of the interdependence of these three factors (Figure 4). If tasks cannot be achieved, morale will fall; members will tend to blame each other or quarrel, thus disrupting the group cohesion, and they will become individually dissatisfied because their needs for status are not being met.

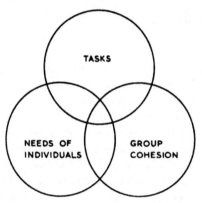

Figure 4

The role of the leader therefore demands that he/she must do certain things:

1 Explain the group's tasks to it.
2 Plan how these tasks might be achieved.
3 Set the standards of performance required.
4 Maintain morale and encourage the group.
5 Keep an eye on its individual members.

The extent to which these functions can be shared with the members of the group is also important. If the leader announces his/her decisions in an autocratic manner, then the time taken to carry them out is likely to be longer than if they were discussed with the group members first so that they fully understood the decisions (Figure 5). The actual amount of participation by the members of the group will in fact depend on some of the aspects already mentioned – how much

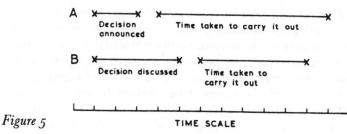

Figure 5

technical knowledge they have of the problem and such factors in the situation as the amount of time available, for example.

In all these ways, then, the functional approach concentrates on what leaders do, rather than trying to analyse what they are. In particular, they must concern themselves with maintaining good relations with their subordinates, each of whom should be given a clear understanding of where they stand in the estimation of their group leader. The sting of criticism can be avoided if group leaders make a habit of discussing members' work with them regularly, assessing progress, praising strong points, and discussing weaknesses. Such techniques can rightly be considered as being non-financial incentives, stimulating subordinates on to greater efforts. Where practical, elements of competition may be introduced – competing against one's own previous best performance, against standards set by other staff or rival departments, or against target times. All these can help individuals to develop through having to extend themselves to meet some form of challenge and thus gain in prestige when successful.

This raises another of the very real problems that senior managers in large organizations have to face. There is in any managerial hierarchy a system of protocol designed to control the methods by which the 'bright young people' can get past the block of their immediate superiors and tell senior people of their ideas. Such a regimen clearly has disadvantages: orderly systems there must be, but a rule such as 'not seeing the person below without the knowledge of the person between' is nothing more than red tape. How can top managers be sure that, below the level of their own subordinates, there are not some really valuable younger managers whose abilities are not being fully used?

There must be some sort of mechanism to expose the talent at lower levels. 'Ginger groups' such as work study and operational research teams which report direct to the top can pass information upwards which might otherwise not be obtained. Unfortunately this gains the teams concerned the reputation of being spies, which makes their own work more difficult and puts their information sources on the defensive. The most effective method, perhaps, consists of several minor administrative practices: to encourage departmental heads to bring their deputies to meetings; to persuade them to set up their own working parties; to use internal courses as a means of eliciting ideas and criticisms, particularly across departmental boundaries. These are all open and recognized methods, built into the regular chain of executive action, by which three rather than two levels of management are brought into frequent contact.

The group leader should also be willing to delegate to subordinates, especially to the younger members so that they can develop their potential. Delegation is a process whereby a manager entrusts a subordinate with the authority to perform a defined task and requires him/her to be accountable for it. Effective delegation is a finely balanced technique: it does not mean giving a person a task and then breathing down his/her neck to make sure it is done properly; nor does it mean allocating work and leaving subordinates to get on with it as best they can. The important thing with delegation is that leaders should grant freedom to act, thus showing that they have confidence in their subordinates. The person to whom a task has been allotted should be allowed to carry it out in his/her own way and not necessarily in accordance with the traditional methods used in the department or by the group leader. They must feel that they are not only responsible for their action but also trusted. The control which managers exercise over delegated tasks is inherent throughout the process. At the outset they provide subordinates with proper job descriptions, see to it that they are adequately trained and are fully briefed on what they want done – in all these ways ensuring that tasks are approached in ways likely to achieve the desired results. Then while they are actually working at their tasks there must be a system of control through personal observation, reporting back, and consultation.

Leaders who take this functional approach rely heavily on their own personalities and capacity for directing and controlling others. 'Technical' leaders, on the other hand, are followed because of their superior knowledge or because they have the services of expert advisers at their command; by exploiting this expertise they are able to help the group decide what common action must be taken. There is a third type – 'institutional' leaders – who rely on a position in the recognized system of discipline, as in the armed forces, the church, or the nursing profession. Authority is here more easily asserted and the right to order and control more quickly acknowledged; at the same time the respect of subordinates is often more apparent for a position and its status than for any personal qualities its holder may seem to possess.

It is also true to say, even of this latter institutional type of situation, that both formal and informal leaders usually emerge in all working groups. Formal leaders are appointed by authority and should have recognized terms of reference within their sphere of competence. Informal leaders represent a group in a manner which fosters its interests, and their behaviour will depend very much on its attitudes. They will reflect the claims and views of the group, and initiate acts of leadership; in this respect, it is conceivable that in different situations the role of informal leader may switch from one person to another. The prestige of informal leaders allows them to rub shoulders on equal terms with other group leaders. Unfortunately, groups may elect them because of their good fellowship rather than their efficiency, and this can lead to trouble.

Switching to the other side of the coin, what is it that individual members of working groups want from their leaders? Much has been implied already in explaining the leadership role. Individuals want the requirements of their job made clear to them, and want to be kept informed of their superior's assessment of their performance. They expect to be treated fairly and justly, of course, seeing no favours shown to one person or another. They want their superior to be accessible and always ready to listen and be helpful. Where subordinates have authority delegated to them, they look to the group-leader to back them up in their decisions and actions. They hope that their leader can inspire loyalty to the group and set standards of behaviour, largely by their own example of hard work and integrity. They must also try to understand the personal characteristics of their superior, because they cannot feel really secure until they have established a good personal contact with him/her; this is often difficult in authoritarian types of organization, where the status of the superior's post may obscure the personality of the individual holding it.

It is well known that there are 'fashions' in personnel management, as in all aspects of life, and there has been considerable renewed interest in the role of leadership in recent years, not least in the pronouncements of people who are themselves among the most prominent leaders of the UK national economy.

Lord Sieff,* chairman of Marks and Spencer, has said that far too few industrial leaders believe in good human relations at work or, if they do, fail to implement such a policy. 'It is no answer to blame the unions: management must face up to its responsibilities for creating good working conditions. People are the most important asset of any organization – they should be treated as individuals who merit respect. Full and frank two-way communication and respect for the

---

*Royal Society of Arts lecture, April 1986.

contribution people can make, given encouragement – these are the foundations of an effective and progressive policy'.

John Harvey-Jones, ex-chairman of ICI, has written a book* on the subject. One point he develops is that in the armed forces (where he received his early training in leadership) training people to make things happen involves the process of: stating intentions, issuing commands, making sure everyone understands them, and then seeing they are carried out. Harvey-Jones succeeded in transferring this apparently simple principle to a large industrial commercial organization where typically messages from above become inaudible a few layers further down in the communications network. His view is expressed, 'The ideal organization, and the one which has the best chance of success, is one where, if you ask anyone from the chairman down to the newest recruit on the shopfloor what the business is trying to do, you would get the same answer'.

Effective leadership can thus be seen to be the kind which generates high levels of subordinate commitment. It follows that it is unlikely that line managers will perform well unless they feel 'ownership for their work'. Some firms go to great lengths to achieve clarity of mission. IBM, for example, regularly surveys staff and management in order to identify any misunderstandings, problems and development needs, with a view to putting them right. British Airways' (BA) campaign in the mid-1980s for 'putting people first' involved 35,000 employees attending a programme for developing people skills, based on the realization that BA's mission needed to switch from 'flying aeroplanes' to 'the business of moving people around the world'.

Statements on qualities of leadership, like the above, may seem to some to be platitudinous. Be that as it may, their practical significance can be judged from the following negative, or at least 'other-side-of-the-coin', quotations taken from letters published in *The Sunday Times* in October 1985:

> Today's management is arrogant, insecure and totally devoid of any consideration for the most important people in their lives – the workers, the employees. There are those who cannot manage their jobs and those who cannot manage people, and many who cannot manage either. For this they are paid very highly and command no respect from their staff.

> Two problems dominate: the enormous cultural divide between manager and managed, and the inadequacy of education and training. Most British companies still consist of three divisions – the board, senior administrators and the rest, or as one chairman put it, 'those buggers down there'.

Making it Happen: Reflections on Leadership (Collins, 1988).

Individual personality

Man is a perpetually wanting animal, new needs emerging as old ones are satisfied, a never-ending process from cradle to grave. Their behaviour in life is entirely governed by the circle of hereditary or environmental influences creating needs within them and their taking action to fulfil those needs. Fulfilment removes the original cause of the needs they feel, as illustrated in Figure 6. Always a person's behaviour can be questioned – what is the motive for that behaviour, and what caused that motive to develop in the first place?

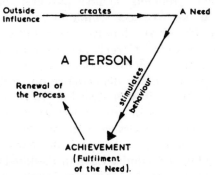

Figure 6   Model of behaviour patterns

The adjustment that people make between their particular motivation, their ability to achieve the goals implied, and the limitations placed on their drive by their environment and opportunities, is reflected in their *personality*. This is the quality that distinguishes them from every other person, whether it makes them outstanding among their fellows or draws little attention from them. Both hereditary characteristics and the environment in which they live affect people's personalities and attitudes. Intelligence is inborn, and temperament is largely controlled by the endocrine systems of the body, which in turn depend on the state of a person's health. The basic forms of motivation – for food, shelter, sex, parenthood – are also inborn, as are certain aptitudes to be mechanical, good at languages, or artistic, for example. Considerable evidence has been gathered to show that physique has a direct bearing on personality; thus the short, stockily-built type of person tends to be sociable and emotional.

Much or little can be made of these inborn characteristics by the way a person is brought up. His/her family and the environment in which he/she lives will cause his/her development to be channelled along lines which prescribe conformity with adult conventions. These differ throughout the world, qualities that are much admired by one race being considered repulsive by others. All sorts of physical, social, and emotional events will have their impacts and help to expand or stultify a person's potential. Acceptable behaviour on all occasions results in society regarding a person as having an adjusted personality.

The normal pattern of personality development throughout life is well understood. Parental control and school instruction instil a sense of values and social obligations early on, so that we in Britain, for instance, learn to repress natural aggressiveness and respect other people's feelings and their property, and accept a measure of responsibility for their welfare. We are taught to value privacy, have great regard for intelligence, and admire certain types of physical beauty. Then in adolescence, rebellion against parental control emerges as emotional needs change. We accept middle age as the best time of life: natural drives for a home and family, a pleasant job with status, the struggle for success – all have largely been accomplished (or, at least, disillusionment has not yet set in). Old age, on the other hand, is not a happy time: there is too much dependence on younger people, and this, in small family units, is often over-burdensome.

Throughout this process of growth we are developing *attitudes* – towards authority, religion, types of people, work, leisure, and a host of other things. Everything that happens is viewed in the light of experience, and judgements and behaviour modified accordingly. It is important for the personnel manager to appreciate that once an attitude is firmly established, it is not easily changed. Thus many people would prefer to change their jobs rather than their attitudes, seeking an environment where they feel at ease and need make the least personal adjustments. In this way it is possible to become blinkered from any further experiences, to reject any opinions that conflict with one's own, and end up with attitudes firmly entrenched as prejudices. These always tend to indicate insecurity or lack of intellectual ability on the part of the person concerned. On the other hand, someone who is confident, perhaps because his/her life is already successful, will risk meeting new challenges and will change and develop his/her attitudes throughout his/her life.

Workgroup sanctions

Individuals at their place of work are judged not only in terms of their own personality and attitudes, however, but also by the way they adapt to the general working situation and, in particular, their ability to work with other people. Except for the rare backroom boffin, all workers are members of formal and informal social groups.

The personnel manager must accept this as a fact of life and advise on ways of encouraging the efficiency of these groups: positive measures can be taken to strengthen their bonds, which will improve the social climate of the organization and hence raise productivity. In the first place, the prevention of strain or disturbances can be tackled from the outset, by taking care to allocate newcomers to groups where they seem likely to fit in. Thus objective selection, proper induction, and the practice of participative management are all designed to ease contact with fellow-workers and supervisors, and enable quick adjustment to the discipline and atmosphere of the organization. The actual formation of groups can be fostered, and the effectiveness of existing groups improved, by such measures as training courses, joint consultative committees, or by sponsoring leisure-time clubs. Where there are signs of disruption in group relationships, then management must take corrective action to eliminate it (*cf.* Elton Mayo's work).

This presupposes an understanding of the ways in which group patterns of behaviour and values are established, maintained, and transmitted. In fact, these are determined by *sanctions* – formal or informal rewards and penalties designed to channel behaviour in certain directions, ranging from smiles and frowns at one end of the scale to fines, suspension, and dismissal at the other end. It is precisely because smiles of encouragement and frowns of disapproval are important that group discipline can be achieved: through them, in particular, newcomers are taught how to conform to group values without recourse to the more serious penalties.

In any large organization, three main types of sanction can be seen in operation:

1 Management sanctions – applied to enforce discipline and control quality of work: 'carrots' such as bonuses and promotion, and 'sticks' like suspension or dismissal.
2 Union sanctions, which have two forms:
   (a) Those aimed at enforcing trade union discipline over members whose behaviour seems likely to bring their union into disrepute or to disrupt the unity of workers' interests: reprimands, fines, and expulsion have varying degrees of impact, while such social pressures as 'sending to Coventry' have a profound psychological effect.
   (b) Those applied against management to make them keep to negotiated agreeements: they tend to run counter to management's own sanctions, of course, and are largely aimed at defending union members against disciplinary action.
3 Workgroup sanctions: these are enforced by workers directly in three ways:
   (a) Against managements for breaking unwritten rules not covered by formal agreements.

   (b) Against their unions for actions regarded as officious or inefficient.

   (c) Against their fellow-workers to uphold approved patterns of conduct within each group.

The differences between these main types of sanctions are closely related to the sort of behaviour which management or trade union members seek to encourage. Management's incentives are intended to pick out individuals with initiative and start them on the promotion ladder, thus rising above their fellows; but trade union and workgroup sanctions are designed to foster loyalty to the group and to resist management's efforts to set workers in competition with each other. The threat of loss of the social life associated with primary workgroups is the most powerful sanction for conformity. The man who becomes a foreman may be made to feel that he has switched to the other side and can no longer be trusted with knowledge of the activities of the group to which he previously belonged. Newcomers to groups, especially youngsters, become indoctrinated with group ideas without even realizing that this is happening, often reaching what they think are their own decisions when in fact they are responding to group influence. One group value that they are commonly taught is disapproval of the promotion-seeker, which suggests that people who do accept promotion tend to reject workgroup pressures and values; for this very reason they may be unable to interpret to top management the real nature of worker attitudes.

Group arrangements are among the most important causes of job satisfaction, absenteeism, and labour turnover. They are particularly important when the work is dangerous or stressful. An optimum design* for working groups suggests that they should be small (five or six in membership), cohesive, cooperative teams, able to take decisions about their own affairs.

But how can these conditions be brought about? To a limited extent, groups will emerge with their own leaders and norms, whether or not planned by management. If very large groups are created, they will divide up into smaller groups; if leaders are not appointed, they will emerge informally; group norms will develop to influence the methods and rate of work. Official arrangements may thus be considerably distorted, with subsequent changes in communications channels and even in incentive systems.

However, all this is true only up to a point, and with highly technical processes consultants have been able to devise effective new group

*'Working in Groups', Michael Argyle, *New Society*, 26 October 1972, page 221.

arrangements. One example is the Tavistock study of Longwall coalmining, the starting point of which was a working group of forty-one miners, divided into three shifts, who never met, doing cutting, filling, and stonework. Since these three interdependent groups never met, there was a loss of cohesiveness and cooperation. Great improvements were achieved by restructuring the men into three different types of groups, each containing all three skills: output then rose by 51 per cent. Cooperative motivation has its own advantages, and must necessarily be fostered when jobs are complementary to one another.

Other group problems could not be solved without changes in technology. Long assembly lines are an example, for this kind of work produces a very low level of job satisfaction. Making lines shorter, or changing their shape into squares so that workers face each other and interact more easily are proven simple solutions. So is the Volvo (Sweden) experience of scrapping the assembly line altogether and having small groups of workers responsible for constructing the entire car.

Group norms are developed about most matters relating to the group's main activities. Most important are norms about the work, including output restrictions and the elaborate deceptions which go with them, and conventions about how the work should be done. There are norms which determine attitudes towards management and unions, and others concerned with social activity – humour, practical jokes, gossip, clothes, appearance, and private slang, the meaning of which may be known only to members of the group. Some norms are created to deal with the external problems of the group (the work and its environment), and others with its internal problems (survival as a harmonious social group). Once developed, the norms are imposed on new members who may conform initially only under pressure, but who usually then come to accept the group's pattern of behaviour. In certain circumstances this pattern may facilitate the communication of new ideas, but some norms may also have the effect of making groups conservative in outlook and resistant to change.

Group dynamics

The study of group behaviour has become more and more sophisticated over the years, culminating in the technique of *group dynamics*, which describes what happens within and between groups when working at tasks. It has been defined as 'the examination of the interacting intellectual and emotional activity of human beings endeavouring to relate to one another cooperatively whilst preserving their personal identity and individual aspirations'.* The aim of such studies clearly is to try to increase the effectiveness of groups in achieving objectives.

People who lack confidence in themselves as individuals or in their groups, who fear they are of little standing in their groups, who expect others of more ability or status to take the lead, who feel they have no great stake in a group problem or its outcome, who resist change or fail to see the need for it, who feel no need to understand others: such people find it difficult to share fully in group activities. Helping them by offering opportunities to discuss their personal feelings in a constructive way, so that increasing awareness can be achieved – this is the special concern of experts in group dynamics. The word 'experts' needs to be stressed, as it is essential that specialists, preferably qualified psychologists, should apply the training techniques involved rather than amateurs who happen to be interested in the subject.

The best known of these techniques is the so-called 'T-group' – a group of people formed with the task of considering how small face-to-face groups work by looking at the behaviour of their own group. The early stages are often frightening to many people who want a clearly defined discussion so that they and the other group members will not get hurt too much. But experience shows that, although some members feel status-conscious at the outset, barriers do come down quickly as the group members settle to talk about why they feel and behave as they do. Over a period of time, the group builds its own identity and becomes intent on examining its methods of reaching agreement about values. In doing so, it discovers personal motivations through studying internal relationships within the group, and it is claimed that the whole conspectus of interaction of individual personalities influenced by wider group pressures becomes clearer.

Specific benefits from T-group training have been listed thus:†

1 Receiving communications: more effort to understand, attentive listening.
2 Relational facility: cooperative, easier to deal with.
3 Awareness of human behaviour: more analytic of others' actions, clearer perception of people.
4 Sensitivity to group behaviour: more conscious of group processes.
5 Increased sensitivity to others' feelings.
6 Acceptance of other people: more considerate and patient.
7 Tolerant of new information: less dogmatic, more willing to receive suggestions.

Personnel Management and Working Groups, Anne Crichton (IPM, 1962), page 9.
†'The Impact of T-Groups on Managerial Behaviour', I. Mangham and C. L. Cooper, *The Journal of Management Studies*, February 1969.

Observers generally agree on the types of change seen: improved skills in diagnosing individual and group behaviour, clearer communication, greater tolerance and consideration, and greater action skill and flexibility.

Further reading

Motivation – a Manager's Guide, William Simpson (Industrial Society, 1983).
On Human Relations, Harvard Business Review (Heinemann, 1979).

4

The employment function

Manpower planning

'Obtaining the best staff for an organization' is the prime function of personnel managers' tasks, but before they set about filling individual jobs, they should consider the overall management problem of making the best use of available resources. *Manpower planning* is concerned basically with budgeting for the best use of labour resources, just as the management accountant budgets for the best use of financial resources. It aims to 'maintain and improve the ability of the organization to achieve corporate objectives, through the development of strategies designed to enhance the contribution of manpower at all times in the foreseeable future'.*

National manpower policy

Looking at the national economy as a whole, the key word in any manpower policy is 'redeployment', covering problems of overmanning and the movement of workers, both from declining to expanding industries and from inefficient to efficient firms within an industry. Nor can people be allowed to work below their capacities because of inadequate training or skill, or because of restrictive practices of management or unions. To achieve growth targets specified for the

* Manpower Planning, Gareth Stainer (Heinemann, 1971), page 3.

national economy, there must be large movements of labour between industries and within industries, and ever more rapid changes in working methods to meet the demands of technological developments. In other words, effective redeployment includes all measures designed to ensure the movement of labour into more productive work. Of prime importance in this is the requirement that those affected by such changes must be helped to adapt to them.

Specific actions involved in manpower planning at national level include:

1 Lump-sum payments to redundant workers.
2 Help provided for workers moving to new areas.
3 Modernization of the Employment Service provided by the Department of Employment.
4 Expansion of the Training Agency's range of training.
5 Helping married women and older workers, who wish to do so, to take or remain in paid employment; employers are encouraged to adopt flexible attitudes towards working conditions, especially hours, in order to utilize these particular categories of labour.
6 Overall government policy to improve employment prospects in development areas and industries which need more labour. Measures include, for example, the building of advance factories, capital grants, and regional employment premiums which offer continuing subsidies to manufacturing firms who expand within the development areas.
7 Since unemployment has become a major problem, job creation, work experience, youth training schemes and a whole range of programmes have been introduced.

All these activities should be based on productivity studies of all sectors of the national economy, designed to establish current levels of economic performance of manpower in different industries and at different places within those industries. Identifying where high productivity already exists will help to make government targets for future economic growth much more realistic. It will also enable labour forecasts based on economic trends to be made more accurately: that is, the numbers required, both by skills and by location.

Within each firm

Whatever effect these measures may have in achieving national productivity targets, the individual personnel manager must obviously

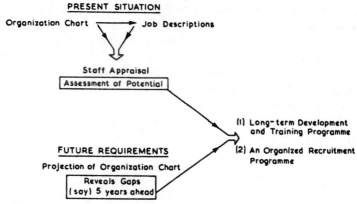

Figure 7

be concerned mainly with his/her own organization's labour problems. The skeleton of a firm's manpower plan is sketched in Figure 7.

The present situation must be analysed in terms of the structure of the organization and the competence of the people working for it. An organization chart will show what their jobs are and the lines of promotion between them. For effective planning, however, more detail is required, and full job descriptions must be prepared evaluating the relative significance of all the jobs listed. The suitability of the existing staff in carrying out their jobs must then be assessed, with some form of rating to enable comparison with the requirements of the different jobs previously described. In particular, the assessment must include a method of identifying those individuals who appear to have potential for development on to bigger and better jobs in the future.

An estimate of future staff changes and requirements must then be made, based on three main sources of information:

1 Knowledge of the age structure of the present staff, and what is likely to happen by way of retirements.
2 Natural wastage – labour turnover statistics should enable a forecast to be made of the numbers of present staff likely to leave during the period under review.
3 The proposed expansion or contraction of the business activities of the organization – based on market research findings, likely technological advances, and anticipation of the prospects of competitors.

Once the comparison between future requirements and present resources has been made, the personnel manager can then devise a long-term training and development programme to prepare for promotion those staff who have been assessed as having the necessary potential. The changing nature of the jobs themselves, apart from any consideration of promotion, can also be catered for in such a scheme of training. Finally, any remaining gaps foreseen will have to be filled by recruitment from outside; but with adequate warning, at least this can be properly phased, rather than personnel managers finding themselves faced with vacancies occurring unexpectedly.

Clearly, the more precise the information available, the greater the probability that manpower plans will be accurate. But, in practice, they are subject to many imponderable factors, some completely outside an organization's control. For example, occasional comment in the popular press about the future state of labour supply and its effect on the national economy almost always ignores the impact that further development in automation, education and training, the merging of firms and productivity bargains might have on production figures in the meantime. Other imponderables include international trade, general technological advances, population movements, the human acceptance of or resistance to change, and the quality of leadership and its impact on morale. The environment, then, is uncertain, and so are the people whose activities are being planned. Manpower plans must therefore be accepted as being continuous, under constant review, and ever-changing.

As far as possible, however, the imponderables should be taken into account by the personnel department in preparing its manpower plans. Obviously there must be a *precise statement of the organization's objectives* to start with, in order to calculate the size of the labour force required to meet them. From the outset, too, managers and supervisors at all levels must be given a clear *understanding of the need for a manpower plan in detail*.

Having said this, there is initially a great need for much more *information* than is usually at present available to the planners; fortunately the increasing computerization of personnel records and control statistics may aid this process. As far as *existing manpower* is concerned, the planners must know everything about the size and composition of their organization's labour force, rates of turnover and absenteeism, the cost of overtime, recruitment difficulties, anticipated results of training activities, and the types of changes in jobs that go on week by week. Comparisons of performance can then be made – interfirm, industrially, and nationally.

Relevant information that should be collected about the *external environment* would cover local provision of housing and public works; social plans and trends, including sickness, retirement, unemployment; reductions in hours of work, and longer holidays; and industrial development schemes. Then, in looking at *labour supply*, its availability would be compared with other areas, as would its distribution in terms of age, skills, membership of trade unions, and sex (including part-time and full-time married women workers). The difficulties of obtaining labour can be measured and expressed as the average length of time taken to fill jobs of varying types of skill and levels of seniority. A forecast must also be made of the *pace of technological change*, particularly the speed with which capital investment is enabling equipment to replace labour.

The whole range of this planning activity will be new to many personnel managers, and will be found to be very demanding. It is truly a managerial task; in no way can such planning become merely a repetitive process, with information being applied to a standard formula; rather it means forecasting, taking action, receiving control information, and constantly adjusting decisions and correcting forecasts to meet an ever-changing situation. The importance of thoroughly developed *communications* in all this cannot be over-emphasized. The planners must be able to obtain the most comprehensive information about manpower locally, industrially, and nationally; they must also be able to present this data to the management team throughout their organization in ways which enable its significance to be fully appreciated.

Stainer* has analysed the strategies involved in manpower planning thus:

1 The collection, maintenance, and interpretation of relevant information about manpower.
2 Periodic reports of manpower objectives, requirements and actual employment, and of other characteristics of the resource.
3 The development of procedures and techniques which will enable all requirements for different types of manpower (including those for new capital projects) to be determined over a wide range of periods in the light of known corporate objectives; and the modification of these objectives where they make unrealizable demands for manpower.
4 The development of measures of manpower utilization as part of the process of establishing forecasts of manpower requirements, coupled if possible with independent validation.
5 The use, where appropriate, of techniques designed to result in more effective allocation of work, as a means of improving manpower utilization.
6 Research into factors (which may be technological, social, or individual) which limit the contribution that individuals or groups can

*op. cit., pages 3–4.

make to the organization, with the aim of removing or modifying such limitations.

7 The development and use of methods of economic evaluation of manpower which adequately reflect its characteristics as income generator and cost, and hence improve the quality of decisions affecting the resource.

8 The assessment of availability, acquisition, promotion, and retention, in the light of the forecast requirements of the organization, of individuals who it has been established are likely to perform well.

9 The analysis of the dynamic processes of recruitment, promotion, and loss to which an organization is subject, and the control both of these processes and of the organizational structure; so that as far as possible the maximum performance of individuals and groups is encouraged without excessive cost.

The manpower planning process in diagrammatic form is illustrated below (Figure 8).

The labour-flow approach to manpower planning – 'current labour inventory' linked to recruitment, promotion and wastage rates and business/technological developments – lends itself to the use of

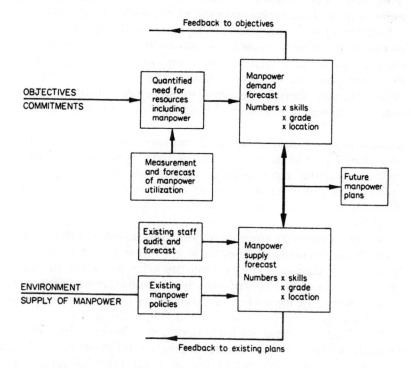

Figure 8   The manpower planning process

computerized spreadsheets, to which quantitatively based demand-forecasting techniques, embracing budgetary information, can be applied. In other words, manpower forecasting can be worked out on a spreadsheet, provided that the problems involved can be modelled, the relevant variables quantified and the key interrelationships specified.

The spreadsheet can then be used to work (very quickly) through 'What if. . . happens' types of questions to give the planner a complete picture of the manpower system, in particular demonstrating that possible solutions to staffing problems affecting one grade, occupation or department can create other problems elsewhere. Promotion rules can be built in, thus providing a model which sets out the established sources for job succession, linked to statements about the perceived quality of people employed in the organization.

Large amounts of data can be input to such a model: for example, the financial costs of recruitment, training, labour wastage and redundancies. Alternative manpower policies can be costed in turn, to give managers an objective basis for choosing between different strategies. In all these ways, spreadsheets present opportunities for new types of hybrid manpower models, incorporating labour flow and budgetary considerations, and hence equip personnel managers much more thoroughly to tackle strategic management problems.

Demographic trends and attempts to deal with the economic recession of the early 1990s are causing manpower planners increasingly to concentrate their attention on two aspects of organization design: re-planning the way work is performed to secure the supply of labour, and altering the authority structure because of the need both to harness the skill of knowledge workers and to improve flexibility. The former derives directly from studies of the labour market and from projections of the organization's manpower supply and demand. The increased use of part-timers in 'back-to-back' mode, attracting more female workers (creches, evening shifts), opportunities for older people − all are examples of action stemming from manpower planning analyses which call for organizational changes.

In both categories there is an obvious reason for the personnel manager to be involved, in order to consult staff and negotiate with them about changes. His/her role may be less clear in effecting changes to the authority structure, where radical reorganization may be necessary to cope with rapid changes of technology or customer requirements or to gain full advantage from the higher proportions of knowledge workers. Such changes are unlikely to happen satisfactorily without the personnel manager's intervention, calling as they do for understanding of the need for rapid cultural change throughout the organization. As well as acting as an agent of change, the human resource specialist must also be deeply involved in the facilitation and consequences of organizational change. For example, reward systems and career development will need re-thinking. Most difficult to deal with are questions of status; for flexible organizations to work effectively all staff must be able to take on new roles without feeling inhibited by existing attitudes towards differing status levels.

The technology to assist the practicalities of manpower planning also advances apace, with software packages (for example, the 'Sussex' system of the Institute of Manpower Studies) which are menu-driven and designed to be used by line managers as well as personnel specialists. Their general aim is to enable both policy options to be evaluated and informed recommendations to be made.

Local employment intelligence

The Department of Employment's local labour market intelligence services cover three main aspects:

1 A range of information recorded in local offices.
2 The positive involvement of employers, for example, through frequent visits and systematic discussion.
3 Regular bulletins to circulate important information.

The records to be maintained include: background information on such things as local transport, housing, educational and training facilities; data on the industrial structure of the area – the main industries and firms, analyses of employees by industries, occupations and age, expansions and redundancies; and data on employment activity – entry into employment of young people, proportion of women in employment, travel-to-work patterns, and figures on placings, vacancies, and unemployment.

For their part, employers appreciate the defined purpose of obtaining and discussing information on changes in labour requirements. In many areas, while acknowledging the confidentiality of data about individual firms, it is possible to make available fairly reliable information on changes for up to a year ahead. Published bulletins include outlines of important developments likely to affect prospects in the area and appraisals of the effect on the labour market to be expected from them; advance information about skilled workers due to become available for employment as the result of closures; analyses of workers registered for employment in a particular industry; and notices about new training courses. For purposes of local comparison, national data on labour turnover, absenteeism, rates of participation of women in employment, and average earnings are available.

Recruitment procedure and code of practice

The basic problem of recruitment is knowing what staff are required and where to get them. This simple statement outlines the procedure that must be followed when trying to select a candidate for any responsible post:

1 Assuming the organization tries to conduct its recruitment in an orderly manner, the procedure will be based on a forecast of manpower requirements as far ahead as possible.
2 Departmental heads will submit to the personnel manager a requisition for the staff they require at the appropriate time.
3 The job concerned will then be fully analysed, to prepare two documents –
   (a) A *job description*, a copy of which will be sent to all applicants.
   (b) A *personnel specification*, for use by the selectors in conjunction with the job description.
4 All likely sources of recruitment must be notified of the vacancy, and advertisements placed where necessary.
5 Applications will begin to flow in, by telephone, letter, or personal calls. The methods for dealing with these will largely depend on the urgency of filling the vacancy. If the procedure has been well planned beforehand, there should be time to ask all candidates to complete an application form and for these to be considered together before going on to the next stage.
6 This will be to interview the candidates. Where there is a large number of them, it may be necessary to do this in two stages, with preliminary interviews held initially in order to make up a short-list for the final interviews and selection later. But when there are only a few candidates, the short-list is virtually settled for the selectors. The successful candidate is then usually chosen after the final interviews.
7 References are normally taken up either just before or just after the interviews. The former applies generally in public services when references are obtained for all the candidates on the list for final interview. In private industry, the common practice is to make reference enquiries only about the successful candidate after he/she has been offered the job; the offer is conditional upon his/her references proving satisfactory, but this method is considered necessary to avoid jeopardizing that person's existing job.
8 The contract of employment must be completed, and suitably worded letters sent to the unsuccessful candidates.
9 Before new employees start, proper reception arrangements must be made for their arrival, and an induction programme prepared. Subsequently some method of follow-up should be observed after

three or four weeks to see how they are settling. Further brief checks should be made from time to time, not least as one way of evaluating the selection decision taken and the success of the methods used.

The need to maintain high professional standards in administering this procedure has been recognized by the Institute of Personnel Management, which has urged a code of recruitment practice upon members, in order to promote good relations between prospective employers and the people who apply for the jobs they offer. In achieving this aim, obligations of both recruiters and candidates should be observed, thus:

Recruiters' obligations

1 Job advertisements will state clearly the form of reply desired, e.g. curriculum vitae, completed application form, and any preference for handwritten applications.
2 Every application will be acknowledged promptly.
3 Candidates will be kept informed of the progress of applications, and be told about the form of the selection procedure, the likely time involved and the policy regarding expenses.
4 Detailed personal information (e.g. religion, medical history, place of birth, family background) will not be called for unless and until it is relevant to the job.
5 Recruiters will not take up any reference without the candidate's specific approval.
6 Applications will be treated as confidential.

Candidates' obligations

1 Response to advertisements will be as requested, e.g. telephone for an application form, provide brief relevant details, send a curriculum vitae.
2 Appointments and other arrangements will be kept or the recruiter informed promptly when candidates discover an agreed meeting cannot take place.
3 Recruiters will be informed as soon as candidates decide not to proceed with an application.
4 Only accurate information will be given in applications and in replies to recruiters' questions.
5 Information given by a prospective employer will be treated as confidential if requested.

The basic concepts of this code have existed since 1970, and it is interesting to observe how social and economic changes since then have borne upon the most recent revision (1990). For instance, the high unemployment situation has led to a large growth in unsolicited applications: advice given is that it is unreasonable to expect big organizations, which may receive many thousands of such applications in a year, to bear the cost of replies, but where SAEs are enclosed, then at least receipt should be acknowledged.

The payment of expenses incurred in attending interviews remains controversial. The IPM continues to advise that reasonable and significant expenses should be met. Actual practice, however, seems to vary, and some employers do not reimburse expenses. In these cases, it is argued that the recruiter's expenses policy should be clearly explained when candidates are called for interview – not at the interview or subsequently. Advice on policy about taking up references before interviews – common practice in the public sector – is also given: in effect, that this should not be done without the candidate's express permission.

A section in the code deals with indirect discrimination. Care must be taken that recruitment methods do not effectively screen out minorities or members of one sex: in particular, it is argued that the 'word of mouth' or 'old boy network' approaches can be unfair, by tending to perpetuate a workforce of staff drawn from the same sources as at present. Indirect discrimination against disabled people should also be avoided by ensuring that, when interviewing, the rule should be to test ability for the job first and to discuss the disability only if adjustments need to be made to allow the applicant to do the job.

Job requisitions

Job requisitions are intended to give recruitment officers enough information about each job to enable them to fill it. They may be presented in an informal manner, verbally by telephone or even during a chance meeting between a departmental head and the personnel officer; or there may be rules insisting on the completion of a requisition form. Whichever method is used, requests should be as detailed as possible, listing the duties of the job, the conditions of employment, and the qualifications, experience, and personal qualities required of candidates. High-level approval is usually needed if the job is additional to the existing labour force rather than a direct replacement for someone leaving.

Linked with the job analysis that follows, recruitment officers' aim should be to gather sufficient information about the job to be able to

REQUISITION FOR STAFF

Staff or Hourly: ....

Location: ....

Job Title:

Date required to start :

Department ....

Details of Duties

Promotion Opportunities : ....

PERSON REQUIRED

Preferred Age ....   Sex ....

Education & Professional Qualifications	Practical Experience required

Special Qualities   (physical, personal, etc) ....

EMPLOYMENT CONDITIONS

Rate of Pay	Hours	Shifts	Holidays	Pension

Addition to existing staff ? .... Addition approved by ....

Requisitioned by .... (Dept.head)   Date ....

FOR USE BY PERSONNEL DEPT.

Name of person engaged :..

Date started : ....

Source of recruitment

Figure 9

answer any questions that candidates may put to them. Hence the advantage of the more formal approach, using a form like the one shown in Figure 9 to make sure that all the points are in fact covered.

Job analysis

In order to avoid the confusion and ambiguity of some of the terminology associated with this technique, the following definitions were agreed between the Department of Employment and the industrial training boards. The general use of these definitions would have obvious advantages:

Job description: a broad statement of the purpose, scope, duties, and responsibilities, of a particular 'job'.

Job analysis: the process of examining a 'job' to identify its component parts and the circumstances in which it is performed. The detail and approach may vary according to the purpose for which the job is being analysed: for example, vocational guidance, personnel selection, training, equipment design.

Job specification: a product of 'job analysis' – a detailed statement of the physical and mental activities involved in the 'job' and, when relevant, of social and physical environmental matters. The specification is usually expressed in terms of 'behaviour' – in other words what the workers do, what knowledge they use in doing it, the judgments they make and the factors they take into account when making them.

Personnel specification: an interpretation of the 'job specification' in terms of the kind of person suitable for the job. The characteristics are often set out on the lines of the NIIP 'Seven-Point Plan'.

Job analysis is a technique which has been evolved to study the detailed content of a job and all the relevant factors that influence it. It has wide applications in many aspects of personnel management, one of which is recruitment.

But before continuing with this main theme, let us examine the technique generally and its other *main uses* in the personnel manager's work:

1 In *filling jobs:* whether by internal transfer or promotion or by recruitment from outside, it is essential to have a detailed description of the vacant job, supplemented by a specification of the sort of person who could do it satisfactorily. Also used for *appraisal.*

2 In devising *training programmes:* the need is to know what skills and knowledge are required to perform particular jobs well, and to make an appreciation of the training necessary to acquire such skills and knowledge.

3 In establishing *rates of pay:* here the emphasis is different, being placed on assessing the relative factors of jobs – how difficult, unpleasant, important they are, for example – and putting wage or salary values to them. In large organizations, it is clearly impossible to have separate rates for each individual, so the vast range must be reduced by placing jobs in grades or categories. Classifying them in this way means closely examining how they resemble or differ from each other, for the overall purpose is to reduce the number of categories to the smallest possible.

4 In *eliminating accidents:* the technique is readily adapted to investigating the hazards contained in jobs as a preliminary to devising methods of eliminating them.

5 In *reorganization*, made necessary in times of growth, contraction, mergers or amalgamation, or whenever the existing organizational structure is seen as a handicap to efficiency. Once again the emphasis is different, for here the analyst is seeking the purpose of all the tasks carried out in the organization and their relationship to each other.

Gathering all this information is a long and tedious task, and one suspects that this is the main reason why so few large employers maintain up-to-date analyses of the jobs in their organizations. Yet it must be apparent that if such detailed information is required to carry out the five functions just listed, personnel managers are not going to be able to operate efficiently unless they conscientiously acquire it by applying the technique of job analysis. Its tedium is perhaps best relieved in practice by carrying out analyses as opportunities present themselves – for example, when a job falls vacant, when its salary scale is being reviewed, or when improvement targets are being set for the person doing it. Personnel managers can thus 'kill two birds with one stone', and it is surprising how quickly they can build up a complete file about jobs. They will also more readily obtain the cooperation of departmental heads in this way, for they will be able to see the relevance of the technique to their own problems.

With a routine or repetitive manual job, the analysis may be carried out simply by watching the person doing it at work. But, of course, many jobs comprise tasks which are not repeated at regular intervals or which involve a great deal of mental work that cannot be seen; in such cases observation must be supplemented by interviews and discussions with the people doing these jobs.

The sources for information about jobs are clearly supervisors and the workers actually doing them, but both have their drawbacks. The former can be surprisingly ill-informed about the detailed content of subordinates' jobs, since it is difficult for them to notice or grasp all the numerous imperceptible changes that happen to jobs in a large department over a period of time. On the other hand, the person doing a job quite naturally tends to 'puff it up', placing greater emphasis on its important aspects and playing down the more tedious, routine side so that the investigator may be left with a false impression. On balance, it is probably better practice to interview the holder of the job first, and then check the information obtained with his/her superior; if any marked differences of opinion emerge, the job should be discussed with them together until a common understanding is reached.

Most people tend to be very sensitive about their jobs, and the fact that these are going to be analysed may cause considerable apprehension. It is essential, therefore, to gain their confidence in the first place and maintain it throughout the exercise. Gaining it is largely a matter of job analysts fully explaining what they are going to do, the methods they will be using, and what the purposes behind their activities are. They can maintain this confidence only by the thoroughness of their investigations, while paying due regard to the normal work of the department which must continue while they are there. Nothing is more likely to mar people's confidence than if they have to return two or three times to each job because they overlooked certain points on the first occasion.

Finally, confidence must be consolidated by staff seeing that the purpose originally explained to them is in fact achieved: if, for example, office staff are asked to cooperate in devising a clerical training programme, but nothing subsequently happens about it, then they are hardly likely to respond when their help is sought again.

For comparison between jobs to be possible, analysts must use the same framework throughout their investigations. This should cover the following points:

1   Initial requirements

(a) What a person must bring to his/her job by way of aptitudes, educational achievement, training, and previous experience.
(b) What training will be given to any newcomer to that particular job.

2   Duties and responsibilities

(a) Physical aspects: what movements are actually carried out when doing the job, and the amount of effort involved; this should include a statement of disqualifications (for example, candidates for some police forces cannot be under 5 ft 8 in in height).
(b) Mental effort: the degree of intelligence involved in the work.
(c) Whether the job is routine in nature, or demands the use of initiative.
(d) An assessment of the difficulty of the job: what its agreeable and disagreeable features are; what the causes and consequences of failure are.
(e) Responsibilities: for controlling other staff, for materials, equipment, and cash.

3   Environment and conditions of employment

(a) Physical surroundings: indoor or outdoor, temperature, humidity, noisiness, dirtiness.

(b) Accident hazards inherent in the job.
(c) The form of wage payment, and frequency of its review.
(d) Other conditions: hours, shifts, superannuation, sickness benefits, holidays.
(e) The prospects of advancement.
(f) The provision of employee services: canteens, social clubs, protective clothing, for example.

4 The social background

(a) The size of the department.
(b) Whether the job means isolation from other people or membership of a working team.
(c) The sort of people with whom the job means contact: senior management, fellow-workers, outside representatives, the public.
(d) The amount of supervision received.
(e) An assessment of the status of the job.

In working through such a checklist analysts must beware of being unduly influenced by the personality and qualifications of whoever happens to be doing the job at that particular time. Rather, they must be conscious of the demands the job may make on any person performing it. It must be clearly realized, therefore, that there is a distinction between the ideal and the minimum for satisfactory performance: the latter can be described as 'essential' requirements and the former as 'desirable' in any subsequent specification.

Job analysis, then, is a tool of management aimed at eliciting the detailed information so necessary if staff problems are to be dealt with satisfactorily. Viewed in this perspective it is a problem-solving device, and as soon as a programme of job analysis has been carried out management must check that the problems concerned have in fact been solved: for example, that rates of pay are more equitable, or that a departmental reorganization is resulting in higher productivity. Otherwise the programme must be revised and tried again, or some new approach adopted.

Returning now to recruitment procedure – once a job has been analysed, the information is readily available to prepare a *job description* listing the duties involved in the job and setting out the conditions of employment. Candidates should be supplied with a copy, so that they have sufficient information to decide whether to pursue their application. The selectors would be given copies too, and they should also receive a *personnel specification* which will present an 'identi-kit' of the sort of person considered suitable for the job available. Again a form should be used for this purpose, as in Figure 10, so that selectors

JOB SPECIFICATION FORM. | Job Title

Age Preferred/ Limits	Sex	Married/ Single	Qualifications
			Essential :
			Desirable :

Previous Experience.
Essential :
Desirable :

ABILITIES REQUIRED	Notes on degree of ability required and the situations In which it would be used.
Intelligence	
Speech	
Writing	
Numeracy	
Administration	
Social	
Initiative	
Ambition	

General comments on personality required, appearance, manner, etc :

Home circumstances likely to affect ability to perform the job :

Figure 10

become used to having this information presented in a uniform manner.

There are many other well-known methods of preparing for and conducting selection processes. For example, the 'vital qualities' approach* seeks to identify the best performers in particular jobs and

*See 'Using Structured Interviews to Measure Job Success', G. Buckingham, *Personnel Management*, October 1985, page 99.

analyse the qualities and range of behaviour which lead to success. Thus a salesperson requires at least a generally acceptable manner, thorough knowledge of the products and the confidence to clinch sales; restaurant staff need pride in their work, a sense of responsibility and some measure of assertiveness. Listing such qualities in job advertisements tends to attract appropriate applicants (and cuts out many who would be unsuitable) and can make subsequent interviews much more pointed.

Sources of labour supply

The techniques described so far have been concerned with knowing what staff are required; the second part of the recruitment problem is where to get them. There are many potential sources of labour supply, and it is most important that the personnel manager should maintain the right sort of contact with each of these and regularly review their effectiveness. Some of the most widely used are official agencies, directly concerned with employment:

1 Local Employment Offices and Job Centres of the Department of Employment: a service both to employers looking for labour and to the individual worker looking for a job. The usefulness of this service generally depends on the state of the market in a particular area — good in those regions where unemployment is high, but not always helpful, especially as regards skilled people, in areas where there is little unemployment.

2 The Department's former Professional and Executive Recruitment service (PER) was privatized in 1988, and continues to operate a nationwide service for filling professional and executive vacancies. With headquarters in Leeds and twenty-three regional offices, PER offers consultancy, executive search and psychometric testing services. It has created an international division in London in anticipation of cross-border moves after 1992, and now uses European media in its recruitment work. The *Executive Post* newspaper continues to appear and is used by PER for specialized vacancies in sales and engineering.

3 Career Advisory Officers offer the same type of facilities for young people finding their first jobs.

4 Schools, technical colleges, and universities — most of these have members of staff with special responsibilities for helping students to find suitable jobs: careers masters at most schools, and university appointments officers engaged full-time on this activity, for example.

5 Private employment bureaux — licensed by local authorities in many large towns, where they usually offer specialized services for secretarial, clerical, nursing, catering, and domestic workers.
6 Ex-service organizations and some police forces have resettlement offices which sponsor candidates for employment, having knowledge available about their previous experience and records of behaviour. In London, an Over Forty-Five's Association exists to help the older man or woman to find work.

A major point needs to be stressed about all these local agencies. Each area may have several hundred potential employers competing for the labour available, and personnel managers thus have to make a special effort to get their voices heard. This can best be done by maintaining close personal contact with such people as the manager of the local employment office, careers advisory officers, careers masters at local schools, and bureaux proprietors. They will naturally call to mind those employers who have appreciated the importance of a personal, friendly relationship, and who have invited them along to see something of the work carried out in their factories or offices (and, indeed, entertained them properly at the same time). Regular, personal contact of this sort is the most certain method of ensuring a fair share of the best available labour.

Continuing with the sources of supply:

7 Trade unions and professional bodies often maintain registers of unemployed members or offer an appointments service. Where industrial relations are good, trade unions can sometimes produce reliable people. The appointments service of a professional association can be extremely useful to the closed membership of that profession. The Institute of Personnel Management, for example, runs one, details being circulated twice monthly with the Institute's publications *Personnel Management* and *PM Plus*, subscribed to by all members.
8 Personal recommendations by existing staff — in many ways the most satisfactory source of labour supply. An employer can usually rely on workers who have been in service for a long time, and they in turn respect him/her. They will not recommend relatives or friends for jobs lightly, because if such people prove to be bad employees, then this would reflect as much on the recommender as on the 'duds'. Some firms positively encourage this method of recruitment by offering financial rewards. This can clearly be a much more successful method of recruitment than a repetitive series of advertisements in local papers which sometimes produces very few suitable applicants.

9 The 'circular letter' — also used where local press advertising seems to have little impact, possibly when it is suspected that the types of labour sought do not even read the local papers. These letters or brochures can easily be delivered to every household in a neighbourhood, through the normal postal service, delivery agencies, or even by boy scouts in 'bob-a-job' week. They tell the local community what jobs are available, explain conditions of employment, and can highlight any attractive features of the work (just as a press advertisement would, but with the added assurance that they will be read by someone in every house). One large dairy company in London used this method when the reorganization of its services created a demand for more milk roundsmen; in this case the 'letters' were delivered to each house with the bottles by their milkmen. One large hospital spent £96 on a similar campaign and recruited thirteen new employees as a result; in the previous month an expenditure of nearly twice that figure on local press advertisements achieved no success at all.

10 'Head-hunting': twenty years ago less than 5 per cent of senior executives owed their change of job to a head-hunter, but nowadays three-quarters of the top appointments are filled through executive search. Some 200 companies make up the 'head-hunting' industry — replacing 'the old boy network' and discreet advertising, and setting out to find a shortlist of those most likely to fill a job successfully. Once a firm spells out its needs to one of these operators, the sector involved is immediately trawled to come up with a shortlist of suitable candidates. The head-hunter's method is simplicity itself: usually phoning every potential candidate in the particular field to enquire whether he/she would be interested in a challenging job. This may cause annoyance to some recipients of such calls, but, in practice, most top executives are only too happy to hear about job opportunities which may improve their careers. Executive search, to use the conventional term, is probably the most expensive form of recruitment, fees commonly amounting to about a third of the annual salary of the person selected. The personnel manager concerned must also always keep in mind that the ultimate responsibility for recruitment is his/hers — no use laying the blame at the consultant's door if things later go wrong.

Advertising jobs

In addition to all the methods mentioned above, advertising vacancies in national and local newspapers, trade and professional journals is consistently undertaken by most employers. This can be a very expensive business, especially display advertisements for senior staff in the national papers, and it is therefore essential that the personnel manager should be sure that the best results are being obtained for the money spent.

It is important to grasp, at the outset, what the purpose of an advertisement is. This is to *attract applications*. The sifting of those that are suitable comes later – there should be no attempt to build it into the advertisement as such. The text should be written so that it contains all the information about a job likely to interest the candidate – its title, to whom responsible, outline of duties, qualifications and experience required, conditions of employment, salary, fringe benefits, any particularly attractive features about the job (which distinguish it from other similar jobs), and the name and address of the firm. Including the telephone number makes it easier for people to apply, especially if application forms have to be sent for first: it requires much less effort to make a phone-call than to write a letter. The wording must be carefully devised and should avoid such vague phrases as 'appealing to people with initiative' or 'strong personalities' – who among readers will believe they do not possess these qualities?

Where vacancies could involve promotion within an organization, they should be advertised internally first, and any subsequent press advertisement should mention that this step has been taken. The embarrassment of receiving an application from one of its own employees can thus be avoided, although this sometimes happens when a box number is used instead of giving the firm's name. This practice is very controversial, but the reasons why a firm wishes to keep its name secret rarely reflect any credit on the quality of its management. In practice, a box number seems to be used mainly when a replacement is sought for an unsatisfactory senior employee who would then be sacked (but if no one is found, he/she is allowed to continue). Personnel managers who place such an advertisement must face up to the fact that they are automatically excluding a large proportion of possible applicants who will not send letters containing personal information to an unknown address. To some extent these difficulties can be overcome by using a double-envelope system. Candidates write out their application and seal it in an envelope; they then list the companies they would not wish to see their letter, and insert this, together with the sealed letter of application, in a second letter. The newspaper's executive responsible for box number replies can then take the appropriate action.

Because of the great expense of advertising, it is imperative to keep records of the response of each insertion, analysing both the number of replies and their quality. It will often be found, for example, that advertising in a professional journal produces the best results, because people of high calibre will look there first when they want to change their jobs, rather than hunt through pages and pages of the national newspapers. This control information can have a dramatic effect on advertising costs when first introduced, quickly eliminating those papers and journals which yield a poor return.

Dealing with applications

All the relevant sources of recruitment having been notified and the job advertised if necessary, applications should now start to arrive. What form should these take: should candidates be asked to write a letter of application, or should they all fill in the same application form? A clear understanding of the purpose of applications and their role in recruitment procedure as a whole should provide the answer to this question. In fact, applications serve three purposes:

1 To enable an initial 'weeding-out' of unsuitable candidates.
2 To act as a frame of reference for the interview which follows, when particular points can be checked and elaboration sought.
3 To form the basis for the personal record file of the successful applicant.

These purposes surely argue the merits of candidates using the same application form, so that they can all be considered and interviewed from a basis of exactly comparable information. The protagonists of the letter of application urge that its layout and content indicate something about the candidate's abilities; this is questionable, since the recipient can never be sure that the candidates have themselves designed the layout of their applications. Again, is this the right time to analyse the candidate's abilities – is it not far better to wait until he/she appears for the interview? The most significant argument against letters of application, however, is that the contents of each tend to be so different. Some people feel conciseness is what is required, others that they must be expansive; almost all leave out important facts or gloss over (with relief?) parts of their career that do not stand too close inspection or which may have little bearing on the vacancy in hand.

None of these drawbacks exist with application forms, which can ask for all the information pertinent to the job. This is no plea for a standard form to be used throughout the organization (there is really no need for a £40,000 p.a. senior executive to be asked about his/her

EMPLOYMENT HISTORY

Name and Address of Previous Employers	Dates		Job Title and Summary of Duties	Reasons for Leaving
	From	To		

Figure 11

shorthand and typing speeds, but it commonly happens). The ideal, which should certainly be practised for senior posts, would be to design a separate application form for each appointment, aimed exclusively at obtaining from candidates the information directly relevant to that job. Thus, for example, although some parts of a building firm's application form could be common to all applicants, different information would be sought from an architect compared with an accountant. Surely, with so much at stake for the prospective employer and the candidates, it is not asking too much for this extra effort to be put into the recruitment procedure.

Those parts of the application form which could be common include:

1 Personal details – name, address, age, married/single, nationality.
2 Education and qualifications.
3 Health – registered disabled?
4 Spare-time interests.
5 Length of notice to be given.
6 Names of referees.
7 Record of previous employment, leading up to the present job, set out perhaps in the manner of Figure 11.

Additional information may then be obtained by way of the candidates' personal assessment of their own experience and abilities. The relevant aspects of the job are listed on the application form and they indicate how much knowledge or experience they think they have of each. Thus the list for an employment officer post might start:

Experience	I	2	3	4
Job analysis				
Writing job descriptions				
Writing job specifications				
Interviewing – operatives				
Interviewing – executive staff				
Use of selection tests				
Use of group selection procedures etc. etc. etc.				

I = No knowledge or experience

2 = General background knowledge

3 = Reasonable practical experience

4 = Very well informed, with long experience

References

References come into the picture at this stage of the procedure, although many candidates in private industry will probably ask for their present employer not to be approached until later. Only occasionally are candidates told to submit open references or testimonials with their applications; in fact, little attention seems to be paid to them when they are unsolicited, and for this reason many firms refuse to give testimonials to employees leaving them, except possibly when they are emigrating.

On the other hand, most employers both in private industry and the public service do ask for references from previous employers. These enquiries usually take one of two forms:

(a) A normal business letter (which will be answered in like manner), outlining the job for which the candidate has applied, and asking the previous employer's opinion of his/her suitability for it.
(b) An enquiry form, with spaces in which the job and application details can be filled, followed by a number of specific questions, for example:
    Are the facts given by candidates about their employment with you correct?
    If not, will you please supply accurate information?
    What were the dates on which he/she started and left your employment?
    What were his/her actual duties?

Why did he/she leave you?
Is he/she, in your opinion, sober/honest/dependable?

But, no matter how detailed the enquiry, the value of the information thus acquired is discounted by many personnel specialists. It is argued, for example, that so much depends on interpretation and this, in turn, on knowing the person who writes the reference, that expressions of opinion about character are worthless. There are legal complications, too, about putting bad references on paper, apart from the natural reluctance of most people to write so ill of candidates concerned that inevitably they will not get the job (although to some extent these situations can be overcome in practice by phone-calls or even visits to discuss a reference with the prospective employer).

Generally speaking, these criticisms are valid, so that the usefulness of references is little more than a means of checking that the factual information provided by candidates about their previous jobs is correct; if not, then they must be asked to account satisfactorily for any discrepancies before their appointment is confirmed. In the public services, where staff move between authorities as a matter of normal career progression, it is much more likely that the officers called upon to write references will know each other, for example, town clerks or hospital consultants; apart from this personal knowledge there are also closer bonds of professional integrity between such staff than can possibly be the case in private industry. More reliance can perhaps be placed on references in these circumstances.

Computerized personnel information systems

Computerized personnel information systems (CPISs) developed into very sophisticated administrative tools during the 1980s. Such an advance is in marked contrast to the alleged lower quality of recruitment work: the state of the labour market, with very high numbers of applications for most vacancies, and organizations' efforts to cut overheads have led to far too many cases of poor standards in recruitment processes. Yet there are now several computerized program 'modules' which offer good systems without overstretching the personnel department's budget.

Dedicated word processors can easily deal with recording the names and addresses of applicants and sending them standard letters. Moving on from the basic stage, there are now available two main types of module: those which combine with an existing CPIS and those which come as stand alone packages. The latter often have an enquiry facility which allows the user to analyse job applicants by several criteria; the former should have the advantage of being able to utilize the system's own enquiry language, report generator and graphics package.

Examples of other features which might form part of a computerized recruitment procedure are:

(a) Recording and budgetary control of costs – a considerable aid to in-house recharging exercises: recruitment can be expensive and a detailed cost analysis of each recruitment campaign is essential for managing such expense effectively.

(b) Interpretation of advertising costs: this depends on the results obtained – attracting 500 applicants for a job, none of whom is suitable, is useless; the criteria should include the number of applicants who could be shortlisted for interview and the number of interviewed candidates who could be offered the job.

(c) Ethnic group monitoring – so as to demonstrate lack of discrimination in the recruitment process; to do this effectively the module must allow for recording the name of each applicant, the job applied for, the applicant's sex, ethnic or minority group and the reasons why the applicant was not shortlisted/interviewed/given the job.

(d) The facility to create internal shortlists by searching the records of existing employees, and maintain a holding file for outside candidates. In this context, recording all details of external applicants, to allow them to be sorted and searched by many different criteria, is a luring prospect: but such systems do require the input of large amounts of data, and the return for effort expended is highly questionable.

The following table* sets out basic data for a computerized recruitment system, bearing in mind that its contents need to be adapted to meet the particular requirements of individual organizations and that all software is intended to save effort:

*'The Recruitment Process', Colin Richards-Carpenter, *Personnel Management*, March 1986, page 57.

Table 2

Basic data for a recruitment system

Internal advertisement start date

Internal advertisement end date

Coverage code (where the job has been advertised within the organization)

Media code (which media have been used for external advertising)

Media date

Post number (where the recruitment module is part of a larger CPIS, the post number acts as a link and provides all the information on the post, i.e. job title, grade, organizational position etc. In a stand alone system such items have to be input separately)

Advertisement reference number

Post closing date

Full name of applicant

Full address (including post code)

Response action code (called for first interview, second interview etc.)

Response action dates

Closing date of hold lists (one of the status codes described above would be to ask applicants if they would like to go on a hold list in case another similar vacancy occurred in the future – this date would tell you for how long you would hold that person)

Standard letter variables:
interviewer
interview venue
interview date
interview time etc.

References sent for date

References received date

Employer's name

Employer's address

Clearance code (this field would tell you that selected candidates had been cleared for such things as security, medical etc.)

Clearance date.

Further reading

Practical Manpower Planning, John Bramham (IPM, 1988).
Job Analysis, M. Pearn and R. Kandola (IPM, 1988).
Towards a Comprehensive Manpower Policy, Manpower Services Commission, 1976.
Recruitment and Selection, P. Plumbley (IPM, 1991 edition).
The Theory and Practice of Systematic Staff Selection, Mike Smith and Ivan T. Robertson (Macmillan, 1987).

5

Selection of staff

Once applications have been received (and references where appropriate) they have to be sifted to decide which candidates will be interviewed. This process demands great care, matching the information provided against the personnel specification, for when a large number of people have applied there is always the possibility of excluding better candidates than those who manage to secure an interview. This is partly a matter of the time and expense an employer is prepared to incur to get the best person, weighing this against the seniority or importance of the job. It has been estimated that the total cost of employing a manager from age 35 to 65 at an average salary of £30,000 p.a. is a staggering £3.4 million, and employers may feel justified in giving preliminary interviews to as many as thirty seemingly good applicants out of a hundred enquiries received. They must in effect decide on a budget for the cost of each appointment to be made.

The interview

Interviews are carried out in many ways: by the departmental manager in small firms, by a personnel officer with technical assistance, by panels of senior executives sitting together, by large committees in some of the public services, and by variations and combinations of all these.

Whatever the form, the three purposes of interviewing remain the same, and if only these were fully appreciated by people charged with responsibility for filling jobs, many of the complaints so frequently heard about the ways in which candidates are treated at interviews would disappear. The purposes are:

1 To enable employers to obtain enough information about candidates to decide their suitability for the job in question.
2 To give candidates all relevant information about the job and the organization.
3 The public relations aspect of leaving candidates with the feeling they they have had a 'fair crack of the whip'.

The first function has been the constant study of specialists in selection for many years and much has been done to perfect methods of getting information from candidates. But the second purpose has been comparatively neglected. Job descriptions may have been sent to candidates, and these may be expanded verbally at the interview, but far too often candidates are not shown the actual place or office where they will be working, nor do they see anything of the people with whom they will work – both vital ingredients in job satisfaction and morale. A group of my own management students once found this to be a significant factor in labour turnover.* Some 300 people in managerial or supervisory posts were questioned, more than half of whom at some stage in their careers had left jobs within a short time of starting (eighteen months). Of these, nearly three-quarters said that one of the factors which caused their rapid departure was disappointment with the way the job turned out compared with how it had originally been explained to them. There was little suggestion of their having been deliberately misinformed, more that they were not given as much information as they might have been, and particularly that no opportunity was allowed for them to see the physical conditions nor become acquainted with their future colleagues.

If the third purpose is kept continually in mind, it will greatly influence the manner in which any interview is conducted. For candidates to feel that they have been fairly treated, they must be given the chance to ask any questions they wish, and these should be answered; some of them may seem trivial to interviewers, but they may be very important to candidates. An employer's ultimate aim should be to send an unsuccessful applicant away genuinely sorry that he/she has not got the job, because it seemed such a good firm to work for. As

*Survery carried out by Diploma of Management Studies Group at the Medway College of Technology.

it is, employers seem quite oblivious to the amount of goodwill they lose in a local community as the result of bad interviewing practices.

The first impression that candidates gain of an organization is most important. Thus their written applications should be individually acknowledged, rather than by a cyclostyled note, and reception staff should be properly trained to deal with personal callers seeking employment, helping them to fill in application forms if necessary.

When an appointment has been made for an interview, punctuality is of the essence, as with any other business engagement. If candidates are early or some delay is unavoidable, then a comfortable waiting room should be available, with up-to-date magazines to look at (including company literature), and with toilet facilities adjacent. The basic physical requirements for the interview itself are a private room, preferably without a telephone, and freedom from interruptions. There is much to be said in favour of furnishing this room informally, say with easy chairs around a coffee table, as many people find interviews across a desk to be intimidating.

Most managers would hotly reject any suggestion that they cannot conduct good interviews, because they see this particular ability as a reflection of how well they can handle people, get them to talk freely, and make judgments on their personalities. Yet interviewing demands skills in which few senior managers have been properly trained. To start with, these skills can be improved by adopting a systematic approach: staff selection is not simply a matter of dropping everything else for a few minutes to chat with the candidates for a job.

Probably the best-known system is the *seven-point plan*,* which is an attempt to list the items that must be considered in any comprehensive investigation of a person's occupational assets and liabilities. The need for the preparation of a full job description and specification has already been stressed, and the first application of the plan lies in doing this under the seven headings from which the technique takes its name:

1 Physical make-up

What does the job demand in the way of general health, strength, appearance, manner, voice?

2 Attainments

What does it demand by way of general education, specialized training, and previous experience?

* The Seven-Point Plan, NIIP Paper No. 1, was written by Professor Alec Rodger and was published by the National Institute of Industrial Psychology.

3   General intelligence

What level is required to do the job (a) satisfactorily, (b) well?

4   Special aptitudes

Does the job involve any special dexterity – manual, verbal, musical, artistic, etc.?

5   Interests

How far does the job require a special interest in, for example, outdoor life, being with other people, artistic expression? Are any hobbies likely to be relevant?

6   Disposition

Does the job call for any of the following qualities – leadership, acceptability to others, reliability, sense of responsibility, self-reliance?

7   Circumstances

How will the pay, prestige, status of job affect the worker's private life?

Having thus evolved the job's requirements, the selector will attempt to link these and the differences shown between the candidates, in order to find the best 'match'. The assessment of candidates should therefore also be carried out under the same headings:

1   Physical make-up

Has the candidate any defects of health or physique that may be of occupational importance? How agreeable are his/her appearance, bearing, and speech?

2   Attainments

What type of education has he/she had, and how well has he/she done educationally? What occupational training and experience has he/she had already, and how well has he/she done in his/her previous jobs?

3 General intelligence

How much intelligence can he/she display and does he/she ordinarily display? (This may be assessed by testing.)

4 Special Aptitudes

Has he/she any marked mechanical aptitude? manual dexterity? verbal facility? artistic or musical ability? (Again, may be found by tests.)

5 Interests

To what extent are his/her interests intellectual? practical–constructional? physical–active? social? artistic?

6 Disposition

How acceptable does he/she make him/herself to other people? Does he/she influence others? Is he/she steady and dependable? Is he/she self-reliant?

7 Circumstances

What are his/her domestic circumstances? How large a family? Does he/she own his/her house? Is he/she willing to travel?

Using this plan conscientiously is an excellent discipline for anyone new to interviewing, as it so clearly assists the process of matching the candidate and the job requirements. With experience, interviewers may learn to take a number of short cuts and can be less formal in their approach. Even so, they should still use some sort of plan, not in the sense of following a stereotyped sequence (because an interview should always be allowed to develop naturally), but rather as a means of checking that all the required information has in fact been obtained.

Some preparation is necessary before candidates actually arrive. Interviewers should carefully study their applications and try to memorize the more important personal details supplied. This is not only good manners, but it also leaves interviewers free during their discussion to concentrate on their main task of assessing candidates. Their initial approach should be friendly and designed to put candidates at ease so that they behave in a normal manner: this is perhaps best done by starting on some subject of mutual interest, which is often revealed in candidates' applications.

Interviewers should follow certain well-established rules during their time with candidates:

1 They must appear interested throughout, and not seem merely to be going through an irksome routine (it is not always easy to concentrate towards the end of a tiring day).

2 They should do the minimum amount of talking themselves, encouraging candidates to speak freely, but without dwelling too long on irrelevancies. Ideally they could say to candidates, 'Now tell me all about yourself' and, provided they stick to the point, speak no more until the end. In practice, of course, they will have to interject occasional questions to get more information or change the subject from time to time.

3 The questions that they do ask should be phrased so that they are easily understood, but cannot just be answered 'yes' or 'no'. Nor should they be leading questions which, by the content or voice inflexion when putting them, suggest the answer likely to score.

4 Interviewers must remain detached. There should be no question of obtruding their own personality into the exchange in order to create an impression; they should not express opinions about episodes in the candidate's career, let alone censure him/her. Nor should they offer unasked-for advice, except possibly to an occasional youngster who obviously needs vocational guidance.

5 They should be aware of their own prejudices, and allow for them and any predilections they have to generalize, to believe stereotypes, or to be swayed by 'halo effects'. Stereotyping describes a form of bias which arises from the tendency to attribute widespread cultural beliefs about groups of people to individuals, such as 'all red-heads are hot-tempered'; alleged national characteristics, for example, overlook the obvious differences between individuals – 'all Germans are hard-working'. Halo effects result from favourable conclusions being reached about individuals, stemming from just one particular trait which they possess. For example, a good attendance or time-keeping record will often result in that person being generally viewed as someone who produces a lot of work of high quality; a likeable person is often judged to be more intelligent than someone who is disagreeable.

6 Interviewers must also beware of superficial first impressions and hasty decisions. One study* of a series of fifteen-minute interviews

*See 'Summary of Research on the Selection Interview Since 1964', O. R. Wright, *Personnel Psychology*, vol. 22, 1969, page 394.

showed that the average 'decision time' was under four minutes. In such cases interviewers could produce little better results than decisions based solely on an application form. It also means that interviewers seek to confirm their early impressions by means of the emphasis they place on particular parts of the interview; and they may consciously reduce the possibility of non-congruent information emerging by their very choice of the subject-areas explored.

7 Notes of fact may be taken during the interview, with the candidates' agreement. But notes concerning interviewers' assessments of candidates should be written after the candidates have left the room and there is no possibility of their seeing them. Research projects* have proved conclusively that it is important to keep notes if interviewers wish to recall information accurately. One experiment involved forty managers watching a video-taped interview, and then answering twenty straightforward factual questions about it. The average score was only ten, and the best results were obtained by those managers who followed their normal practice of keeping notes.

8 There can be no hard-and-fast rules about the length of time an interview takes; so much depends on the candidate, the type of seniority of the job, and the methods used, that it can vary from ten minutes to a couple of days. With experience, interviewers will learn to gauge how much time they need for each type of applicant.

9 Perhaps the overriding consideration is to be as thorough as possible. In particular, there should be no reluctance, for whatever reason, to examine closely any areas of doubt about a candidate's career. A new job is a vitally important event, likely to affect a person's life and have some direct impact on a firm's affairs for many years to come. There must therefore be no evasion of responsibility and the questioning must be exhaustive. Naturally, too, candidates will try to put themselves in the best light, slanting their answers to impress their audience (on occasions, even telling lies). Where they suspect this is happening, interviewers must probe and crosscheck as much as they can.

Interviews of likely candidates are usually started by personnel officers; they may then pass them on to the departmental head concerned, or they may interview candidates together. Whichever method is used, the personnel officer's advisory role must always be kept in mind and the departmental head's decision accepted as final. This responsibility is clear, and removes any likelihood of the personnel department being blamed later if candidates turn out disappoint-

*'Improvements in the Selection Interviews', R. E. Carlson *et al.*, in *Personnel Journal*, 1971, page 268.

ingly. It also has the advantage of allowing departmental managers to show candidates something of the place and the conditions under which they will be working.

The main qualification of good interviewers is their ability to establish an empathy with candidates, 'becoming one' with them. This presupposes that they have done their homework and thoroughly know the job and anything else about the organization likely to interest candidates. Interviewers themselves need to be intelligent, well adjusted, emotionally mature so that they stay unshockable, and well aware of their own biases and prejudices. Good health and freedom from strain or fatigue are also essential.

Panel interviews

Many of our public services are run by elected councils or management committees appointed by appropriate ministers. One of their major responsibilities is the selection of their senior officers, administrative and technical, and usually interviewing panels (sometimes twenty or thirty strong) are formed for this purpose. Councils and committees are frequently criticized as amateurs in an increasingly professional world, and this is very apparent as far as staff selection is concerned: it is a task for which very few members have ever received any training at all. The consequence is that most senior officers in local government and health service administration (two of the largest employers of labour in the UK) can relate numerous selection 'atrocities' within their personal experience.

Is there anything, then, to be said in favour of this system which, by law, must be carried out in this way? The trouble is, of course, that some public authorities still do not employ specialist personnel officers, so there is no expert in selection methods available anyhow. In this case, perhaps it is better to have a panel – at least the members can prompt each other and hope to cover the whole field of enquiry between them. And since the filling of senior posts is so often a matter of promotion as well, this method offers some guarantee of objectivity and fairness.

But there are serious disadvantages. One which increases as the number on the selection committee grows is the difficulty of putting candidates at their ease. How can they be expected to relax and behave naturally, as they would in the job if appointed, when they sit on a solitary chair surrounded by a large group of people all of whom may be complete strangers to them? Apart from their effect on the candidates' nerves, large committees often become confused in their procedure: important aspects of candidates' experience are overlooked, questions are repeated, and members sometimes seem more intent on impressing each other than considering the candidates.

If selection panels are to be used, they should follow a more constructive pattern. Their size should be limited to a maximum of six, each of whom should be properly introduced to the candidates in turn. They should agree areas of questioning between them so that there is no repetition or 'hogging' of the time by individual members. Above all, they should carry out the necessary preparation by studying the job descriptions and personnel specifications issued beforehand, and try to acquire some training in the methods of finding out if candidates possess the qualities needed to do the jobs successfully.

Selection tests

Most employers take their decisions about whom to select for a job when the interview stage of the recruitment procedure has been concluded. An increasing number, however, seek further evidence before making up their minds, by asking candidates to take a number of tests which have been devised to try to measure certain aspects of an individual's total personality in an objective and accurate manner. The main types are:

1 Intelligence tests of general mental capacity.
2 Special aptitude tests of particular talents.
3 Proficiency or trade tests in particular fields, for example, typing, or reproducing the main elements of a work task.
4 Tests which explore certain aspects of personality.

Intelligence tests can give a useful general indication of candidates' mental calibre, thus helping to assess if they are likely to be bright enough to meet the demands the job in question would make on them. Spearman's work on measuring intelligence is well known: he explained what he called the 'g' factor thus – 'we are divided by schooling and experience and we differ in our aptitudes, but below this we share a deeper basis of common ability'. Clearly, any reliable measure of 'g' can be of great help to a recruiting officer.

Special *aptitude tests* are widely used in giving vocational guidance when considering school-leavers for certain types of apprenticeships, or when someone is seeking an entirely new type of employment (for example, computer programming). All sorts of aptitudes can be tested – mathematical, mechanical, practical–constructional, musical, for example – and here again these tests can be useful in many ways, not least in cutting down the wastage from expensive training programmes for young people.

Proficiency and trade tests are perhaps the most straightforward, since basically they test ability to do the work involved. Thus if a job demands a certain level of ability in calculating, a 'maths exam' can easily be devised to find out if a candidate is good enough. Similarly, shorthand and typing tests are commonly given to applicants for secretarial work. Sometimes only part of the job, its 'key factors', can be tested: this calls for specialist advice to ensure that these factors are a fair test of competence, and that they are properly standardized and scored. Security of the tests is another problem: their content needs to be changed from time to time to prevent local candidates passing on knowledge of the tests.

Personality tests are intended to measure such aspects as emotional stability, social attitudes, and various traits of character. There are two main types – the *questionnaire* and the *projective*. The first simply asks a series of questions: unfortunately some candidates seem to find it easy to anticipate what answers score best and it then becomes necessary to complicate the process by building in some form of lie-detector. The most famous example of the second or projective type is the Rorschach ink-blot test – but many selection experts reject the basic concept that any one test can reveal a complete character study, which is the claim made. Long training and great skill are required in interpreting the results of such tests, and even then there is little evidence that any more useful information is obtained than from the interview or from other simpler, less costly methods. Personality tests for specific vocations (for example, salespeople) can also be a waste of time and effort: the simple truth is that different people succeed for different reasons and people are just as likely to sell large quantities because customers feel sorry for them as they would if they have an expansive, charming personality. Many of the tests that have been advocated over the years are suspect, both as regards the qualifications of their inventors and the psychological validity of the tests themselves.* Nothing can over-emphasize the potential danger of such tools in the hands of people with power over others' careers. For this very reason, many candidates for managerial jobs, aware of the controversy that rages about these tests, are extremely reluctant to undergo them.

Intelligence, aptitude, and proficiency tests can provide useful additional information in an objective manner about certain abilities

---

*See 'Personality Tests, the Great Debate' (*Personnel Management*, January 1991, page 38) which starts by demonstrating little or no correlation between the results of personality tests and success in subsequent job performance. In turn, that assertion is critically challenged by the testimony of six practitioners in the field of psychological testing, and the presenters told 'to re-think their claims more open-mindedly.'

which are perhaps difficult to discover by interviewing alone. The best claim for personality tests seems to be as a catalyst before the interview; once people have been told the results of such tests, they seem much more prepared to let their hair down and discuss their character traits than if the interviewer had questioned them directly. Validity and reliability are the key considerations about all tests – 'where valid instruments exist, one should measure rather than make far less reliable interview estimates . . . Performance on certain tests is positively correlated with success in certain jobs. It is, of course, interesting to speculate on the reasons for these correlations, but the predictive value of these tests is justification enough for their use'.* But it is the unease that people feel about these inexplicable correlations that makes tests the subject of so much controversy. Personnel managers responsible for advising on recruitment and promotion should use any means of objective measurement available, but where limitations are known to exist, tests must be very carefully chosen, properly administered, accurately scored, and sensibly interpreted.

Group selection techniques

In the case of senior appointments, or where a number of candidates have to be considered for one vacancy, still more information can be obtained by giving them a task to carry out as a group and observing how they react to each other. The point about this technique is that people in senior posts spend a good deal of their time thinking up ideas and then trying to persuade their colleagues to agree with them. It is very difficult to judge a candidate's ability to succeed in this vital role merely by interviewing him/her, but group selection methods can give some indication of how each candidate is likely to get on with other people.

The standard method can be described quite simply as putting a small group of candidates into action together, observed by a panel of selectors. This panel should be small, with not more than four members, experienced people of good judgment who have been properly trained to know what they are looking for and how to find it. The group of candidates should be about six in number, so that adequate time can be allowed for each person to contribute to the discussions: these should take place without interruption from the selectors. The setting in which the group works should be comfortable and as informal as possible; seating at a round table is a sound practice, for there is then no obvious chairperson.

---

*Letter to *The Financial Times*, 4 April 1966, from Mackenzie Davey, chairman of a firm of management consultants.

Actual procedure can vary considerably, from direct discussions on general subjects or problems put to the group by the selectors, through to complicated prepared briefs for 'committee sessions' when each candidate in turn acts as chairperson or advocate of his/her own ideas for solving a particular problem. (This latter method is used in the three-day Method B technique of the Civil Service Selection Board.)

While these discussions are going on, the selectors are observing the intellectual and social skills of the candidates and the attitudes of mind they display. Afterwards, the panel will analyse the effort made by each individual – the number and quality of his/her contributions to the discussion, whether they were well expressed, to the point, and positive. Above all, they will consider what influence the candidates have had on the group, the extent to which they have dominated it, whether they helped it to achieve its task or prevented it from doing so, and the ways in which they made their criticisms and received any directed at them. Their intellectual skills would be reflected by the evidence they give of thinking logically, clearly, and in a flexible manner. Evidence of social skills will be seen in their relationships with other members of the group, if they are tactful in what they say, and if their own personality makes an impact. In the group discussions something of their attitudes and approach to life should be detected: whether, for example, they tend to be positive and constructive or negative and critical. Finally, certain other elements of their personality – initiative, self-confidence, and dependability – might also be revealed.

The important thing to remember about the group selection method is that it is but one way of providing additional information about candidates. It is not a substitute for any other aspect of the selection procedure; the evidence it produces must be added to and compared with that derived from other sources. Summing up, in fact all types of selection tests and group observation techniques can have some value in helping to determine candidates' abilities, assess their disposition, and evaluate their attitudes; but they should all be applied by well-trained staff. Improperly used they can be a waste of time and the results can be downright misleading.

The popularity of selection techniques

A survey* of a sample of one-third of *The Times 100 Index*, carried out in 1986, provided most interesting information about the use of selection

*See 'Selecting the Best Selection Techniques', P. Makin and I. Robertson, *Personnel Management*, November 1986, pages 38–40.

techniques. Interviews were universal, with more involvement by line management than by personnel department staff: in 61 per cent of organizations staff from the personnel department were always included, while the corresponding figure for line management was 77 per cent. There was a clear preference for two or three interviewers to be involved, rather than just one, and only 12 per cent of organizations used one interviewer rather than two or three. Panel interviews with five or more members were not very common, with 66 per cent of organizations reporting that they were never used.

In terms of popularity, the use of references ran interviews a close second, being used at some stage by 96 per cent of organizations. In contrast, psychological testing was relatively little used; nearly two-thirds of organizations never used personality tests and over 70 per cent never used cognitive tests (e.g. critical thinking, perceptual ability). On the increase was the use of assessment centres – 21 per cent at the time of the survey, compared with 7 per cent in 1973.

Validation

Following up the success achieved by candidates appointed under a recruitment procedure is essential if the effectiveness of that procedure is to be kept under review. Selection is essentially a prediction, and it is not easy to prove how good predictions are. Usually one person is chosen from a group of candidates – even if he/she does turn out well, how can the selector ever be sure that one of the rejected members of the group would not have done better? How can success in a job be measured, anyhow? Is it a matter of visible results achieved, an assessment by a superior, a personal feeling of satisfaction, salary progression – or some combination of all these factors?

There can therefore be no strictly scientific measure to validate a recruitment procedure. Nevertheless a great deal can be learned from both successes and failures if proper records are kept. In practice, the latter approach might well be the more fruitful, studying the reasons for failure and the sequence of events which finally indicated that a person had failed. If evidence then emerges of some shortcoming in the selection methods used, corrective action can be taken. None of this can be done, however, unless follow-up is planned from the outset with an efficient system for keeping the necessary records.

If the interviewer is asked from the outset to predict the applicant's likely success in performing the various component tasks of the job being filled, then these records will enable feedback to be quite specific. Such an approach, rather than trying to assess overall suitability, will mean that the interviewer's own achievements and failures can be more readily identified. It has another advantage in forming the first step in the successful candidate's career development programme. For once the 'whole job' concept of suitability is rejected, and recognition given to the fact that very few candidates ever start as perfect matches with job requirements, then selection can also be seen as beginning the process of defining training needs.

Further reading

Psychological Testing – A Practical Guide, John Toplis, Vic Dulewicz and Clive Fletcher (IPM, 1987).
The Skills of Interviewing, Elizabeth Sidney and Margaret Brown (Tavistock Publications, 1961).

6

Aspects of employment – transfer, promotion, termination

The Contracts of Employment Act 1972*

The first main provision, in Section 1 of the Act, gives both employers and employees rights of minimum periods of notice to terminate employment. The following periods obtain for employees: if they have been employed for more than thirteen weeks but less than two years, they must receive at least one week's notice; more than two years but less than five years' employment entitles them to two weeks' notice; more than five years but less than ten years, four weeks' notice; between ten and fifteen years, six weeks' notice; and over fifteen years' employment, eight weeks' notice. Section 2 sets out employees' rights concerning minimum payments that must be made to them during these periods of notice, and these payments must now be linked with the provisions of the Redundancy Payments Act.

Section 4 obliges employers to give employees written particulars of their main terms of employment. The contract or agreement between them must name the parties, state the date when the employment begins, and set out:

*Amended by the Employment Protection Act 1975, which requires employers to provide written information for their employees about certain aspects of their disciplinary rules and procedures; and subsequently consolidated into the Employment Protection (Consolidation) Act 1978.

1 The rate of pay, or the method of calculating it.
2 The intervals (monthly, weekly, etc.) at which remuneration is paid.
3 Conditions relating to hours of work.
4 Conditions relating to holidays and holiday pay, payments when absent through sickness or injury, and provision for pensions.
5 Length of notice to be given and received for termination of employment.
6 The date on which a fixed-term contract is to end.
7 Information about the calculation of accrued holiday pay due on the termination of employment.
8 The employee's right to belong to a trade union.
9 To whom the employee can apply for redress of any grievance relating to his employment.

Industrial tribunals are empowered to hear complaints relating to any alleged breach by either party of the contract of employment.

Experience in putting Section 4 of the Contracts of Employment Act into practice has varied. It is sometimes difficult to incorporate all conditions relevant to a person's job in a single letter. For this reason, many employers send a much shorter letter, simply confirming the engagement and briefly welcoming the newcomer; a separate document is then enclosed setting out terms of employment. Another method is for an employment handbook to be used to explain conditions common to all staff. For management and executive appointments, most organizations get their legal departments to draw up a full-length contract; special conditions may have to be agreed for such staff, and perhaps an undertaking about the organization's trade and manufacturing secrets signed (sometimes including the Official Secrets Act, for example in the aircraft industry). Apprentices are generally employed under the strict provisions of their indentures which specify the obligations of both firm and apprentice to each other.

It should perhaps be added that the personnel manager's role as 'the social conscience of the organization' takes attitudes toward contracts beyond purely legal requirements into consideration of the total range of mutual obligations between each individual and the organization for which he/she works. The notion of a psychological contract conceives that the individual has a variety of expectations of that organization and that the organization has a variety of expectations of him/her. These expectations cover not only how much work is to be performed for how much pay, but also involve the whole pattern of rights, privileges and obligations between worker and organization.

Transfer of staff

In the previous chapter the problems of filling jobs by outside recruitment were analysed. They may also be filled, of course, by the internal transfer or promotion of existing employees.

Transfers from one job to another may be temporary or permanent, but in any event they will call for a certain amount of management control by the personnel department. First the transfer request itself must be dealt with: this may come for the worker concerned, from his/her supervisor, from the head of another department, or may be made necessary by rises or falls in trading activity which have an impact on the organization as a whole. The way a transfer request is handled often calls for considerable tact and diplomacy. If it is made as a result of a minor difference of opinion between a worker and his/her supervisor, the best initial approach may be to try to patch up the difference. If a transfer proves inevitable, then the search for a suitable alternative job must start, and this must be undertaken in a manner that will calm any suspicion the receiving supervisor may have that he/she is being asked to take someone who is a troublemaker, a poor workman, or who has otherwise been disagreeable in his/her previous department. Very often there are financial difficulties about making transfers, too: when the new job carries the same rate of pay (which is what the word 'transfer' implies) there is no problem; but if it carries a lower rate, then the person transferred sees it as a demotion. It is clearly no solution to maintain his/her previous rate in these circumstances, as this will only cause trouble between him/her and those workers in the new department who are doing similar work. Resolving such differences calls for great powers of persuasion on the personnel manager's part, and also makes follow-up of the transferred employee necessary to check the success of his/her diplomacy.

When the transfer request emanates from employees themselves, it is usually because they want to broaden their experience by working elsewhere or because they do not like the work, the place where they have to do it, or the people they have to work with. From departmental heads' point of view such transfer requests can be a confounded nuisance, especially when they have gone to great lengths to train their team of workers up to a level where they operate well together and are producing good results: they now have to face the prospect of seeing part of their efforts destroyed. This dilemma serves to emphasize the importance of senior executives maintaining close contact with supervisors and their subordinates. Managers must try to be constantly aware of people's feelings towards their jobs, so that personal antipathies in the workplace are never allowed to develop to the point where someone asks to be transferred elsewhere. At the same time, it must be recognized that change is the natural state of affairs in industry, and that it is abnormal for a working situation to remain static. If this is accepted, then managers will see that it would be foolish to obstruct transfers of their staff made necessary by these changes. Indeed, healthy relations between management and employees will mean that transfers can be made with goodwill on both sides, since those affected will appreciate their firm's problems and difficulties.

Finally, *job rotation* is a form of staff transfer which is commonly used for training purposes. Its success is partly due to the fact that the need to learn is so obvious when the trainee is deliberately put into an unfamilar situation. Even so, it is a method about which there is considerable controversy. It may be a good means of introducing youngsters into business life, but is it efficient at more senior levels? For example, technically qualified people of high ability are often prepared for general management by placing them for short periods in various commercial departments. But how much benefit derives from an unqualified person actually working in a specialist department for a few months? Since they can rarely make any constructive contribution, they may be more a hindrance than a help, and it is clearly wasteful that their own technical ability should be squandered simply looking over other experts' shoulders. Are there not better methods – training courses, or even carefully prepared book lists – to enable them to appreciate the various branches of general management? Apart from these considerations, it is obviously bad for morale if the staff of specialist departments regard the trainee as a 'high flyer' patently being given opportunities for promotion which they feel are being denied to them.

Staff promotion

The management of an organization should always make every effort to provide opportunities for their subordinates to obtain promotion, as personal advancement is undoubtedly one of the best inducements for people to stay with an employer. While it is not necessarily good practice to fill every vacancy in this way and never bring in 'new blood', it is very encouraging for employees to see that the best jobs do not go to outsiders very often. An organization's promotion policy might well be that, other things being equal, it will give preference to internal candidates for senior posts, and that it will advertise all vacancies involving promotion within the organization before placing them in the press.

Another aspect of policy is whether promotion should be based on seniority or merit. If the former, able younger people are likely to become impatient about 'waiting-for-dead-men's-shoes' and will leave to look for better prospects elsewhere. In the long run, this may mean that an organization comes to be managed by second-rate people who have stayed, possibly because they are not of sufficient calibre to make a move. On the other hand, the use of merit alone can cause difficulties; for example, unions often distrust the sincerity of management mainly because the measures of ability used by many supervisors in identifying merit are open to question and give rise to charges of favouritism. Such allegations can only be refuted by managers showing that they have evolved effective controls to recognize merit objectively. Nevertheless, seniority cannot be ignored; although it is no substitute for competence in the job, it can be used as a deciding factor when all other things are equal.

Unfortunately, it has truly been said that the best way to avoid promotion is to be good at your job. In trying to implement an internal promotion policy, often the most difficult task is to get departmental heads to agree to part with promising subordinates: they are naturally reluctant to lose a good worker and resistant to the idea of having to train a successor. That personnel managers must be able to persuade them to overcome these feelings is obvious, for once employees have an inkling that they are in the running for promotion they will become very disgruntled if they find their way barred by their present departmental head; and if resistance to training new people were allowed to prevail, then the whole policy of promotion from within would be stultified. The process of persuasion can be greatly helped, however, if personnel managers are able to produce a satisfactory replacement for the promoted person with as little delay as possible.

Promotion usually means several things to the person concerned: higher status, both at work and in the community outside; more pay; perhaps the substitution of greater job security and fringe benefits for direct financial incentives; and a more senior position, from which he/she should be able to render a better return to the organization. For this last reason, if no other, a comprehensive promotion programme* should be evolved, covering these details:

1 The relative significance of jobs must be established by means of techniques (already described) for the analysis, description and classification of jobs; this must result in the lines of promotion between jobs becoming clear.

---

*See also discussion of a company's manpower planning programme in Chapter 4, page 71.

2 A method of assessing the potential of staff for promotion must be introduced, rating individuals against the job requirements already specified.

3 Whenever a senior position falls vacant a decision has to be taken whether it would be better to fill it internally or to go outside to recruit someone with different experience, a broader outlook, and a fresh mind. Bearing in mind the cost of training a newcomer into the firm's methods, and the dismay that its present employees may feel at being passed over, external recruitment would seem to be justified only if there is no obvious candidate within the firm.

4 The question of training for promotion must be resolved. The sensible answer surely is for firms to plan ahead as far as possible and send employees on supervisory and management training schemes in advance of promotion. Those selected will then feel that their firm is taking an interest in their careers, and they will be ready to step into gaps as they appear.

Some large organizations tackle the problem presented when numerous internal candidates are available by using the administrative device of a *promotion board*. This may carry out two functions: deciding who is eligible for promotion by means of a series of tests and interviews, and trying to select the right people for actual vacancies. The composition of such a board may be flexible, but it should be small, with perhaps only the works manager and the personnel manager as permanent members; where a particular vacancy is being considered, they could then be joined by the head of the department concerned and the manager of the candidate's department. The same members of the board should also interview outside candidates if that step is taken.

Such a board would be guided in its task by the promotion policy of the organization. Certain aspects of it – external recruitment or internal promotion, seniority or merit – depend on 'other things being equal'. Making them so largely depends on operating a programme such as that just explained, for success means that the organization will benefit by having several internal candidates available when positions fall vacant. Even so, being realistic, it is unlikely that all members of an organization will support its promotion policy, no matter how carefully it has been prepared. Discontent will inevitably exist among those who do not progress in their careers; such employees will be left with feelings of personal inadequacy, which the experienced personnel manager must expect to become rationalized into grievances against the methods by which their more fortunate fellows were selected.

Termination of employment and ACAS Code of Practice

Termination of employment may take one of three forms: lay-off or suspension, discharge by the employer, or resignation by the employee. Lay-offs and suspensions are temporary in nature and represent actions by the employer, usually taken in the hope of re-employing the workers involved in the near future. Lay-offs are occasioned by lack of work, as when bad weather prevents outside building activity: those laid off are then recalled when work becomes available again. Suspensions are usually imposed for breaking rules and regulations and last a fixed short period of time.

Until appreciation of the principles of scientific management* was driven home by the post-war reality of full employment, it was regarded as the sole prerogative of management to hire and fire labour. This concept is accepted as being both unethical and impractical in industry today, so that workers are now protected against arbitrary discharge.

A legal definition of the reasons sufficient to justify the fair dismissal of an employee, originally set out in the Industrial Relations Act, was repeated in the Trade Union and Labour Relations Act 1974, and, in practice, amounts to the following: redundancy – provided the selection for redundancy was fair; legal impediment – provided the employee was offered any suitable alternative employment; non-capability – provided adequate training and warnings have been given; misconduct – providing warnings, excepting summary dismissal, suitable to the offence have been given. On the other hand, the 1974 Act specifies a number of cases where dismissals may be unfair – relating, for example, to employees' rights to join trade unions, strikes, and lockouts.

The procedures involved in terminating an individual's employment must, above all, be designed to ensure fairness. This is emphasized in the Code of Practice on Disciplinary Practice and Procedures in Employment, prepared by the Advisory, Conciliation and Arbitration Service, which came into effect in June 1977. The code recommended that:

(a) All employees should be given a copy of the employer's rules on disciplinary procedures; these should state which employees they cover and what disciplinary actions may be taken, and should allow matters to be dealt with quickly.

(b) Employees should be told of complaints against them and given an opportunity to state their case; they should have the right to be

*See Chapter 1, page 5.

    accompanied by a trade union representative or fellow-employee of their choice.

(c) Disciplinary action should not be taken until the case has been fully investigated; immediate superiors should not have the power to dismiss without reference to senior management, and, except for gross misconduct, no employee should be dismissed for a first breach of discipline.

(d) Employees should be given an explanation of any penalties imposed, and they should have a right of appeal with specified procedures to be followed.

(e) When disciplinary action other than summary dismissal is needed, supervisors should give a formal oral warning in the case of minor offences or a written warning in more serious cases.

(f) Special consideration should be given to disciplinary action in exceptional cases: these would include night-shift workers or those in isolated locations to whom the full procedure is not immediately available; no disciplinary action beyond an oral warning should be taken against a trade union official until a senior or full-time official has been consulted; criminal offences outside employment should not be treated as automatic reasons for dismissal.

Legal action cannot be taken against an employer solely because of not complying with one of the code's provisions. However, an industrial tribunal may take into account whether or not the employer complied with the code.

    For ten years 1978–87 the code played an important part in the deliberations of industrial tribunals, to such an extent that apprehension grew over 'legalism' – the increasing tendency to rely on case law. At the same time tribunals themselves came under criticism, from some employers for being burdensome and from some unions as being biased towards employers. For these reasons, when the ACAS prepared a revised code of discipline in 1987, it was rejected by the Secretary of State for Employment.

    As a practical alternative, the ACAS therefore published an advisory handbook.* Although this offers advice on good practice it is important to appreciate that it does not have the status of a code of practice: i.e. there is no legal requirement on an industrial tribunal to admit its contents as evidence, although clearly an employer who follows its advice may expect this to be taken into account. The handbook is intended to complement the existing code, which remains in force, taking into account case law and the development of good practice

---

Discipline at Work – the ACAS Advisory Handbook, 1988.

during the previous ten years. Conduct at work, absence and substandard work are the main topics, and a positive approach is adopted, aimed at seeking improvement in any unsatisfactory situation; the emphasis, in fact, is on avoiding disciplinary action except where absolutely necessary.

When employees themselves resign, important management action should follow in the form of exit interviews to try to find the real reasons why they are leaving. These reasons may well reflect on the efficiency of the organization's management and lead to a review of its policies and practices on pay, training, promotion, working conditions, and the quality of supervision. One fundamental aspect of policy about resignations that must be settled is the lengths to which a firm is prepared to go in order to dissuade someone from leaving. This question frequently arises when people have been expensively trained or when they have knowledge of secrets or working methods that their firm might be anxious to keep from competitors. Should the salary promised by their prospective new employer be matched or improved upon? If so, what will be the reaction of their present colleagues doing similar work – can all-round increases be justified?

The arrangements that have to be made when employees leave are quite complicated and personnel managers need to insist upon receiving full information from departmental heads about intending departures, so that the right procedure can be followed. Assuming that attempts to persuade employees to stay are unsuccessful, an exit interview should be arranged. Apart from this, a certain amount of paper work is involved, notifying the details of the departure to such people as the wages staff, pension fund officer, social club secretary, and security officer, so that they can have everything ready at the time they leave. Departmental heads should be asked to complete a leaving report, assessing the employees' performance while working for them, which is then filed for future reference purposes. The key question on this form might well be – 'Would you re-employ this person in your department: if not, why not?'

Redundancy

Industrial development and economic changes involve risks such that no organization can unconditionally guarantee security of employment to its workers. But at the same time, if a sense of loyalty is expected from these workers, a firm must in return show a sense of responsibility towards them in times of uncertainty as well as when conditions are stable. Anxiety can be greatly diminished at such times if agreement is reached beforehand on a policy designed to keep redundancies to a minimum and to mitigate their impact on the individual. Redundancy means having a labour force surplus to productive capacity. It is a situation that arises usually as a result of a marked fall in demand for a firm's products or because the reorganization of working practices or capital investment in new equipment reduces the number of workers required. When this happens, employers are obliged to meet obligations imposed by the law on redundancy, as set out in the Employment Protection Act 1975, the Employment (Consolidation) Act 1978 and decided cases. Relevant guidance on good policy and practice was offered even earlier in the Industrial Relations Code of Practice 1972. The question still arises, however, as to what employers might do in the name of good personnel management over and above the minimum requirements of the law.

In past attempts to formulate redundancy policies, trade unions and the workers they represent have usually emphasized seniority and length of service – 'last in, first out'. For their part, management naturally prefer to consider efficiency and argue that quality of workmanship must be the main factor: their logic is that an efficient staff will allow the organization to maintain its competitive power, thus reducing the likelihood of further redundancies and enabling them to expand the labour force again as soon as economic conditions improve. In fact, these opposing views can be integrated in a policy statement such as this:

> Management will tell workers and their trade union representatives of any redundancies in advance, will consult with them on methods of dealing with the situation, and undertake that the criteria for selecting the employees to be affected will not depend solely on the opinions of the selectors but should take account of such measurable factors as length of service, attendance records and assessment of work performance.

Such a policy demands that employees be assessed as to their qualities of workmanship before length of service is considered, and clearly must embrace the labour force as a whole, not just that of the few departments which may happen to be directly affected. This assessment should be an exercise in joint consultation between management, supervisors, and shop stewards, aimed not at choosing those to be dismissed but at grading the abilities of people they all know well.

If threatened redundancy seems likely to be only temporary in nature, as when demand fluctuates seasonally, then the best practice may be to create some sort of reserve fund so that good workers can be retained; the firm will not then have to face the prospect of recruiting inferior workers later when demand revives. The earnings of the people retained would be made up to their previous average level from this fund, as long as they were prepared in the meantime to do work other than their normal jobs, for example, maintenance tasks or labouring.

A number of other measures can be taken to keep redundancies to a minimum:

1 Marketing policy can be reviewed, including the possibility of an increased selling effort at lower prices.
2 All recruitment can be stopped (except where this may lead to increased sales), thus allowing natural wastage to account for some of the surplus jobs.
3 Part-time working, subcontracted work, and overtime should all be cut as much as possible.
4 Work-sharing and short-time working should be allowed wherever practical, although both should be recognized as uneconomical and must therefore be limited in extent and duration.
5 Some workers likely to be redundant can be transferred to other sections or plants within the organization and provided with facilities for retraining.

If the redundancy is permanent, with no prospect of re-employment, the longest possible notice should be given and the organization should do its best to help employees find alternative work. Executives in the personnel department itself can help initially by contacting their opposite numbers in other local firms to tell them of the types of skills of employees being made redundant and to find out if there are any vacancies available. These people should then be allowed time off with pay to attend interviews for new jobs. Similarly, facilities should be offered to the staff of the local employment office to come to the firm's premises during working hours to meet the people concerned and interview them, as a preliminary to finding them new jobs before their period of notice expires.

Another aspect of the problem that could be settled by joint consultation is the method of dealing with certain special categories of labour, in particular, older workers, married women, foreign workers, and shop stewards.

Normally the first people to be asked to leave are those workers who have carried on beyond the statutory retiring age. Looking at seniority from a different angle, too, it might be possible to bring forward the departure of those who are nearing the retirement age, although this could only be done by offering financial compensation or if they were otherwise eligible for pensions. This seems a just step to take if it allows a large number of younger people, who usually have more pressing domestic responsibilities, to stay. When pensions are not available, however, the opposite view can be put with some force – that the younger employees should go first because they will find it easier to get other jobs than the older employees.

Married women are usually well up on the list of those to be made redundant. In fact, when their husbands are working there are obvious economic reasons why many unions argue that they should be the first to leave: they certainly should be discharged before men whose families are wholly dependent on their employment. A very serious social problem arises in the case of immigrant workers: although there may be little objection to their being offered jobs when labour is short, the common attitude is that they should be made redundant before local labour. Thus the worker's country of origin becomes a factor in the redundancy situation. In fact, in all three of these cases there are elements introduced over and above the normal controversy between seniority and efficiency, and it is in clarifying policy on such points that joint consultation can prove its strength or weakness.

The position of shop stewards is a problem in itself, and many industrial disputes have been caused by their dismissal or transfer through redundancy. The whole procedure must clearly allow for no favourites; yet at the same time stewards are the workers' chosen representatives, and they will react strongly if there is any suspicion that they are being victimized for having served their cause. If they are dismissed or transferred, their choice is being diverted and they are forced to elect another official. It therefore does seem reasonable to make an exception here and allow shop stewards to continue in their jobs for the duration of their union appointments.

Much of the procedure outlined above relies heavily on joint consultation for its successful implementation. But even where the practice of this technique is so advanced that workers can share in deciding policy of this nature, final decisions must remain in the hands of management, who, more than ever in such a serious situation as redundancy, must be conscious of their overall responsibility for the firm's efficiency. Nevertheless, to avoid all charges of injustice, management could further demonstrate its goodwill by submitting the names of those to be dismissed to union representatives for comment or even to try to get their agreement. 'Comment' would give them the chance to suggest other names, with reasons for these alternatives; 'agreement' would assure everyone concerned that the selection had been carried out strictly according to the negotiated policy.

Most individual organizations with progressive redundancy policies include provisions for severance pay to help soften the initial impact of possible unemployment. The need for such provisions was lessened by the Employment Protection (Consolidation) Act 1978 which stipulated that all employees with a minimum period of two years' service are entitled to lump-sum payments if their jobs cease to exist, as follows:

1½ weeks' pay for each year of service between ages 41 and 65 (60 for women);
1 week for years between 22 and 40;
½ week for years between 18 and 21.

Thus the scheme provides payments, based on a combination of length of service, age, and normal pay when dismissed, which are intended to compensate workers for their loss of job expectations and to encourage them to move. The wage-related unemployment benefit scheme, introduced under the National Insurance Act 1966, is intended to cushion any unemployment before they find a new job.

The most up-to-date version of the guidance contained in this section is offered in the IPM's Redundancy Code, published in February 1984, with brief sections on the purpose of a redundancy code, legal aspects, avoiding compulsory redundancy, redundancy agreements, implementing redundancies and assisting redundant employees.

The usefulness of such a code is perhaps best seen in a historical context: the original Redundancy Payments Act dates back to 1965, yet practical difficulties still arise and the courts have been seen to change their attitudes over the years to such matters as defining redundancy, voluntary redundancy and dismissal, employers' entitlement to rebates, prior consultation with individual employees involved, and selection criteria for redundancy.

A report on a survey* of redundancy arrangements, published by the ACAS in 1987, revealed that, in selecting people for redundancy, there has been a clear move away from the principle 'last in, first out' — towards a basis which gives greater priority to the skills and experience which may need to be retained within an organization in order to maintain a balanced and effective workforce. The survey also shows that there has been a continuing formalization of redundancy arrangements, with 70 per cent of the 470 employers sampled having written redundancy conditions and nearly 50 per cent having agreements with recognized independent trade unions. This increase in formalization, in management's view, has had a positive impact on industrial relations, making cooperation with trade unions on the introduction of new technology and working practices much more likely. It was also found that 85 per cent of the workplace arrangements allowed for

*Redundancy Arrangements: the 1986 ACAS Survey, Occasional Paper No. 36.

employees to volunteer for redundancy, while 65 per cent made provision for pay-offs higher than the statutory minimum.

A new form of specialist personnel consultancy has grown up in the wake of large-scale redundancy programmes, offering a service of 'outplacement', helping firms to divest themselves of surplus employees in a manner which generates the minimum of union opposition and local community hostility. In fact, the principal task undertaken is that of advising individual employees who lose their jobs, if possible persuading them to move elsewhere within the organization and thus retaining their skills, experience and goodwill.

Outplacement counselling is largely in the hands of private consultants, so management has to be prepared to add their fees to any redundancy payments already due to be made. To have maximum effect, the outplacement agency should be called in before the workforce is laid off, to allow time to set up, make contacts, interview and 'market' those concerned. It will need to talk to local enterprise bodies and depending on the particular circumstances, liaise with the Small Firms Service, local Employment Service offices, the Rural Development Commission or any other body that can help to provide an 'integrated partnership' approach to the problem. Generally the agency will then arrange a series of seminars to explain how it can help those who may be at a loss about what to do after being made redundant.

The consultants usually set up an on-site Job Shop, sometimes with the help of local job centres, but mostly offering employment possibilities which they have found themselves through contacting and visiting other local employers (jobs often not previously advertised). The team may have to set about re-educating those on the redundancy list in how to go about finding work; threatened by the prospect of losing their regular jobs, some find it hard to think objectively about the relevance of their existing skills or the directions in which their experience might take them.

At all times the needs of the individual should be paramount. The consultant can help with form-filling and interview technique, and with advice on setting up in business when required. When dealing with senior staff, good outplacement agencies make life easier by providing a structure at a time when the normal day-to-day routine has disappeared. The best agencies provide an office, secretarial services, telephone, personal stationery, photocopying and fax machines, a database and a reference library. The client is encouraged to attend regularly and meet other redundant people who, with their varying backgrounds, can support and help each other.

The outplacement consultative process follows a well-tested route. After initial registration and settling-in, clients are invited to take stock. What have they achieved in the past? What have they most enjoyed doing, and vice versa? What do they want to achieve from a new job? What are the priorities in their personal lives? Careful plotting of such points leads to the creation of an ideal job specification — a target to aim for and a standard by which to compare available opportunities and future offers.

The CV then has to be put together, along with marketing letters which list past achievements — both designed to attract the busy executive, with more detailed information being available later. The next stage is targeting the desired job, and here telephone and secretarial back-up can be most useful. Networking is the main process of finding the desired job and identifying the person taking the final decision about it. Many senior jobs are never advertised: sometimes they are handled by an executive search service ('headhunter'), but often they are only in the planning stage when the all-important contact is made. Networking starts with friends and former colleagues — anyone who is prepared to spend time discussing the job search problem.

It is part of the ethos of most outplacement consultants that they deal only in the corporate market, not taking fees from people in the throes of redundancy. Nor do they believe in thrusting clients into jobs — it is up to the individual to decide what he/she wants to do. The evidence is that managements increasingly are realizing that it is in their interests to accept some responsibility for those made redundant: it is good for the morale of the remaining workforce, it is good for the future when they need to recruit, and it is good for their economy that people should be in work. When individuals are advised to seek retraining, it is important that there should be a guarantee of employment at the end of it. In all these ways, outplacement is a big step in the right direction, offering essential counselling and back-up when things seem at their blackest, and boosting individuals' confidence by showing that someone does care and can give every assistance.

The problems of unemployment

The basic tasks of personnel managers were described at the outset* as those of obtaining and retaining an appropriate labour force for their organization. They are carried out, depending on the scale of the organization, in the setting of national, regional and local demands for and supplies of labour, and at the present time in the general context of

*See Chapter 1, 'Definitions'.

high levels of unemployment. Local situations are undoubtedly upper-most in the minds of the majority of personnel managers but a broad understanding of the contemporary unemployment situation, predictions as to its future, and attempts to solve the associated social and economic problems are important – because personnel managers can contribute positively towards these solutions.

Current unemployment figures seem stark for two main reasons: the fact that, post Second World War, it was possible for the government to implement policies leading to full employment successfully for some 25 years; and fears that, although much of the high unemployment is attributable to world recession, it demonstrates features of a permanent nature which cause continuing anxieties even as economic recovery grows apace.

It is easy to state objectives – for example, 'the creation of a national economic strategy capable of restoring a competitive and technological grip on world trade, and a labour market strategy capable of recognizing and exploiting every possibility for employment growth consistent with this'.* The practical problems which then arise, however, are wide in range and controversial as regards proposals for their solution.

Part of the difficulty lies in the crude nature of unemployment statistics which seek to define the size of the problems. Such statements as 'over 2 million, or 9 per cent of the nation's workforce are unemployed' impress with their gravity but have little meaning unless the distribution of the unemployed by gender, age, skill, duration and location is also analysed. Detailed statistics also show that the incidence of unemployment is heavily weighted towards the unskilled, the young and the old, and those living in the traditional areas of manufacturing industry.

Another conclusion must be that a large measure of long-term unemployment is an unavoidable result of rising overall levels of unemployment, and thus becomes a very significant item for attention in any programme designed to mitigate the effects of unemployment. It is a truism that long-term experience of unemployment reduces an individual's ability to find work and his/her skills atrophy, so that an increasing level of unemployment makes any return to full employment more difficult. Even when re-employment is secured, it often involves a process of down-grading, with successive jobs being less skilled and lower paid.

Dealing with the scepticism and hostility of those affected by long-term unemployment is never easy. Making the new scheme compulsory or voluntary is one point at issue. In support of the latter view, it is

---

*Manpower Studies, No. 7, IMS, University of Sussex, 1984.

argued that such programmes must attract by what they offer, and that the greatest attractions are demonstrably high quality of training, quality outcomes and, for as many participants as possible, jobs at the end of the programme. By the same token, providers should not be compelled to participate – for unwillingness on their part, for whatever reasons, would damage credibility and adversely affect what the programmes offer.

The focus of all such training must be concerned with more than 'starting gate' or basic skills. It must range upward to higher level skills, including high-tech, while accepting that this may need special provider funding arrangements within the overall framework. Administratively, 'local training plans' are envisaged, designed annually with the advice and guidance of the local advisory body of the Training Commission.

Forecasters concern themselves with prospects for reducing levels of unemployment, but even those who take an expansionist policy view – based on packages of economic tools involving continuing monetarism or international reflation – do not hold out much hope for a fall in unemployment below two million by the end of the decade.

Another problem relevant to the individual personnel manager is the fact that one deep-rooted cause of unemployment in the UK is our inability to coordinate income and employment policies. Employment in manufacturing has continuously declined since the 1960s, although this has been countered in some measure by an increase of some 2.5 million jobs in the service sector. A further contraction in the demand for labour can be seen in the widespread push for productivity growth. Taken together, these factors have influenced not only massive increases in the number of unemployed, but also far-reaching shifts in the structure of employment: that is, from manual to non-manual occupations, from full-time male to part-time female employment and from manufacturing to service activities.

The overall quality of the labour force must also be taken into account. This is not simply a matter of improvement in the general level of education: more important, it is concerned with re-educating and retraining the labour force during their working lives so as to respond quickly to changes in demand for particular types of labour. If the labour force of the future is to cope with rapidly changing technology, while retraining remains inadequate, then the possibilities of permanent exclusion from job opportunities will inevitably increase.

Assuming the continuation of the world recession and economic policies centred on the control of inflation through monetarism, what practical steps can be taken to reduce the level of unemployment? The answer to this question is that five schemes appear to have emerged as the most promising among the very many ideas put forward in recent years: they relate to employers' recruitment and retention policies, employment subsidies, work-sharing, training and community initiatives.

The first need is for employers to review their recruitment and retention policies with a view to achieving, long-term, greater employment security and stability among their labour forces. At the moment, it is argued, employers take too short-term a view of prospects and therefore tend needlessly to accentuate cyclical fluctuations in hiring and firing. Such practices produce considerable, but unnecessary, costs of adjustment – money which would be better spent on the longer term improvement of the quality of the labour force. In other words, employers should treat labour more like a capital investment when financing the implementation of major manpower changes; not, it is suggested, through large-scale redundancies but, where merited longer term, through retention and retraining.

Second, employment subsidies are generally regarded as being means of influencing employers' policies short-term. They have proved to be valuable not so much in the creation of jobs directly, as in influencing the distribution of unemployment – in particular, by improving the job prospects of disadvantaged groups. Experience has so far shown job creation through subsidies to be either very expensive or on a very small scale, with a strong suspicion that many claims for subsidies have been for jobs which would have been created anyway. The conclusion must therefore be that subsidies are attractive and effective as policy options only when employers have a perceived need to recruit, and not at times when economic necessity causes large cuts in employment.

Third, there are the job creation effects of work-sharing initiatives, by reductions in working time. In practice, however, the results achieved in this respect have been negligible. Early retirement has often been used by employers as a means of shedding labour, rather than as an opportunity of opening up jobs to young people; that is, the high cost to employers of securing early retirement has been offset by overall reductions in manning and by very low replacement rates. Suggestions regarding overtime reductions have rarely been implemented because employer and employee in many organizations have mutual interests in maintaining high levels of overtime. Again, longer holidays cannot easily be covered by creating new jobs. In practical terms, a shorter working week offers the best chance of work-sharing, although its potential has not yet been realized in the UK because compensating productivity increases have been readily available. Job-sharing is, however, still regarded by many personnel specialists as providing worthwhile short-term benefits, despite the shortcomings associated with part-time work. Somehow public opinion needs to be marshalled to ensure that reductions in working time are continued in ways which genuinely create new jobs.

There appears to be particular scope for more part-time jobs to be made available for some groups of the unemployed. In the case of school-leavers, for example, many would probably find a gradual transition into full-time work attractive. Part-time contracts also offer the obvious advantages of providing training and experience, while allowing both employer and employee to make up their minds about each other should full-time vacancies arise. Part-time staff also provide a pool which can be called upon during holidays, absence or in very busy times. These advantages are further pointed up when the flexibility of part-time working is fully grasped: alternate weeks, short days, groups of days, are among many possibilities. It is important, too, to consider part-time opportunities when cutbacks seem to be necessary: rather than abolish full-time jobs completely, the personnel manager may well advise at least a partial switch to permanent part-time employment.

The fourth means of assisting the unemployed is through training, but this must be linked closely with the subsequent availability of jobs; new skills acquired during training courses quickly deteriorate unless they are actually used in employment. It must also be understood that learning new technical skills is not enough in itself – rather, trainees must be taught how to identify, acquire and apply relevant knowledge and skills in such ways as to enable them to act confidently and be able to use those skills in unfamiliar surroundings. Ideally, therefore, training should be aimed not at teaching a single specific skill, but an adaptable, flexible, and redeployable set of competencies.

Fifth, another small-scale contribution towards reducing unemployment lies in the large number of community initiatives being taken throughout the UK by public agencies, local authorities and local businesses. In particular, job creation has been encouraged by assisting small firms and cooperatives and by attracting investment. Although the results in any one community may be measured in terms of only hundreds of jobs at best, nevertheless such initiatives are usually designed directly to meet specific local needs, such as off-setting a major closure in an area, and hence are likely to be well-targeted. Not that the cumulative effect of these schemes is negligible; by 1984 some 130,000 places in community programmes had been filled.

Along similar lines, American experience of neighbourhood revitalization might be adapted. (Such programmes are not altruistic, but demonstrate enlightened self-interest in that their aims embrace the long-term prosperity of organizations taking part.) One practice is that of large corporations with government contracts setting aside a certain proportion of subcontracting work for local small businesses, thus helping them to create new jobs. This is a particularly interesting concept as there is a noticeable tendency for subcontracting to grow in every industralized nation as large companies shrink to a hard core of basic activities and buy in the rest. Other ideas prompting companies to take on greater responsibilities within their local communities perhaps stem from the examples of British Steel and the National Coal Board which, instead of abandoning communities in which they have closed large employing operations, have set up separate businesses whose tasks are solely concerned with job creation. These ideas include the following:

(a) Providing seconded managers to help local people get new businesses started.
(b) Encouraging employees at all levels to be involved in community affairs.
(c) Earmarking spare plant, equipment and factory space for local job creation.
(d) Encouraging small businesses to produce and market products developed by large businesses but not launched for reasons of scale or strategic fit.
(e) Buying goods and services locally wherever possible.
(f) Taking on a few more young trainees each year than are currently employed.

The main employment programmes offered by the Government's Employment Service are fitted into a framework for advising clients, which aims to give coherent help to those who most need it. The framework includes: a *Back to Work* plan, giving individual guidance on how to find work; review of all claimants unemployed for thirteen weeks, and selective interviews of those with skills in demand; a unified advisory service allowing continuity of contact by skilled advisers; systematic follow-up of those not taking up jobs or places offered on training programmes; an intensive burst of help for those unemployed for two years; more case loading of those with particular difficulties to give concentrated assistance in identifying causes of their problems and access to opportunities. The new framework will also make clear to clients their statutory obligations to be both available for and actively seeking employment. Claimants who have been unemployed for two years or more may be required by benefit regulations to attend Restart Courses; such an extra and intensive effort is felt to be necessary at this stage to stop the gradual drift into very long-term unemployment.

New Client Advisers of the Employment Service have the role of offering positive assistance to the newly unemployed to help them back to work as soon as possible. *The Restart programme* enables everyone unemployed for six months or more to be invited every six months to an in-depth interview which aims to provide help and guidance, assess individual needs, and overcome disadvantages. *Restart courses* aim to help those aged 18 or over who have been unemployed for six months or more to reassess their strengths and skills, rebuild their confidence and motivation, consider their options in detail, and decide what action to take to get back to work.

Job clubs are places where people get together to work at finding jobs. They are shown the best ways to search and apply and how to perform well at interviews, with access provided to resource centres where newspapers, stationery, stamps and telephones are available free. Then the *Travel to Interview Scheme* gives assistance to unemployed jobseekers to go to interviews beyond their normal daily travelling distance of the home area.

Jobshare pays £1000 to employers if they create part-time jobs for unemployed people by splitting full-time jobs or combining regular overtime. *Programme Development Funds* are money allocated to Employment Service Regional Directors to fund locally devised and innovative projects in areas of deprivation that help the most disadvantaged clients take up work, training or self-employment. *The Job Interview Guarantee* scheme offers employers help, for example, job preparation courses, to find suitable longer-term unemployed people if they guarantee to offer interviews to these applicants.

Employment Training (ET), the programme for unemployed adults introduced in 1988, offered a new feature with its starting-up funding of up to £20,000 for training agents. These agents are responsible for trainee recruitment, counselling, assessment, individual action plans and referral to a suitable training manager, and they are paid fees accordingly. In turn, training managers are responsible for the delivery of the action plan, to include directed training and practical training on projects or with an employer.

Trainees receive training allowances based on previous state benefits (plus £10—£12) and are paid travelling expenses, lodging allowances and child care costs.

People who have been unemployed over six months are eligible for ET, with priority going to 18—24 year-olds who have been unemployed for six to twelve months and those aged 18—50 who have been out of work for more than two years.

All ES programmes are open to people with disabilities, often with relaxed entry conditions. In addition, there is a wide range of services and schemes for those who need special help, including: disablement resettlement officers who can help with special occupational counselling and advice; the disablement advisory service of local teams which help employers to implement good policies and practices towards people with disabilities: the employment rehabilitation service, and other special schemes covering loans of equipment, grants for adaption of premises, fares to work, trial periods of employment: the sheltered employment programme provides jobs for over 20,000 severely disabled people who need sheltered conditions or support to hold down jobs; and the sheltered placement scheme allows people with severe disabilities to work alongside other workers in a variety of jobs and locations.

The nature of economic depression, seemingly world-wide during the early 1990s, meant that unemployment levels in the UK continued to grow and required constant attention and new ideas to deal with the problem. *Initial Training* (IT) is a scheme launched in 1989 to tackle the difficulties of collapsing confidence and rusty skills which may prevent long-term unemployed people from making the most of a full-time programme like Employment Training. It has the aim of preparing people more fully for entry into training by helping them to develop clear aims, appropriate attitudes and motivation as well as the basic skills needed to cope in a training environment. An important feature of the IT scheme is that trainees can participate on a part-time basis while retaining their existing benefits. Such flexibility is very helpful to those with domestic commitments especially sole parents, the disabled, or people recovering from illness who need to enter ET gradually. A smooth transition from IT to ET is most important and in many cases participants are able to spend brief trial periods with their prospective ET provider before leaving the IT programme.

Another comprehensive package of measures to help the un-employed was promulgated in 1991. *Employment Action* was a new programme designed to offer up to 60,000 people a year the chance to keep their skills up to date by work experience on local projects. Aimed at people who have been unemployed for six months or more, work experience is planned for two main areas: one-off projects of local benefit, particularly in the inner cities; and reinforcing the existing activities of voluntary organizations, aimed at people with recent service sector experience.

Other main features of the project are: new help for more than 100,000 in a year finding a job, aimed specifically at those experiencing unemployment for the first time who need advice in assessing the opportunities open to them; 15,000 more placed on ET particularly for people with learning and literacy problems, to enable them to develop new skills; 100,000 extra opportunities in the Job club programme, designed to meet the needs of specific groups; and an expansion of Restart courses to help people unemployed for six months or more to re-enter the labour market.

Job generation will be more easily achieved if it is consistent with changes in patterns of work – in the form of part-time jobs, service sector employment, non-manual occupations and female participation, as well as changes in the organization of work within firms to increase the flexibility of labour – rather than hanging on to a vanishing traditional model of full-time lifelong jobs on which so many current 'solutions' to the problems of unemployment still seem to be based.

Finally, it must be recognized that any new policies may achieve only a small percentage of their job creation potential. This is an inevitable consequence of the volatile nature of the labour market: maximization of results must therefore be the practical aim, rather than an ideal policy which suffers no leakages. In other words, a multiplicity of approaches and diversity must be encouraged – for the problems of unemployment demand not a panacea but a wide variety of initiatives, each of which can make some contribution in its own way.

Economically speaking, some pundits seem to rely on the theory that there is a fixed amount of employment in the British economy and the trick is to spread it around more thinly (hence 'fairly'). The fact is that Britain as a country simply does not produce enough manufactured goods. Many of the present Government's measures for improving the climate – for example, training and start-up incentives – are sound in themselves, but do not tackle the central defect of the economic situation, the wholesale retreat by business from large sectors of the manufacturing economy. British business has allowed itself to be virtually expelled from whole areas, particularly where high quality precision manufacturing is required: machine tools, plastics processing equipment, office equipment, cameras, motor cycles, half of the domestic motor car market – to the extent that we are now net importers of manufactured goods. Here lies the main challenge, to recapture these markets, and the answer does not lie in the otherwise commendable courage of one-person and other small businesses.

The only way these markets will be reclaimed, and generate the jobs which go with them, is by the formation of new companies of sufficient size to recruit management and engineering talent commensurate with the task. No sophisticated research or time-consuming innovation is needed – the target is the production of goods which are similar to imported products, but just a little bit better in quality and design. The proper sources of capital for such large-scale enterprises are the banks. This should be seen as an opportunity for them to play a part in the renaissance of Britain similar to that played by their counterparts in Germany and Japan in the 1950s and 1960s.

Meantime, among the current figure of about 3 million unemployed in Great Britain, of particular concern is the plight of school-leavers unable to find jobs. Over the years a bewildering number of suggestions of ways to tackle the problem have been made, many of them by personnel management specialists: the practice of 'job release' is one, allowing jobs to be created for young people by arranging the premature retirement of older workers; cutting overtime seems to be another equitable idea, sharing the jam which goes on top of the cake: for regular overtime for some, while many others receive dole payments, is hardly the mark of a just society; Temporary Employment Subsidies, Youth Employment Subsidies, Small Firms Employment Subsidies, premium grants payable to employers who engage additional trainees for approved training, financial grants available to employers who provide opportunities for college-based students to gain industrial experience, the Employment Transfer Scheme, the Job Introduction Scheme for Disabled People, and the Youth Opportunities Programme – all are examples of positive steps taken to try to reduce unemployment figures.

7

Special categories of the labour force

The rate of natural growth in the working population* is of basic concern to personnel managers carrying out their manpower planning functions:

Table 3

Great Britain: active labour force projections
(*thousands*)

1993	27,349
1995	27,490
1997	27,706
1999	27,888
2001	28,102

However, within this trend of a slow rise in the total size of the labour force lies what has been termed 'a demographic time-bomb' associated with an ageing population and a considerable fall in the numbers of school-leavers during the 1990s. In detail, it is anticipated†

*Fuller analysis — male, female: all ages, working age — appears in the *Employment Gazette*, May 1992.
†*Defusing the Demographic Time Bomb*, NEDO and the Training Agency, 1989.

that the structure of the labour force will change in these significant ways:

• The adult labour force in most parts of the UK is projected to expand, so that by the year 2000 there will be some 2.3 million more people aged 25–34 in the workforce than there were in 1988, more than off-setting the 1.3 million fall in the under-25s during the same period.
• There will be many more women in the workforce, making up some 45 per cent in total; many will be returning to work after periods of absence, and they will make up over 90 per cent of the increase in the workforce during the 1990s.
• The workforce is 'greying'; by 2000 a third of the total will be 45 years of age or over.

The same demographic trends of a decrease in young people (over the 35 years up to 2025 the number of 15–19 year olds coming on to the labour market in the European Community will decline by up to 15 per cent) and the gradual ageing of the workforce are affecting all countries in Europe as well as the USA, Japan and, to a lesser extent, SE Asia. The reduced numbers of young people entering the labour market and deficiencies in education and training systems are leading to an increasing problem of skill shortages and mismatch between labour supply and demand. Many employers are realizing that they face a hostile labour market in the years ahead as the demand for professionally and technically qualified manpower continues to rise, for recruitment of such staff has always been heavily dependent on new skill supplies from further and higher education.

Employers recruit young people for many reasons: convenience, lower labour costs, tradition, as 'seed corn' for their skills stock and career systems. In most organizations there is considerable scope to break this mould and Table 4 lists the options available:*

*Employment Gazette, February 1990, page 66.

Table 4 Some adjustment options

Improving access to young recruits	*Reducing need for young recruits*
Recruitment and selection	
Intensify existing youth recruitment effort Improve pay and/or benefits for young people Widen the youth net: • lower or abolish recruitment filters and replace with new selection procedures • reduce hiring standards	Direct substitution of adults for young people • women re-entrants • mature workers and re-entrants • former employees (returners) • long-term unemployed • ethnic minority adults • disabled re-entrants • adults with learning difficulties Extend recruitment efforts for adults: • new recruitment channels • more careful selection • identifying and breaking down inappropriate barriers (qualification, age, experience)
Retention	
Establish new or improved career paths for young people	Opening new work channels: • part-time working options • job sharing or job splitting • remote working New contractual arrangements: • annual hours • school term contracts • sub-contracting arrangements
Improve induction for young people	Improve induction of adults Better selection of recruits New career paths (horizontal as well as vertical movement) Career breaks and 'caring' sabbaticals Childcare schemes Improve awareness of employees' benefits Changes to work organization and job design targeted at improved job satisfaction Better monitoring of reasons for leaving

Table 4 Continued

	Training and development
Improve or establish own label YTS programme	Remove age barriers and develop adult employees: • improve access to training and development
Improving other youth training programmes Link improved training with guaranteed career paths	• Re-skilling, upgrading

	Other
Build a reputation as a good employer • establish or improve schools/colleges liaison • work experience programmes for pupils and students • develop career packs, open days, etc.	Relocate premises Introduce productivity initiatives Encourage redeployment of staff

In the context of these labour force projections the tasks of personnel management may be summarized as — making the best use of the labour force available locally, training employees in order to work in the most efficient manner, and ensuring that their skills are utilized to the maximum.*

A recruitment crisis is inevitable as the twentieth-century ends, and this will need to be tackled realistically: that is, not by concentrating on the declining pool of young people, but rather by widening recruitment prospects to include older workers, the unemployed, women returners, people with disabilities and ethnic minority communities. Other innovative approaches embrace jobsharing, intensive reskilling training programmes, and special contracts to allow mothers to work only during school term-times. Certain categories of the labour force — married women, the disabled, elderly workers — present particular problems to the personnel manager, but tackling them positively will certainly go some way towards improving the effectiveness of the total labour supply.

*A case study of how one organization is tackling the 'demographic time-bomb' appears as an appendix to this chapter.

Married women

For most women paid employment is now a taken-for-granted activity and they spend the greater part of their lives in the labour market. At the same time almost all wives have a primary role looking after the home and family and a secondary role as wage earners, while the opposite is the case for their husbands. This has consequences for women's position in the labour market and their attitudes towards work. Broadly, women do not participate in the labour market on the same terms as men over their life-time and the conditions under which they offer themselves, for example as part-time workers, may go some way towards explaining the segregated and secondary nature of much of the work they do. While paid work is an increasingly important aspect of women's lives, most accept or accommodate to a domestic division of labour and achieving a balance between home and work which this entails.

It is now normal practice for women to work full-time until the birth of their first child. What is striking is that very high proportions of women return to work after having a child, and that they are doing so ever more quickly. Even so, women with children still fall into two broad groups: mothers who work between births and return to work soon after their latest birth and mothers who more closely approximate to the two-phase pattern and do not return to work at all until their last child is of school age. Not surprisingly, since paid employment is now the norm for the majority of women, traditional family-orientated views are declining in the long term as women's level of education rises and they spend more of their lives at work. One major survey* has shown that only a small minority of women (25 per cent) supported the long-standing belief that 'a woman's place is in the home'; rather, a large proportion agreed that married women have the right to work if they want to and do not work just for pin-money (71 per cent and 66 per cent respectively). In addition, most women accepted that working is beneficial for a woman. Even so, paid employment was rarely seen as a central life interest; it is accommodated to and balanced with domestic demands, and for most women takes a secondary role in their lives to family commitments.

Husbands' attitudes are clearly also important in this context, and the conclusion of the survey was that husbands can hardly be described as enthusiastic supporters of their wives working. Only 14 per cent of wives working full-time said their husbands would prefer them not to work, but only a minority (43 per cent) of working wives

Women and Employment, Jean Martin and Ceridwyn Roberts (HMSO, 1984).

agreed it was definitely true that their husbands were pleased that they worked. Husbands of working wives, however, rarely felt that wives should not work or that their wives' main job was to look after the home. The over-riding impression emerging from the survey was one of husbands tolerating their wives working, though in many cases they did not want it to interfere or conflict with their own work or domestic life. Women's part-time working in part may be seen as an accommodation to this view of the desirable balance between paid and unpaid work.

In examining the reasons why women want to work, a distinction must be drawn between two groups: women in the labour market (either working or unemployed) and 'domestic returners'. The reasons for wanting work usually given by the latter differ from those of other groups, largely because the differences between women wanting full or part-time work are so pronounced. Overall, financial reasons for working are paramount in all groups, but women already in the labour market emphasize financial need or financial autonomy much more than women returning to work do. Even among women wanting part-time work, domestic returners are less likely to mention financial reasons and more likely to mention the sociability work afforded them. This difference is so marked that the adult company dimension of working is clearly a more salient factor for women returning to the labour market than it is for women already in employment. Domestic returners are likely, too, to be less concerned than working women with the quality of a job; that is, they are not choosing to look for a better job, as most people already working do, but are simply looking for *a* job. Women wanting part-time work, in particular, tend to trade off aspects of a job, such as good pay, security and the opportunity to use one's abilities, in favour of convenient hours.

Management action to make the employment of married women more effective involves a new attitude towards training them for skilled jobs and the need to recall and make better use of the skills which married women acquired before leaving work after marriage or to have children.

It is interesting to reflect here on the role of the personnel manager in advising departmental heads about patterns of staff behaviour. Many common assumptions about the alleged unreliability of married women employees as regards attendance, time-keeping, sickness, and labour turnover have been questioned and proved wrong by recent surveys. Obviously much depends on whether the women have small children, and some firms insure themselves against possible unreliability by not recruiting women with young families. The fact remains that as far as regular work habits are concerned, the record of married women is generally as good as, if not better than, that of single women.

Older women can also be relied on to bring a steadying influence to their jobs, and skills and training from previous employment may well include such characteristics as the ability to deal with the public, operate complex machinery, and supervise junior staff. Thus, while married women will always try to adjust their employment to meet their domestic requirements, those employers who help them to do so will reap the benefits of dependable service.

Personnel specialists should also be able to capitalize on what is known about the motivation of married women in working, in order to attract them into their firm's employment. To start with, the fact that the majority of part-time workers are over thirty-five indicates that financial considerations rather than domestic circumstances determine whether a woman will look for full-time or part-time jobs. There may be economic pressures which force young married mothers to work full-time when no part-time jobs are available, but older women, whose husbands are at the peak of their earnings, can afford to be much more selective. Thus, although the financial motive is always present, only in a small proportion of cases during early years of marriage does actual necessity seem to be involved. The majority look on their work more as a means of obtaining higher standards of living for their families – buying better furniture for the home, running a car, taking holidays abroad, for example. The psychological uplift of not having to be 'careful' over money and the desire for personal independence are other relevant aspects of the financial motive. The desire for companionship is very important, especially to those women who find themselves left alone all day after being used to looking after children. The routine of housework and shopping can become very depressing in such circumstances, and they particularly enjoy the prospect of being kept young by going back to work with a friendly crowd of younger people. In any case, married women today have much more time on their hands than their mothers, and certainly their grandmothers, had; the days of very large families have disappeared so that, whereas a mother spent some fifteen years nursing her own babies at the turn of the century, this has now fallen to an average of only four years.

In theory, personnel policies should always reflect equal conditions for all staff, with no special treatment for particular groups. Nevertheless, conditions of supply and demand in the labour market inevitably mean that concessions must be made when necessary to obtain the required amount of labour. In practice, these concessions usually take the form of:

1 Shorter hours or longer lunch-breaks to allow family shopping to be done; a retail shop is sometimes provided on the premises.

2 Unpaid leave of absence for domestic reasons, such as children's illness or husband's holidays.
3 Fitting hours in with husband's shifts whenever possible.

There is a negative side to this subject as well, for many organizations place certain restrictions on the employment conditions of married women: making them the first to be declared redundant, not considering them for promotion, excluding them from pension schemes and sickness benefits (especially if part-time), and in some cases giving them only temporary status. Some of these policies need to be changed if a realistic attitude is to be taken towards employing married women.*

Skill is one thing, responsibility another. Although many married women resent the humdrum nature of their work and would like something more challenging, they do not on the whole want to be supervisors and thus add further responsibilities to their domestic commitments. If they possess any organizing talents, they prefer to use them at home where their sense of status and security are centred. Above all, they do not want to take their work home with them, which a supervisor with problems often has to do. Nor is there much financial incentive to accept promotion, for supervisors do not usually get piece-rates or the chance to earn more money before holidays or at Christmastime. There is also a marked reluctance to move above friends whose companionship was one of the main reasons for coming back to work in the first place. Even so, many managers recognize particular qualities in married women as supervisors − experience of life, maturity, and tolerance, for example, plus the ability to handle other married women and recognize excuses for what they are. To draw on these skills in the future, however, may very well mean offering much more realistic financial incentives at supervisory level, further concessions as regards hours, and a more elaborate structure of deputy or relief supervisors to cover times of family crisis.

An important amenity that employers might themselves provide, if they feel convinced that they will thereby recruit staff who would not otherwise come to them, is a day nursery to look after employees' children during working hours. The costs of establishing, equipping, and staffing such a unit must be carefully considered by management beforehand, in relation to the number of new employees likely to be recruited, and any decision should be based on these factors:

1 How many married women with children are actually available for employment (information from local employment offices).

*Since the Sex Discrimination Act 1975, women may not be discriminated against because they are married.

2 How much competition there is from other employers for this type of labour; the possibility of combining with any of them to provide a nursery.
3 What facilities are already available in local authority and private nurseries in the area.
4 The costs involved in providing accommodation and facilities to the standards required by the DSS.
5 The extent to which these costs can be offset by charging mothers who place their children in the nurseries.
6 The net expected gain in staff.

Personnel managers or their welfare assistants have a direct role to play in easing the adjustment of married women to the working situation, by appreciating their difficulties and problems and by helping to solve them. More and more general practitioners in the community are protesting about the 'working-wife syndrome' – the increasing number of patients who present themselves near the stage of nervous and emotional collapse, asking for some sort of tonic to remove their irritability, tiredness, headaches, insomnia, and indigestion. 'The usual story is: get up at 7 a.m. or earlier; do some rapid housework, including breakfast for the family; leave home at 8 a.m.; work all day – often standing all the time – shopping in the lunch break or on the way home; and return home to a bleak house with unmade beds, breakfast dishes unwashed, at about 6 p.m. The evening is spent in catching up on neglected housework and the weekend in washing, shopping, cleaning, and mending. . . . The cause of this syndrome is sheer overwork. The attempt to run a home – especially if there are children – and yet spend 8–10 hours a day away from the home doing another job is almost impossible.'*

The need for welfare officers to be available to give friendly advice to women who show signs of reaching this state is obvious. It is partly a matter of providing services and making concessions over working conditions, as already described, but fundamentally calls for acceptance of the fact that married women must be allowed to put their families first. For example, when a woman returns after a few days off work, she should not be subjected to a nerve-racking inquisition with threats of dismissal included for good measure; rather she needs an understanding discussion of her domestic problem. Financial advice should be made available for young married couples, too, so that they do not come to rely so heavily on the wife's income that her absence from work can cause a family economic crisis over domestic debts.

*Letter in *The Lancet*, 5 February 1966, from Dr J. F. Hanratty.

Older people

In light of the working population scenario described above, employing organizations need to look carefully at their own demographic structures and should analyse carefully the evolution of their labour markets. The current tendency to get rid prematurely of some older staff will have to be revised. To keep older personnel efficient, more extensive forms of training and recycling will become important. Parallel structures which do not block promotion for younger employees may become more common, on the one hand; on the other, some organizations have facilitated the creation of new firms in which opportunities are offered to the older manager. Some older managers can also be re-employed as external consultants or assigned to special tasks.

Clearly the waste which results from condemning to inactivity a growing part of the population is wrong. The basic need is for flexible forms of 'retirement' which would enable people to enter into a second or third 'career' and thus contribute positively to the national weal.

With higher standards of living, improved health, and better medical services, people stay fitter for work much longer. The average age of the working population has increased steadily over the past two decades, and now that so much concern is being shown for making the most effective use of available manpower, a great deal more needs to be done in tackling the problems of all those people who, because of their age, meet with special difficulties in obtaining or retaining jobs.

The time at which these difficulties arise varies with individuals, the area where they live, and their occupation, and depends not only on their physical and mental ability but on the nature of the work, the attitudes of their employer and workmates, and the state of the local labour market. Although knowledge about the processes of ageing is still very incomplete, it is well established that a feeling of continued usefulness has great psychological benefits. In later middle age, most people try to move away from jobs which make severe demands on them for speed, agility, or sustained heavy muscular effort. They are quite capable of doing work which requires less effort, of course, and can offer positive advantages in some types of jobs, for example, those requiring accuracy and attention to detail, and those in which judgment based on experience is called for. Some skilled workers also make very good instructors for young craftsmen. The qualities that older people generally bring to their work, such as regularity of time-keeping and conscientiousness, must not be overlooked.

The National Advisory Committee on the Employment of the Older Worker found that 60 per cent of employed persons preferred to stay on at work when they reached pensionable age. Their reasons were mainly financial, but also because they feel fit enough and want to carry on working, even when they have enough money to be able to retire. Main reasons for retirement are ill-health or lack of opportunities to continue working: employers tend to give the latter as a reason for enforcing retirements rather than dismissing people for inefficiency or incapacity for work.

The difficulties of employing older people are varied and complex. Individual mental and physical shortcomings may prevent them from doing many types of jobs that call for quick reflexes. Often there is marked resistance from younger workers to their continued employment, because they may block promotional opportunities.

The phrase 'too old at forty' still has some significance, although in recent years there has been a noticeable tendency for age limits in staff advertisements to be extended. The cost of providing pensions rises according to age when joining a superannuation scheme. Most of this financial burden falls on the employer's shoulders, which is a sound reason for not engaging an undue proportion of staff above middle age; again, many pension funds exclude the entry of men and women above a specified age (sometimes as low as fifty). In a redundancy situation, it is common practice for pensioners and those nearing retirement to be discharged first, in order to preserve the security of young employees with family responsibilities. Sometimes the age structure of an organization becomes unbalanced in relation to future work requirements, and firms have been known to retire older workers compulsorily to inject some younger blood into the organization.

Professional and executive jobs tend to be the most stable, but older people who lose such posts often find it difficult to get other work. Some go into premature retirement if they can afford to; some have to take employment which makes little use of their professional abilities; some find only part-time jobs. Others have to change not only their employment late in life, but also their profession: for example, regular servicemen of the armed forces. Such people can only rarely offer experience worth much to a prospective employer and in most cases they are philosophical about the inevitable reduction in pay and status, especially if there are some prospects of improvement once experience has been gained. Direct help is given by the Civil Service, which offers some posts, without age limits, in both clerical and executive grades for competition by ex-regular members of the forces. Specialized employment bureaux have been created to help, too. The Ex-Officers' Association, the Regular Forces Employment Association, and the Over Forty-Fives' Association are the best known, and there have been examples of professional men banding together to provide their own self-help service in finding new jobs. Even the psychology of the problem has been tackled in the attempt to change employers' attitudes. The National Advisory Council strongly recommends that phrases like 'the normal age of retirement' should be replaced by 'the *minimum* pensionable age', thus directing the employers' attention away from the concept of statutory retirement.

Finally, many employers do their best to give practical help and advice to their employees as they near retirement. The actual burden of work in the late years can be eased by transfer to lighter duties or by shortening hours to allow travel that misses the discomfort of rush hours. The very last stage of their training can take the form of courses run by local technical colleges intended to prepare people for the transition to retirement and the leisure it brings, and the employees concerned can be put in touch with many clubs and other agencies which will help them to occupy their time.

Disabled workers

A disabled person is one who suffers from some physical or mental impediment on a permanent basis.

The basic intention when offering employment to someone who is disabled is to help him/her to rehabilitate him/herself to a normal life. But finding suitable jobs for handicapped people has to be approached in two ways – from the points of view of both individuals concerned and the groups with whom they will be working. In practice, the first need is to give them the opportunity of training to do jobs which are within their capacity. The members of the group about to receive them must also be educated so that they have some insight into their problems. The average working group seems to find little difficulty in making the necessary adjustment, but it can be a matter of fine balance: if people are too kind to disabled people and want to help them when they really do not need it, or if they make them an object of pity, they may eventually cause them to become too dependent and lose their self-respect.

The problems of disabled workers were originally tackled by voluntary agencies, but these have long since been extended by legislation and other state action. The Employment Department Group supports a range of measures to help people with disabilities to gain and keep employment. The two largest, in terms of people potentially recruited or assisted, are the 'Quota' scheme and the Disablement Advisory Service (DAS) – the success of which can be measured statistically in that 76,900 people with disabilities were placed in jobs during 1989–90.

Responsibility for administering the Quota scheme (which dates from the Disabled Persons Employment Act 1944) is currently vested in the Employment Service. The terms of the scheme place a duty on employers with twenty or more workers to employ at least 3 per cent of registered disabled people in their workforce. It is not an offence for an employer to be under quota: but it is an offence for an employer under quota to recruit anyone other than a registered disabled person without getting a permit from the Employment Service. In fact, it appears that only about a quarter of employers are in line with or above the required percentage, although it is also accepted that the 3 per cent quota is unattainable for all employers. One factor which seems to have contributed to this situation is the decreasing number of people with disabilities choosing to register: it should not be assumed that a declining number of registered people with disabilities can be equated with a fall in the total number of people with disabilities who are active in the labour market.

There is considerable evidence* of goodwill towards employing people with disabilities, but this has to be tempered with an awareness that the employer may well be presented with problems. To help tackle these DAS teams carry out a variety of functions: they seek to generate company policies which promote positive actions and attitudes toward the employment of people with disabilities; they advise employers on how to retain staff who become disabled, and on how to meet their Quota obligations. They also play a valuable role in promulgating the voluntary Code of Good Practice on the Employment of Disabled People; this goes further than merely listing good practices – it sets out specific and realistic objectives which employers, employees and their representatives can aim for, together with assistance available to that end. DAS teams also market the video *It Worked Fine*, which complements the Code of Good Practice by targeting more junior personnel and management staff.

Men and women with extreme disabilities can be offered work in sheltered workshops, run by such organizations as Remploy Ltd. These represent an attempt to compromise with the mixed motives of people who are unable to face the world at large but do not want charity, who need to feel that they are giving their best and being paid fairly for it. However, it is sound psychology to insist that people protected in this sheltered environment should transfer to normal work as soon as possible. Those who are unable to do so, the chronically disabled, can sometimes be found work at home: for example, making poppies for the British Legion.

The Employment of People with Disabilities by Judy Morrell: Employment Department Group, Research Paper No. 77, 1990.

Most people returning to work after prolonged absence due to sickness or injury face difficulties. Some return too early and are unable to meet the demands of their previous job. Some stay away too long because of doubts about whether they could cope with the work. A few firms have their own rehabilitation arrangements which are instrumental in getting their own sick or injured people back to work. This often calls for ingenuity on the part of supervisors in adapting methods and machinery to assist rehabilitation. Some workers who cannot manage their old jobs or who have lost their confidence may be transferred to work that requires less effort or concentration. Far too often, however, the net result of these good intentions is that the worker concerned is resettled into a simpler or less responsible job, which amounts to a downgrading and loss of expectations if not an actual reduction in earnings.

The considerate attitude of employers would best be channelled along lines of sending workers who are in this unfortunate position for retraining in new skills. Much more should be known about the role of the Department of Employment's Rehabilitation Centres in this respect; in particular, greater publicity about them should be directed at employers who all too often seem quite unaware of their existence. There are now twenty-seven of these units spread throughout the country, capable of providing training courses for some 14,000 people annually. Some units offer residential accommodation, the others can find lodgings for their 'students' if necessary. The average length of the courses undertaken is about eight weeks. The great majority of cases are referred from hospitals or by general practitioners on completion of medical treatment. Most of the rest are spotted at local employment offices and are considered likely to benefit from such courses of retraining even though some of them have no permanent disabilities.

The scope of the courses is intentionally wide, in order to help as many people as possible. They encompass:

1 Those who need special help, subsequent to medical treatment, to adapt themselves to return to work or to find the most suitable job.
2 Those who find the stress of their present jobs too much for them.
3 Those who have become unemployed because of industrial change, especially older workers.

Each person's training is designed to meet his/her individual needs and there is no set syllabus. Courses are planned and controlled by a case conference, the composition of which clearly indicates the care given to these problems. Its members are the rehabilitation officer in charge of the unit, a doctor, an occupational psychologist, a social worker, a technical person in charge of workshops, and a resettlement officer who is in contact with local employment offices for subsequent placement purposes.

The basic aim is to stimulate the environment and conditions which the rehabilitated worker will meet when he/she returns to normal employment. So the workshops are given a factory atmosphere and the trainees are engaged on genuine production work subcontracted from government departments and local firms. This covers a wide variety of semi-skilled activities and machine operating, but craft training can also be offered at other government training centres.

Thus experts are used – vocational guidance from occupational psychologists and practical assistance from workshop supervisors who are craftsmen selected for their ability to help people – to improve disabled people's physical capacity, restore their confidence, and enable them to find out what work is most suitable for them. At the end of the course, the case conference discusses a report with them, and this is sent off to the local employment office in their home area where it is hoped they can be found a job along the lines recommended.

It seems that this rehabilitation service could help many more workers than it actually does, especially since the directing staff are prepared to gear individuals' programmes towards their employers' requirements or the potential openings available on their return to work. The benefits clearly are mutual: workers return to gainful employment in a manner which uses their skills and abilities to the highest possible degree, and employers are helped to use their labour force to best advantage, particularly by reducing the length of absence on long-term sickness.

A review of rehabilitation services was carried out in the early 1980s, culminating in a report in 1984, 'Proposals for the Development of the MSC's Rehabilitation Service'. The proposals concentrated on disabled people, on assessing their current employment potential and on providing appropriate help which would lead to employment. Techniques which would help the resettlement of clients into jobs were to be developed and more effort devoted to initial placing action.

In addition to the twenty-seven ERCs, it was proposed to set up a new network of ASSETs – Assistance Towards Employment Centres – to provide vocational assessment services in areas of the country not previously covered: they were to offer assessment and guidance services in-house and also provide rehabilitation through placements with local employers. Each ASSET centre would offer job search training and provide access to current local vacancies as well as assisting clients to make applications through a Jobclub.

Race Relations Act 1976

This legislation was passed to strengthen the protection offered to immigrants in the spheres of housing, employment, and the provision of goods and services, and establishes that a person discriminates against another if on the grounds of colour, race or nationality he/she treats that person less favourably than he/she would treat others. Provisions of earlier legislation (the 1968 Act) continue, so that the following actions by an employer are unlawful, if they involve discrimination: refusal of work to a qualified person; refusal of the same terms of employment, conditions of work, or opportunities for training and promotion as are made available to other persons employed in the same circumstances; and dismissing someone in circumstances in which other persons employed on the same type of work would not be dismissed. It is also unlawful to impose any unjustifiable requirement or condition which, although applied equally to all people, is disproportionately disadvantageous to members of a particular racial group (this will not, for example, prevent an employer recruiting the best person for a job but will help to ensure that any requirements or conditions imposed are relevant to the work to be done). The Act also ensures that a person who asserts his/her rights under the legislation or intends to take any other action under the Act (for example, giving evidence at an industrial tribunal hearing) will be protected against victimization.

Acts of discrimination, which are unlawful when committed by trade unions or employers' associations, include: refusing admission to membership on the same terms as other applicants; refusing a member the same benefits as other members; refusing to take the same action on his/her behalf as on behalf of other members; and expelling him/her.

A powerful new Commission for Racial Equality (CRE) was established by the 1976 Act, replacing the former Race Relations Board, with overall aims of eliminating racial discrimination and promoting racial equality and good race relations. Its powers of investigation and enforcement are similar to those of the Equal Opportunities Commission (see page 250), although in the employment field most individual complaints are dealt with by industrial tribunals.

During its first year of operation the CRE published a number of guidance documents proposing that the ethnic origins of workers should be monitored and encouraging positive action programmes to overcome the effects of past discrimination and to counteract disadvantages.* This is not to advocate quotas, which clearly would be

*The need for these emerged clearly from PEP report *Racial Disadvantage in Britain*, D. J. Smith (Penguin, 1976).

absurd in certain circumstances; rather, records of ethnic origins would enable an employer to check there was fair recruitment of minorities. No exception should be taken if such records were to be used in an equal opportunity programme that had been clearly explained to employees and job applicants. The CRE also commented that an effectively monitored equal opportunity policy enables employers to identify groups who are under-represented in certain jobs or sections and may provide a defence for an employer in the event of a complaint.

The IPM advocated a similar 'affirmative action' policy as long ago as 1970, pointing out other practical benefits of monitoring. A record of race can be used to validate personnel policies and check the theories of line managers about productivity, training time, labour wastage, and absenteeism. It can also assist in making policy decisions on such matters as leave for Hindu or Moslem religious festivals.

Unfortunately the lack of success of this policy, although backed by legislation and the work of the CRE, is underlined by a recent report which confirms that little has changed over the years – in fact, 'the British job market has changed little in its hostility towards black workers, except that it precludes more of them from working altogether'.* People of Asian and West Indian origins are more likely than white people to be unemployed. Those in work tend to have jobs with lower pay and status than white workers, with black workers generally earning about £20 a week less than white workers. Such findings must be seen in some measure as an indictment of personnel managers since they must share the responsibility for the failure of employers and senior management to take more positive steps to combat racial discrimination.

The CRE's determination in this respect is reflected in its publication of a new *Code of Practice* for the elimination of racial discrimination and the promotion of equality of opportunity in employment, although time alone will judge if this has the desired effect. The practical application of the Code started on 1 April 1984: it does not in itself constitute law, but its provisions may be admitted in evidence before an industrial tribunal (so that it operates in the same way as the ACAS Code of Practice on discipline).

The Code's two most important recommendations on the responsibilities of employers concern the implementation of equal opportunities programmes and the monitoring of such programmes with the aid of analysis of ethnic origins of the workforce and of job applicants. Specifically the Code recommends that:

*'Unemployment and Ethnic Origin', *Employment Gazette*, June 1984, page 260.

(a) Employers should adopt, implement and monitor an equal opportunities policy.
(b) The policy should be clearly communicated to all employees.
(c) Overall responsibility for the policy should be allocated to a member of senior management.
(d) Where appropriate, the policy should be discussed and agreed with trade union representatives.
(e) Training and guidance should be provided for supervisory staff and other relevant decision-makers to ensure they understand their position in law and under company policy.
(f) Employers should monitor the effects of selection decisions and of personnel practices and procedures to assess if equal opportunity is being achieved.

The information needed for effective monitoring will best be produced by records showing the ethnic origins of existing employees and job applicants. A comprehensive method of monitoring, suggests the CRE, should include analyses of: the ethnic composition of the workforce of each plant, department, section, shift, job category and changes in distribution over periods of time; and selection decisions for recruitment, promotion, transfer and training, according to the racial group of candidates and reasons for those decisions.

Further help and guidance can be expected from the Race Relations Employment Advisory Group made up of representatives from the CBI, TUC, local authorities, large language training interests, and minority groups directly involved with industry; its remit is to review the ways in which efforts are being developed to permit equal opportunities in employment.

Prejudice is rampant, of course, among both management and workers, with many stereotypes held concerning all immigrants, about such things as their intelligence, reliability, laziness, cleanliness, and the amount of supervision required. This is particularly unfortunate in the case of young coloured workers, many of whom were born, brought up and educated in Britain. They thus have the right to expect equality of opportunity and for their skills and abilities to be developed and used to the full.

Undoubtedly the greatest single factor contributing to prejudice is the language problem. It is very difficult to make acceptable social contacts at work or in the community unless people can converse clearly together. The natural reserve of English people makes them appear aloof to people who cannot speak English well – and this is the way that stereotypes are formed. The language problem also makes life difficult for supervisors: they seldom have time to learn how to handle people who find difficulty in understanding instructions and who often have different temperaments from their fellow white workers. Different welfare provisions are also needed, especially for Asian workers, to cater for their particular eating, clothing, and toilet habits, which can cause serious friction if not carefully observed.

A particular problem which has emerged in recent years is that concerning promotion and the immigrant. The fully integrated labour force is not simply one which appreciates wages, benefits, and job security. The research findings of behavioural scientists about status, loyalty, and access to opportunities for advancement apply as much to immigrants as to British employees. Nothing illustrates this more clearly than promotion policies, for a keen practical distinction can be drawn between non-discrimination and equality of opportunity.

All the evidence seems to suggest a lack of carefully thought-out policies and a failure to recognize that new types of workers demand new policies, procedures, and skills. One solution which does not work is that of confining promotions to departments which very largely or wholly employ immigrant staff. The pursuit of such a 'promotion-by-necessity' policy continues segregation in practice, and does nothing to help other workers accept and respect immigrants as equals or as capable of holding authority.

There is something of a 'vicious circle of self-fulfilling prophecy'* about the situation. First-line management form a stereotype of the immigrants' inability, for whatever reasons, to do certain jobs, and this is reinforced by open hostility among some white workers. In the past some immigrants may have been badly selected for upgrading, or may have been given a rough ride by their British fellow-workers. All these factors accumulate to dissuade immigrants from seeking promotion to jobs which existing supervisors do not believe they can do and white workers do not want them to do. The overall result can only be one of wasted potential which creates negative attitudes, and which the immigrants themselves see as being unjust. They do have special needs and difficulties, and it is not enough to give them training in groups dominated by British supervisors operating traditional attitudes and patterns of behaviour at work. A willingness to rethink policy along more positive lines is essential; in turn, its application must be carefully monitored by senior management, preferably along the ethnic monitoring lines suggested by the IPM and emphasized in the CRE's Code of Practice.

*'Promotion and the Immigrant', Tony Jupp, *Personnel Management*, April 1974, page 30.

Discrimination and equal opportunities

Despite all the best efforts in legislation and codes of practice over the years, a considerable level of racial discrimination in employment still exists and sex discrimination is dwindling only very slowly. Disillusion among ethnic minorities and women is evident and, most important in the employment context, there is misuse and waste of human resources.

The IPM therefore published an Equal Opportunities Code (EOC) in 1986, taking the view that personnel managers have a special leading role in combating discrimination. While they can use the sex and racial discrimination laws and the EOC and CRE Codes, an IPM Code seemed appropriate to reinforce the major laws and the 'statutory' codes with interpretations, emphases and additions specially relevant to the roles of personnel managers. The new Code covers sex and racial discrimination in employment, and also sections dealing with discrimination on grounds of age and against the disabled. The policies recommended are intended to ensure compliance with the law, thus helping with cases of alleged discrimination before industrial tribunals; they also serve to promote an environment which enables the organization to tap the widest possible sources of talent.

The IPM's basic recommendation is that personnel managers should promote the publication and adoption of positive equal opportunities programmes within their organizations, with these characteristics:

(a) They should cover discrimination on grounds of sex, race, age and disablement (plus religion in Northern Ireland); the causes of discrimination are different for these groups, and each kind should therefore be considered separately.

(b) They should be based on policy statements issued and publicly supported by top management.

(c) They should be promoted from the highest level to those in key management posts, especially those with major roles in recruitment and development decisions.

(d) They should be publicized continuously by every channel of communication, e.g. house journals, works committees and briefing groups, and by all managers and supervisors to their subordinates.

(e) They should not be imposed from above but be produced in consultation between personnel departments, line management, trade union and employee representatives.

Policy statements alone will achieve little or nothing, however; they must be supported by action, by training and by publicity. Above all, the working of the programme must be monitored.

Personnel managers have a special role in all this – that of leading, persuading and convincing. To do so, they must, *inter alia*, demonstrate their expertise in the field. First, they should study and master the basic legislation: the Equal Pay Act 1970, the Sex Discrimination Acts 1975 and 1986, and the Race Relations Act 1976. Second, they should be familiar with the more important cases on which issues of principle have been decided (EAT, Court of Appeal and House of Lords). Third, they should be able to quote freely from the two 'statutory' Codes of the EOC and CRE. Finally, they should know where to go for information and expert advice: the employment departments of the EOC and CRE; the Race Relations Advisory Service of the Department of Employment; the Information and Advisory Services of the IPM; the MSC's Disablement Advisory Service, through local job centres.

The *realpolitik* approach of the European Community saw first the exposition of its principles on equal opportunities, then since 1982 their gradual translation into practice with a series of action programmes. The principles have been concerned to expand female participation in the workforce and to promote equal opportunities at work. They have covered many aspects of employment: preparation for it (education and training): manageability, combining occupational and family responsibilities; treatment at work, pay and working conditions; and retirement (social security).

The first action programme (1982–5) aimed at ensuring observation of the principles by the development of community legal action and by promoting equal opportunities in practice. It aimed at a better balance between the sexes in employment to eliminate the idea of a traditional division of roles in society between men and women, encourage participation of women in sectors where they are under-represented and at high levels of responsibility in order to achieve a better use of all human resources. Under the programme work was begun on a range of areas – raising awareness, respect for the dignity of women at work, flexible working arrangements, vocational training, sharing work and domestic responsibilities.

A second action programme (1986–90) was even wider ranging, highlighting seven areas where new or continued action was necessary to create real opportunities at EC, national, local and occupational levels, including: information and development of mechanisms of existing equal treatment provisions; action to promote diversification of vocational choice; more positive action on employment opportunities, with revision of unjustified protective legislation; measures to encourage the participation of women in high-tech jobs; social protection and social security (review of provisions and gradual individualization of rights); measures to promote the sharing of family and job responsibilities through awareness raising, childcare facilities and flexible working patterns; and information and sensitizing campaigns to change attitudes.

The 1987 recommendations on vocational training were aimed at encouraging greater participation, particularly of younger women, mothers, underprivileged women and women returners, in training schemes, with special regard to modern technology, occupations in which they were traditionally under-represented, and in self-employment. They encouraged the cooperation of all training bodies in taking a proactive approach to women's training and adapting courses to their needs, including the recognition of domestic management skills. In 1988 the commission set up the IRIS of training programmes for women to stimulate and support the above objective. IRIS runs demonstration projects, promotes the exchange of information together with a central information reference base, and organizes seminars and publications. All EC training programmes now contain equal opportunities provisions.

Under the current action programme more networks of experts have been set up to provide a forum for national exchange of information and to stimulate work in particular areas. These include networks on the media, child-care, local employment initiatives, women in the senior civil services, equal opportunities in education and positive action for women in industry.

However, despite all the legal and social initiatives and the sustained increase of women in the labour force, the commission's first annual report on employment (in 1989) made it clear that progress in actually achieving equality has been slow; women still remain largely confined to traditional occupations, relatively low-level jobs, and to forms of work which do not provide the same levels of protection and benefits as many 'masculine' jobs; average female pay is still only 80 per cent of the average male pay in the EC. The Social Charter* re-affirms the need for equal treatment to be assured and for equal opportunities to be developed, but substantial progress remains to be made at EC, national and occupational levels, both in setting minimum standards of conduct across the community and in developing attitudes and structures to ensure that women are able to contribute to, and benefit from, the single European market on an equal basis. Personnel practitioners have a clear responsibility to

---

*At the time of writing, not yet ratified by all EC member states (including the UK).

ensure that positive action is taken to turn these initiatives into reality.

A new form of discrimination problem has more recently arisen over the medical condition of AIDS. In 1986 the Department of Employment sent a booklet of advice to some 400,000 employing organizations, warning against discrimination against people with AIDS. It stresses that person-to-person transmission of the virus does not occur during normal working activities and that employees should be reassured on this point. Lack of this basic knowledge may cause unnecessary fears which could lead to discrimination against those who might be affected.

On dismissal, employers are urged to take a balanced view of all the circumstances: whether an individual can continue to work satisfactorily, the possibility of a move to different duties, any medical advice received and whether continued employment is against the employee's, the employer's or the public's interests. Dismissing employees who are infected, or suspected of being infected, simply because of pressure from other employees would in many cases expose the employer to a claim for unfair dismissal. Suspending them might serve only to reinforce the groundless fears of their colleagues. Most importantly, knowledge of an individual's infection must be treated in confidence and disclosed to others only with the employee's permission except where, on the basis of medical advice, it is necessary to protect the safety of others.

Appendix: what can be done about 'the demographic time-bomb?'

This illustration describes the action taken by the supermarket chain Tesco,* the position of which caused particular concern since almost half its retail workforce is under 25 years of age and its business expansion programme (twenty new stores a year) envisaged the recruitment of an extra 10,000 people annually.

In practical terms, two main problems had to be tackled: ensuring a share of the contracting young labour force, and finding alternative ways of recruiting the staff needed.

A three-fold strategy was determined as regards competition among employers for the decreasing pool of young people: in the short term, increased pay and relaxing one rule to enable the recruitment of 15 year-olds for evening work; in the medium term, a revision of the school-leaver programme which had evolved from the Youth Training Scheme (YTS); and in the long term, improved links between Tesco and the education sector. 'Career Start' became the in-house version of YTS: participants have fully-employed status from day one, and each store has its own training facilities and staff trainer – over 500 places were filled when the scheme was launched. Reinforcing links between school and work has included such schemes as: compacts, to prepare students for work by setting goals such as punctuality, attendance and completing courses of work: teacher secondments to give them insight into running stores which turn over £millions a week; and generally developing excellent relationships between Tesco and local schools and colleges.

At the other end of the scale a major alternative source of labour has proved to be the 55 plus age group. Initial experiments in the Crawley area were very successful, with high recruitment figures and a 76 per cent level of retention over the first year. The scheme was broadened, with similar success, throughout London and East Anglia, and produced an unexpected bonus of a good response from people in their 30s and 40s; the campaign drove home the message that at Tesco age does not matter.

There was also some surprise at the substantial numbers of people past normal retirement age who came forward: policy was therefore changed to increase the maximum ages of employment (previously 60 female, 65 male) to 70 for both sexes. Existing employees who reach retirement age can be re-engaged if they wish and, subject to

---

*'*Facing the Demographic Challenge*' by Pat Lennon, Tesco: reported in the *Employment Gazette*, January 1990, page 41.

annual health review, can carry on working while retaining their service-related benefits. Experience has shown, too, that these older people do not need training to the same extent as youngsters: having themselves been customers for so long, many of them can turn their personal experience round and provide service to the same high standard that they would expect to receive themselves. Absenteeism among older employees is low — they seem reluctant to take time off for minor health problems. Stability is very high, and there is some evidence that their example encourages other employees to stay on too. They have helped to improve staff relations within stores, so that younger staff no longer go to supervisors every time they have a query: it is much more comfortable to ask 'Uncle Fred' or 'Auntie Freda' instead.

About 200,000 women return to work annually, and Tesco is convinced of the need to look after them, mothers in particular. Experiments with term-time working and job-sharing are in place. But the main problem for women with children who want to work is how to look after the children. Tesco have two pilot schemes: providing childcare or crèche facilities, and paying mothers childcare allowances which they can then use to employ child minders.

Lastly, following the success of the mature entrant scheme, the long-term unemployed were targeted, with a poster campaign on the theme 'Just because you're out of work doesn't mean you're out of the running'. Another technique has been termed 'priority hiring': the idea is to provide a week's pre-interview training to people who have been out of work for some time and who may have forgotten how to present themselves at a job interview.

Further reading

Equal Opportunities Code (IPM, 1986).
Ethnic Minorities and Employment Practice, N. Jewson, D. Mason, S. Waters and J. Harvey: Employment Department Group, Research Paper No. 76, 1990.
Women and Employment, Jean Martin and Ceridwen Roberts (HMSO, 1984).

8

Staff assessment

Experienced managers generally agree that in the past there has been a lack of precision about efforts to make the optimum use of staff and labour resources, compared with the much more meticulous attention paid to the material and financial resources of an organization. Clearly, every firm is anxious to find good supervisors and managers, and most of them would acknowledge that it is more important to their future growth that such staff should come from within their own ranks rather than be recruited from outside. Apart from general techniques and practices, there is, too, the fundamental concern of personnel management for getting the best out of each individual working in an organization. Yet the procedures for achieving these dual aims of securing growth and fulfilling employees' potential are haphazard and leave much to be desired. Many managers feel instinctively that they carry dead-wood in their departments, but seem unable to do anything about it. The fact that employment in the public services, in particular, carries a high degree of security of employment prompts many administrators to complain that they have to put up with staff whose shortcomings are well known, but for which, again, there are no remedies.

Theory

The theory of the role played by each individual in an organization is quite clear-cut, and is most simply explained in terms of a diagram (see Figure 12).

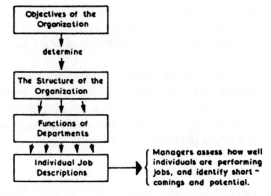

Figure 12   The organization and the performance of individuals within it

The objectives of the organization will determine its structure in the first place. For example, if a manufacturing company intends to export most of its products, its structure will be different from what it would be had it decided to concentrate on distribution direct to retailers in this country.

Any large organization must be subdivided into departments and sections, all with their own defined contributions to make towards achieving the purpose of the organization as a whole. Each department then splits down to separate tasks that have to be carried out, and these, too, must be precisely described. At this basic level, it surely then emerges as a clear responsibility of the departmental manager to assess how well the individuals allocated to these tasks are performing, to identify and correct their shortcomings, and to report on their potential for advancement to bigger and better jobs within the organization. It should be emphasized from the outset that this is a continuous reponsibility, not simply a matter of formal reports at particular points in time.

Purposes

Thus the overall purpose of a staff assessment scheme is to improve the efficiency of an organization by trying to get the best out of the individuals working for it. Within this concept, staff assessments are used in practice for four other specific purposes:

1 Salary reviews – as a means of measuring how much of an increase one employee should be awarded in comparison with his/her fellows (some personnel managers believe that salary reviews should be kept separate from performance appraisals, however).

2 The development and training of individuals – to fulfil the potential or correct the shortcomings revealed by their reports.

3 Planning job rotation – the movement of staff to broaden their experience.

4 As an aid in making promotions – the assessments can provide useful information when internal candidates are being considered for vacant senior posts, especially in a geographically widespread organization where those responsible for filling such posts may not know the candidates personally at all well.

Procedure

There are four distinct stages in the process of staff assessment. All employers who apply the technique carry out the first, that of a written report prepared at fixed intervals by an employee's immediate supervisor. Many go on to the second stage – a discussion between the person reported on and a senior officer, who may or may not be the writer of the report. Very few, however, seem to make much attempt to take the third step, that of obtaining some sort of positive contribution to the process from the employee reported on. Finally, no assessment scheme can be successful unless it is completed by a careful follow-up of the recommendations made about each individual.

There are a number of well-known hurdles to be overcome if reports are to be written effectively. The first is that of ensuring that the writers are objective: clearly it is important that they should be so, and avoid any personal friendliness or antagonism that they may feel towards particular subordinates. The danger of overmarking is very real, especially when it is known that the subordinate concerned is nearing consideration for promotion; but it is obviously unfair to everyone involved – the person himself/herself, his/her competitors for promotion who may have been marked realistically, and those more senior managers who are faced with the responsibility of making the promotion.

The best safeguards against subjectivity seem to lie in the design of the form itself. The more detailed this can be made, the more demanding will writers find it. Provision should also be made for the reports to be reviewed, and commented on by more senior executives: by the writer's own boss certainly, and if possible (as in the Civil Service) by his/her boss, too. The original reporter, knowing that his/her best efforts are subject to this close perusal and comment, will feel under considerable pressure to meet the required standards of objectivity.

The second problem to be tackled is that of securing uniformity of assessment among the report writers. This is very difficult where an organization has numerous units in different parts of the country or may even be international in its operations. Undoubtedly, the best way to deal with this is by arranging training sessions for reporting officers, when instructions can be given verbally and any difficulties discussed fully on the spot. The inclusion of a case-study in such sessions, asking those attending to assess an imaginary employee, is very useful. When the results are correlated and analysed, individuals become well aware of their own tendencies to be harsh or lenient in making their assessment, and can correct these when preparing actual reports. Experienced personnel managers have concluded, in fact, that highly capable managers tend to mark harshly, while those of less ability are over-generous (believing that good reports on the staff in their departments will redound to their own credit).

The difficulty of ensuring a common understanding of the meaning of the questions contained in the form, and what is required in completing it, can also be overcome to a large extent in these training sessions. One simple exercise to emphasize the reality of this semantic problem is to ask the group to rank in order, 1–14, the following words, commonly used in assessing staff:

adequate, average, competent, excellent, exceptional, fair, good, inadequate, indifferent, ordinary, poor, reasonable, satisfactory, superior

The subsequent process of ironing-out individual disagreements about the shades of meaning of these words reinforces the lesson that assessors must give very careful and objective thought to what they write.

In addition to the training session, comprehensive guidance notes must be issued to everyone taking part in the assessment scheme, giving precise instructions about its purposes and the way in which the report forms should be completed.

Content of report forms

Personal details of employees reported on will appear first, with their job title, and the length of time they have spent in their present post. This may seem to be stating the obvious, but it can be more important than appears at first sight. It will show how long superiors writing the report have known them and their work. If this has been only a short time, they may have to reserve their judgment; if it has been for many years, they would clearly know their work better than anyone else in the organization.

The report aims at assessing employees' performance in their job during the period (usually a year) immediately preceding it. It is important to be quite clear what the job actually is, and the second part of the form should therefore be a brief job description, outlining the main duties undertaken. There is abundant evidence (see Chapter 1, page 23) that departmental managers do not know the jobs of their subordinates in precise detail, so this part of the form might well be filled in by the employees being reported on; at the very least, it should be the subject of consultation and agreement between the two people involved. Special note should be made of any changes in duties since the last report, and any new qualifications obtained could also be added here.

The main part of the report then follows, assessing effectiveness in performing the job that has been described. This is normally done under a number of headings, as in the examples appended, often in the manner of a graded scale of marks, supplemented with comments giving evidence for the grades awarded. Their various attributes are summarized in a general assessment, together with some sort of 'pen-picture' to describe their personalities and attitudes of mind towards their jobs and the organization.

Assessors must then give their opinion about employees' suitability for promotion, including the level of the jobs to which they might aspire and an indication of when promotion might be given. The safest guideline here, as with the writing of references, is for assessors to consider if they themselves would welcome the people concerned if they were to be promoted to senior posts in their own departments.

To ensure that positive action is taken about employees' shortcomings, separate notes should be made of these.

Then the main 'action section' should follow, clearly specifying what must be done, either to fulfil the potential that they show or to correct their deficiencies; this might include personal guidance by senior executives or specialists, a change of duties within the organization's provisions for job rotation, or attendance at particular training courses.

The forms will be signed by the assessors and passed on to their superiors for any additional comments and counter-signatures, thus ensuring that reports are seen by executives at least one level removed from the staff under review.

Finally, the report form should contain a section for notes on follow-up in which entries can be made to show how and when the recommendations for action are carried out. The assessment procedure as it affects any individual should not be regarded as 'closed' until these notes on action are added.

When the forms are countersigned, they are usually sent to a central personnel records section. One particular advantage claimed for doing this is that personnel managers can readily pick out those staff whose reports indicate potential for the future, and who would therefore benefit from training in supervisory and management skills. Such timing can then be properly planned on an individual basis.

In summary, the content of a staff assessment form may be illustrated as in Figure 13.

Most space on the report form is usually taken up by the assessment of the employee's performance of his/her job. Present practice is for this to be done under a number of headings, such as: *knowledge of the job*; *initiative*; *management and supervision*; *output*; *expression on paper*; *figure work*. In turn, these headings are frequently qualified by explanations or

---

Content of staff assessment form

1 Personal details.
   Job title – time spent in that job.
2 Job description:
      including changes in duties since last report.
   Any new qualification obtained.
3 Assessment of performance:
   Headings . . . . | Comment column:
         . . . . | giving evidence for
         . . . . | the grades awarded.
         . . . . |
4 Overall assessment.
   Pen-picture of personal qualities and attitudes.
5 Suitability for promotion:
      level to which he/she might aspire;
      when promotion might be given.
6 Notes on present deficiencies.
7 Action to be taken:
      to fulfil potential shown;
      or to correct deficiencies.
8 Signed – by writer of report.
9 Comments and counter-signature of the report-writer's superior.
10 Follow-up – to record how and when the recommendations for
       action were carried out.

Figure 13

key-words intended to direct the thoughts of the assessors along the lines intended, in a uniform manner. Thus:

Output – effectiveness, speed, reliability, diligence.
Expression on paper – intelligibility, precision, style, cogency, lucidity, conciseness.

In practice, some sort of design compromise usually appears in the layout of forms. The job assessment is asked for under headings, with a graded scale, but a comments column appears at the side of each graded assessment. Where this is so, it is important that this column be used freely, and it should therefore have its own appropriate heading. The simple word 'Remarks' is itself too general to guarantee the desired informative comment; far better for it to read – 'Remarks – in explanation of the grade awarded', and assessors are then forced to weigh their judgments carefully.

However thorough may be the training sessions arranged to prepare managers for writing reports about their staff, caution dictates that they should also be given comprehensive *guidance notes* to remind them about the purpose of the assessment scheme, its rules, and the correct approach to their responsibilities towards their staff.

Here is a typical list of such reminders as they affect the written report part of the process:

1 This report is required as a means of assessing present performance in the job, for planning each individual's career development, to pick staff for particular types of training and job rotation, and to help in selecting suitable applicants for promotion.
2 The immediate superior of the person reported on should write his/her report.
3 The job description, on which the report is based, should be prepared in consultation with the person reported on, to ensure that it is an agreed outline of his/her basic duties and responsibilities.
4 Where space for 'Remarks' is provided on the form, this should be used freely to explain the grades awarded.
5 These grades should reflect actual performance, and where this has been affected by special circumstances (e.g. ill-health or unfortunate domestic events), separate notes to this effect should be added in the 'Remarks' columns.
6 The report deals with the employee's performance during the preceding twelve months only. There should, therefore, be no looking back to previous reports, nor should duplicate copies of this report be kept.

7 All reports are strictly confidential; their contents must not be disclosed to nor discussed with anyone not concerned with them in the course of his official work.

8 Each report should normally be commented on and countersigned by a departmental manager or some other appropriate executive senior to the person who writes it.

9 Executives who have the duty of writing reports are reminded, above all, that they have a continuous responsibility to keep their subordinates informed of their opinions about the ways they perform their jobs: this should cover both good as well as unsatisfactory performance. No 'below average' grading should ever be recorded under any heading without the subordinates concerned having previously been told verbally of their deficiency and thus having been given the opportunity to correct it.

A useful case study* taken from the public sector concerns the Trent Regional Health Authority: having gone through a thorough internal restructuring as a result of the Griffiths report on the management of the National Health Service, it was decided at the highest level that appraisal could play a key role in redefining goals, generating clarity of purpose, and generally building commitment to a new sense of corporate identity. The idea of using performance appraisal and staff development as an instrument for inducing a 'culture shift' and influencing attitudes was readily adopted by the chairman and members of the Authority.

Thus the crucial top-level support was obtained as was the commitment of the executive team of chief officers. Meetings with other senior staff demonstrated that an appraisal scheme could succeed, provided that it focused on meeting the need to define priorities and responsibilities and also aimed at systematic development of individuals and their careers. Subsequent discussion in the joint staff consultative committee revealed support in principle for performance review, but management was left in no doubt that a primarily top-down judgmental approach to appraisal would not be acceptable.

Nevertheless, once a 'problem-solving' climate had been achieved, agreement was readily reached that appraisal ought to be part of the management process, that it was not an 'optional extra' and had to be compulsory for all staff, and expected of all managers. Extensive training support was clearly necessary at the time of introducing the scheme.

*Reported in *Personnel Management*, May 1986, pages 34–5.

Staff representatives pressed on the uses and ownership of appraisal documents, and argued that formal appraisal, if it was to be successful, should simply reflect continuous feedback on performance as part of normal working relationships. The prevailing concern of staff, however, reflected in every subsequent training workshop, was the need for reassurance that appraisal would be truly developmental in tone and not a cloak for harsh reckoning. Building trust and confidence, and demonstrating that the values of the management system are congruent with the appraisal process, are therefore crucial in securing genuine commitment to the scheme and achieving positive results.

Forms and written records are not considered to be vital features of the system. What is more heavily stressed is the simple need for dialogue and exchanges of views, in a relatively formal setting, at regular intervals, between bosses and subordinates, aimed at producing agreement and an action plan for the immediate future.

In an attempt to build on the concept of appraisal as a routine feature of the management process, and a constant aspect of manager–subordinate relationships, a decision was taken to avoid a once-yearly organization-wide 'appraisal time'. This would have been an intolerable burden on managers and therefore counterproductive. Instead, formal reviews are timed to coincide with each individual's anniversary of appointment, thus spreading the load of work involved and minimizing the threat of great peaks of demand on managers' time.

The personnel department's role, apart from providing training support and advice if needed, is, first, to demonstrate model appraisal behaviour by piloting the scheme within the personnel department, and second, to 'trigger' reviews by sending each employee an appraisal booklet on his/her anniversary. This sets out in detail the principles and objectives of the appraisal process, advises staff of their entitlement to a formal review, and encloses a few blank sheets of paper with headings for an initial self-assessment process. At the same time the manager concerned is advised that this has been done.

In order to stress the responsibilities of managers, one of the sheets in the booklet asks, 'What have you done to develop staff who work for you?' Personnel and training officers monitor the system, to the extent of asking about action plans at intervals. The keeping of records of appraisal interviews is regarded as a matter for the participants, since the privacy of the dialogue is to be guaranteed in an attempt to develop openness and confidence. The key objective, apart from the achievement of effective exchanges of views in an interview, is the production of an action plan, created as a working document and shared by the individuals concerned.

The sophistication of appraisal systems seems to know no bounds.

Indeed the accolade of featuring in the Peterborough column of the *Daily Telegraph** has been awarded, in this manner:

New paper avalanche hits Civil Servants
Britain's Civil Servants, already buried under a mountain of paperwork, are appalled by the introduction of a new 'Staff Appraisal Package' which itself needs a five-volume 'Staff Appraisal Training Package' to understand. The new system takes a third again as long to process as the old method of staff reporting. In some cases, where a Civil Servant has a particularly large staff, it means that as many as 100 extra working hours a year will now be spent writing reports about subordinates.

Like anything to do with the Civil Service, the new report forms are long-winded affairs. The latest ones run to eight pages and include contributions from the employee concerned, his boss, his boss's boss and his boss's boss's boss.

But the real problem, initially, is understanding how the new system works. To that end the Management and Personnel Office has produced: a 36-page volume on 'The Role of the Jobholder'; 34 pages entitled 'Notes for Guidance – Effective Reporting'; a 59-page work called 'The Role of the Reporting Officer'; 58 pages on 'Effective Appraisal', and a 39-page book called 'Maintaining Standards – the Role of the Countersigning Officer'.

The correspondence page contained a lengthy letter of defence, written by a senior civil service personnel manager, a few days later – but!!

The second stage: discussion of reports

Most staff assessment schemes provide that, when written reports have been completed, they should be discussed with the people concerned. This discussion might take place between appraisees and their immediate superiors, or departmental managers themselves might inform them of their contents. In some of the nationalized industries a panel of senior officers is formed for this purpose.

The extent to which the discussion is based on the written report varies widely in practice. In some cases, it seems to play no part at all; in others, the 'main highlights' are mentioned, or only those aspects which have caused adverse comment; and at the other extreme, the people concerned are sometimes given the report to read and sign an acknowledgment that they accept its contents.

The important thing to realize is that these discussions are essential in any assessment scheme which is used as part of a promotion

*15 March 1986.

selection procedure. If employees do not know what is being written in their annual reports, and at the same time are repeatedly unsuccessful in their efforts to gain promotion, then clearly they will come to view the whole assessment process with the utmost suspicion, and it will fail in its overall purpose of trying to get the best out of individuals in their jobs.

It should also be realized that these discussions have a particular importance at certain stages in the development of people's careers:

1 After they have occupied any new post for about eighteen months, when they have had time to decide if it is turning out right for their career.
2 At about thirty, when they wonder if they have made sufficient progress in their job, for they are now at the age when they must do something about it.
3 At the age of forty when they wonder if they should carry on with the same firm for the next twenty-five years until they retire; if not, it may be 'now or never' as regards changing their job.

Most large organizations now readily accept the need to deal with the progress of staff by means of these frank discussions. Yet there is much evidence that this is done badly by many heads of departments who feel uncomfortable at the very intimate contact forced on them by the process, when their normal day-to-day relationships with subordinates may be based on personal friendships in a fairly free-and-easy atmosphere. Apart from the embarrassment of the departmental manager in this situation, there is another very real problem from the employees' point of view. Up to this point they have been in the dark: they know nothing of what their report contains until they face their boss across a desk and are told something of its contents. Is it fair to expect anything constructive to emerge as a result? The initiative is entirely in managers' hands – their subordinates may mumble some appreciative or defensive remarks, go away, discuss what was said with their spouses that evening, sleep on it, and then kick themselves the following morning for not having reacted in an entirely different manner. But the opportunity has gone, at least until the same unsatisfactory process is repeated in a year's time.

Depending on the purpose of the assessment, various attempts have been made to overcome this difficulty. For instance, one procedure involves issuing the report form in triplicate in the first place: departmental heads make their assessment on one copy: they hand the second to the subordinates concerned who make their own self-assessment; they then come together to discuss their respective findings, and complete the final, third copy between them. The purpose of this procedure is the further training of the individual under review with a guarantee to honour the recommendations that the manager–subordinate pair jointly agree.

Another precise analysis of the effectiveness of job appraisal reviews was reported by the Behavioural Sciences Research Division of the Civil Service Department.* A survey of appraisal interviews given to 252 officers in one government department revealed that the handling of negative performance feedback is fraught with anxiety and difficulties, and therefore tends to be avoided. At the same time, it was abundantly clear that those interviews in which discussion of the interviewee's deficiencies took place were the most effective in producing positive results in terms of the number of post-appraisal recommendations for action and the proportion of officers who felt that such interviews increased their sense of job satisfaction. They were also the appraisals to which the interviewees responded most favourably; most of them welcomed a full, frank discussion of their performance at work and saw this as the most useful function of the whole process.

The survey revealed the most common fault to be, predictably, that of interviewers talking too much. This is highly significant because training courses on appraisal techniques usually advocate the 'problem-solving' approach which encourages subordinate officers to do most of the talking, the interviewer's main purpose being to help them to think their own way through job problems and provide solutions for them. This approach contrasts with the traditional 'tell and sell' style of superiors who tell their subordinates what they think of their performance and what they should do to improve it (the interviewee thus having little say in the matter).

A series of rating scales, assessed by the interviewees who took part in this study, gives an indication of the good and bad points of technique. Figure 14 summarizes the results and speaks for itself: for ease of presentation, the responses for each item have been condensed into just two categories.

A positive contribution from the subordinate

No matter how good staff procedures and practices of personnel management may appear on paper, the concern of each member of an organization's staff is always: 'How does this affect me as an individual?' A deliberate attempt must be made to improve the present

*'An Evaluation Study of Job Appraisal Reviews', C. A. Fletcher, *Management Services in Government*, November 1973, pages 188–95.

'Tell and sell' style	Percentages		'Problem-solving' style
1 The interviewer did nearly all the talking in the interview	54	46	I did most of the talking in the interview
2 The interviewer seemed wholly concerned with assessing my work performance over the last year	50	50	The interviewer seemed chiefly interested in improving my work performance in the year ahead
3 I took the line of least resistance when criticized	23	77	I discussed the assessments with the interviewer when I did not agree with him/her.
4 The interviewer did not allow me to offer my viewpoint on the way I coped with the job	6	94	The interviewer allowed me to put forward my own views on how I coped with the job
5 The interviewer seemed to have made up his/her mind about things before the interview started	28	72	I got the impression that the interviewer was willing to change his/her views on things in the light of what I said.
6 Almost all the ideas for getting round job difficulties came from the interviewer	45	55	I provided most of the solutions to the problems we discussed
7 The interviewer made no attempt to understand my feelings about the job	11	89	The interviewer made every attempt to understand the way I felt about the job.
8 The interviewer did not appear to be paying attention when I was speaking	6	94	The interviewer listened most attentively whenever I spoke
9 The interviewer did not invite me to put forward any ideas or suggestions about the job	14	86	The interviewer continually pressed me for *my* ideas and suggestions about the job
10 The interviewer did not really make my own thoughts about my job any clearer	38	62	The interviewer helped me clarify my own thoughts and ideas about the work

Figure 14

methods of appraisal discussions to enable staff reported on to play a positive role in the process. The integration of the views of bosses and their subordinates is essential if assessments are to be accepted as forming part of a staff development programme; without full consultation and discussion with subordinates, the results will smack of manipulating people to the organization's ends rather than constructive staff management.

The best way of getting something worthwhile from these discussions is to persuade departmental heads to regard them as presenting opportunities rather than as unpleasant chores. This will undoubtedly call for some fundamental rethinking on the part of those managers who have been brought up on the belief that the demands of their organizations and the needs of the people working in them compete with each other. In emergencies staff know that more is expected of them; they seem somehow to be inspired to rise to these challenges and cooperate to get the job done. The worker who mutters 'If I were boss for a day, I would show them', or colleagues who rush off when the hooter sounds to dig their gardens or paint their homes, may seem oversimplified examples. But they nevertheless illustrate the point that hard, demanding work both spurs people on to high performance and is a major source of satisfaction for a whole range of human needs. This concept points to a tremendous unrealized potential for greater organizational effectiveness.

Why then are so few managers able to use the full capacities of their staff to increase productivity by expanding their contributions to their jobs? Surely it is largely because they concentrate on what is wrong, on solving problems and overcoming obstacles, rather than on where they want to go and the prospects of getting there through the fuller use of the individual talents of their staff.

Contrast the conventional form of staff attitude surveys with the opportunity presented by a properly conducted appraisal discussion in which the employee plays a positive role. At present, the former concerns itself with finding out how 'happy' staff are, if they are 'proud' to work for their employer, whether their fringe benefits are to their liking, and if their bosses treat them in a kindly manner – all stemming from the basic assumption that work is nasty, and that management's task is to make things pleasant by way of compensation. Replace this with the contrary assumption (proved by the way they respond to crises) that staff in fact have both the capacity and the desire to increase their productivity. The appraisal discussion then presents the opportunity to strive for improvement by posing questions such as these to each individual:

1 Do you fully understand your job? Are there any aspects you wish to be made clearer?
2 What parts of your present job do you do best?
3 Could any changes be made in your job which might result in improved performance? (Consider work-load, equipment used,

financial resources available, ability of juniors, help from seniors, and physical environment.)

4 Have you any skills, knowledge, or aptitudes which could be made better use of in the organization?

5 What are your career plans? How do you propose achieving your ambitions in terms of further training and broader experience?

There would be an obvious advantage to staff being given the chance to think about these points beforehand – so they could well be set out as a printed questionnaire and handed to the employee a few days before his assessment discussion. Prepared with the answers to these questions, individuals can make a positive contribution at this discussion, while their management superior can seize any opportunity that presents itself to link operational needs of their department with its employees' readiness to increase their output. Peter Drucker, whose own 'manager's letter'* is another variation of this effort to get subordinates more positively involved in their own personal development, summed up the concept thus in an address to the Industrial Society in April 1964:

> Look for strength in your people and load that strength. Never be concerned with what people cannot do but with what they can, and give them that to do.

Clearly the style adopted by the manager in an appraisal situation, in controlling interaction with the appraisee, is crucial. A spectrum of such styles exists in practice. At one extreme there is a dominating attitude – the manager who writes out a report form, hands it or reads it to the subordinate and asks for an acknowledgment signature; at the other extreme, the abdicating style – the harassed line manager, pressed by the personnel department to submit completed reports, who simply hands out the forms to staff and asks them to complete them. Between these extreme ends of the spectrum there are four other styles a manager can adopt: telling, advising, joint and self-assessment.

Linking this concept to the contingency theory of leadership† – which propounds that there is no one best style of management; rather there is a variety of styles, each appropriate to different situations – it emerges that the appraisal style most likely to be effective will be determined by the subordinate. Thus relatively inexperienced employees, feeling their way into new jobs and concerned about their

---

The Practice of Management (Heinemann, 1969), page 127.
†See page 26.

personal career development, are likely to seek considerable feedback from an appraiser. That person, in turn, is likely to adopt a telling or advising style, making the running during most of the discussion. Those same subordinates, faced with the self-assessment style of appraisal, would undoubtedly feel extremely uncomfortable, because they have not yet developed the requisite frames of reference for assessing their own performance or the skills required to analyse problems of performance and to propose solutions.

The converse also applies: a very experienced employee with good job knowledge and skills, a confident performer with a high level of ability and able to view his/her own performance objectively – were the manager to adopt a 'telling' style, that subordinate would probably feel and show frustration and aggravation at not being able to express opinions. In fact, the appropriate style would be either the joint or self-assessment approach.

In an ideal world, all employees would move along this spectrum of participation, taking increasing levels of responsibility for their own appraisals. They would gain satisfaction from their increasingly significant contributions to the process. The manager would benefit by having staff able to step back and assess their own performance, to identify areas where they could sharpen up their skills, to generate ideas on how they might achieve increasing levels of effectiveness, and to be committed to achieving objectives and strategies.

Follow-up

Whatever form the assessment takes, the long-term success of any scheme will depend on the effectiveness of follow-up. Everyone involved in the assessment process is concerned here – the personnel manager, the departmental head, the report writer, and the employee himself/herself.

Personnel managers' responsibility lies mainly in the actual administration of the scheme. In large organizations, for example, they will have to arrange the timing of reports, region by region, or department by department; obviously they will not want several hundred reports arriving on their desks on the same day. Correct phasing will even out the workload, and also enable the action recommended, in terms of training courses or job rotation, to be spread throughout the year.

Departmental managers also play a key role, for it is their duty to direct and control the ways in which their executive staff assess their subordinates. If they merely accept the reports submitted to them uncritically, then the assessors in their turn will give less consideration to what they write and become increasingly careless in this aspect of their work. For their part, the assessors will be most concerned with what they see in terms of results and appreciation of their views. Nothing is more certain to frustrate them and lead to carelessness in the preparation of reports than to see that their assessments appear to carry little weight when promotions are being considered or training programmes developed.

The remaining element essential for success is that the assessment scheme must have the confidence of all staff who are subject to annual reports. This, too, is most readily secured and consolidated by the results that flow from the assessments, when staff see that the promised action is being taken to change their duties, to train them in some new aspect of their work, or that they are being considered for promotion. Frank discussions about their progress and deficiencies may raise high hopes for the future; these hopes must never be dashed because of lack of follow-up.

Criticisms of reports on staff

Staff appraisal schemes have been applied to the problems of executive development for many years, dating, for example, in the British Civil Service from 1910. Some organizations are well satisfied with the results obtained, while others are currently experimenting with new schemes in their efforts to improve methods of personnel control. Even so, the development of the technique of *management by objectives* has undoubtedly sprung from well-founded criticisms of the conventional type of staff appraisal.

Although the procedure, and the guidance notes that go with it, may emphasize that it is performance of the job that is being assessed, there is, in the event, still a great deal of subjective opinion too much concerned with personality aspects, seemingly trying to measure the employee against the standards of some mythical ideal manager. Second, it so often happens that the recommended action includes job rotation and, more especially, training courses outside the organization. All such recommendations tend to evade the responsibility of individual managers to give personal guidance to their subordinates. They should not be allowed thus to abdicate their duty to develop their own staff and hand over the complexities of executive training to a specialized personnel department. On the contrary, they must be made to appreciate that this is essentially a job-centred function which can only properly be fulfilled by line managers.

The so called 'crown-prince complex' also inevitably emerges from a system in which the central personnel manager reads through all assessments of staff in order to pick out those with the best potential for development. But concentration on these, and on such people as graduate trainees (of whom there is often a high turnover, in any case), must mean some neglect of all the other staff who also need guidance to improve their job performance. Indeed it is alleged that existing staff assessment schemes place far too much emphasis on the whole question of promotion, instead of being a means of getting staff to do their present jobs better and thus naturally outgrow them.

The final major criticism concerns the use of a graded scale to assess various attributes of each individual. Most of these scales have a middle grade, representing average or standard performance. The difficulty of ensuring uniform marking by managers throughout a widespread organization has already been mentioned, and this assessment of average performance makes the point. What does 'average' mean in this context? It cannot be the standard that each manager personally expects, because these would obviously differ. Can it be a measure of comparison with a number of people whom a manager has already known in the assessed employee's post? Again experience may vary, even though the net is cast more widely. What about factors such as age? Should special allowances be made if the holder of a post is much younger than normal, or should the attitude be that he/she is being paid the rate for the job and must therefore measure up to it? Even with the most detailed report forms, comprehensive training sessions and precise guidance notes, it still remains very doubtful if all these difficulties in ensuring uniform practice in working can be overcome.

Group assessments

One system that has been developed to try to overcome the dangers of the subjective approach involves assessments being made by a group of appraisers working together. This group would consist of the immediate superior, possibly the boss, and two or three other managers who know something of the person being reviewed and the quality of his/her work.

The personnel department plays a direct role in this process by providing the last member of the group. Where top managerial staff are being assessed, personnel managers themselves, or their colleagues in charge of management development, might take part; with lower levels of staff, a personnel officer attached to the local unit will join the assessment group. The function of these personnel department representatives is to act as 'appraisal coordinators', taking no active part in the actual appraisal, but being responsible for seeing that it is carried out in a thorough and comprehensive manner. This check is necessary because, although the final assessment will include much the same information as the conventional staff assessment form, the actual discussion between the group of appraisers is informal. At its close, the coordinator is responsible for writing the assessment report, summarizing what the four or five appraisers have concluded.

This method clearly decreases the likelihood of any personal bias in favour of or against the person being assessed, and it is claimed that a balanced judgment is reached by virtue of the number of managers taking part. The presence of the coordinator greatly helps to secure the desired uniformity of assessment throughout an organization.

Assessment centres

Still rather unfamiliar, but growing in terms of the number of organizations using them to appraise staff performance, are assessment centres. Rooted in the War Office Selection Board methods of the Second World War, which were designed for officer selection, assessment centres provide a broad approach to the identification of managerial potential among existing staff. They involve the multiple assessment of several individuals by a group of trained assessors using a variety of techniques such as games, simulations, problem-solving exercises, tests, and group discussions.

The purposes, like other forms of appraisal, are concerned with the assessment of potential and the identification of the development needs of individuals. Typical of the approach is this statement from the briefing letter sent by one company to participants in the scheme – 'It is important to understand that the major purpose of the assessment centre is to allow a group of tutors (senior company managers) to assess the nature of your potential for development. The methods and final results will be discussed openly with you. The centre should also provide you with an opportunity to review your present abilities and to consider your future career – it can therefore be a helpful and worthwhile experience for you.'*

One strong claim for the usefulness of this approach is at supervisory level, where it is considered to be virtually impossible to predict accurately management potential from current performance in non-supervisory positions. The assessment centre, in fact, provides the opportunity to observe an individual's performance in a number of situations which simulate a variety of realistic supervisory problems. Normal practice is for the participants to be selected initially by their

Performance Appraisal in Perspective, D. Gill, B. Ungerson, and M. Thakur (IPM, 1973).

immediate superiors, who obviously consider that they have the potential for promotion to a higher level.

Assessors are usually line managers two levels above the participants: they are thus people who should have a thorough knowledge of the jobs for which the participants are being assessed. Sometimes consultant psychologists become involved when psychological tests form part of the programme. Assessors require preliminary training, of course, in order to become familiar with all the exercises used and to obtain practice in the observation methods.

The culmination of the assessment is a final report compiled from information drawn from several sources: the tutors' assessment of the participants based on test results and observation of their performance in the activities at the centre; the participant's own assessment of himself/herself; and the assessments of participants by other participants. The report may also suggest how the participant's skills and abilities can best be used within the organization.

An interview is then held when one of the assessors discusses all the details of the report with the participant. If there is general agreement with the assessment, the tutor and participant discuss ways in which any strengths that have been identified can be used, in terms of future roles and activities which the participant might successfully carry out. Emphasis is placed on considering the things he/she can do well and deciding how these things can be built on. Where there is disagreement, the tutor must try to find the reasons for the differences of view: if it persists, a note of the discussion is included in the report. A copy of the final report is sent to participants, before it is sent to their immediate boss.

The advantages claimed for this approach follow logically. Apart from achieving the purposes originally stated, substantial staff relations benefits are claimed, in that this form of assessment appears to be an open, objective, and fair way of assessing potential and making promotion decisions. Assessors develop skills in observation and evaluation, hence deeper self-awareness; one company has described assessment centres as 'the best method of management training we have yet discovered'.* The method helps to overcome the problem of employees who suffer from bias on the part of their superior. Finally, it can act as a motivator, participants returning to their normal work with a realistic self-assessment and a plan for their own development.

The operation and benefits of assessment centres are well-illustrated by the example of Rover,† where a competence-based model has

---

*ibid.
†*Case Study*: Rover, David Bower and Andy Embury, *Personnel Management*, June 1991, page 52.

been created in order to establish clear and rigorous assessment criteria. To this end a 'map' of eight dimensions of competence was devised, encompassing strategy, business, resource management, communication, quality, professional, consultancy and organizational development. The first five could apply to senior managerial staff in any service function, while the other three are more functionally specific. Each attracts a cluster of four competency groupings, together representing a clear set of behavioural benchmarks and assessment criteria.

The 'map' was developed by personnel department staff in the Rover group: its concise nature and use of language specific to Rover generated interest and established credibility with senior managers and, subsequently, with participants. Along with assessment, equal weight is now given to learning and development. The assessment criteria are made freely available to participants, who are offered enrolment by self-assessment. Simulations and exercises have been devised to measure agreed competence benchmarks and provide a challenging and satisfying development experience. Short 'learning interventions' are introduced at various points, focusing on ideas and techniques both useful as part of the programme and with wider applicability back at work, including presentation skills, structured thinking and strategy development.

To capture sufficient data for a robust appraisal a statistical profiling technique is used, asking the assessors to record observed behaviour against those mapped benchmarks of competence measurable as part of each exercise. Assessors are rotated between exercises to help eliminate the possibility of bias. Standardized ratings against specific behaviour drawn from the map allow comparisons to be made between participants' behaviour and performance, set against the observed performance of the whole group. Using a specially designed computer program, profiles are built up by analysing the ratings of observed individuals' performances across the range of simulations and exercises. Each profile is thus a composite and does not reflect significantly the result of a strong or weak performance in a single exercise.

Individual scores and profiles can be compared with the group's average to identify individuals' relative strengths and development needs.

The real value of the profiles, however, lies in the feedback and development planning process, for individuals can judge their own performance relative to that of their colleagues and in the context of business need. A debriefing session aims at identifying strengths and development needs and hence to agree a personal development plan with the individual.

Rover management considers that the shift from assessment to a development centre approach has been very successful: using competence-based criteria gives greater visibility and credibility to the process and offers spin-off benefits in performance appraisal, training objectives and for succession and development planning purposes. Challenging exercises which reflect real business issues are more acceptable to participants and offer more realistic assessments, while statistical profiling gives more focused assessment, greater consistency and the basis for a more systematic approach to researching performance competencies.

Further reading

Appraisal for Staff Development: a Public Sector Study, Ronald Wraith (RIPA, 1975).
Performance Appraisal in Management, M. R. Williams (Heinemann, 1972).
Staff Appraisal, G. A. Randell, P. Packard, and J. Slater (IPM, 1984).

9
Management by objectives

Management by objectives is the best example of participative management – the ultimate acknowledgment of the fact that the most positive effect on morale can be obtained by allowing staff to share in management decisions which affect their destinies. The philosophy behind the technique can be traced back to Plato's concept of man's inherent desire to strive for 'excellence' – a quality which we most readily associate perhaps with saints, musicians, or artists, but also an obvious attribute of leadership and the good manager. It calls for a steady self-discipline, rigorous standards, an abhorrence of mediocrity, and refusal to accept the second-best: challenging managers' personal skills and their integrity in seeking the best for its own sake.

The best-known exponent of the theories of human behaviour from which the practical concept of management by objectives has developed was Douglas M. McGregor.* The basis of his argument, expanded in his famous Theories X and Y, is that past understanding of the nature of man is in many ways incorrect and that, under proper conditions, unimagined resources of creative human energy could become available within the organizational setting.

Theory X states that the central principle of organization is that of control and direction through the exercise of authority, with these premises:

The Human Side of Enterprise, Douglas M. McGregor. Copyright 1960. Used by permission of McGraw-Hill Book Company.

1 The average human being has an inherent dislike of work and will avoid it if he/she can.
2 Because of this human characteristic of dislike of work, most people must be coerced, controlled, directed, threatened with punishment, to get them to put forth adequate effort towards the achievement of organizational objectives.
3 The average human being prefers to be directed, wishes to avoid responsibility, has relatively little ambition, wants security above all.

With Theory Y, the central principle is that of integration – the creation of conditions such that staff can achieve their own goals *best* by directing their efforts towards the success of their organization. The premises are:

1 Work is as natural as play or rest. Depending upon *controllable conditions*, it may be a source of satisfaction (and will be voluntarily performed) or a source of revulsion (and will be avoided if possible).
2 External control and punishment are not the only means for achieving effort. A person will exercise self-direction and self-control in the service of objectives to which he/she is committed.
3 Personal satisfaction can be the direct product of effort directed towards organizational objectives.
4 Most people, under proper conditions, learn not only to accept but to seek responsibility. Avoidance of responsibility, lack of ambition, and emphasis on security are generally *consequences of experience, not inherent human characteristics*.
5 The capacity to exercise creativity in solving problems is widely, not narrowly, distributed in the population. But under modern working conditions, the intellectual potential of the average human being is only partially utilized.

The technique of management by objectives can most simply be seen as the application of Douglas McGregor's Theory Y in practical terms, seeking as it does to make a deliberate attempt to link improvement in managerial competence with the satisfaction of individual personal needs. This calls for a fourfold approach:

1 Clarification of the broad requirements of each job.
2 Establishing specific targets for defined periods of time.
3 The management process during these target periods, and the help given by superiors.
4 Appraisal of the results at the end of the target period.

This strategy must be based on a very clear understanding of what the words 'target' or 'objective' mean in a business situation. It is axiomatic that unless you know where you are going, you will not get there. So in the first place an objective implies moving forward or making progress; but to do this, managers must fully appreciate where they are moving from (the present position), where they are moving to (desirable results), and when they are required to get there. The second implication about setting objectives is that they will involve changes, and naturally these are intended to be for the better. So the overall aim of the technique may be described as taking action to obtain improvement in the measurable results being achieved throughout an organization.

A business is primarily concerned with its affairs today, with seeing that all is going well at the moment. But it must also have a clear vision of its future, set out in terms of objectives at all levels – for the board itself, for subordinate formations, for operational units, and for the individual managers working within these units. All these objectives should appear in writing, clearly stating the present situation and future aims in the utmost detail. Objectives are useless unless they are broken down into statements of the *precise actions* that must be taken to achieve *specified results* within a *given period of time* by *individual members* of staff.

Applying the technique

Just as work study and O & M specialists have studied factory and office workers in the past, so the work of managers will now be studied by staff teams, the members of which must obviously be knowledgeable about management by objectives and must also be skilled job analysts. These teams will want to deal with an entire operating unit at a time, starting with the production departments (where the 'real work' of the business is carried out) and moving to the service sections later.

Within each unit, the advisory team will apply a four-step procedure:

1 Identification of the 'key result' areas of the business, i.e. those in which positive results must be obtained if it is to succeed.
2 Analysis of the work of every executive in these areas – carried out by the holder of the job himself/herself, advised by one of the team's analysts.
3 This produces a performance improvement guide which the executive, boss and analyst will discuss together, until agreement is reached between them on specific targets for improvement.

4 Since time limits will have been set for the achievement of these objectives, performance reviews must be carried out when the due dates arrive, to decide whether or not the desired results have been obtained, and why, and to formulate new objectives for the next period.

Having decided in which production unit the management by objectives team is to work, the process starts by means of a series of meetings between its head and the team in order to resolve clearly what the key areas of the unit's activities are, and how results in these areas can be precisely measured. A lengthy list of these might emerge, examples being: profitability, the manufacturing programme, utilization of machine capacity, quality of the product and customers' complaints, and the level of productivity of operatives. There are four main aspects of business activity which can be used to identify the key result areas of the work of any department or of any individual's job. These are – the *quantity* of work done, its *quality*, the *time* taken for activities to be completed, and the *cost* involved in all this.

Having identified these key result areas, three questions must then be asked:

1 What particular problems are associated with each area?
2 How are acceptable standards of performance defined and measured?
3 Who is responsible for initiating action in each of these areas?

When the management activities associated with the unit have been established in this way, and are commonly understood, the tasks of each executive (say, foremen upwards) can be analysed. This should be aimed at producing a guide document which is very different from the job description mentioned in Chapter 4, being essentially concerned with providing a framework for improvements in performance. The initial documentation for this can be a single foolscap sheet of paper (A4), divided into four columns, as shown in Figure 15.

The first column will list a number of aspects of the job where any improvement in results will clearly contribute to the achievement of the objectives to be specified: obvious examples are rate of production, control of costs, wastage rates, quality of goods, and productivity of employees. For each of the points listed, executives concerned, in discussion with the analysts, should then be able to suggest targets, representing improvements in performance which they themselves feel confident of being able to achieve. There can be no generalizations here: each target must be quantitative and measurable in terms of business results. Thus 'to reduce scrap' is too vague an objective; it

Key Result Areas of the Job	Targets for Each Area	Control Information Required	Review notes— Lessons learned From working methods. Follow - up.

Figure 15   Guide to performance improvement

must be expressed in precise terms, such as, 'to achieve a 10 per cent reduction in scrap rates in my department within the next three months'. Of course, control information must be made available to individuals taking part in this procedure, so that they can monitor their progress towards achieving their objectives; for example, if one of their objectives concerns improving quality control, then they have the right to ask to be supplied with information about amounts of items rejected at the inspection stage and the number and nature of customers' complaints. The last column has a variety of uses: notes can be kept for future reference about the success or failure of the particular methods used in trying to achieve objectives; further training needs of the individuals concerned can be identified; and any obstacles preventing objectives from being reached should be noted, especially if they are beyond their control and require action by more senior management to remove them.

When this analysis is finished and the guide sheet completed, it must be fully discussed by employees concerned with their boss, both parties advised again by the analyst. The most important aim of this discussion is to reach agreement on a number of clear objectives for executives concerned, with time limits for their realization, together with notes on any additional training or assistance from other senior staff they may need in order to achieve them. Further meetings may then be necessary to make a detailed analysis of the steps which must be taken to realize each objective.

A specimen sheet has been part completed by way of specific example: it is for a recruitment officer and is presented as Figure 16.

The departmental managers must, of course, maintain a control system to remind them of the review dates for each of these objectives. All that is necessary here is a simple barchart (Figure 17), listing their

Key result areas	Targets	Control information	Remarks
1 Maintaining labour force at full strength.	(a) Special campaign to recruit twenty additional married women operatives within the next two months.	(a) Information on availability from employment office. Weekly returns on recruitment and labour turnover.	Read available literature on problems of employing married women. Watch for supervisors' prejudices.
	(b) Organize a day nursery in the factory grounds, to open within the next six months.	(b) Local authority regulations. Number of mothers using it? Number of mothers recruited because of it? Weekly cost statement.	
2 Time taken to fill vacancies.	Average to be reduced from three weeks to two weeks within the next six months. (a) Standard job requisition procedure to be introduced within the next month.	Time taken to fill each vacancy to be recorded.	

	(b) Start new applications procedure within the next month, encouraging personal visits or phonecalls.	Effect on appointments diary.	Organize reception staff to be able to deal with callers.
3 Cost of recruitment services.	Reduce advertising costs by 25 per cent within the next three months.	Record of response received to all advertisements placed in press and journals.	

Note: Further notes might appear in Remarks Column at the end of each target period.

Figure 16   Part of a performance improvement guide for a recruitment officer

subordinates, their targets, and the dates by which the targets should be achieved.

Each review is based on the simple question – have they, or have they not, reached this objective? If they have, the next stage is to look again at this particular key result area and consider if its performance standards can be raised even further; otherwise, the 'achieved objective' becomes the normal standard of performance for that task. If the target has not been achieved, this is no occasion for recriminations; rather, it calls for a detailed consideration of all factors which prevented its realization, and how these might now be overcome. In these ways the review process throws up new targets for the next period of time, again specifying precise objectives in terms of business results, what assistance will be required from more senior managers, and what additional training is needed to improve employees' ability to meet these new demands.

The introduction of the management by objectives technique into an organization in practice may call for a certain amount of strategy. No matter how much individuals participate in agreeing their own objectives, and no matter what reassurances may be given about not achieving them, there may still remain some fear of failure, for it is difficult to remove entirely the traditional concepts of punishment for not reaching targets. It is essential, then, to gain people's confidence in the technique at the initial stages. This can perhaps best be done by setting fairly easy targets at the outset, so that staff will soon lose any apprehension they may feel about the demands of this new approach to management. In fact, the experience of organizations already using the

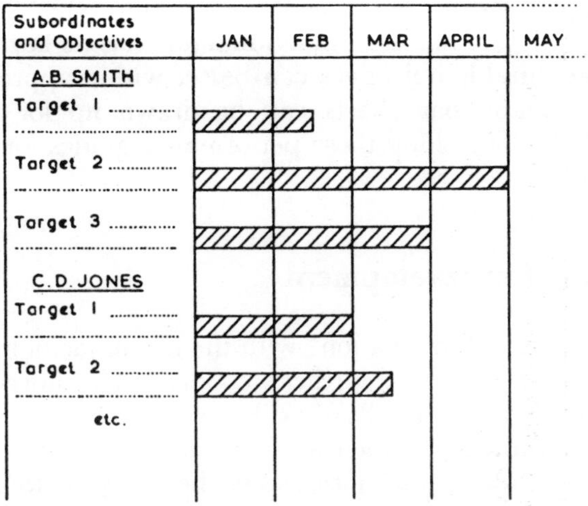

Subordinates and Objectives	JAN	FEB	MAR	APRIL	MAY
A.B. SMITH					
Target 1	▨▨				
Target 2	▨▨▨▨				
Target 3	▨▨▨				
C.D. JONES					
Target 1	▨▨				
Target 2	▨▨▨				
etc.					

Figure 17   Bar chart: control of objectives

technique shows that in the initial stages only about half of the objectives set are actually achieved. The main reason is that, human nature being as it is, staff devote most energy to those areas in which they enjoy their work, tending to neglect the more unpleasant or difficult areas and miss targets set in these as a result. Of course, as time goes on and the easier objectives are achieved, then those which are more difficult can no longer be avoided.

Unit improvement plan

A logical refinement of the process of preparing individual improvement guides is to build in a system of suggestions for overall organizational improvement. While their jobs are being analysed, executives can be asked to indicate any problems or obstacles which they believe to be impeding their efforts to improve their performance and achieve their objectives. These may be internal to their own department and they may be able to suggest action to deal with them on the spot; or they may be attributed to other sections of the organization (for example, drawings arriving late, or delays in dispatching products to customers) which will require action to be taken by higher levels of management. When all the staff concerned have thus commented on their problems and suggested means of solving them, a large number of points calling for action from top management may well emerge. Indeed, taken together, all these points may form a pattern from which objectives for improvement of the unit as a whole can be defined (the reorganization of work processes, or the reallocation of labour between departments are examples). After all, each operational unit, just like each individual job, has its key result areas for which measurable objectives can be set within appropriate time limits. Once again, bar charts can be drawn up for use by top management in controlling these performance guides for whole production units.

The formula for development

Linking the theory of motivation* with the technique of management by objectives has led to yet a further step forward in efforts to improve the efficiency of an individual's work. People can be inspired to greater efforts by the challenge of their jobs: satisfaction accrues from being given responsibility, so that jobs should be designed to increase the

*See Chapter 3.

demands made on the abilities of employees to achieve some personal fulfilment of their own potential. In this context, managers have the task of exerting pressure on their individual subordinates to acquire new skills or knowledge that can be used in their jobs. This may well, in turn, involve the provision of more advanced training to enable staff to gain a wider point of view and develop new attitudes.

This concept readily fits in with management by objectives, and with the task of top management of controlling the risks of their businesses. If senior managers will agree with all staff who report to them specific objectives which both meet important business needs and at the same time demand of individuals an enlarged body of knowledge or skill in order to achieve the objectives, then the key step in personal development will have been taken.

Growth of the business capacity of individuals is most rapid when they have to accomplish something entirely different from what they have been doing in their jobs in the past. But they must clearly know what is expected of them, appreciate its importance to the organization and to themselves in terms of career progress, and eventually be told whether or not they have accomplished these new tasks successfully.

The *formula for development*, then, may be summarized as in Figure 18.

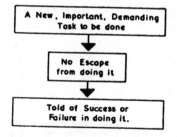

Figure 18   Formula for development

Conclusion

At the beginning of Chapter 8, Figure 12 set out the role of the individual in an organization and the need for performance to be appraised from time to time. This can now be amended (Figure 19) to take into account the technique of management by objectives.

Such a process clearly overcomes the 'insuperable' difficulties of conventional staff appraisals – subjectivity of marking and uniform standards – and ensures a positive approach to the whole problem of securing organizational growth, by concentrating on the deliberate expansion of the human resources available and directly seeking to improve the job performance and enthusiasm of individual managers working in it. This sort of analysis has resulted in management by objectives being eulogized as 'a new way of life for managers', or the first really comprehensive total system of management. The claims advanced to support these glowing statements include:

1 No organization should run except in terms of its aims and objectives. Its very existence presupposes aims. Action presupposes objectives. It is therefore essential that all organizations systematically set, define and review their aims and objectives. Manangement by objectives provides the framework.
2 Effectiveness can be calculated only in terms of attaining aims and objectives.
3 Organization must have regard to objectives, not 'vice versa'. Management by objectives exposes organization obsolescence.
4 The resources of any organization are limited and must be

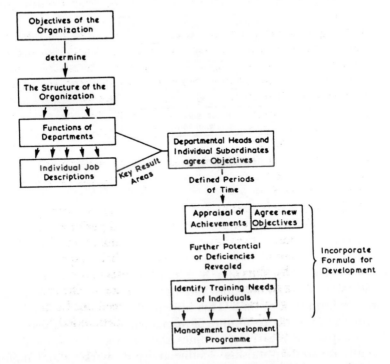

Figure 19   The role of the individual within an organization

allocated to satisfy priorities. But focusing on objectives and analysing them critically, management by objectives helps this process.

5 It is essential that all parts of an organization pull in the same direction. Management by objectives specifically directs that the objectives of individual managers must be consistent with the objectives of the organization.

6 Management by objectives ensures that people look at their own work, and that of their subordinates, in terms of results, and not in terms of processes. It identifies and concentrates attention on the more important elements of managers' jobs.

7 'Our greatest asset is our human resources' – this is a meaningless phrase unless something is done by way of applying the findings of behavioural scientists, including:

(a) people prefer to be involved rather than commanded;

(b) motivation is diverse and complex, but there is a need for much greater emphasis on 'job enrichment';

(c) people like to know where the organization is going, where they fit in, what they are supposed to be doing, and how they have done; if possible they want to monitor their own performance;

(d) people want to contribute and have their contribution appreciated.

8 Any organization needs to make the best use of the talents and ideas of all its members. To achieve this, managers must create a climate of work in which constructive suggestions can flow naturally as part of the process. Management by objectives performance improvement guides are so designed, and also pinpoint the responsibility for carrying forward the ideas that emerge.

9 Organizations need to develop their managers' abilities. The appraisal of performance will reveal and lead to the correction of factors which have impeded the attainment of objectives. Potential will be systematically uncovered also, so that training needs become exposed.

10 Motivation is increased by participation in target-setting, and by a connection between career progression and performance records.

11 Communications throughout the organization improve as managers become more clearly aware of their responsibilities.

12 Management by objectives may reduce costs in a number of ways:

(a) by leading to improvements in operational efficiency;

(b) by drawing attention to work which need not be done at all;

(c) by showing when new methods are demanded, rather than simply improving on the old.

13 The increasing use of specialists has the danger of their taking narrow professional views about management problems. Manage-

ment by objectives (MBO) harnesses their specializations to the general objectives of the organization.

MBO – practice and problems

Numerous case-studies have appeared in various publications over the years, the majority describing successful applications of MBO, but also pointing out the problems which must be overcome if failure is to be avoided. To illustrate the former, an analysis of forty-five projects* carried out in different government departments during the period 1968–73 showed a wide variety of tangible and intangible benefits. These ranged from a staff saving of 13 per cent to 'more attention being focused on priorities', better delegation by managers to their subordinates, a 'flow of innovative ideas', improved communications, and the usefulness of having clearly defined job objectives when staff move between posts. The general impression gained by Civil Service Department advisers was that MBO is now commonly seen not so much as a means of gaining certain selected objectives, but rather as a comprehensive approach to better management in which an organization's activities are planned and controlled by reference to its essential purposes and the atmosphere is one of participation and constructive change.

Experience over the years has shown how the threads, contained in the sections of theoretical analysis above, come together. Of the basic problems to have emerged, one† seems to arise from the fact that some organizations, in their implementation process, have lost sight of the philosophy which underpins MBO techniques. Thus, in some cases, relative failure can be attributed to management's attempt to use MBO as a method of propping up existing authoritarian ideologies, at variance with the participative approach necessary for success. The distinction between control from above and self-control is of the essence, and when collaborative techniques are used to bolster an authoritarian managerial structure, it is small wonder that cooperation and commitment do not increase; indeed, the level of organizational tension will often rise.

In such circumstances the superior-subordinate relationship may become the focus of win–lose struggles. It is open to the subordinate,

---

*'mbo in the Government Service', C. J. Hancock, *Management Services Bulletin*, 1974, pages 16–26.
†Cf. 'Management by Objectives in Perspective', C. F. Molander, *Journal of Management Studies*, February 1972.

for example, to attempt personal targets at the expense of organizational objectives. These targets may also be selected because they are simple rather than complex; or are readily quantifiable; or where high risk programmes are avoided in favour of maintaining the system in its present form.

It is widely recognized that senior managers increasingly find themselves working as members of groups, yet it seems that target-setting and reviews are rarely carried out on a group basis. Predictably, the common result is increased tensions between and within management groups, when individuals strive independently to reach their own targets and standards. Staff/line conflicts are frequent enough in any event; in trying to achieve agreed targets, many staff managers, not least personnel specialists, must have the cooperation of colleagues who function outside their control. The behavioural sciences offer solutions to such problems. Motivational theory clearly demonstrates that objectives which are settled within groups will secure greater commitment from individual managers than those given to them by an external authority. It may well be, therefore, that MBO would be most effective if target-setting was undertaken on a group basis. If relevant groups of subordinates set targets in conjunction with their superiors, who in turn accepted targets arrived at through their own group efforts, two main results would emerge: individuals would feel genuinely committed to those targets; and there would be less of the intergroup friction which so often arises when targets are set without reference to all the staff who may be affected, directly or indirectly.

The application of this group approach in practice can be seen in the development of *Quality Circles* − USA and Japanese management inspired − among the most important participative management experiments of recent years. A typical quality circle (QC) is a voluntary group of six to eight people from the same workplace who meet for an hour every week under the leadership of their supervisor to solve work-related problems in their department. Members of the circle select the problems they wish to tackle, collect the necessary data, apply systematic problem-solving techniques in working towards solutions, present their findings to management for approval, implement their solutions wherever practicable, and monitor their effects. In undertaking these activities, it is argued, people learn new skills and develop their abilities, while the team approach also helps to engender a spirit of trust and respect for one another's abilities. The organization benefits by tapping the knowledge and experience of its labour force at all levels, while individual employees make direct contributions to real problems and develop greater feelings of commitment to the organization.

The 1980s saw a considerable growth in the number of organizations practising quality circles — by 1985 it was estimated* that some 400 were taking part; a National Society of Quality Circles came into existence and by 1988 it had 120 organizations in membership and distributed its newsletter to some 250 subscribers. All this is in contrast to the early days of QCs in Britain when questions were asked about their suitability to the manufacturing environment. It is a measure of their durability that today the questions are more about how to evaluate QCs, how to put them to best use, how to overcome the difficulties experienced in running them, how to maintain enthusiasm, and how to integrate QCs with other management techniques — that is to say, the novelty has worn off and QCs have become a permanent feature of many organizations.

Most immediately their importance lies in the commentary they offer on attitudes to change in traditional ways of work organization. Employees, it seems, have greatly welcomed the opportunity to make a contribution to their work situations offered by QCs. Trade unions, understandably have been cautious, even hostile: QCs sometimes challenge working arrangements hard won through collective bargaining and tough negotiations; in the long run they may even threaten jobs: and in targeting tasks carried out by individuals they contrast with collective action.

Especially interesting, however, is what QCs reveal about the attitudes of managers. Generally speaking, senior managers are very enthusiastic and most of the initiative on QCs comes from them. Middle managers and first-line supervisors take rather a different view; they would appear to be the biggest stumbling block to the introduction of QCs, and have undoubtedly been responsible for many failures. Many explanations have been put forward to account for this reaction: they feel threatened, are unable to cope with this participative style of management, and remain unconvinced of the need to concede what they perceive of as managerial authority — explanations which express volumes for the hold which traditional authority relationships have over people who should be regarded as major change agents. If nothing else, the experience of QCs points to one clear conclusion: there must be considerable changes in managerial attitudes and the structure which underpins authority relationships before there can be any significant developments in the participation and involvement of many more people at work in Britain.

Another problem which occurs in large organizations is that from time to time major changes in policy or procedures are imposed

*'Quality Circles', by Ron Collard and Barrie Dale, Chapter 15 in *Personnel Management in Britain*, edited Keith Sisson (Blackwell, 1989).

externally on managers who see such changes as damaging to their efforts to achieve objectives already agreed. Examples would be new projects, market developments which demand that resources be reallocated, and new government legislation or policies.* Dealing with such situations in practice depends essentially on the time-span involved. Frustrating as changes may seem at first sight, if the change or new development is to be spread over a period of years, say, then one of the key result areas in the job descriptions of the managers concerned could be – 'To plan for the introduction of . . . (what the change is).' Thus each manager would become committed to examining the required change, and the normal MBO methodology of control and feedback would come into play – even seeking improvements to that change concurrently with its application. Revised objectives of individual managers and the organization as a whole would thus be properly dove-tailed. Idealistic as this sounds, it would certainly be a great advance on what normally happens at the moment in trying to adapt to changes.

In terms of current management thinking, MBO must be seen in the context of organization development (OD): that is, in a conceptual scheme of planned organizational growth which is itself clearly aimed at maintaining a participative managerial style. OD must be planned, managed from the top so as to be organization-wide, and designed to increase effectiveness through interventions in the organization's processes using behavioural science knowledge. Techniques for formulating the changes implied in such growth will include MBO, although a prerequisite for its successful implementation may well be the provision of sensitivity training for effective team functioning.

MBO is a catalyst for change in the sense that, used as an incisive instrument for organizational analysis, it will expose weaknesses and thus point the way to more effective management. The identification and integration, vertically and horizontally, of the objectives of each manager and part of the organization will at the very least reduce enervating conflicts between line and staff, project teams and functional managers, and may even cool down the traditional battle between sales and production staffs. This must surely be the main practical value of management on a team basis, with managers contributing to the objectives of the whole rather than a part, and accountable for meeting their agreed contribution of those objectives.

MBO then can be justly claimed to offer the ultimate solution to the problem of participation, because right down through the management hierarchy it emphasizes the self-control elements of taking

*'Management by Objectives – Quo Vadis?', C. G. Pearce, *O & M Bulletin*, February 1971.

decisions, and subsequently evaluating results, directly aimed at optimizing efficiency. As a dynamic system of management, it can show employees how they contribute individually to the total achievement of their organization. Thus a sense of participating in the whole develops, coincidentally with the satisfaction of personal needs in the work situation. It is not simply a matter of freedom from the traditional type of authoritarian control; employees come to see themselves as an integral part of the total organizational system and not as mere cyphers chasing targets imposed from above. They are made responsible for creating the reality of the situation.

For individual managers, MBO also offers a real chance of providing an environment for job enrichment. Participation in controlling their task, the revealing of constraints or obstacles to progress (some of which may then be removed), the very process of discussing the job in detail with a superior – all add to enrichment. And achievement, recognition, and further responsibility are all inherent in the concept. But the attitudes of top management are crucial here: the installation of the ongoing processes of MBO must be positively encouraged, and decisions taken quickly about the constraints and weaknesses exposed; otherwise managers down the line will become disheartened and initial apprehensions about MBO as merely a gimmick may be confirmed.

Further reading

The Human Side of Enterprise, Douglas McGregor (McGraw-Hill, 1960).
Management by Objectives in Action, John Humble (McGraw-Hill, 1970).
Management by Objectives in the Civil Service, John Garrett and S. D. Walker, CAS Occasional Papers, No. 10 (HMSO, 1969).
Quality Circles Handbook, David Hutchins (Pitman, 1985).

There is also an excellent series of films produced by AB-Pathe Ltd, and featuring John Humble: 1 *Management by Objectives*; 2 *Defining the Manager's Job*; 3 *Performance and Potential Review*; 4 *Colt – a Case History*.

10

The training function

The purpose of training is to give employees at all levels sufficient instruction and guidance to enable them to perform their jobs effectively and prepare themselves for promotion. The personnel manager's task is to give advice and coordinate the training policy and programmes of the organization as a whole, but all line managers must directly control the development of the skills and potentials of their subordinates. The fact that the vast majority of all training takes place on the job makes this responsibility clear. Going off to outside courses or visits are infrequent experiences; the true training situation exists where there is a gap between the standard of performance demanded by a departmental head and that actually being achieved by the individual subordinate, and the main purpose of training is to close that gap.

Management of the training function itself is a fourfold process:

1 Assessing the need – determining training requirements for all types of staff, deciding priorities, and defining standards.
2 Programming – plans and procedures aimed at fulfilling the needs: policy on internal or external courses; individual development plans; deciding the best techniques appropriate to each type of training.
3 Organizing – how best to use the staff, finance, and facilities available for training purposes.

4 Evaluating – how well the results meet the original needs; budgetary control of resources.

The importance of adequate resources for training cannot be overemphasized. To this end, attitudes at board and senior management levels are crucial: all too often they are negative,* with training activities not being regarded as contributions to the 'cutting edge' of the competitiveness of their organizations. Training must not be classified as an overhead, to be cut back when times are hard; rather it must be viewed positively, as an investment leading to identifiable income.

In recent times it has become fashionable to advocate 'continuous development' – self-directed, lifelong learning at work through work itself. To this end the IPM has published a code† to help all senior managers to broaden their views about learning and training, to help them firmly to anchor their learning activity in the organization's business activities, and to emphasize that learning within the organization must be managed on a continuous basis. In the belief that this is the way to successful growth of both the business and the people working in it, the code is presented under these headings: policies, responsibilities and roles, the identification of learning needs and opportunities, learner involvement, the provision of learning resources, benefits and results.

Background

The recent history of training in Britain centred on the work of the Manpower Services Commission (MSC), which was created by the Employment and Training Act 1973, transformed into the Training Commission in 1988, and subsequently reduced in status to the Training Agency of the Employment Department. Its history is important to personnel management because of the many valuable lessons to be learned.

The MSC disseminated a set of ideas linking education and training in an effort to reverse Britain's steady industrial decline, acting as a catalyst to persuade politicians and industrialists to re-evaluate the place of training in the modernization of the British economy. Technological advances were clearly fundamental, and a concomitant training revolution was also required. At the heart of the MSC's

---

*See *A Challenge to Complacency: Changing Attitudes to Training* (MSC/NEDO report, December 1985).
† *Continuous Development: People and Work*, the IPM Code (June 1987).

philosophy was the goal of explaining to the workforce the way in which wealth is produced and used in industry: on the one hand, in terms of enterprise and efficiency, emphasizing the role of entrepreneurial activity in opening up new markets and business activities; on the other, elevating labour as a factor of production, with investment in human capital as crucial for economic performance.

For the MSC a long-term objective, a matter of decades rather than years, was to shift attitudes towards training and to elevate it on the political agenda. It advocated manpower as the key resource, the country's most valuable asset, and argued that it should be in the forefront of government, industrial and company investment strategy (not a residual factor as so often happens). In fact, British training and retraining policy is in part aimed at social objectives, including improving the opportunities of disadvantaged individuals in the labour market — being evaluated primarily in terms of its contribution to the relief of the suffering experienced by casualties of the system, rather than its impact on economic efficiency. At the same time, the rate of return on resources invested in training is crucial: in terms of profitability it often appears to offer a less attractive form of investment than most to businessmen. Nor was the MSC successful in disengaging training from the obsession which public policy had with 'skill-shortage' problems; yet relating training to such shortages and the number of skilled vacancies notified by job centres forestalled any appreciation of Britain's wide training malaise. Once again the politics of managing mass unemployment took precedence over the economics of human capital in the debate on vocational education and training. Essentially policy makers failed to distinguish between three types of initiative: reforms designed to raise the rate of productivity growth by upgrading the nation's stock of skills; reforms to improve the inflation-unemployment trade-off through reducing short-term skill shortages; and reforms to provide a more equitable distribution of job opportunities by means of job creation for the long-term unemployed. Furthermore, policy makers assumed that state intervention was supplementing the training efforts of employers, whereas in fact it often served only to bolster industry's arrogant and generally ignorant attitudes towards manpower. Obviously the social role of training is important, but the concept of government provision can only work in an environment where employers themselves are prepared to invest more and respect what the Government does in addition.

Britain's training problems have been compounded in recent years by the attitude of the trades unions. Irrespective of the definition of skill in terms of human capital, the determination of skills has largely been in the hands of the powerful craft unions which controlled the supply of skilled labour at the workplace through the apprenticeship system. This outdated form of training conferred other powers such as demarcation of work, levels of wages for skilled and unskilled workers, and the duration of training. Subsequent arrangements for promotional training and the retraining of established workers have been even more defective.

Of course, the attitude of government is also vital. If policy makers are to learn from the MSC's failures, public expenditure must be put into supporting in-house training rather than training for the general labour market. Future policy must directly bear on attitudes and at the same time reduce the cost of training to individual firms. The guiding principle must be that new policies must work with the trends of profitability and enterprise, and not against them. Tax incentives should be used, not to increase the amount of training as such, but rather to increase organizations' training capacities by giving them an incentive to produce a stake in training as an organizational activity.

Such statements underline the stark fact that hitherto Britain has lacked a credible training strategy at the level of the firm. Elsewhere in the world, in Japan, Sweden, the USA, for example, most emphasis is placed on retaining the 16–19 year olds in higher education: take-up rate is near 75 per cent but only just over 50 per cent in Britain. A move towards the German type of dual system is perhaps the best practicable solution: there, provision for 16–19 year olds is employer-based, with 90 per cent of the cost of youth training paid for by employers. Such a model strikingly demonstrates that employers' commitment to young workers is a sound indication of their willingness also to pay for the training and retraining of established workers.

Trainers themselves must be constantly concerned with their own effectiveness and the need, above all, to take an active rather than a passive role: no longer must training be seen as an 'add-on' service to be used on request, but as a consultative facility as regards both delivery and evaluation. New opportunities within organizations should be sought and explored, using training as a strategic intervention.

The most promising approaches to training are four-fold; their interdependence, with combinations of two or more, often produce the best results:

1 Open-learning systems where self-instruction modules tailored to varying time-spans lead to credits; although currently popular, little is known about how things go wrong with such studies, and feedback on training benefits is poor as is setting of priority needs.

2 Responsive training, by contrast, is demand or need orientated: it may have specified or open-ended objectives, to prepare people to cope with new problems (simulated working environments are examples of this type of training).

3 Facilitating workplace training, using such techniques as 'job-setting' where people are made responsible for complete areas of work rather than just one function: an alternative is 'work-setting', designed to broaden the scope of a person's work experience. Overall these methods have advantages in overcoming the problems of transfer of theory to the workplace, and they also reduce the cost risk of purchasing learning materials which may soon become surplus to requirements.

4 'Collective competence' – the emphasis being placed on performance rather than learning by providing support services for groups to perform their own roles more effectively; this approach can be strengthened by job aids, making technology more intelligible, accessible and user-friendly, incorporating educational elements into the design of systems, and working with technology to solve real problems.

The tools for managing learning in the workplace are:

- A comprehensive set of understandable standards of competence describing the whole work role; they must cover not just the tasks involved, but the communication, problem-solving and human relations competences which are so important in the real working world.
- Means of assessing and recognizing the achievement of these competences continuously – with clear and open objectives, and methods of review, assessment and for accrediting performance; these are some of the key factors in motivating managers and employees alike.
- A systematic way for employees to look forward and plan future achievements with their line managers; the learning contract is a tool increasingly used in human relations development, and the language of competence provides the objectives to be discussed and the methods for achieving them.
- A process of accreditation, which in turn calls for the general recognition of achievements; standards incorporated into National Vocational Qualifications (NVQs) built around a life-time credit accumulation system are therefore crucial.
- A cohort of supervisors and line managers trained and committed to their roles in management development and assessing and

recording achievement; such roles are not burdensome overheads, but an integral high added-value part of the work of supervision itself.

These tools should serve to provide the focus for the use of both traditional approaches to learning and the application of new technology and methods. Learning outside the work place will always be necessary to achieve competence, but it is the workplace itself and standards of performance required there which should increasingly drive the appropriate use of off-the-job learning. Learning contracts are an important tool for harnessing the talents of workforces to the organization's and individual's objectives: they both motivate employees to learn or develop and aid the identification of relevant and cost-effective courses and other learning opportunities.

The organization of training

In 1988 the Manpower Services Commission gave way to the Training Commission which in turn became the Training Agency within the Department of Employment. Many of the functions hitherto exercised by these bodies have since been allocated to the nationwide network of Training and Enterprise Councils (TECs) — but it is argued* that there is still a role for the *Training Agency* (TA): the national coordination of objectives and standards of training, the dissemination of information on good practice, making international comparisons, identifying special skills shortages, and research; to these must be added such existing tasks as helping disabled people find a place in the labour market (the TA funds four colleges for the disabled) and the work it does with the Open University and the National Council for Vocational Qualifications (NCVQ).

A radical reform of Britain's training structure followed the White Paper *Employment for the 1990s*, with a new framework announced aimed at meeting employment needs and increasing the country's international competitiveness. A National Training Task Force (NTTF) was set up to oversee the new efforts; local employer-led groups were invited to establish the TECs, to plan and deliver training and to promote the development of small businesses at local level; and a Business Growth through Training (BGT) programme was launched to help companies develop training strategies to meet their business objectives.

*At the time of writing the work of the TA appears to hint at its preparing for abdication as training supremo: (its days are numbered?).

The NTTF's brief was to develop new local training arrangements and to promote greater investment by employers in the skills of the workforce. To this end its early work had the priority of establishing a national standard for investment in people which could then be used by TECs in their own local activities. Thus the pilot phase of the 'Investors in People' programme had six criteria:

1 The business should have a flexible plan for the future, including objectives for developing its people.
2 Top management commitment to developing people should be communicated to employees.
3 The development needs of all employees should be assessed and reviewed regularly.
4 The business plan should include a budget and systems for training and developing people.
5 Responsibility and authority for ensuring the appropriate development of people should be given to all line managers.
6 The business benefits arising from investment in training and development should be evaluated.

Four key principles for reform underpin the creation of the eighty-two TECs which cover England and Wales (and twenty-two Local Enterprise Councils in Scotland):

- Training and enterprise must have a local focus; the economic and social conditions of every community are different, and what works in one may not work in another. If national policies and programmes are to be effective, they must be tailored to meet the special needs of people and employers at local level.
- The delivery of training and help for small businesses should be employer-led. Business itself is best placed to identify key skill needs and to ensure that quality and relevance of training and business assistance meets these needs.
- Local employers must be given powers to make real decisions.
- Whatever arrangements are put in place, they must promote radical reform, strive for excellence and be rewarded for good performance.

Funds amounting to £3 billion a year finance the TECs, each having an annual budget in the range of £20–£50 million. Each TEC has to formulate a business plan which forms the basis of its contract to operate the training and enterprise programmes of the Employment Department. The plan covers the TEC's vision of its role in the local community, an analysis of the local labour market, an inventory of existing training and enterprise provisions, and a statement of both three-year strategic objectives and detailed plans for its coming year of operation.

In planning the activities of TECs, great emphasis has been placed on flexibility so as to make its main programme, *Employment Training* (ET), highly responsive to the needs of both individuals and employers in the labour market. The objective of ET is to equip unemployed people, especially those out of work for six months or more, with the skills they need to find and keep jobs. (Skill shortages in industry are a major concern, especially with the advent of the single European market in 1993.) In practice, the emphasis on flexibility means freedom to – decide arrangements for the guidance of all entrants to the programme; decide how training should be designed and how training providers are funded; settle the terms and conditions for trainees; provide ET to people unemployed for less than six months; and enable individuals to train for longer than the existing limit of twelve months (within an agreed budget).

People who want to join the programme are referred first to a training agent who provides assessment, counselling and guidance, and agrees an action plan with each trainee. Training managers are then responsible for arranging a mix of practical training with employers or on projects and directed training to meet the requirements of the individual's action plan. Over a thousand training managers and nearly 200 training agents operate the programme throughout the country, with a budget of £900 million enabling them to provide training places for up to 250,000 trainees annually. Trainees receive a training allowance of £10 a week more than their unemployment benefit entitlement, and they may also receive help towards fares and other expenses.

The types of organization contracted to run ET cover a wide range of private and public employers, local authorities, training organizations and the Skills Training Agency. (In 1990 there was a Civil Service buy-out of the sixty Skill Centres: forty-eight of them subsequently continued in being, thus forming a viable private sector network of training provision with good coverage of the major centres of population in England, Scotland and Wales. Named the Astra Group, it plans to retain a strong base in craft training, but may also expand into supervisory and junior management skills courses, if market opportunities arise).

Examples taken from the earliest practical strategies planned by TECs serve to illustrate the range of activities undertaken:

- Advice and financial support to help small companies to set up their own training schemes (Herts).

- Links with European employers and colleges to share knowledge and expand work experience and training opportunities (Dorset).
- Vocational traineeships for young people (Thames Valley).
- Sixty new gateways giving easy access to training and business assistance activities (Devon and Cornwall).
- Raising standards of employee training through a system of kitemarks and awards (Cheshire).
- More and improved management training for women (Teeside).
- An economic regeneration forum (Wearside).
- Joint action with local tourist boards to tackle skill shortages in the tourist industry (Cumbria).

Business Growth through Training (BGT) is a £1.4 billion programme introduced in 1990 aimed at unifying the assistance available to companies. Services include help to people who own their own firms, with relevant, flexible and accessible training available for busy owner-managers; help for small businesses to plan and implement the training and development of their employees; and targeted help to individual training organizations and local bodies such as TECs to tackle acute skill shortages in particular areas. With the aim of involving up to 100,000 employers by the end of its first year of operation, BGT offered five options each designed to improve business competitiveness:

1 Helping small businesses to produce better business plans.
2 Providing training seminars on business planning.
3 Contributing to consultancy costs to enable medium-sized firms to strengthen their management's capability.
4 Assisting firms to pool efforts when key skills are in short supply.
5 Allowing selected firms to develop innovative training solutions.

The *Youth Training* (YT) programme gives all eligible young the opportunity of a broad-based vocational education and to achieve a qualification or credit towards one. It stresses the importance of raising the level of qualifications of new entrants to the workforce and emphasizes results, such as vocational qualifications, rather than time spent in training (as in the traditional five year apprenticeship schemes). It offers the chance to gain specific skills of relevance to work and to improve the employment prospects of young people.

The Training Credits scheme gives young people who have left full-time education to join the labour market an entitlement to train to approved standards. The initial pilot schemes are being expanded year by year, with the eventual aim of offering Training Credits to all young people by 1996.

The Government's White Paper of 1991 contained proposals for a number of education and training initiatives, with the main aims being:

• To ensure that high-quality further education and training become the norm for all 16 and 17 year olds who can benefit from it.
• To increase the all-round levels of attainment by young people.
• To increase the proportion acquiring higher levels of skill and experience.

The White Paper sets out proposals to achieve a fully integrated system of education and training, to bridge the traditional academic–vocational divide, and to build up a partnership between employers and the education system. Specific initiatives to make education more relevant to the needs of working life includes:

• The Technical and Vocational Education Initiative (TVEI), which aims to equip all 14–18 year olds in full-time education for the demands of working life.
• Work-Related Further Education which aims to link vocational education to the needs of employers.
• The Enterprise in Higher Education Initiative which aims to make higher education more relevant to the world of work.
• Compacts, whereby employers guarantee jobs with training, or further education followed by a job to young people in inner-city areas, provided they reach agreed targets as regards punctuality, attendance and academic performance. (Initial achievements of the scheme were impressive: a network of some sixty Compacts linked schools with local businesses, involving 90,000 inner city youngsters and 9000 employers; during 1987–91 the scheme generated 27,000 job opportunities for school-leavers). During the recession of the early 1990s, however, it proved increasingly difficult to guarantee jobs after training, and the further challenge remains of developing the Compact approach across the country.
• Education Business Partnerships, which aim to encourage a range of activities to help young people reach their highest potential and prepare them better for work.

The National Council for Vocational Qualifications (NCVQs) was set up in 1986 to reform and rationalize the vocational qualifications system in the UK. It aims to make qualifications more accessible and more relevant by basing them on standards of competence set by industry, and to establish a coherent framework — the National

Vocational Qualification (NVQ) — based on defined levels of achievement to which qualifications in all sectors can be assigned or accredited. The first priority was to have the framework from the most basic level to the management supervisory level (I–IV) in place by the end of 1992. Eventually the NVQ structure is expected to cover all occupational levels up to and including the professions. It is also intended to develop broader-based NVQs to allow young people to keep their career options open and assist older adults wishing to make a career change. Every British education authority is now taking part in the TVEI, conscious of the need to prepare young people better for working life.

The policy of forging closer links between schooling, higher education and the workplace was furthered in the White Paper *Education and Training for the 21st Century*, aimed at setting out a strategy to boost the numbers of young people continuing in work-related education and training and to raise standards. In brief:

- By 1996 every 16 and 17 year old leaving full-time education will be offered a training credit worth typically £1000 to spend on training towards NVQs.
- These NVQs are to be introduced as quickly as possible and colleges will be required to adopt them.
- Two new Diplomas, one Ordinary and one Advanced, will combine academic and work-related qualifications.
- Compacts will be extended nation-wide.
- The National Record of Achievement, a burgundy folder enabling individuals to summarize their achievements in education and training, will be used by the great majority of school-leavers.
- New ways of managing the Careers Service will be encouraged, including partnerships between LEAs and TECs.
- Business leaders will be given more influence in post-16 year old education through TECs: these in turn will have expanded roles in running training credits, Compacts, the careers service and local colleges.

An essential complement* to all this government activity and the training framework provided by the NTTF and TECs at national and local levels, is training at industry sectoral level, without which local efforts might well be poorly focused. This is provided by a network of voluntary *Industrial Training Organizations* (ITOs), each responsible for defining its sector's training needs and ensuring that

---

*Training Infrastructure — the industry level, by Bill O'Connell, *Employment Gazette*, July 1990, page 353.

action is taken to meet them; also for providing the lead in establishing standards for key occupations.

ITOs are the descendants of the Industrial Training Boards originally set up after the Industrial Training Act 1964, which were replaced by voluntary and non-statutory training organizations (NSTOs) in the early 1980s; that name was subsequently replaced in common usage by ITO embracing both statutory and independent bodies. A National Council of ITOs was established in 1988 with the purpose of maintaining and developing the effectiveness of sectoral training arrangements. The policy document *Employment in the 1990s* proffered the logical extension of the belief that independent activities responding to the wishes and needs of employers are preferable, and it is likely that the few remaining ITBs will eventually be replaced by independent non-statutory bodies.

The ITO network of 117 bodies covers just over 80 per cent of the nation's workforce. There is no single 'model' because each industrial and commercial sector has different requirements and particular needs: many provide direct training services, others do not; some are funded by subscriptions from employers, others by grants from trade associations; all are employer-led, some have trade union and education members on their executive councils, others do not. Despite this diversity in operations, all ITOs have the following roles in common:

• Defining, monitoring and reviewing future skill requirements and training needs in their sectors, including spotting the skill and training implications of changing technology, international trends and the new ways in which skills are applied.
• Providing the lead in establishing the standards of competence for key occupations and arranging for learning achievements to be accredited.
• Advising the Government and education system about sectoral developments and their effects on training.

The ITOs also provide important services to those concerned with the organization and delivery of training, which can save both time and money — for example, avoiding duplication by sharing knowledge and expertise, by jointly researching skill needs and developing relevant training materials, by getting 'the training message' across to member employers in their sectors, by publicizing TECs/LECs and their roles and establishing effective links with them, by relevant ITO experts participating in specialist committees, and by providing all-important sector-specific labour market information.

The New European Social Fund (ESF) was created in 1989 to finance resources for a wide variety of innovative projects designed to enable many thousands of unemployed people to get jobs and training. In the UK £650 million was allocated during 1990–91 to assist labour markets as regards both employment and vocational training programmes.

The aim of the ESF dates back to the Treaty of Rome 1957; it is to create a central fund, to which all member states of the EC contribute and from which cash is allocated by the European Parliament to help iron out labour market inequalities within the Community. There are two guiding principles:

1 Additionality, the Fund supplementing member states' own expenditure on employment and training measures.
2 Matching funding, whereby ESF support is matched pound for pound with funds from a public body.

Areas and groups of people in critical need are targeted; in Britain these are mainly the regeneration of areas seriously affected by industrial decline, combatting long-term unemployment for those aged over 25, helping young people under 25 into the labour market, and promoting the development of rural areas. The practical results are such that in 1989, for example, the ESF helped over 2500 projects in Britain, involving over one million trainees. The projects ranged from vocational training in the media to a course in Gwynedd in modern office technology taught in both English and Welsh, and covered subjects as diverse as welding and hotel reception skills. Crucially ESF resources went to areas of industrial decline such as Cumbria and Strathclyde.

TECs throughout England and Wales are increasingly appreciating the benefits of working with the ESF. For example, the East Lancs TEC has used ESF money to set up a project to help women returners to work, providing skills training in information technology and work experience placements. The flexibility built into this project enables women trainees with family commitments to study where and when they want, so they can fit in their learning with their daily schedules. Targeted at those over 25 and out of work for more than twelve months, the project offers practical help to those who want to return to work, and provides an alternative skills supply for employers rather than rely on school-leavers to meet their skill needs.

Administrative arrangements agreed in 1990 mean that Brussels no longer gets involved with individual projects, but simply approves broad programmes of work submitted by member states. So now it is up to the individual member state to select and approve project bids — a change which clearly increases local control of ESF spending and should ensure that the most useful projects are supported.

Induction training

Induction training is carried out in order to help recruits to an organization to overcome their sense of strangeness, secure their acceptance by existing employees, and develop in them a sense of belonging. A large proportion of labour turnover occurs during the early weeks of employment, mainly because no effort has been made to enable newcomers to feel at home: they thus become unhappy and leave to find another job in a more congenial atmosphere. This type of training is in effect an introduction to the organization's purpose, policies, and practices, seeking to establish the right links between individuals, their work, and their outside life in the community, by explaining:

1 Their place in the organization.
2 The relationship between their work and the finished products.
3 The relationship between their firm, its industry, and the world outside.
4 How they can put their point of view to management.

In small firms this introduction has to be done informally, largely by the recruit's immediate supervisor. But in large organizations a planned induction programme is often given. A typical example is:

1 Welcome by a director, whose talk would include a history of the firm.
2 Films showing firm's activities — flow of production, from raw-material sources through to the marketing of the finished article.
3 Talk on personalities of the firm, including an organization chart.
4 A conducted tour of the works.
5 Talk about social and welfare facilities available.

Such a programme would be carried out as frequently as the number of recruits warranted it, and would be organized by members of the personnel department. It is essential that directors and other senior executives are involved in the talks, however: this adds prestige to the occasion and gives the newcomer a sense of importance.

Clearly the content of this type of course would be of common interest to all newcomers no matter how junior or senior their positions may be. In particular, office as well as production workers should be included, and the relationships between different grades of staff made clear, so that at least they start off by feeling members of one team. But this general information would then have to be supplemented by supervisors in each department, to provide the more domestic details. These include: a tour of the department, explaining how each job fits in to the main flow of production, and departmental rules about time-keeping, refreshment breaks, accident prevention, protective clothing, the actions to be taken in the case of emergency, procedure for reporting sickness, and observance of hygiene. In explaining how new workers can put their views to management, arrangements for joint consultation and the structure of works committees should be outlined, together with the firm's policy about trade union membership. The purpose and procedures of any suggestion scheme might be included at this stage. On wider personnel issues, recruits must be told whom to approach among management if they want help with any private domestic matters. The training officer should explain the firm's promotion policies and any schemes to help employees improve their qualifications or broaden their education. Finally, it is important that all aspects of remuneration are clarified: methods of payment, incentive and bonus schemes, profit-sharing, superannuation and sickness benefits, and any other compulsory or voluntary deductions from pay.

All this information given verbally may be consolidated in the form of an employees' handbook, setting out the organization's policies, rules, and regulations in black and white. When the newcomers have settled in and had the opportunity of reading the handbook, the last stage of the induction process should be a formal follow-up session when questions would be answered and any points of misunderstanding removed. This may all appear to involve considerable effort, but unless special attention is given to the problems of integrating new employees with the organization, the risk of high labour turnover with its attendant costs is great.

Particular attention should be given to the induction of school-leavers taking their first jobs; their reception will not only give them an impression of that particular firm, but may colour their attitude towards industry for the rest of their lives. Special emphasis should therefore be laid on the background to the job and its relation to the outside community; and on encouraging them to equip themselves for better jobs in the future.

Job training

All jobs in industry and commerce call for the exercise of certain skills and the application of different forms of knowledge, and they will not be carried out very effectively unless these skills and knowledge are properly imparted in the first place. This means that learners must be made aware of what they are doing, and why, and then be allowed actually to do the job for themselves. Skills are thus taught through a mixture of demonstration, explanation, and practice. The majority of people seeking jobs, especially school-leavers, are attracted by promises of proper training, the effectiveness of which is usually reflected in the rate of turnover among people during their first few weeks with a firm.

Job training methods generally fall into two types, depending mainly on the size of the organization and the resources it can devote to training. These are:

1 The understudy method, popularly known as 'sitting next to Nelly', when the learner is attached to someone proficient in the job and picks it up by copying that person.
2 The use of a separate training section, set aside especially to teach jobs to newcomers before they actually start work in the main production areas.

The success or failure of the first method undoubtedly lies in the hands of the experienced person giving the instruction. No matter how skilled they are at their job, unless they are good at teaching it too, their efforts and those of the learner will be of little avail. There is the possibility of their using bad working methods – short cuts that they may have evolved during years of experience which might not be suitable (sometimes positively dangerous) to teach to someone new to a job. If they are on piece-rates, and the demands of production are all important, they may have little time to devote to trainees who will become bewildered by the speed of everything around them and the impatience of their instructor. In any event there is likely to be considerable wastage of materials by the learner and also the risk of damage to valuable production machinery.

With so many disadvantages to this method, the concept of having separate training facilities is obviously to be preferred. Full-time qualified instructors in properly equipped training workshops can exercise much better control and ensure that the correct methods are taught. The learners receive the full attention of these instructors whose thoughts are not absorbed by production demands, and emphasis can be placed on gradually building up skill at the job before transfer to the main production areas (in the process, induction is helped, too). Nevertheless, when the transition does take place, it still becomes a traumatic experience for many workers who find the change from the unreal and less urgent atmosphere of the training room to the pace of the factory itself more than they can cope with. This is a matter of great concern to management who naturally do not wish to see expensively trained recruits leaving soon after starting on actual production. Everything should be done during the training period, therefore, to simulate real working conditions – inspection of the products made, with constantly increasing rates of output emphasized, for instance – in order to develop confidence.

Of course, in small organizations it may be physically impossible to have separate arrangements. The numbers of people to be trained and the frequency of demand for courses determine the methods used. Costs therefore need to be examined very closely in the light of these factors, with special regard to the savings in time taken to reach proficiency when newcomers are dealt with separately (as much as a half in many cases, compared with 'sitting next to Nelly'). Where traditional methods have to be used, supervisors must be careful in selecting the instructors: often people who have themselves recently learned the job are best, provided they can also be given some guidance on how to teach newcomers satisfactorily. On the other hand, if separate training is undertaken, supervisors must realize the importance of maintaining personal contact with trainees intended for their departments. This in itself can be a problem to those supervisors who are conscious of their own initial lack of background education. Nevertheless, they must be made to accept that training and development can never be completely delegated elsewhere, for by their very nature they are part of every supervisor's responsibilities.

A good example of job training in practice is the programme used by Nissan Motor Manufacturing (UK)* in launching the new model Primera car in 1990. To cover a diverse group of production manufacturing staff, the company ensured that the production line management team took the lead responsibility for training each operator to a specific standard on his own task and two others. Supervisors and team leaders were trained in instruction techniques and training was then conducted largely on the job. The company adapted a Japanese-style 'skills index monitor' to measure and display the level reached by each individual. The thoroughness of this approach won Nissan the NTTF Patron's Award for 1990.

Personnel Management, January 1991, page 10.

Further reading

Getting Off to a Good Start, Alan Fowler (IPM, 1983).
Managing the Training and Development Function, Allan D. Pepper (2nd Edition, Gower, 1992).
Training and Development, Rosemary Harrison (IPM, 1988).
Training Interventions, J. Kenny and M. Reid (IPM, 1986).

Training supervisors and managers

Both policy and practice for the training and development of supervisors and managers should be based on the technique of manpower
planning within an organization.* The fundamental concept quite
simply is that it is better to plan for job succession through internal
promotion whenever possible, rather than wait to see if anyone is
available when senior posts become vacant (and then perhaps have to
search outside the firm for suitable candidates). In trying to put this
concept into effect, and make training arrangements as a result,
responsible managers will base their plans on the answers to these
questions:

1 Are we providing adequately for our future requirements for senior
   staff?
2 Are we promoting the right people at the right time?
3 Are we getting the best results from existing foremen and managers?
4 Are we doing all we can to help our staff prepare themselves for
   promotion to supervisory and managerial positions?

Supervisory training

The basic problem in training supervisors is to get them to accept new
ideas and to build up confidence in their technical knowledge,

*See Chapter 4.

organizational ability, and social skills. Concern for solving this problem has grown consistently since the war for a number of reasons. Full employment brought about great changes in the general social climate, while the increased importance and influence of trade unions have had a direct impact on the industrial climate. The constant demand for higher productivity has led to increased specialization and radical changes to machinery, equipment, processes, and working methods. The trend towards larger units with more complex organizations in turn has caused relationships between employees to become impersonal, detracting from the significance of individuals and stifling their sense of responsibility. Almost everything that can be done to counteract these influences and enable individuals to feel that their contributions within a vast organization are important depends ultimately on the calibre of first-line supervision – thus emphasizing the vital nature of this aspect of training. Discipline based on pre-war 'carrot and stick' concepts of fear and insecurity is now inappropriate. The alternative, discipline by consent, does not occur spontaneously in the absence of sanctions – it requires qualities of leadership based on understanding of subordinates' points of view. This at a time, too, when the status of first-line supervisors is in question, particularly since their authority is constantly being eroded by the activities of specialists, such as production planners, quality inspectors, and work study engineers.

The main requirements of any supervisor are that they should regularly achieve production targets and increase productivity. To do so, they must be technically competent, be able to administer their department and organize its work, and establish proper relationships with their subordinates, colleagues and superiors in both line management and service functions. Their training should therefore be designed to:

1 Keep abreast of the current technical demands of their job.
2 Provide them with all the background information about the organization's policies and activities that they must know in order to act effectively and confidently.
3 Teach them the techniques and methods of management appropriate to their level and how they might best be applied under existing conditions.
4 Instruct them in the principles of personal leadership and develop their ability to exercise them effectively.
5 Teach them to cope successfully with changing conditions.

Of course, there is an enormous diversity in supervisors' jobs, depending largely on the size of firm and type of department, but

certain forms of training are suitable for them all. One investigation*
concentrated on the problems facing supervisors and the areas in
which their performance was often inadequate. There are two ways of
identifying the problems – individual interviews and a 'critical
incident report' procedure. Critical incidents are recorded by asking
supervisors at the end of their working day to describe briefly in
writing the problem they found most difficult to cope with that day.
These reports can then be analysed to detect what needs are common,
and general training schemes developed. In addition, specific job
training can be designed and given separately to individual supervisors.

A wide variety of external courses is available for training supervisors, but these should always be introduced cautiously, at a pace
which allows both the desire and ability to learn to be fostered.
Otherwise, the results achieved are likely to be disappointing and any
early hopes which may have been raised in the minds of senior
management will founder. In any event, external training should
always follow an internal course about the firm's history, activities,
organization, policies, practices, and procedures, which will provide a
general background against which subsequent training can be viewed
in perspective. It makes no difference whether this programme is
implemented on a group training basis or through a series of talks
given by appropriate managers in the normal course of their work, as
long as a properly planned syllabus is devised initially and then
consistently adhered to. There must be a thorough preliminary
appreciation of supervisors' jobs and their place in the organization (by
applying the technique of job analysis) before they attend any external
training courses.

The best known is Training Within Industry (TWI), a well-
established nationwide training service which has preserved an
excellent reputation for keeping up-to-date with changing times. In
the 1990s there exists a wide range of training courses designed to
meet the needs of employers in developing people's skills leading to
increased flexibility, improved safety, quality control, and the more
effective use of human resources. Most of this training is intended for
supervisors and managers, but there are also courses available for
training officers, clerks, secretaries and sales representatives.

TWI training officers are experienced in a wide range of training
provision and can design programmes to meet the specific needs of
particular employers. Standard courses are available to individual
employers either on their own premises or on an open basis at TWI

*DEP *Training Information Paper No. 2*, P. Warr and M. Bird (HMSO, 1968).

designated venues to serve the needs of a number of employers in the same locality.

The supervisory and management programmes are based on two principles: that the step from shop-floor to supervisor calls for a change in outlook and the use of the more intangible skills of supervisors; and that supervisors and managers must develop skills in the broad areas of leadership, communication, human relations, safety, and instructional techniques. The present range of standard programmes includes – interviewing techniques; developing leadership; effective interpersonal skills; job relationships; staff development for office supervisors; managing the human resource; safety skills; and time management. Courses last from two to four days and are conducted for small groups of up to about twelve people. The trainer utilizes the experience of the group members in examining and discussing various problems of supervision and management.

Safety training courses are designed to assist in the development of skills needed in obtaining and maintaining a safe working environment. The safety skills course can be adapted as appropriate for safety representatives, supervisors, managers and office staff. Sales training courses are available tailored to meet the needs of firms in retail selling techniques, selling by telephone, selling techniques for field sales representatives, and 'successful selling'. Other courses available cover effective report writing, and social and organizational skills for secretaries.

Instructors and training officers can be offered tutorials on any of the programmes mentioned above, to enable them to provide in-house courses. In addition, in order to develop the necessary training skills, courses are offered on basic and advanced trainer skills. Employees responsible for preparing export/import documentation can be trained in the complex procedures involved. If a firm has been able to identify specific problems of documentation, trainers may be engaged on a daily basis to train small numbers of staff on the firm's own premises, geared to the firm's needs.

Highly formal training is normally associated with large organizations which have all sorts of teaching aids and comprehensive facilities available. The principles apply equally to small firms, however, where entirely individual training, carried out in the privacy of the offices of appropriate senior staff, can be given with considerable benefits. The small firm also has the advantage that training can be implemented at optimum speed; in big companies, the numbers involved in training programmes are often so large that time-lags inevitably occur between training courses, and their impact may consequently be diminished.

Interest and enthusiasm generated through special training efforts will wane, in any event, unless something positive is done to prevent this happening. Apathy or misunderstanding on the part of colleagues or superiors may well frustrate supervisors when they try to apply the knowledge they have acquired from training. Here again their own line managers are clearly responsible for proper follow-up and encouragement. The firm's training officer can also help by organizing:

1 *Departmental competitions:* for example, in 'good housekeeping' or safety.
2 *Discussion groups:* a forum for raising problems, keeping up with current technical developments, and also a useful means for communicating news about the company and any changes likely to occur.
3 *Exchange visits:* to see how other factories are run, or even to work in them for short periods of time.
4 *External refresher courses:* providing the opportunity to exchange experience with other supervisors from a wide variety of activities and backgrounds.

Management development

The job of a manager can be analysed into five types of activity, thus:

1 *Defining the organization's aims,* which will be achieved by the coordinated efforts of all staff.
2 *Planning* the best use of all available resources (labour, money, equipment, accommodation, time, and ideas), in order to achieve these aims.
3 *Taking action* to put plans into effect.
4 *Measuring* the results achieved by this action, and *comparing* them with specified performance standards.
5 *Taking corrective action* if there is any deviation from the recognized standards.

Apart from the necessary qualifications and grasp of administrative principles, this analysis of management shows that it differs from the work of other employees by demanding the use of judgment, the balancing of arguments, and the taking of decisions. The distinguishing feature of management training, therefore, is that it aims to cultivate these skills.

In as far as management is now regarded as a profession, training for it may be said to go through the same three phases as all professional education. First, background studies orientate students towards their chosen career (science for the engineer, for example): for management, this background is often considered irrelevant, although nowadays there may be some bias towards economic or sociological subjects. Second, there is the phase of on-the-job learning – a carefully controlled and supervised apprenticeship, with actual responsibilities slowly increasing as time passes. Parallel with this is the third aspect, a series of supplementary experiences – courses on special topics, attachments, secondments, reading lists – providing off-the-job training with the aim of achieving better performance on the job. External courses are thus seen as carefully timed supplements to development, which can be evaluated in terms of improved knowledge and skill when the trainee returns. This event itself demands that the climate of opinion in the working group concerned is such that criticism and suggestions will be encouraged or indeed expected of the returned member.

At the national level, the director of the MSC has argued the case* for a management development initiative which comprises the following ten points:

1 Every organization to have its own MD plan, consciously and systematically formulated, for every level of management and every function.
2 The plan to be determined by the board of the organization, based on a training audit professionally conducted on an annual basis.
3 Every manager to have his/her own personal development plan, agreed with senior management, and containing both immediate and long-term objectives.
4 Nationally agreed standards of expertise and performance appraisal.
5 Managers to acquire appropriate professional qualifications before taking up a post, and constantly update them.
6 Every manager to have access to learning opportunities throughout his/her working life.
7 By 1995, a comprehensive and reliable system of modular provision and modular course material available across a very wide spectrum of management functions, skills, education and training.
8 The prime learning medium to be that of best practice, implying the development of a very wide range of case material.
9 The development of nationally recognized centres of excellence in management education and training.
10 Reports to be given voluntarily – e.g. in organizations' annual reports – on the progress being made. Some authoritative body,

*BIM, Industry Year Conference, March 1986.

such as the IPM or BIM, should publish an annual report to the nation on management development.

The emphasis in management training, then, must be placed on the development of individuals, and they should be allowed every opportunity of trying their hands at bigger jobs by deputizing for their superiors. People concerned must also be made aware of the importance of a planned career and of the self-development steps they must take, through personal study and reading, to equip themselves for promotion. For their part, all senior managers must accept that the organization's dependence on the successful career development of their subordinates must take precedence over the convenience of their own local operations. They must therefore be prepared to give up subordinates for other jobs and take on in their place people from elsewhere in the organization who will be less knowledgeable but are themselves in need of instruction and broader experience.

This method of transferring staff to gain experience is a common means of training. As already mentioned, job rotation* is very useful in developing people early on in their careers, but may not be such good practice at senior levels. Where it is used for management trainees, great care must be taken in handling relationships between them and other staff within the departments through which they move. Trainees who are clearly destined for top jobs can arouse great jealousy, so their own behaviour needs to be circumspect and tactful at all times. If they are given projects to carry out, the limits of their authority as regards departmental supervisors must be precisely defined, and it is better for them not to be given a completely free hand.

Many universities, polytechnics and colleges of higher education have management departments, and the Diploma in Management Studies is now recognized as a qualification demanding a high calibre of student. Visits to other organizations can be of great value especially if the trainees are briefed beforehand on what they can expect to see: points of similarity and contrast with their own organization's structure and methods should be indicated and discussed on these occasions. It might even be possible to make mutual arrangements for trainees to spend longer periods of time with each other's firms, if potential advantages are obvious.

Many organizations send their managers on residential courses at a variety of staff colleges and management centres. The Management College at Henley and the Business Schools at London and Manchester are perhaps the most famous of these in Britain; but several banks

*Chapter 6, page 113.

and many large private companies, for example, have their own staff colleges – all offering courses designed to stretch the intellectual ability of those attending and to provide close contact with other practising managers. External courses perhaps have the added advantage of getting members away from the possibly parochial atmosphere of their own industries.

But the key factor in all these approaches and methods is the continuous interface between managers concerned and their own immediate superior. One important question in any performance appraisal scheme is to ask the boss – what specific action do *you personally* intend to take to develop your subordinates or to remedy their shortcomings? Only after they have together considered what can be done to bring about development and improvement should they call in (if at all necessary) the management training specialist. Even then, senior staff must be pressed further to secure an absolute commitment to action. A written policy, for example, will indicate sincerity about training: 'The achievement of effective results in the development of his immediate subordinates will be an important fact in the appraisal of a manager's results.'

A practical case-study of management development in action is the work of the Public Service Training Council in Northern Ireland.* Examples of its activities include:

(a) 'Action centred' MD programmes: an essential feature is that each participant, with the support of his/her boss, brings a substantial live problem to the course. This becomes a link between the various workshops and a vehicle for development, since each person becomes part of a problem-processing group. Apart from the first workshop – which concentrates on self-knowledge, self-analysis and ways of approaching problems – the remaining workshops are structured by the participants themselves as needs become apparent.
(b) Leadership and team-building: this programme emphasizes management styles and teamwork, using an outdoors background to drive lessons home.
(c) Forums on issues facing the public service: these are short, sharp sessions – half a day or less – when managers come together to discuss the challenges facing the public service (not time-consuming, but effective).
(d) Special interest groups: to help build communications bridges between organizations and departments, with the Council sup-

*See 'Making Public Servants into Managers: the Northern Ireland Experience', J. Maquire, *Personnel Management*, February 1985, pages 32–4.

porting short courses and seminars, e.g. for personnel management or finance department staff.

(e) A microcomputer training resource: the object of this is to develop good course design, test it and then transfer it to other training departments.

Another management development technique which is widely used in the USA and is on the increase in the UK is variously termed 'mentoring' or 'preceptorship'. The basic concept is simplicity itself: senior people, usually working in the same organization, take juniors under their wing and help their business education and training in any way possible. To take one practical example: qualified members of the Institute of Health Services Management offer preceptorship to young staff working in the health services who are preparing for the Institute's examinations. The keyword of the concept in practice is 'flexibility', so as to encourage as many members as possible to help in this way, but having regard to the personal limitations of some individuals. Hence a range of services is on offer: basically, being able to answer questions and offer advice about the examination syllabus; through discussions on current management topics and reports, and arrangements for visits to specialist departments and managers, to formal seminars and tutorials for groups of students at the other extreme. Such a scheme itself depends heavily on the preceptors, in turn, receiving appropriate training to understand and fulfil their roles.

Awareness of the growing need for individuals to be more active in managing their own careers, but also of their need for support in doing so, is exemplified by the BBC's *Career Point* programme*, of which career development workshops form a central plank. These two-day workshops, involving as many as 80−100 participants at a time, encourage staff to think about their careers (especially when cut-backs seem inevitable) in the context of their lives as a whole. A series of exercises helps them work out the range of their own skills, what is important to them in their working lives, and whether their present jobs fulfil their needs. They then plan ways of achieving their goals, so that they go away with a clear sense of what they are and where they are going.

The sessions are led by volunteer managers and staff from across the BBC's functions who have been specifically trained for this task. This is intended itself to be developmental experience for them, no less than for those attending the workshops, giving them training skills and enabling them to meet people from parts of the organization with which they would otherwise have little contact.

***Personnel Management Plus*, December 1991, page 16.

As well as attending career development workshops, Career Point gives staff the chance to use a resource centre where an interactive computer program customized for the BBC helps them to identify their own skills, interests and 'work values' — what is important to them in their jobs. The results are linked to a database of about 2000 internal jobs.

Many of the people who work out their goals by means of the workshops or computer programme need no further help. Others ask for career counselling, which usually means talking to their boss or personnel officer, or seeking specialist counselling, which may include psychometric testing. Another follow-up to the basic career development sessions is provided by career-planning workshops, planned to build participants' confidence and give them practical job-search skills.

Management competences

National standards of management competence, published by the Management Charter Initiative (MCI) in 1990, now form part of the framework of NVQs set up by the National Council for Vocational Qualifications. Overall competence is defined as the ability to perform the activities within an occupational area to the levels of performance expected in employment: this goes rather beyond the dictionary definition, 'sufficiency' or 'adequacy', to mean an observable skill or ability to complete managerial tasks successfully. Units of competence, or modules, describe what people need to be able to do, and incorporate standards which reflect full overall competence in a job. Performance is essentially expressed in output terms which incorporate knowledge, understanding and necessary personal qualities.

The MCI's purpose is to develop a set of generic competences and standards in discrete zones of people and resource management, relevant to different levels (first-line managers, middle managers, higher level strategic management). It is also trying to establish a much-needed framework and language in the areas of communications, numeracy and personal effectiveness. In so far as assessable standards of performance in core competences — for example, operations, finance, people and information management — can be agreed, these can then be used as training objectives and be incorporated into generic management qualifications, attesting to skills which are transferable between management jobs.

The MCI, which is now the lead or standard-setting body for management and supervision, suggests that the standards can be used for NVQ awards, as guidelines for organizations in developing their staff, and for appraisals. A complementary personal competence model has also been issued which individuals or assessors within organizations can use as a development tool: it looks at how managers actually behave and describes ways of achieving the standards. These standards are designed to be generic, common to the vast majority of management jobs, and can thus be used by employers and other lead bodies in developing standards for management occupations within their own industries. An example of a detailed statement of generic competences at middle management level is shown in Table 5.

Table 5 MCI middle management generic competences

| *Basic units of competence and associated elements* | |
Units	Elements
1 Initiate and implement change and improvement in services, products and systems	1.1 Identify opportunities for improvement in services, products and systems
	1.2 Evaluate proposed changes for benefits and disadvantages
	1.3 Negotiate and agree the introduction of change
	1.4 Implement and evaluate changes to services, products and systems
	1.5 Introduce, develop and evaluate quality assurance systems
2 Monitor, maintain and improve service and product delivery	2.1 Establish and maintain the supply of resources into the organization/department
	2.2 Establish and agree customer requirements
	2.3 Maintain and improve operations against quality and functional specifications
	2.4 Create and maintain the necessary conditions for productive work
3 Monitor and control the use of resources	3.1 Control costs and enhance value
	3.2 Monitor and control activities against budgets
4 Secure effective resource allocation for activities and projects	4.1 Justify proposals for expenditure on projects
	4.2 Negotiate and agree budgets

Table 5 Continued

Basic units of competence and associated elements

Units	Elements
5 Recruit and select personnel	5.1 Define future personnel requirements
	5.2 Determine specifications to secure quality people
	5.3 Assess and select candidates against team and organizational requirements
6 Develop teams, individuals and self to enhance performance	6.1 Develop and improve teams through planning and activities
	6.2 Identify, review and improve development activities for individuals
	6.3 Develop oneself within the job role
	6.4 Evaluate and improve the development processes used
7 Plan, allocate and evaluate work carried out by teams, individuals and self	7.1 Set and update work objectives for teams and individuals
	7.2 Plan activities and determine work methods to achieve objectives
	7.3 Allocate work and evaluate teams, individuals and self against objectives
	7.4 Provide feedback to teams and individuals on their performance.
8 Create, maintain and enhance effective working relationships	8.1 Establish and maintain the trust and support of one's subordinates
	8.2 Establish and maintain the trust and support of one's immediate manager
	8.3 Establish and maintain relationships with colleagues
	8.4 Identify and minimize interpersonal conflict
	8.5 Implement disciplinary and grievance procedures
	8.6 Counsel staff
9 Seek, evaluate and organize information for action	9.1 Obtain and evaluate information to aid decision making
	9.2 Forecast trends and developments which affect objectives
	9.3 Record and store information

Table 5 Continued

Basic units of competence and associated elements	
Units	Elements
10 Exchange information to solve problems and make decisions	10.1 Lead meetings and group discussions to solve problems and make decisions
	10.2 Contribute to discussions to solve problems and make decisions
	10.3 Advise and inform others

At senior management level, the NatWest Bank's use of high-performance managerial competences* as a tool for management development includes the following examples:

Concept formation: builds frameworks or models or forms concepts, hypotheses or ideas on the basis of information, becomes aware of patterns, trends, and cause/effect relations by linking disparate information.

Conceptual flexibility: identifies feasible alternatives or multiple options in planning and decision-making, holds different options in focus simultaneously and evaluates their pros and cons.

Developmental orientation: creates a positive climate in which individuals increase the accuracy of their awareness of their own strengths and limitations, and provides coaching, training and developmental resources to improve performance.

Achievement orientation: possess high internal work standards and sets ambitious yet attainable goals; wants to do things better, to improve, to be more effective and efficient; measures progress against targets.

A grid covering eleven such competences is used, the other seven headings being − information search, interpersonal search, managing interaction, impact, self-confidence, presentation and proactive orientation.

The significance of MCI lies in the fact that some 1000 employers, representing more than 25 per cent of the UK workforce, have joined in this effort to develop recognized standards of management practice. MCI also endorses management training arrangements which meet its declared standards of quality, including assessment and validation processes which lead to national awards and professional qualifications: to this end a national network of assessors has been set up

---

Personnel Management, September 1989, page 55; based on *Managerial Competence*, H. M. Schroder (Kendall Hunt, Iowa 1989).

to deliver direct endorsements and inspect provision at training centres.

Looking to the immediate future, MCI's objectives into the mid-1990s are:

- To establish standards for managers at all levels, reviewing and up-dating them in the light of experience and the changing business environment; and ensuring their acceptance by industry and commerce as valid and valuable for purposes of recruitment, identification of training needs and appraisal.
- To work with awarding bodies to design a comprehensive framework of standards and endorsed qualifications, to be recognized as valid by anyone working in management education, training and development; and to achieve joint status with awarding bodies and professional institutions.
- To start a research and development programme which focuses on internal comparisons and forms a UK base for international standards.
- To achieve recognition for Accreditation of Prior Learning (APL) as a building process and part of a continuous personal development strategy for managers.
- To set up local networks nation-wide to work in conjunction with TECs or LECs to so that they are seen both as vehicles for change and as leaders in local management education training and development.

Yet another initiative has sprung from the growing realization that a long-term, sustained and proactive programme of investment in people is essential for survival in today's environment of intense economic pressures. But employers need encouragement to adopt and show commitment to an attitude which places employee development as a top priority. The Investors in People (IIP) initiative is designed to do just that. Under the auspices of the NTTF, TECs, the CBI and other business organizations, the initiative is focused on the IIP Standard, which sets out the policies a company must follow in order to achieve the IIP status. It stipulates that an Investor in People:

- Makes a public commitment from the top to develop all employees to achieve business objectives.
- Regularly reviews the training and development needs of all employees.

- Takes action to train and develop individuals on recruitment and throughout their employment.
- Evaluated the investment in training and development to assess achievement and improve future effectiveness.

Recognized companies who meet the Standard are entitled to display the IIP logo in their publicity material as a symbol of quality – although the main point is not just the award of the Standard, it is about encouraging organizations to improve their employee development and thus benefit from improved business performance.

The circuit scheme

The *circuit scheme* of exchange visits is another useful training device for senior staff, whereby teams of managers visit each other's organizations, with collective meetings arranged between the teams and between individual specialist executives making up the teams. The purpose is for each person to report back on the differences in method, approach, and costs observed, and suggest points about his/her own organization which might be investigated. Where such exchanges can be made, teams might be made up of a representative of general management, an accountant, a production engineer, a work study officer, salesperson, and personnel officer.

Obviously this can be done much more easily in the public services than in private industry where secrets have to be safeguarded against competitors. Where this method has been tried between administrators from different hospitals, for instance, quite dramatic results have been achieved. Examples of the conclusions from one such series of meetings include: resiting of time-keeping clocks; supervision over certain grades of staff to be strengthened; a new telephone system to be introduced; variations in costs for cleaning services to be investigated; further discussions to be held on the benefits of direct labour or contract labour for maintenance work; and the saving of appreciable sums of money by making certain medical equipment locally. The general feeling was that the exercise was a great stimulation to all those who took part in it. Members of each of the teams gained some new idea that they were anxious to put into practice, and they all felt that their outlook had been considerably broadened.

Training personnel managers

One important report* advocates the use of modular training schemes in training specialists in management through an initial course, cohesive and theoretically orientated but providing introductory practice in basic skills, and a second stage involving a selection of appropriate modules, each of which would deal in depth with specific areas of personnel management. The content of the initial course, for people entering personnel management, would be related to the kinds of work likely to be encountered early in their careers. No attempt would be made at this stage to provide a package of knowledge and expertise in techniques for use later in higher posts, for this would be educationally inefficient and, because of the rapid development of personnel work, would be out of date by the time of use. A fivefold structure is put forward as the best means of achieving this early understanding of personnel management:

1 Basic knowledge – for example, industrial and trade union law, how ITBs operate, and the main sources of staffing information and statistics.
2 Behavioural sciences.
3 Industrial psychology.
4 The organizational role of personnel, especially manpower planning.
5 Fundamental techniques – for example, job analysis and interviewing.

Subsequent training should consist of short, intensive courses on particular techniques or aspects of personnel management in which there is a desire to specialize. Teaching in this manner should be much more effective than in general courses; it can incorporate the most recent developments, and is likely to stay fresh in the trainee's mind. The modules themselves could change from time to time, reflecting the development of training needs.

The whole concept can perhaps be best presented in the form of a modular diagram (Figure 21), illustrating the subject-matter of the specialized, intensive courses.

The DE report *Training for the Management of Human Resources*† went into greater detail in analysing the training needed by professional specialists to enable them to function as an integral part of an

---

*'A Modular Approach to Training', the 'Edinburgh Group', *Personnel Management*, July 1969, page 28f. For more recent views see the 1985 IPM report 'The Personnel Professionals', Philip Long.
†HMSO, 1972.

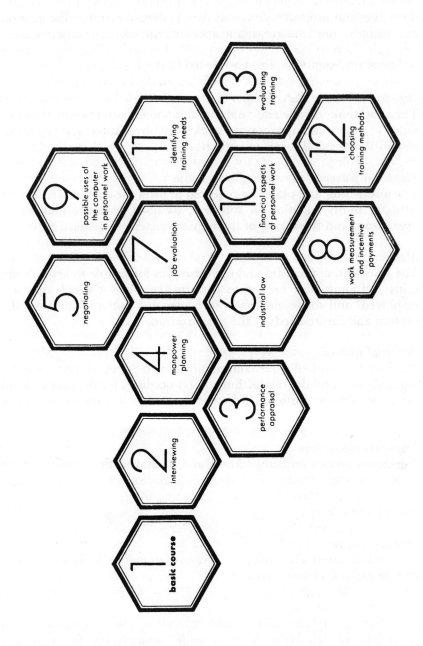

Figure 21 Modular diagram

organization's management team, making a cost-effective contribution towards achieving its overall objects. The report suggests that there are three levels of intensity: common core knowledge and skills; general knowledge of function areas; and specific practitioner competencies.

The main functional areas are listed thus:

Organization review and anaylsis
The continuing review and analysis of an organization's operations in order to determine appropriate work structures, roles, relationships, responsibilities and levels of authority.

Manpower planning, recruitment, and selection
The forecasting and planning required to meet the present and future needs of an organization for sufficient qualified people to man all its operations, and the taking of the necessary steps to acquire them.

Manpower training and development
The provision of facilities and opportunities for people to acquire the skills and knowledge needed to perform the jobs for which they are employed, and to develop their own personal potential to meet the present and future needs of the organization.

Industrial relations
The promotion of effective communications between all parties in an organization, and the establishment of procedures for the resolution of personal and institutional differences, e.g. by means of collective bargaining and joint consultation.

Employee remuneration
The development, implementation, and administration of appropriate systems of remuneration (including, for instance, job evaluation, wage and salary structures, incentive payments, fringe benefits, and non-financial rewards).

Employee services
The establishment of satisfactory services relating to the safety, health, and welfare of all employees.

Administration and records
The design, implementation, and control of adequate records and administrative procedures to provide information for planning purposes and for the documentation of all employed personnel.

The ways in which these functions, and the degrees of competency required to work in them, interact are illustrated by Figure 22:

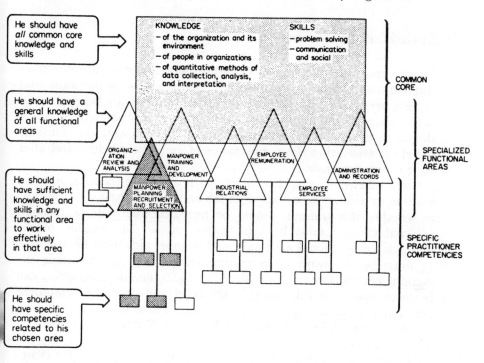

Figure 22

It cannot be over-emphasized that, as with any other profession, training in personnel management must be kept up-to-date. Having moved through the historical welfare, scientific management, industrial relations and manpower planning phases, the professional has now entered the human resources management era – aimed at getting the best out of people while matching that achievement to the organization's objectives. New technology, computers, for example, is moving closer to the business management side; all such knowledge is now essential.

Personnel management is expanding into areas as complex as finance, statistical analysis and the compilation of carefully-targeted remuneration packages aimed at wooing scarce skills. Thus, for example, training courses for personnel department staff nowadays typically contain financial topics such as setting up and operating share option and profit-related pay programmes. They are also likely to include health insurance, removal and relocation services and payments, and leased cars. It is part of the personnel manager's job to decide which of the fringe benefits are most important in each case.

Evaluation of training

The purpose of evaluation is to determine whether or not the objectives and content of training courses are consistent with the aims and current needs of the organization; if these objectives are being reached in the most effective and economical manner; and, if not, what changes should be made. In the final analysis, of course, evaluation must be based on measuring the performance of employees before and after their training periods.

Comprehensive evaluation starts with assessing training plans in relation to defined needs based on job and task analysis. Decisions as to whether this training should be provided internally or through external courses must be kept under review. The quality of the methods, instructional materials, and training aids must be assessed, as must be the ways of measuring students' progress during the training period. The results achieved on the completion of training can be examined, and subsequently the level and quality of employee performance can be appraised over a period of time.

The methods of evaluation have been listed* thus:

1 Comparison with the findings of educational research: for example, can programmed instruction be applied in specific courses to increase learning speed?
2 Comparison with job performance requirements, with continuous review to ensure appropriate adjustments.
3 Inspection of instructors, using a checklist of desirable qualities.
4 Written achievement tests, examining ability to apply the information received during training.
5 Questionnaires to trainees: these may be of limited value if trainees have no standards of comparison.
6 Questionnaires to supervisors – both to identify training needs initially and to specify the results of training.
7 Trainees' interviews – useful in highlighting specific problems.
8 Observation of performance on the job, before and after training.
9 Study of records and reports analysing achievements.
10 Proficiency tests: shorthand and typing, for example.
11 Analysis of problems and accidents, seeking their causes.

*Training and Development Journal, May 1968, page 38f.

12 Research with matched groups, one having received training, the other not – obviously a time-consuming business.

As well as the purposes stated above, evaluation may also be used in a way which contributes to the learning process among course participants. The first step is to ask them and their bosses to complete questionnaires before courses begin, briefly explaining their expectations and what they hope to achieve through taking part. Short questionnaires should also be completed at the end of courses, focusing on learning and what might be applied back at work. Some time later, both participants and their bosses should again be asked to complete questionnaires which review the effects of the courses.

The primary advantage of such a process lies in helping potential participants concentrate their thoughts beforehand and their actions afterwards, thus providing a closer integration between training activities and normal work experiences. Also, by requiring the boss to comment at several stages on the subordinate's needs and progress, it may encourage the boss to accept greater responsibility for staff training. In some respects it is little different from requiring participants to arrive with written expectations and to depart with individual action plans. The main advantages are that the boss becomes directly involved and the stages of learning and evaluation are linked together.

12

Wages and salaries — the national scene

Employment is first about work, about sustaining a business or service, about enabling activities to grow or survive on the basis of their usefulness. The details of renumeration and working conditions, assuming reasonable initial standards of each, come at best second to that. Mentioning the direct obligation which an employee has to an employer when he/she contracts into employment sounds Victorian. But equally there is a message of the high level of obligation which a modern employer must take in relation to the employee. Business success in any enterprise depends in large measure on employers not only meeting their obligations in that way, but also that they actively work to join their employees to the objectives and problems of the business so that they are jointly understood and possibly shared. The pursuit of these new conventions is very important for both employers and unions in a changing, competitive world in which everyone's livelihood and standards are at stake.

Current practice as regards remuneration emphasizes flexibility — systems which link pay to performance, output, productivity, profits or labour market conditions. Variations are seen in the starting pay of recruits, reflecting the individual's qualifications and experience or local skill scarcities. Local and regional allowance schemes are also common in areas where the labour market is tight or where the cost of living is relatively high.

There are four broad types of incentive-based systems, two based on individual performance and two on collective performance:

1 Use of management's assessment of performance to determine the level of an individual's basic pay, frequently referred to as 'merit pay'; this is a method of varying pay by allowing managers discretion to decide the criteria which determines pay: in the formalized performance appraisal schemes operated by large organizations, these criteria are often explicitly defined, but in small firms pay is more usually settled by a manager's subjective assessment.

2 Bonus schemes reflecting individual's performance include piecework, payment by results and commission paid on sales, all of which are clearly discernible from basic pay (unlike merit payments which are usually consolidated into basic pay). A distinction must be drawn between bonus schemes which pay a fixed sum on attainment of a particular level of output or sales and schemes where payments vary according to the precise level of output or sales: the former (sometimes called 'a threshold bonus') is similar to basic pay in the sense that employees expect to obtain it for a reasonable amount of work; the latter is more flexible and more sensitive to the individual's effort and level of performance.

3 Collective bonus schemes based on output or productivity, with a distinction drawn between those relating to a group of workers, section or department and those relating to the whole organization. These types of bonuses have a long association with manufacturing industry, where they provide the flexibility to respond to fluctuating workloads on production facilities; they apply most frequently to manual workers and sales staff.

4 Collective bonus schemes based on profits, with a distinction made between profit-sharing schemes and employee share plans. Both these types of incentives were much encouraged during the 1980s. As regards the former, in some cases the amounts paid are a matter of management discretion, in others they take up a fixed percentage of profits; similarly, with the latter, a mixture of management discretion and fixed relationship to profits can be seen in the allocation of shares.

Nevertheless, in the majority of organizations in both the private and public sectors, the pay and conditions of employees are still determined by collective bargaining — that is, through agreements negotiated between employers' and workers' organizations. Such agreements cover not only rates of pay, but may include working hours, special allowances for overtime, night duty and shift work, piecework rates and other incentives, guaranteed minimum weekly payments, holidays, allocation of work, apprenticeships and redundancy arrangements.

Individuals applying for a job may make their own private deal with a prospective employer, irrespective of the conditions of their new fellow-workers. An entirely different situation obtains when that employer is a member of an association which has signed an agreement with relevant trade unions about the conditions under which all workers in that industry will be engaged. The obvious advantages of this type of arrangement are that, on the one hand, all workers gain equality of conditions, and, on the other, employers know that their competitors who have signed the same agreement will not have lower wages costs than themselves. Indeed, the significance is wider: for the terms of agreement are usually observed by employers throughout an industry, even if they are not actual signatories. Similarly, of course, the terms apply equally to all employees and not just to those who are members of the unions that successfully negotiated them (hence the main reason why union members object to working alongside non-union workers).

The development of collective bargaining practice has long rested on the principle that it is a voluntary system, depending on the mutual consent of both sides of industry and their loyal acceptance of decisions reached. This principle carries the implication that there will be no outside interference in the manner by which wages are settled: but economic circumstances in recent years have dictated otherwise, and there has been a large measure of policy control exercised by the Government, especially in the public sector.

As far as the content of collective agreements is concerned, basic wage rates are the prime consideration, of course: these are settled nationally in the first place, but usually leave scope for subsidiary or local agreements (as in the building industry). Trade unions always seek to maintain differentials between occupations, based on elements of skill, danger or variety in the work, and the actual scarcity of labour. More than one-third of all industrial workers in this country are at present operating on piece-rates or bonus systems. Most of these involve agreements made at national level, although some are based on district collective bargaining; agreements made at the level of the organization itself are also commonplace. Among these levels, two-tiered settlements at the levels of the organization and of the industry of which it is part often form the basis for pay especially in large organizations. In such cases the level of settlements usually mirror closely the national agreement.

A survey on recent changes in payment systems* indicated that management decision had become more important in settling pay

*Employment Gazette, August 1991, page 457.

than any level of collective bargaining. An individualization of wage and salary payments has occurred with greater use being made of both personal bonuses and assessments of each individual's work performance. Two themes emerged from employers' comments on the principles which guided their determination of rates of pay in the current economic scene: one is the need to contain costs in order to maintain and improve profitability and to ensure continued competitiveness; the other is the need to compete in the labour market and overcome the difficulties of recruiting, motivating and retaining the right employees. Flexible payment systems can contribute to the achievement of both these objectives, especially individual incentive and merit payments: these provide opportunities for selective wage increases for key staff which might otherwise not be possible. Thus the aim of employers in developing flexible pay systems seems less concerned with establishing a direct and measurable link between output or productivity and remuneration, such as is implied by traditional payment-by-results schemes, than with providing recognition for valued employees. Higher output or productivity is taken as an act of faith flowing from the accordance of this recognition.

Factors in negotiating wages

The conclusion of most wage negotiations is a compromise, decided by the effective strength of each party's case. Their arguments have traditionally been based on the following factors:

1 *Increases in the cost of living*

Negotiations on this point revolve around movements in retail prices, since these directly influence the purchasing power of wage packets. But the volume of industrial production, labour costs, import prices, and wholesale prices all in turn affect the Index of Retail Prices, thus limiting the extent to which it can be used in wage negotiations. In any event, a narrower view of a particular industry usually needs to be taken, whereas the Index of Retail Prices is more a reflection of the state of the national economy as a whole. It may also be more important to consider earnings rather than basic wage rates: published sources (e.g. *The Employment Gazette*) provide this information, so that average earnings for average hours worked can be compared with movements of retail prices to show whether real wages have risen or fallen. The Government also argue that the Tax and Prices Index, introduced in 1979 and designed to reflect the impact of tax changes as well as price rises on incomes, is a more accurate basis for pay negotiations.

2 Tradition

The history and development of different industries and the unions associated with them vary greatly and have brought about differences in approach towards negotiations. Improvements in conditions do not always relate mainly to wage rates: factors of security of employment, higher status for manual workers, fringe benefits, shorter hours, and longer holidays – all these to some extent depend on traditional attitudes taken towards negotiations by both employers' federations and unions. The amount of progress already made generally as regards wages or various aspects of working conditions will also be a significant factor in determining the future policy of both bodies.

3 Prosperity of a firm or industry

Making sure that its members get 'a fair slice of the cake' is, of course, a main concern of every trade union, and frequent references will be made during negotiations to an industry's record of production and its financial position. The difficulty of applying this information, however, lies in apportioning the credit for improved performance, for example, between the shareholders' additional investments in new machinery and any increased effort on the part of the labour force. Higher dividends often lead to demands for higher wages: it is a complex subject when so many factors – such as managerial ability, financial turnover, size of funds for capital development, and delivery dates – all contribute to the higher dividend payments. But the fact remains that if the shareholders are consistently being made more prosperous, trade unions will press the claims of their members at the same time.

4 Pay relativities

Relationships between the pay of different groups of employees lie at the heart of all pay determination. Relativities are inherently complex, being influenced by economic, social, and institutional factors which are often difficult to reconcile; but two factors are of major importance – the labour market and fairness.

In so far as pay relativities reflect differences in skill and responsibilities sought for particular kinds of employment, they help to distribute available manpower between jobs, occupations, and industries in accordance with the varying demands for workers' services. But, on the other hand, people's views of the fairness of their pay in relation to that of others frequently lead to pressures for changes in wage levels, and these may conflict with the operation of market forces. Fairness is subjective in the first place, and liable to change in meaning as circumstances change.

Collective bargaining usually facilitates the settlement of pay differences within single negotiating units (differentials), but there is no machinery for dealing with pay differences between different negotiating units (relativities). Although adjustments to relativities which occur all the time improve the position of some groups in relation to others, the effects are often offset wholly or in part as the result of later negotiations in which those others seek to restore their former relative positions.

Claims for changes in relativities are based largely on comparisons, which may be made between specific jobs with broadly similar skills and responsibilities, or they may be expressed as a generalized reference to movements in average pay for all jobs or for some large category like manual or non-manual occupations. Negotiators rarely confine themselves to one type of comparison, nor do they wish comparisons to be the sole determinant of pay; furthermore, each group has justifiable reasons for preferring one kind of comparison to another. There is no simple, universal set of pay comparisons which can be urged on all groups, and no single technique of general application for solving relativity problems.

Thus the task of devising procedures for considering claims by groups for a relative improvement of their position in the community is formidable – not least because of the absence of agreed criteria for deciding what relationships should be changed, and how this can be done in a manner that is fair to both beneficiaries and those whose relative position would become worse. Fairness, after all, is in the eye of the beholder, and the basic objectives of trade unions are to protect and improve the lot of their members – not to be fair to each other or to the community at large. The great practical difficulty is the need for consensus: on the assumption that the amount available for all wage increases is limited, other groups of employees must bear the cost of any special treatment. In other words, the relative position of some workers can only improve if others suffer.

5 Comparability

Where the type of work carried out in different industries is similar, then wage rates in them will tend to keep close together. But, however equitable this approach may appear in theory, many practical problems arise over the enormous amount of detail that accumulates during comparison studies; analysis takes a long time, interpretation varies, and inevitably there are considerable delays in settling a claim.

While pay is the most important element of any comparison, the total remuneration packet also has to be examined. The quantification of conditions of service and pension arrangements is clearly less straightforward than that of cash remuneration. Then there are other less tangible factors such as job security, labour supply, and the efficiency of labour utilization. Experience shows that comparability requires careful and detailed work of an ongoing kind; information has to be gathered systematically and methods standardized. One argument, therefore, is that a longer-term view should be taken of the role of comparability, and that the collection of information and refinement of methods can only be carried out satisfactorily and on a thoroughly acceptable basis by a permanent body.

By emphasizing consistency, equity and rationality, the comparability approach appears to give a sense of fair play to any pay settlements. Even so, it is still powerless to overcome a number of the harsh facts of life associated with bargaining, notably:

(a) The disruptive influence of power bargaining tactics;
(b) The ability of the employer concerned to pay the recommended increases, particularly in the public sector;
(c) How difficulties in measuring productivity can be taken into account: the seemingly obvious statement that employees of an organization with low performance levels should earn less than those in organizations with high levels of productivity is, in fact, fraught with practical difficulties of measurement.

Government intervention

There have always been exceptions to the principle of complete freedom of action on the part of employers and unions in wage negotiations. The need for some form of compulsory control during wartime was obvious, of course, but apart from this there has been the need to afford extra protection to less well organized groups of employees. The best known examples in practice are wages councils,* the Employment Protection Act 1975, and Fair Wages Resolutions. The Government's own role as an employer, directly or indirectly, of nearly a quarter of the total working population also has an obvious influence on policies concerning wages and conditions.

*At the time of writing, the Government is considering legislation to abolish wages councils.

Wages councils

An estimated 2.7 million workers in Great Britain have their conditions determined by agreements which are enforceable at law, rather than being based on the voluntary acceptance of collective bargains. Examples of the types of workers covered are: baking, boot and shoe repairing, hairdressing, laundry workers, milk distribution, tailoring, the retail food trade, road haulage, and toy manufacture. Regulations affecting the wages and conditions of all these workers are decided by wages councils, the activities of which are provided for mainly by the Wages Council Act 1959, which consolidated a large amount of previous legislation. The other significant statute is the Agricultural Wages Act 1948, covering some 800,000 agricultural workers.

The constitution of a wages council allows for equal numbers of members representing employers and workers, together with not more than three independent members (often drawn from universities and the legal profession): the Minister usually appoints one of these three as chairperson. In fact, the Minister appoints all the members of wages councils, bearing in mind the main types of establishment and classes of workers affected and the principal centres in which they are employed. Since the Employment Protection Act 1975, council's powers have been extended to include fixing minimum wages, holidays, holiday pay, and all other conditions of employment in the industries to which they relate.

Wage regulation proposals must be published in the *London Gazette* and details must be sent to every employer affected. In turn, employers must exhibit the proposals so that workers can read them. Employers or workers may then make representations to their wages council within fourteen days and, after considering these, the council will submit its proposals with such amendments as it thinks fit to the Minister. The Minister will then either make a wages regulation order to give the proposals legal effect, or refer them back to the council for reconsideration as a whole; the Minister cannot reject or amend the proposals submitted. Wages regulation orders made by the Minister to give effect to the proposals of wages councils are issued as statutory instruments, and wages paid to workers must not be less than the minimum fixed by these orders. Employers must keep records of payments of wages for three years and these must be made available to the Wages Inspectorate.

The objectives of the twenty-six wages councils currently operating are historically those of protecting unorganized workers and promoting collective bargaining. About three-quarters of the employees covered are women and ethnic minorities, with part-time workers and home workers (mainly women) also substantially represented.

From July 1986 major changes came into effect – removing all young people under 21 (some half million) from statutory wages regulations, and confining wages councils to setting only a single minimum hourly rate and a single overtime rate. The Government's view was that such changes would lead to a significant increase in job opportunities: for it was claimed that the previous system inhibited the creation of more jobs, as it was simply not economic for employers to offer young people jobs at the wages required.

Having given due notice of these changes however, the Government had to face a political rebuff from the International Labour Organization which pointed out that almost all countries in the world now operate minimum wages systems and none excludes young workers.

In a review* of the consequences of abolishing six wages councils, researchers in Cambridge University's Department of Applied Economics found that underpayment of subsequent national wage agreements was concentrated among female workers. Their conclusion was that the most important effect of abolition was to increase the size of the unregulated sector and therefore the potential for low pay. Since these harmful effects occurred in industries where it was thought that minimum wage regulation had been superseded by binding voluntary collective bargaining arrangements, the effects of abolishing the whole wages council system, including that operating in industries where the level of union membership is insignificant, would likely be very severe. Clearly there should continue to be legal protection for those at the weakest end of the labour market. Statutory minimum wage-fixing machinery should be retained, although perhaps with greater responsibility given to the parties negotiating the agreements and a reduced role for the independents.

The Employment Protection Act 1975

Whether wages and conditions are settled by collective bargaining or by regulations issued by wages councils, the Government has given workers an extra measure of protection by the Employment Protection Act 1975, the provisions of which enable a trade union or an employers' association to make a claim to ACAS that an employer is observing terms and conditions of employment which are less favourable than the recognized negotiated terms and conditions for the trade or industry. If there are no such terms and conditions, a union or an employers' association may claim that an employer is observing terms

Industrial Market Structure, Industrial Organisation and Low Pay, Christine Craig *et al*, Cambridge University Press, 1982.

and conditions of employment less favourable than the general level in the same trade or industry in the district. ACAS may settle the claim by conciliation, but if this fails the claim can be referred to the Central Arbitration Committee which may make an award.

The Government as an employer

The Government itself employs a very large labour force — some 4 million people working in the public sector as civil servants, local authority employees, or for the nationalized industries and other public authorities: i.e. more than 20 per cent of the total labour force. The basic problem is that most of the work is in 'non-productive' services, with inflexible wage rates which often compare unfavourably with those in private industry. The Government has the problem of reconciling its role as the employer of large numbers of workers with its wider responsibilities not to allow wage increases which might harm the national economy. The public sector has features which make it relatively easy to control wages: the Government clearly has the necessary authority as far as its own employees are concerned, and the wage negotiating machineries for many public services are entirely centralized and uniform.

Recent attempts at incomes policies under Conservative governments have accepted the difficulties of controlling pay in private industry and commerce, and indeed the undesirability of trying to do so. Controls accordingly have been confined to the public sector, serving as examples for the private sector to follow, with government exhortation to spur them on but not to force them. The fact remains that the attempts to effect incomes policies in 1970–2, 1972–4 and 1975–9 were all destroyed in the end by strikes in the public sector; the last, for example, during the 'winter of discontent' when unions in a number of public services imposed selective strikes until the government gave way with a series of settlements which shattered that particular attempt at operating an incomes policy (and soon afterwards resulted in its electoral defeat).

The current government favours a policy permitting free collective bargaining, subject to monetarist fiscal controls which include cash limits in the public sector, and insists that the nation's economic difficulties arising from inflationary pressures will never be solved unless wage increases are restricted to what can be afforded and that incomes should not be allowed to rise on average faster than the average increase in national productivity and economic growth. Guidelines have been laid down annually for public sector pay increases within the cash limits imposed on the different services' budgets. Beyond doubt the level of pay settlements in private industry has diminished sharply in recent years — but whether as the result of government policy or the rapid rise in unemployment is open to debate.

One approach, often regarded as the most likely to succeed, was based on the concept of comparability, whereby public sector unions professed that they would be satisfied if the pay of their members was set by comparison with that of other workers. This was the basis on which the Civil Service pay research unit operated for many years, with enviable results in the eyes of staff working in public services other than the Civil Service. General acceptance of the concept was founded in the fact that there were in existence: the Civil Service system, including separate arrangements for industrial civil servants; three review bodies — for doctors and dentists, for the armed forces, and for the 'top salaries' group; and arrangements whereby the pay of policemen and firemen, having been set at an appropriate level, should be adjusted annually in line with average earnings.

The whole question of government control in this area remains topical. Solving the problems of unemployment and achieving an object of rising living standards without inflation requires steady economic expansion, careful price scrutiny, fiscal and social service measures designed to protect people with low or fixed incomes, measures to ensure the public accountability of private firms with significant market power, and broad agreement with the unions for the planned growth of incomes. A policy based on these factors carries conviction, because it clearly operates to the benefit of the majority of the population.

The last formal incomes policy ended in 1979, followed therefore by the longest period in twenty years when the private sector has been free to negotiate changes in payment systems. Some companies claim to have used this freedom to manage their payment systems so that these can contribute to organizational goals rather than simply respond to pressures.

The integration of pay structures, initially embracing all staff groups or all manual workers, but latterly to bring both together, requires the wider use of analytical rather than whole-job systems of job evaluation. The increasing impact of the equal pay for work of equal value regulations has had a similar impact on the spread and type of job evaluation systems. Demands for greater flexibility have encouraged broader gradings, and the need for less bureaucratic impediments has fostered a move towards fewer factors in job evaluation systems. The general trend for relating pay to performance and results, together with a greater concern for individual rather than collective recognition, has meant more emphasis in ways of assessing contributions. Reliance on flat rates and on service-related incremental scales are being challenged both by those who see such systems as inhibiting any drive for improved results and also by employees seeking more recognition for their personal efforts. The long-running movement towards single staff status, linked to the wider use of new, pace-setting technology, also has implications for remuneration systems which will avoid overtime pay.

The Equal Pay Act and the Sex Discrimination Act

The perennial controversy about equal pay and conditions for men and women doing the same jobs was statutorily resolved by the Equal Pay Act 1970, through its three main provisions:

Section 1 (4) requires pay to be equal where it can be shown that a woman's work is the same or broadly similar to the work of a man in the same employment;
Section 2 (5) refers to job evaluation: jobs normally done by both men and women must be evaluated by the same criteria, and must not be given different ratings because of the sex of the workers concerned;
Section 3 refers to collective agreements; if these contain discriminatory clauses, they may be reported to the Industrial Court (now the Central Arbitration Board) which is given power to amend them.

Individual men and women who believe they have a right to equal treatment under the provisions of the Act and whose employer does not agree with them can apply to an industrial tribunal for a decision. Legislation of this nature is one thing, however, but does it get to the root of discrimination against women in employment? Feminists have always claimed that women's pay is low because the male and female labour markets are separate, the latter mainly confined to lower-paid jobs. If that analysis is correct, the position can only be improved fundamentally by allowing women to take jobs hitherto reserved for men. Employers' attitudes and prejudices thus remain the chief obstacles to real progress.

The problems of the training and maximum utilization of the married woman returning to work when her children are old enough need to be dealt with (see Chapter 7). It is believed that such employees are often absent and that their wastage rate is high, but research shows that, as the level of women's employment rises, so their reliability and stability increase: in other words, the better the job, the greater are the efforts made to hang on to it.

In the long term, equal pay offers considerable potential economic gains. Faced with higher labour costs, employers will seek to make better use of women at work. The integration of the male and female labour markets should, in turn, have a double benefit: women will produce work of higher value than at present, and their influx into new occupations will ease any existing shortages of manpower, which is a root cause of wages drift.

The whole question of discriminating against women – not only in employment and training, but in education, housing, the provision of goods, services and facilities, and advertising – was tackled in the Sex Discrimination Act 1975. This makes it unlawful to discriminate on grounds of sex or marriage as regards recruitment or opportunities for training or promotion, or in actions which may be detrimental to employees such as short-time working or dismissals. The only exceptions are the clergy, armed forces*, and cases where a person's sex can be shown to be a genuine occupational qualification for a particular job.

Complaints are heard by industrial tribunals after initial consideration by officers of the independent Advisory, Conciliation and Arbitration Service, who try to help the parties reach a settlement. A tribunal, satisfied that unlawful discrimination has occurred, can award compensation or recommend a particular course of action. If the discrimination is in a general form, then the case may be forwarded to the Equal Opportunities Commission (EOC) for consideration. The main functions of the EOC are: to investigate areas covered by the Act and to take action to eliminate unlawful practices; to assist and represent individual complainants in appropriate cases; to conduct enquiries into matters affecting the relative positions and opportunities of the sexes; and to conduct research and take action to educate and persuade public opinion. When an unlawful practice is disclosed, the Commission has the power to issue 'non-discriminatory notices' which can, if breached, be enforced through the civil court. It can also seek a general injunction, in the public interest, dealing with unlawful discriminatory practices.

Further legal requirements were added to this area by the Sex Discrimination Act 1986, in particular, provisions which effectively outlaw differential retirement ages for men and women. It is now unlawful discrimination to dismiss a woman on grounds of age when men in comparable circumstances would not have been dismissed. In effect, organizations have had to harmonize the retirement ages of men and women: e.g. ICI and the Prudential Corporation have done so at the ages of 62 and 60 respectively. Other important aspects of the Act

---

*The Synod of the Church of England has recently voted in favour of the ordination of women; the armed forces' rules are being changed or relaxed in practice.

included Sections 7 and 8 which provided for the removal of a variety of hours-of-work restrictions which had hitherto been placed on women and young persons, and this was followed up in the Employment Act 1989.

Good equal opportunities practice is about the sort of culture and ethos nurtured in British industry, commerce and public service, and its application depends on a number of factors:

- Employers should not assume that direct, basic and unsubtle discrimination is not happening in their organizations.
- They must use effective public relations and outreach methods.
- Look thoroughly at their selection processes and make sure they are working fairly and efficiently to bring through candidates who are really suitable.
- Train all staff who participate in the recruitment and selection process.
- Use training and development programmes so that those with otherwise full abilities and potential can catch up on the skills and qualifications needed.
- Recognize the key role of positive action/developmental training for all staff at all levels.
- Be aware of the need for grievances and particularly cases of racial abuse and harassment to be dealt with firmly and sensitively.
- Recognize the need for objective performance setting and measurement.
- Give a strong lead from the top.

13
Wages and salaries – the individual and productivity

Within the framework of government policy and national wage agreements signed by employers' federations and trade unions, each individual organization has to work out its own salvation. Its personnel manager will be expected to advise on how best to build up a wages structure which must, primarily, be attractive enough to ensure the recruitment and retention of a labour force of the right size and quality to meet the circumstances in which production is carried on. It will need to offer financial incentives to stimulate improvements in performance. Its own brand of personnel policy and attitudes towards human relations will also have an effect on remuneration, and it will have to take into account local representations on such matters as differentials. There is no one 'best' pay system capable of universal application for the benefit of all, and because of the difficulties involved, it is imperative that pay should always be regarded as a most important aspect of management policy. One thing is certain – that inefficiency will follow from a poor wages system, even though the opposite cannot be proved. Highly paid executives may regard the minor anomalies of a complex pay structure in a large organization as trivial in the extreme; but the workers affected will see them simply as examples of unfairness, and their irritation will inevitably strain industrial relations.

By definition, managers should be agents of innovation, constantly seeking improvements in the use of production facilities for their organization to survive in an era of constantly rising costs. In fact, most managers feel themselves to be prisoners of their wages structures – for every change presents the unions with negotiating opportunities and confirms the benefits of intransigence. There may be many other serious defects in any particular wages structure: informal limits on work-efforts may hinder productivity; methods changes may be negotiated and subsequently forgotten; 'wages drift' realizes earnings over and above productivity agreements; supervisors become frustrated at the lack of discipline and corruption of work standards; unnecessary overtime is 'engineered'; senior managers have illusions about incentive schemes which they believe encourage high effort, but which supervisors know have long since been out-manoeuvred. The personnel specialist's role in such situations must in effect be to return to first principles and then consider all relevant details in advising on a wages and salaries system appropriate to his/her own organization.

Differentials

All large employers have established ranges of wages and salaries and use a variety of more or less scientific methods to calculate the relative worth of the complete list of jobs from shop-floor employees to senior executives. Unfortunately, in practice the usefulness of this evaluation of *differentials* is marred by a number of factors, especially where local scarcities of certain skills distort wage scales and bring about a labour auction.

Even when these problems have been tackled, the maintenance of differentials remains one of the most common sources of industrial strife, and emphasizes the need to consult personnel managers, in their role as administrators of wage agreements, before any variations are made in rates of pay. The best intentioned actions by management, such as giving a slightly higher rate to reward the particularly good work of one small section of workers, can have the most far-reaching consequences. For as soon as the wages of that group are raised, the differential between their pay and every other group's pay is destroyed. There will inevitably be a clamour for these differentials to be restored, not by removing this recent rise, but by adding it on to all employees' wages. If this happens in a federated company, then its rates of pay will become higher than those of other firms, and a chain reaction will exert pressure on the federation for a general increase in wage rates. Thus a rise of a couple of pence an hour for a handful of workers in an obscure factory could result in a nationwide claim throughout that industry involving millions of pounds. For this reason it is essential that any alterations in rates of pay should be made only after due process of negotiation, and that any variations should be permitted only within the framework of existing agreements.

Incentives

These agreements do not preclude the many forms of *incentives* which are commonly offered to stimulate production, nor the techniques of *job evaluation* and *merit-rating* which are widely used to try to distinguish between individual effort.

In an industrial setting, incentives are anything which cause people to work harder, urging them to some form of action and at the same time satisfying their subjective desires. The worker's main interest is earning more money, while management is concerned with reducing costs: it is therefore to both their advantages for the best conditions for work to be established, leading to more output, less effort, higher earnings, and lower costs. In this way incentives can achieve cumulative benefits, increasing efficiency which thus makes better incentives possible.

On the practical side, payments made under incentive schemes must stand up to certain tests. In the first place, workers must be satisfied that the output required is within their capacity, that they are being offered a just rate for the job, and that proper skill differentials are being maintained. Once time and output factors have been determined, management must not subsequently reduce the rate paid unreasonably. Payments must be easy to calculate so that workers can know how much they have earned up to a given moment. Any incentive scheme must offer an adequate income, taking into account abnormal conditions outside workers' control, and in some cases minimum earnings are stipulated.

The main types of financial incentives are:

1 Flat payments added to a basic wage or salary, such as annual or cost-of-living bonuses and profit-sharing schemes.
2 Payments based on rate-fixing – the work is measured and a price per piece or time allowed for the work is settled by negotiation, usually between local management and shop stewards. Both workers and management may benefit directly from the cost saving which results from increased effort, as in the Halsey and Rowan schemes.
3 Geared incentive schemes – used where the volume of work

fluctuates and earnings need to be related to average output. Bonus payments may start at a low level of output, but tail off at higher outputs, in order to stabilize workers' earnings.

4 Accurate work-measured schemes – the normal piecework concept where payment is directly proportionate to additional effort and higher output; this means that the work content of jobs must be measured beforehand, and methods and conditions must be standardized. Gangs or groups of workers, as well as individuals, may be rewarded in this way, earnings being determined by dividing total production bonuses between the members on an agreed basis. (Operators of steel melting furnaces may use this method, for example.) A variation of this type of payment is the commission earned by many salespeople, based on turnover or sales; this, too, may be paid to individuals or on a group basis, and in some cases represents a very high proportion of total income.

5 Lieu bonuses – these are sometimes paid in working situations where additional payments cannot be linked directly with production: they are, in effect, payments to compensate those workers whose jobs do not allow them to earn production bonuses, such as men employed on machine maintenance work.

6 Measured day work and high day rates – both depend on the initial calculation of the amount of work expected to be done in a normal eight-hour day and agreement on this through joint consultation. Under measured day work, employees are paid time rates, plus a bonus awarded so long as they maintain the agreed level of output. The high day rate method simply means that they receive a high time rate so long as they keep up the standard of output agreed.

Incentive schemes are intended to stimulate improved productivity, but their introduction is often only one feature of a series of complex organizational changes taking place at the same time, and it is quite impossible to isolate the effects of the changed pay structure in itself. Indeed this had led many progressive firms to suspect the effectiveness of piecerates, and they are abandoning them in favour of high time rates or measured day work linked with sophisticated work study and job evaluation techniques.

The advantages claimed for piecerates are:

1 They may contribute in part towards solving the problems of raising productivity.

2 The pace of work is maintained with the minimum of supervision.

3 To a large extent workers can set their own pace, choosing when to speed up and when to ease off.

4 Workers on piecerates can be relied on to keep the flow of raw materials moving steadily, so it need no longer worry management.

But there are drawbacks as well:

1 It does not automatically follow that people on piecerates work as hard as they can, for group pressures often impose limits on output.
2 In practice, piecerate systems are often not settled objectively, but are calculated on an assessment of what an acceptable weekly wage packet would be; some systems are so complex that they take up far too much management time, spent in manipulating jobs so that all employees receive reasonable wages.
3 New rates are subject to such compromises, in the attempt to avoid friction, that exceptionally high earnings result once workers see how they can gain from the new system; inequalities of pay between departments often emerge in this way, too, making it difficult to transfer labour within the workplace.
4 Piecerates encourage wages drift, because even when higher rates can be justified in terms of increased productivity, they often result in claims from time workers who want the previous differentials to be restored.
5 There is a fundamental concern that piecerates undermine trust, reflecting management's lack of confidence in their employees' willingness to work, and, indeed, their own inability to get them to work.

This last criticism is particularly telling since many large organizations have introduced such methods as measured day work to try to find an alternative to the traditional piecework. But, although management may undertake the most careful preparations of such schemes, the fact remains that they have to be put into effect by first-line supervisors. Throughout British industry, it seems that only a small proportion of these supervisors possess the background training and qualities to meet the additional leadership demands made by this new situation and which are now required in large measure to motivate the workers under their control. Piecework rates must therefore be expected to continue to play a major role in wage determination.

At the same time, experience suggests that measured day work may provide a greater incentive to effort than time rate payments and prove less of a stimulus to conflict than payment by results. The OME report *Measured Daywork** concluded that this system of payment helps both employers and workers to meet their objectives. Employers can

*Office of Manpower Economics (HMSO, 1973).

forecast both output and costs better, will find more flexibility in manning, fewer sectional disputes, and easier maintenance of quality. Workers can rely on stable incomes, especially when employers agree to maintain levels of pay during delays and breakdowns, and can look forward to greater opportunities for job enlargement and enrichment. Even the economy at large will benefit through a more structured wage system, less wage drift, increased performance, and fewer disputes.

These advantages will accrue, however, only if certain dangers are guarded against. Pay relativities tend to be highlighted by measured day work and can lead to pressure for comparability-based pay claims. There is also a risk that effort and performance may drift downwards unless the scheme is well maintained. So measured day work, like any other pay system, can degenerate. For it to be successful, managers must maintain and use control data, review work standards periodically, and be aware of the continual need to improve the ways they employ people.

Job evaluation

Job evaluation is a technique of assessing the worth of each job in comparison with all others throughout an organization. Job contents are fully described, and a variety of methods may then be used to enable one to be compared with another. These include 'job ranking', 'job classification', 'points rating', and 'factor comparisons' – each resulting in a progressively more detailed analysis of jobs as such, without regard to the abilities of the persons doing them. The biggest problem in job evaluation is that of counter-balancing the personal judgements of the departmental heads who make the assessments; although jobs, not people, are being studied, friendliness towards or dislike of particular subordinates may well play a part. Again, trade unions are very interested in payment differentials between jobs, and may exert such pressure that the results of systematic assessments become distorted. Even so, it is sensible to allow full negotiations on job evaluation to take place, as a positive step towards ensuring confidence in the scheme among those employees affected.

Thus job evaluation (JE) is primarily about investigating common characteristics of jobs and using this information as a basis for more systematically identifying those jobs which are more demanding as regards those characteristics than other jobs. The traditional methods for processing JE are severely handicapped, however, because of a lack of appropriate analytical tools. In most organizations JE means painstakingly assembling large quantities of detailed data about each job, resulting in a single piece of information (*viz* a grading for the job concerned). In practice this approach has become a bye-word for suspicion among those involved: too often it involves overstating the real requirements of the job, knowing this statement will be 'beaten back' by the grading committee — a guerilla mentality which really has little place in improving industrial relations or the general level of productive endeavour.* Line managers and employees, whose jobs are evaluated and who have to live with the results, spend considerable amounts of time, worry and effort preparing their submissions; personnel managers and other senior staff take just as long in debate and then pass judgements which, even when well received, do little to enlighten the recipients as to the organizational or business logic underlying the result.

A solution must be found which uses people's time more effectively and delivers more meaningful information to those who need it. Most importantly the solution must appear as an attractive aid to management, to help it to design and monitor jobs which organized work appropriately. During the past decade new tools have been developed to assist in this process, some concerned with making existing JE systems work more quickly, some with improving the consistency of evaluations (thus increasing the 'felt-fairness' of the process among end-users), still others with making the whole process more understandable and acceptable to those affected.

Encompassing all these objectives a solution has been designed using three common tools:

First — a rigorous, structured approach to analysing jobs in accordance with agreed corporate values; typically, after consultation with different parts of the organization, a job analysis questionnaire (JAQ) is constructed. This may contain up to fifty questions, focusing on every significant issue (in the view of those involved) relevant to assessing the relative value of jobs. The same JAQ should then be used to cover all jobs throughout the organization and, with some initial assistance from trained job analysts, it may be completed directly by line managers and job holders. The JAQ differs from the traditional job description in one important way — there is no mention at all of the specific activities carried out by the job holder. This enables the approach to focus on demand-side issues which are common to all jobs (for example, external contacts, internal contacts) and hence can be used directly as a basis for assessment, rather than on the detailed tasks of each employee, which are ever-changing and are therefore not a suitable basis for rigorous comparison. The

JE: a modern-day 'genie' for management information, Steve Spencer, *Employment Gazette*, June 1990, page 306.

immediate advantages of the JAQ are that it is generally easier to complete than writing a job description and that it helps to increase the credibility of the process by making the criteria used to compare jobs explicit and understandable to end-users. The less obvious benefits, in terms of information quality, are that data are captured about jobs in a common format, leading to the formation of a jobs database which can be used for in-depth analysis of the demand side of the labour equation.

The second analytical tool uses the common format to apply statistical analysis to explain the nature and strength of the relationships between the data components assembled and hence measure the relative size or value of each job. Using a carefully controlled sample of representative jobs, mathematical models can be designed to calculate very accurately the score of a job, based solely on the data supplied from the JAQ. This set of techniques (including independent verification) enables most sources of inconsistency to be removed from JE, and the more rigorous assessment process means that those who conduct the evaluations can do so much more efficiently, by reviewing and approving results, rather than pondering separately over all the detailed information.

The third significant tool in the process is the personal computer (PC). In contrast to a decade ago, when the deliberations of grading committees often meant long delays in reaching decisions, the PC takes over the storage, analysis and management of data and, when programmed with the mathematical evaluation and validation models mentioned above, enables the whole process of evaluating, checking and scoring a job to be carried out in a few minutes. Conventional evaluation by an experienced evaluator relies on him/her having a 'mental algorithm' through which he/she processes information from a job description to yield an evaluation judgement ('given this balance of facts and practice in the past, that means a rating of x against this factor or criterion') in a points factor based plan. At the end of the process a job score is produced. Computerized systems essentially try to reproduce this process using expert systems and mathematical algorithms.

Evaluating jobs more accurately and speedily may, in fact, be only the first stage in a more ambitious scheme for creating truly valuable information about the demand side of organizations' work. The long-term success of businesses depends primarily on their ability to optimize the use of their human resources — to ensure that all employees are challenged, but not overstretched, by their work; to identify the need for training and development where and when it is required; and to plan for succession and career development to accommodate the future needs of both the business and its workforce.

Such decisions cannot all be made centrally: a balance must be achieved between corporate consistency and standardization, on the one hand, and sensitivity to local needs and competitive advantage on the other. The tools and techniques of the more recent JE systems are providing the means for deciding how much usable management information can be unleashed to these ends.

Management also has planning responsibilities for ensuring that the organization's future demand for human resources is as closely matched as possible. A computer-based JE process can be used as a true expert system to enable users to obtain detailed feedback on design issues, involving individual jobs and organizational structures, and the identification and prioritization of options for moving or replacing the holders of specific jobs. This career and succession planning module enables the user to search the database for other positions which may provide a variety of types of career move for any given job holder. The advantage of such an approach is that it enables totally objective role-related criteria to be used to plan employees' movements throughout the organization rather than basing these decisions on supply-side characteristics of the individuals themselves. Indeed roles can be shaped to provide appropriate challenges and support mechanisms, and the expectation of career progress can be more clearly communicated to those within the target population.

More powerful software is now being designed better to link data about the demand-side aspects of jobs to performance/potential assessment techniques such as competency analysis — to aid job/person matching, resourcing, and the development of more specific and effective training programmes. Macro-level systems may also be created to integrate the analysis of organizational structures, corporate culture and business performance as a top management aid to designing and managing organizations more effectively in the long-term.

Acquisition of skills and competencies can successfully drive pay systems for groups of employees whose roles are broadly similar, and demonstration of competencies can be a highly effective performance measure in both flexible and more traditional organizations. In both cases considerable rigour is needed in developing such contribution-based approaches, and line managers require higher levels of skills themselves to manage these complementary processes. But a method of measuring and valuing the relative importance of organizational roles is still required as the fundamental determinant of relativities on which individual, market and performance factors can be built: the need for defensible pay decisions will always be with us.

A development of some importance to job evaluation was the equal value amendment to the Equal Pay Act which enables any woman to claim equal pay with any man (and vice versa) if she believes her work is equally demanding under such factors as effort, skill and decision-making. Previously a claim could only be made where the claimant's work was either the same or broadly similar to that of the comparator or where the work of both had been rated as equivalent under a common job evaluation scheme. It follows, of course, that an employer can seek to have an equal value claim set aside where the work of the two employees cited has been rated differently under a common job evaluation scheme.

Another consideration is the impact of new technology and the tendency for what once were very different office and shop floor jobs to become more similar. Pressure on job evaluation results, for example when a production job, which in the past involved hands-on control of machinery, now relies on operating a computer terminal – the comparison with office clerical tasks is obvious.

The third major influence is the trend towards harmonization – the move to single status for groups of employees traditionally operating under different terms and conditions and where pay and benefit levels have been determined on different bases. All parties must agree the acceptability of the job evaluation methodology to be used (not the easiest of goals in a multi-union situation). Harmonization and the requirement for flexibility go hand in hand – so the impact on blurring established job boundaries is substantial. The range of factor choice and weightings must be such as to ensure fair relative measurement of all jobs covered. Above all, changes in attitude are essential.

Merit-rating

Merit-rating attempts to recognize and reward the personal abilities that individuals bring to their jobs, measured by the extent to which their output or the quality of their work exceeds the minimum that can reasonably be expected for their basic rate of pay. This definition may appear straightforward, but many problems have to be solved when trying to put a merit-rating system into practice. First, the desirable qualities relating to each job and their relative importance have to be decided, so that the right weight can be attached to each. The actual method of rating must be settled, and a formula devised for converting the ratings into cash payments. Policy about the duration of a merit award must also be determined beforehand – is it to be permanent, or reviewed from time to time? If the latter, what procedure of warnings or appeals must be created to cover the possible removal of merit awards?

Clearly any scheme will stand or fall on the fairness and consistency of the ratings. As with job evaluation, the personal attitudes of departmental heads need to be carefully guarded against. Many tend to be overgenerous in their attempts to get as much money as possible for their subordinates; others are unperceptive enough to hope that top management will think that a department holding a large number of merit awards must necessarily be efficient, thus redounding to their own credit. The basic trouble, of course, is that the assessments asked for concern factors which have to be judged subjectively, so that there are likely to considerable differences in the standards of assessment between departmental heads. These can only be prevented by a rigorous training programme to try to ensure that they all understand the scheme in the same way.

Whether such training can also overcome the other criticisms levelled at merit-rating is another matter. These allege that any system of award based entirely on the personal opinion of the boss is bound to cause friction, since it is wide open to charges of favouritism; and that, in any event, length of service will be the factor uppermost in supervisors' minds when considering the awards. These points can only be refuted by recording that, on the other hand, many managers and personnel specialists clearly see merit-rating as an incentive and a means of rewarding sound all-round performance, both in terms of immediate cash payments and as an indicator for future promotion.

Suggestion schemes

Another type of financial incentive directly linked with improved performance is the suggestion scheme, now operated in a very large number of organizations up and down the country. Suggestion schemes have existed in one form or another for over a century, and indeed appear to have been revitalized during the 1980s. The Industrial Society and the UK Association of Suggestion Schemes know of at least 500 employers which operate them: 103 of these, replying to a questionnaire* in 1988 covered 1,083,000 employees, claimed total savings of £16 m during the previous year, with an average saving of £1250 for each suggestion adopted.

In common with the principles of joint consultation and joint production committees, suggestion schemes operate on the theory that the boss cannot know everything about work processes, that workers are experts in their own fields, that their detailed knowledge

Employment Gazette, August 1990, page 391.

of the jobs and operations performed in their departments is of great value, and that they have some desire to share actively in the success of their organization. A *suggestion scheme*, then, is a type of incentive designed to stimulate this particular motivation and desire on the part of the workers, by offering them payments or prizes to encourage their ideas on improving efficiency.

The sort of ideas required can generally be summed up as:

1 Improving the quality of any product.
2 Improving production, by economy in materials, avoidance of waste, better methods, or modified designs.
3 Improving processes or general workshop procedure.
4 Improving safety and welfare of employees.
5 Suggestions for new products.

The initial problem to be overcome when launching a suggestion scheme is the reluctance of people to put forward their ideas. This may be due to a variety of real or imagined reasons: fear of making fools of themselves in their mates' eyes; fear that the foreman may interpret any suggestions as implied criticisms of his own efforts and retaliate in some way; fear that ideas may be rejected, then filed away and introduced later without recognition or reward; fear that they will lose patent rights on inventions by disclosing them to the company.

The mechanics of the scheme must therefore be designed to overcome these fears. In the first place, arrangements can be made for all suggestions to remain anonymous (except to the administrator of the scheme) until after they have been fully considered, so that neither an employee's mates nor his/her supervisor need know about the idea. This can easily be done by providing suggestion forms with perforated sections, but numbered on each part. Suggesters write their idea on the middle section and sign the bottom half; they post the suggestion, after tearing off the top slip for their own record. The secretary of the scheme then tears off the bottom section, for his/her reference, which leaves the suggestion part to be considered by the panel of judges: only after they have reached a decision may they be told the identity of the person concerned, when the secretary brings the two parts of the form together again. Distrust of the scheme, shown by the fear that rejected ideas will be used later, can be dispelled by dealing quickly and scrupulously with all suggestions, and, above all, by giving the fullest reasons to suggesters whose ideas are turned down. Strictly speaking, inventions made on a company's premises, using its equipment and in its time, are that company's property; but enlightened employers nowadays take out joint patents with the employee concerned and thus safeguard his/her interests as well as their own.

Suggestions should be considered by a panel of people, possibly a section of the Joint Production Committee, with representatives of both management and workers. They should be able to call on whatever technical advice may be necessary to evaluate a suggestion. A decision should be reached as soon as possible, together with an assessment of how large an award should be given to the suggester. The chairperson of the panel therefore needs to be an executive sufficiently senior to pledge the company's credit in this respect.

Wherever possible, the size of the payment should be related to the savings as a result of the suggestion, either as a lump sum or as a percentage of these savings. Promotion, wages increases, royalties on sales – these are other established methods of rewarding the person with ideas. Payments are often made, too, for the 'good try' – the idea which is rejected for valid reasons but where it is obvious that suggesters have put considerable thought, effort, and time into formulating their ideas.

It is usual for a rule to be made about the eligibility of staff for awards. In some cases all are included, but many schemes allow only the lower-graded workers to take part, on the grounds that thinking up improvements is part of the supervisor's or manager's normal job. When the scheme is so restricted, to perhaps the less articulate part of the labour force, it is important to offer help in writing up suggestions or drawing any diagrams needed to explain them.

Finally, if a suggestion scheme is to have permanent impact, it must be given continuous publicity, backed by obvious enthusiasm from top management. Methods used might include:

1 *Poster publicity*, bright and arresting, and frequently changed. (Over-humorous examples do not produce the most creative results.)
2 *Pay-packet enclosures* – making sure that employees are reminded of the scheme at regular intervals, in a manner that gives them the chance to read at leisure what the scheme has to offer.
3 *A departmental suggestions league* – a prestige competition between departments, with additional awards or a trophy given to the department that scores the highest total of successful suggestions.
4 *Directors' special awards* – given annually to the best suggestions put forward, in addition to the normal award already made. These could be substantial amounts in outstanding cases and would have great publicity value as reminders of the benefits that might come to anyone from taking part in the suggestions scheme.

The main requirements for a successful suggestions scheme can thus be summarized as – good publicity, worthwhile awards, and, above all, swift and fair treatment. All suggestions should be acknowledged immediately, and the actual results announced within a few weeks. Sometimes delays are unavoidable if prolonged tests have to be carried out; the suggester should be kept informed of these. Nothing will discredit a suggestions scheme as much as unnecessary delays or inadequate explanation of what is happening about the suggestions submitted.

Profit-sharing

Profit-sharing schemes fall mainly into four broad types: Inland Revenue approved profit-sharing, with a proportion of profits allocated to employees and the shares held in trust; approved save-as-you-earn schemes, based on savings contracts with the option to purchase shares at the end; various forms of partnership; and executive share option schemes, by definition with only a partial coverage of employees.

Such arrangements confer on labour a share of the success of a business and must therefore, in the first place, be regarded as incentives to greater output. But they are also obviously intended to have a psychological impact on employees in terms of loyalty, thrift, and a sense of security, which in turn can help build up the reputation of the organization as a good employer. There are other objectives, such as the preservation of the spirit of capitalism and the linking of earnings with the prosperity of the business cycle – but these seem too remote and academic to make much impression on the average employee.

The theoretical advantages of this type of incentive are: that it stimulates a greater collective interest on the part of all employees, from senior managers to shopfloor workers; that everyone becomes most conscious of the need for economy and prevention of materials wastage; that suggestion schemes become much more realistic as a means of improving efficiency; and that costs of labour turnover are greatly reduced, because people establish a much closer personal link with the organization. Unfortunately, these theoretical advantages are opposed by several practical disadvantages. The profit share-out is often so small or so long in coming that it loses its impact as an incentive, and, in any case, the efficient worker is no better off than the inefficient. Workers have considerable suspicions that their employer may be getting proportionately more than they are; accounts are difficult for them to understand, so that they become uneasy when profits are low; above all, they are conscious that profits are influenced by factors outside their control. Trade unions generally oppose profit-sharing schemes for two reasons; first, that dissension is caused between workers when, as is often the case, some are included in the arrangements and others left out; second, they fear that the underlying purpose is to win workers over to management's point of view. Not that this is necessarily so, for even shareholders sometimes complain about such schemes, particularly that workers share in the profits but suffer nothing when there are losses.

Despite these doubts, however, employee share ownership programmes (ESOPs) are now among the more fashionable ways of providing employee participation and motivation. Since the Finance Act 1978 and further tax concessions granted in 1984 and 1985, some 3000 approved employee share schemes have been submitted to the Department of Inland Revenue. Hitherto share ownership has mainly been confined to executive staff, but now over 1.5 million people in the UK own shares in the company they work for, with every indication that this figure is likely to grow rapidly in the near future.

Salaries

One of the distinguishing features of 'staff status' is the receipt of salaries rather than wages. A salary is normally expressed in terms of an annual figure, and is paid monthly by cheque or transfer into a bank account, whereas wages are paid weekly in cash. Earnings tend to remain steady, month by month, since salaried staff are seldom paid for overtime nor under any piecerate system. In private industry, most salaries are a matter of private negotiation between the employer and the man/woman concerned, although there has been a rapid growth in recent years in white-collar unionism, as executive and professional staff strove to restore differentials that existed in the past between their earnings and those of manual workers. The Association of Scientific, Technical and Managerial Staffs under Clive Jenkins's leadership was a case in point, with draughtsmen, for example, being urged not to accept jobs for salaries less than the recognized scales.

There are many differences in pay policy between staff and manual workers. Salary scales tend to be much more progressive, not stopping at the age of twenty-one as for craftsmen, so that salary increases act as incentives in place of production bonuses. Rate-for-age scales apply in many professions, sometimes rising until the age of thirty.

In most of the public services, salaries increase by fixed annual increments, which are often not as large as individuals may receive in private industry. It would be wrong, however, to infer from this that comparable jobs are better paid in the private than the public sector; there may be some temporary lagging behind from time to time, but periodic negotiations sometimes result in quite dramatic boosts for the scales themselves. Nevertheless, there are difficulties in the application of fixed scales and increments: when people reach the top of their scale they have no prospect of any further increase until that scale itself is reviewed; and it is impossible to reward differences in the quality and ability of individual staff or in the amount of effort they put into their work and the success they achieve.

In private industry, salaries are usually periodically reviewed on an individual basis. Obviously this method does allow flexibility in recognizing standards of performance, types of responsibility, and the degree to which success depends on personal effort; age and length of service can also be taken in account. On the other hand, this method can so easily give rise to anomalies and the discontent that follows. Employers traditionally try to keep salary payments secret; if there are variations in the amounts paid to individuals, then the reasons for them are not published, in an attempt to avoid any embarrassment that might arise from personal grievances. The personnel manager's advice on salary administration will no doubt be based on the principle that there should be no anomalies, and that corrective action should be taken immediately if it is found, for example, that higher salaries than existing staff are paid have to be offered to attract newcomers. The least that should be done, where salary maxima have been settled for particular jobs, is for the staff concerned to be told how long it should take them to reach these levels, assuming satisfactory work on their part.

Salary reviews usually have the following features:

1 The personnel manager administers a procedure which calls for periodic recommendations (usually once a year) from departmental heads: these are based on merit.
2 External features, such as changes in taxation and the cost of living, are also taken into account at this stage.
3 A continuous comparison maintained with the salary levels of other organizations, by studying staff advertisements or exchanging information with other local firms who employ the same categories of staff.
4 There are special considerations relating to some types of staff:

   (a) The differential between supervisors' salaries and the total earnings of individual employees under their control is a perennial problem that is only partly covered by the better general conditions offered to the foreman.
   (b) In order to attract youngsters of the right calibre for future development, it may be necessary to offer them high initial salaries, which may lead to slower progress as they get older.

(c) Similarly, research staff tend to be highly paid early on in their careers, so that if their interest in research wanes later on and they want to switch to general management, there is little scope left to recognize any managerial ability they may show.

One study* of the values and remuneration preferences of managers in one large British company revealed, *inter alia*, that although they varied considerably in their detailed views about pay, there was very strong support for remuneration based on individual performance, and there was also consistent support for remuneration to be sufficiently flexible to handle special individual cases. The administrative structure required to manage a salary system designed so as to provide motivational stimuli must have these characteristics: flexibility, to cope with individual differences; provision of the fullest information about the remuneration system of all managers involved; and the means of monitoring the effects of the system on performance.

Salary structure

The overall concern, of course, is to relate individual salaries to relative jobs and merit. In pursuing this aim, comparison with similar jobs elsewhere has only a very limited use because job titles and the responsibilities they carry vary enormously from company to company. Systematic evaluation of job content is the only real answer, which in turn demands the writing of precise job descriptions from the outset.

But even when it seems that individuals are being properly paid, the question of whether the salary structure of the organization as a whole is correct still remains. This question has been analysed by Harry Pearson,† Director of Personnel of Rolls-Royce Ltd, to show what salary levels should be within an organization, taking its size into account. 'The structure of salaries is subject to a general law, known as Pareto's law, which says that in any large organized society there is a definite relation between income and the number of people having this income.' The graph in Figure 24 illustrates that if n is the number of people with an income greater than S, then if log S is plotted against log n, an approximate linear relationship will result. This graph, plotting the income of the labour force in Great Britain, clearly shows a mathematical relationship between a salary and the number of people with that salary or greater. The salary structure of any organization should in fact appear as a straight line when plotted in this way. Salary

Motivating Managers Financially, Michael White (IPM, 1973).
†'How to Pay Salaries', *Management Today*, December 1966, page 62.

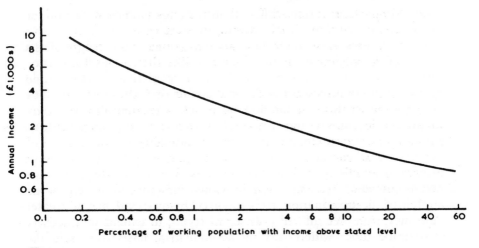

Figure 24

administrators should carry out this exercise for their own organizations, and if there are marked deviations from 'the straight line', they should look closely for the reasons.

Productivity bargaining

Productivity bargaining is the process through which management hope to obtain greater efficiency by offering improvements in wages, and perhaps better working conditions, in exchange for the elimination of restrictive practices. This simple definition, however, must not be allowed to obscure the vast amount of investigation, analysis, and hard negotiation that must be put into the satisfactory conclusion of such agreements. Work systems must be analysed to decide where change is needed, deep-rooted traditions of worker behaviour must be modified, and intergroup jealousies smoothed over by giving carefully considered reassurances about the future.

Management must take the lead in this because it is basically concerned with the efficient use of resources to produce the best results. The search for improvement and the introduction of the changes that this often entails are management tasks – but workers and their unions will resist if the achievement of these tasks brings insecurity of employment in its wake. Nevertheless, unions recognize that in the event they can do more for their members in an efficient firm than in one that is inefficient. Hence an understanding of management's problems develops, to form the basis for negotiation and cooperation aimed at removing both inefficiencies in production on the one hand and workers' grievances on the other.

In no circumstances is productivity bargaining to be thought of as a means by which management can buy itself out of trouble. There is no question of bribing workers to abandon restrictive practices, and passing on to the customer additional labour costs thus incurred. The concept is essentially a method by which wage improvements are financed, not through higher prices but from the cost savings made as the result of agreed changes in working arrangements.

These bargains are, of course, local agreements, and they have already been criticized as being inflationary since they inspire wage claims elsewhere (to maintain previous differentials) which by no stretch of the imagination are supported by any evidence of greater efficiency. Another difficulty arises in trying to extend productivity bargaining more widely, say on an industrial basis. It lies in the essential thorough preliminary analysis of the working system which can only be done locally and under the control of managements who will accept a direct responsibility for administering any changes which they may subsequently negotiate. On the other hand, the concept must not be allowed to provide an excuse which enables control over rising wages and inflation to be subverted. Such bargains can only be allowed when it can be proved that productivity actually has increased.

There are many other subsidiary problems involved in the process of negotiating these agreements. The rewarding of improved productivity by increasing basic wages immediately exposes the salaries of supervisory and managerial staff. A reappraisal of the management structure must therefore be carried out, preferably before the stage of negotiating with trade unions begins, with an intensive investigation of the responsibilities and relative earnings levels of all salaried staff. Not that this is a straightforward matter of salary administration. Restrictive practices and job demarcation are virtually non-existent among salaried staff, so there is little to bargain for by offering more pay for increased productivity in this respect. In reality, of course, other factors are at play besides labour cost and effort put into the job; salary administration demands that account is taken of the availability of managerial and supervisory skills, the added responsibilities that follow technical changes (including the working arrangements of the productivity agreement), and the constant revaluation of job gradings.

But although productivity bargaining has made a real contribution to improved labour relations in recent years, it cannot be regarded as the panacea for all industrial troubles. The concept can only be applied successfully where management is imaginative, takes the initiative in identifying the practices that it wishes to modify, and carefully calculates what it is prepared to pay, in terms of cash and security of employment, to obtain the required concessions from its workers. Second, experience has shown that wage increases can most easily be absorbed in those industries, like oil refining, where the capital–labour rate is high. Third, it is difficult to negotiate productivity bargains on a national scale: it seems that local flexibility and adaptability are key factors in agreements. Fourth, productivity bargaining may only be successful as a once-and-for-all experience.

The Conservative Government's commitment since 1979 to a return to free collective bargaining, albeit within a straitjacket of cash limits throughout the public sector, inevitably meant that the management of large organizations increasingly needed to concentrate their attention on containing, and indeed trying to reduce, unit labour costs. Only when this is achieved will systems of collective bargaining be able to work smoothly, and output, efficiency, employment prospects, and pay be improved. Coincidental with this need for a new approach has come an upsurge in interest in participation at the workplace. Thus wage negotiations in the near future could provide managements and employee representatives with opportunities to arrive at more mutually acceptable levels of pay and productivity, aimed at providing high remuneration and low unit costs.

An ideal pay and productivity plan should have low installation and running costs; be mutually agreed and not imposed; recognize productivity improvement; recognize inflation and contribute to its reduction; provide employee participation in measurement and methods; be simple and easy to understand; non-subjective in application; offer stability and choice of earnings level; and incorporate regular audit and up-to-date procedures for monitoring management effectiveness.* In practice, the components of such a plan must include: simplified low-cost work measurement; a stepped pay band structure; self-financing productivity improvement; and a dynamic pay policy.

Simplified low-cost work measurement involves using techniques that have been developed in recent years, in part to overcome the problems relating to costs, technical weaknesses, and industrial relations conflict, which have been attributed to traditional work measurement. It is based on the statistical sampling of variables, defining activities and tasks rather than 'elements', and using the language of the skill concerned rather than that of work study. Employees thus become better able to set their own standards from these data which they have helped to develop and which they

---

*'How Pay Systems Can Succeed', I. G. Smith and P. Hesketh, in *Management Today*, November 1977, page 99.

understand. The techniques are guaranteed to produce effective control standards for at least 90 per cent of all direct and indirect activities at a guaranteed tolerance of plus or minus 5 per cent over the control period. Experience also shows that the controls can be monitored for about one-third of the costs of maintaining a traditional work measured system. Measurement and control of the variability of work (rather than aiming at its elimination), and the fact that most employees in the local workplace are paid weekly, have a significant bearing on the design of an organization's pay structure.

This approach has also served to remove much of the disagreement and suspicion, hence poor industrial relations, caused by doubts about the technical soundness of rating by work study engineers. Conflict is alleviated largely by providing consistency of rating at a set level of performance on the British Standard Scale, which has proved acceptable to trade unions, and by recognizing that participation in work measurement is a prime requirement for the success of the proposed system.

The stepped pay band pay structure also has a valuable function in the approach, since it offers the advantages of measured day work and piecework systems without any of their disadvantages. It allows workers to choose their own speed of activity and rewards them accordingly. It stabilizes weekly earnings and is claimed to cut the cost of clerical bonus calculations by up to 80 per cent.

A typical stepped pay band pay structure includes four steps:

Table 6

Performance range	Contribution	Pay level
75–85	Learning	80
86–95	Intermediate	90
96–105	Standard	100
106–115	Super	110

Employees are allowed to choose their own step, and are checked for a period of four weeks to ensure that performance is maintained. There are simple rules for employees moving up and down the steps, which again the unions have accepted. Apart from providing consistency of earnings, such a system also contributes substantially towards arresting wages drift and thus reducing inflation.

Self-financing productivity (SFP) requires the active and willing cooperation of employees, for their knowledge must be tapped to help reduce costs. It is also vital for management to invest in new plant and processes with confidence, knowing that this will be acceptable to employees. SFP schemes require first a basis for creating the value-added element, and then a method of sharing it out equitably. The overall effect may be, say, a 50–50 sharing of savings between employees and their firm – thus increasing the pay of the former and lowering the costs of the latter. The employees' share is paid out after an agreed period of effort, possibly at the end of the first year, only after the savings have actually been earned. These savings can then be taken by management as a basis for negotiating a dynamic approach to pay in the ensuing period. Subsequent additional payouts can only be financed by further methods improvements, not only from employees but from the methods department and from more capital investment on the part of management.

Recent analyses of the effectiveness of productivity schemes* suggest that there are two main lessons to be drawn. First, many organizations prefer to sweep away past practices and undertake a fundamental reform of productivity, working time and payment systems. Although achieving productivity gains in a piecemeal way by taking particular initiatives (for example, tightening up working practices) can be done, there are dangers in doing so without also undertaking fundamental reforms. Second, unfreezing the current situation requires a catalyst. Flexible hours schemes — usually the annual hours approach — have been used as the vehicle for change because the scheme drives at the very heart of the productivity equation through reducing ineffective time by new hours arrangements and working practices, introducing more plain-time hours and reforming the wage-working time bargain. Reported productivity gains have often been impressive, yet without any sense of exploitation: employees can gain very significantly, not least through sharing the greater wealth created by raising productivity.

Performance related pay

The inability of successive governments' economic policies to eliminate inflation have made all employers acutely conscious of a key payment issue — how to improve rates of pay without adding significantly to labour costs. A recent development in the UK to this end, particularly in the public sector, is the practice of relating pay to individual performance at work. In fact, performance-related pay (PRP) schemes attempt to link some proportion of pay not only to individual output

---

*'Making Time for Productivity', Philip Lynch, *Personnel Management*, March 1991, page 30.

but also to other indicators of performance, such as quality, flexibility, contribution to team-working and ability to hit targets. In 1988* it was calculated that such schemes formed part of the overall pay settlements in about a quarter of all businesses for manual workers, well over a half for sales and clerical staff, and about two-thirds for supervisors and managers.

The benefits most commonly cited are improvements in the commitment and capability of staff, raising the skills base of employees, being able to identify training and development needs more easily, and improvements in job satisfaction and sense of achievement. Where it is applied to all staff PRP offers a good opportunity to harmonize conditions of employment between staff and manual workers. Similarly, flexible working can be encouraged where it is included as a performance criterion.

One distinct contribution of PRP is its potential to improve communication and business awareness among employees. Especially when one objective is to make organizational and individual criteria for success the same, a clearer focus emerges on such factors as quality, costs and delivery, and employees are rewarded for performance which is directly related to the aims of the business.

Improvements in communications, both upward and downward, tend to centre on regular appraisals: these get the supervisor and job holder to sit down together for a set period to discuss frankly in performance and development terms, the job, relationships with the supervisor and the rest of the team, and requirements for future development. Employees can be given more information about the business and what it is trying to achieve, and although this in itself cannot guarantee cooperation, it does at least improve feedback to employees who, in turn, are able to add to the process their own ideas on how work might be arranged, done differently or better.

Successful PRP schemes clearly provide the means for improving individual and organizational performance in a cost-effective way, and they appear to have three main features† in common. First, they do not seek an immediate payback, but conceive PRP as part of an overall package of human resource initiatives designed to improve employee motivation and performance in the long term. Second, senior management is committed to an effective and valid performance-appraisal procedure, supported by accessible training programmes and introduced by consultation rather than imposition. Third, they seek to relate the objectives of the payment system to

---

*Performance Rewards 1987–8, Reward Group, 1988.
†'Performance-related Pay on the Shop-floor', Nick Kinnie and David Lowe, Personnel Management, November 1990, page 45.

those of the organization and in particular, set out to link the criteria for individual reward to factors crucial to the success of the business.

The future of remuneration systems

The history of the development of industrial relations in the UK highlights a number of permanent 'truths' about the determination of levels of pay. Three particular key factors are:

(a) That pay, and differing views about the objectives of a remuneration system (see Fox, quoted on page 17), will always be a cause of disagreements between management, employers and trade unions.
(b) Economic necessity forces people to go to work but, once there, pay becomes an issue, relative to other 'quality of life' factors, only if it is considered to be unfair.
(c) That without broad acceptance by employees and trade unions, pay systems are unlikely to operate effectively.

While these may be truisms, there are several other new factors which will undoubtedly powerfully influence thinking about pay structures in the future. One is the impact which *new technology* is having throughout industry and commerce, producing a trend indicating that there will be more 'white-collar' than 'blue-collar' jobs during the 1990s. Robotics and other computer-controlled machinery will take manual workers away from their tools and their products and on to keyboards and VDUs. Office workers, including managers, will also work with automated machinery. The roles of both will include planning and scheduling, and the impact of the individual on the work system will be more immediate. Broader skills, deployed more flexibly, will be required, with obvious implications as regards recruitment, training, work organization and changing the balance between occupations. Clearly some jobs and skills will become redundant, while elsewhere new jobs and skills must be created.

Organizations where these changes in work-patterns are best understood, and which take deliberate action to focus on resolving the consequent white-collar pay structure problems, will be at an advantage over those where the changes are allowed to happen haphazardly. The challenge to management is that of negotiating detailed changes to work-patterns and associated pay structures in advance of the introduction of new technology, rather than waiting until its full impact is known. New systems need to be designed to harmonize with new business objectives.

The word '*harmonize*' also relates to new opportunities to eliminate blue-and-white-collar status differentials which have caused so much resentment and friction in the past. Attempts to do so will place further emphasis on the discussion and negotiation of changes in methods of payment, levels of pay, merging of grades and career progression.

Then, again, the *quality of working life* is also affected by new technology, by wider education and by changing social values – all bearing on the way jobs are designed, the effectiveness of management style, and how trade unions react to the ways in which their members are affected. The aim of all attempts to improve the quality of working life is to secure the best fit between what an organization requires of its employees, so that it can survive and prosper, and what those employees need from it for their survival and prosperity; and pay structures need to be re-designed in many organizations to reinforce this approach.

Another factor concerns speculation that the *development of microelectronics* will help to satisfy organizational needs to remain competitive by encouraging flexibility and increased efficiency, especially through greater decentralization and smaller profit-centres or independent business units. Microelectronics will make the control of such devolved units easier and would be likely to reduce the complexity of payment systems. Not only that, but working in smaller units would enable the removal of that remoteness felt by many employees, with links between pay and performance being more clearly understood.

Dramatic changes to traditional ways of work are also anticipated during the next few years and these, too, will influence the design of payment systems. Examples which have already been widely debated include job-sharing, shorter working hours, earlier retirement, much more working from home, subcontracting, and more part-time employment. Add to these the technological developments mentioned above, and 'net-working' may well increase, with 'employees' working from home and being paid fees for services rather than salaries.

Speculation about the future of wage systems must have some regard to the concept of a *national minimum wage*. Politically, the concept is supported in the UK by the Labour Party, but strongly opposed by the Conservative Government; a new factor in the debate, however, takes into account trade competition within the European Community and the advancement of the 'level playing field' argument against those producers who seek an unfair advantage by paying very low wages.

Over a period a minimum wage policy probably could be designed to improve the circumstances of the lower-paid and enable them to enjoy a tolerable standard of living. A minimum wage could also provide a genuine impetus to better labour efficiency. Although many other factors affect this, it is notable that some countries with comprehensive minimum wage structures also have higher levels of labour productivity than the UK; what happens seems to be that where employers are forced over a period to increase low rates of pay, the more successful will manage to raise labour productivity, while the less successful will go out of business and their workers tend to move to jobs with the more successful employers.

To be fully effective and to minimize adverse effects (for example, fewer jobs), a minimum wage policy would need to be part of a broad package of measures designed to achieve specific results: first, it would have to mitigate unjustified attempts to restore differentials; second, it would have to provide further stimulus for investment in training both managers and staff as part of a policy to raise labour productivity, add to the quality of product and generally to improve the employee relations environment; and, third, it would have to provide some incentive to increase capital investment in the industrial sectors most affected and to improve competitiveness.

Clearly there would need to be close cooperation between government, employers and trade unions in order to introduce such a system as effectively as possible — and for the foreseeable future there must be real doubts as to whether such a degree of cooperation is likely to be forthcoming. Nevertheless, one conclusion* is that in the right circumstances a statutory minimum hourly rate of about 45 per cent of median male earnings would have some side effect, but might have favorable long-term consequences for productivity.

Objectives of future payment systems

The success of all management tasks depends, in the first place, on clear definition of objectives – and so it is with designing remuneration systems. The outline above of factors bearing on the future demonstrates that any new remuneration systems need to recognize job-role changes that cross traditional skill barriers and the relevant industrial relations processes which evaluate the significance of such changes. In summary, objectives regarding remuneration will need to be concerned with enhancing overall organizational performance and the key role of the employee in that process rather than, as in the past, emphasizing reward for quantities of work done.

Specifically, a remuneration system based on such objectives will have to:

Personnel Management, October 1991, page 41; Chris Curson, Chairman of the IPM working party on the national minimum wage.

(a) Avoid tying payments systems to standard patterns of work (as in piecework systems).

(b) Reward results and above standard performance, rather than pace of work.

(c) Facilitate job redesign and the introduction of new jobs.

(d) Provide for the effects of decentralization, with responsibilities being pushed downwards.

(e) Give individual employees more opportunities to make decisions about their daily work.

(f) Provide for the development of broader skills and increased mobility and flexibility.

(g) Encourage employees to take greater interest in customer needs, improving quality and meeting delivery dates.

Determining the system

Industrial relations history suggests that it will commonly become the task of a joint steering committee to determine the objectives and devise the form of any future payment structure. Because such a committee – typically consisting of company payment specialists, line managers, employees and their representatives – would involve everyone who is directly affected, and would have detailed local knowledge, greater commitment to the system could be expected and greater enthusiasm to make it work. The proposals from the joint steering committee would then be passed to the formal negotiating machinery.

This suggested approach fits well, for example, with one of the important conclusions of the Department of Employment Research Paper No. 36* – that those firms in which there had been extensive consultation with a wide range of management specialists and levels within the organization (including shop stewards and shop-floor workers) had by far the best results.

The process of change will not happen overnight, of course; it will be gradual, responding to the demands of the organization's particular situation. Above all, flexibility will be needed to cope with new forms of work arrangements, including multi-skilling and new roles, and with greater employee involvement in day-to-day decisions about their work.

Labour costs may not remain such a large proportion of unit costs: for example, increasing investment or energy costs may result in more attention being paid to getting the best returns from those factors

Effects of Incentive Payment Systems, UK 1977–80, A. Bowey et al.

rather than from labour. Multi-factor incentive schemes may therefore become more prominent, with rewards on an organization-wide basis related to a combined index which reflects the utilization of several inputs – a range of energy sources, machinery (capital investment) and labour.

Existing payment systems may be subjected to the following influences:

(a) A new stimulus may be given to *measured daywork* – the BIM has estimated that some 12 per cent of establishments with incentive schemes use this method – because its approach offers a good fit with possible future trends towards allowing individuals or groups of employees greater freedom in the way they organize their work (including agreeing 'contracts of performance'), increased flexibility between jobs, employees' desire for stability of earnings and towards annual salaries for all staff, and the need to cope more readily with increasing rates of change.

(b) Profit-sharing or share ownership schemes* – as already mentioned on page 265 – form part of the slow growth of 'financial participation' in Great Britain. The spread of such schemes is expected to increase in future, provided that there is no change in the tax structure, for several reasons: springing from the urge to be competitive, overall company performance will receive more attention than conventional incentive schemes; the greater use of computers in process control will affect the relevance of work-measured incentive schemes; and there is likely to be further development of participative management styles, with financial participation schemes as their logical corollaries.

(c) It can be argued that *incremental scales* – usually rigidly applied and linked only to experience and length of service – are ill-suited to the increasingly perceived need to reward flexible work-forms, to push decision-taking and responsibility lower down the job hierarchy, and to increase the discretionary element in jobs. Future trends may therefore be towards merit salary structures and the growth of 'incremerit' structures, whereby advances beyond say the mid-point of a scale would be reserved to those whose performance is consistently above average. Clearly such developments would have to be accompanied by effective performance appraisal schemes. Safeguards necessary to achieve the

---

*'Profit Sharing and Employee Share Ownership in Britain', Gillian R. Smith, *Employment Gazette*, September 1986, pages 380–5, offers an excellent survey of this subject. The article covers the history, legal position, extent, objectives of schemes, alternatives, methods of introduction, size of rewards, and evaluation of schemes.

confidence of everyone concerned would require schemes to be open (i.e. not secretive), be seen to be fair, and be practised in ways which reduce subjectivity to a minimum.

(d) Flexible work demands will also lead to the *acquisition of multi-skills*, perhaps through modular training, and methods of rewarding those skills will need to be developed. One approach might be to pay employees according to the number of skill modules possessed, thus encouraging the creation of a flexible workforce at a controlled pace, whilst at the same time ensuring the standards the organization wishes to secure from each job-holder. Individuals would have some choice in extending their skills (and increasing their pay) or remaining as they were.

From the above analysis two main pointers emerge indicating clearly the need for future remuneration systems to reward employees for using their talents to the full and for accepting change. First, if employees give of their best consistently, then organizational effectiveness will be enhanced. Second, where such a climate is created, employers will see themselves as having a high quality of working life. It has also come to be recognized that remuneration systems which are employee-orientated and geared to treating people positively are less likely continually to raise industrial relations issues.

In the context of these considerations, the conclusion emerges that the most significant development in the coming years will be the design of integrated organization-wide remuneration systems.* The modern success of Japanese business offers many good examples of such systems. Generally speaking, a major factor in all Japanese pay systems is length of service, reflecting the deference given to age and authority. Promotion is usually slow, with a certain time having to be spent in any grade irrespective of how competent the individual may be. No big Japanese company pays on the basis of individual output, although most pay a company bonus which is negotiated annually with the trade unions and is geared to overall company performance. A number of pay components may be involved:

(a) Basic pay, dependent on age, academic background, employee record and length of service.
(b) Pay for the job, with classification into levels according to job knowledge, skills, responsibilities, mental and physical loads, and working environment.

---

*An existing example of such a system – at the Berkshire Brewery of Courage Central, with seven interlocking organizational structure levels and three job related skill levels/pay indices – is explained in the *Employment Gazette*, April 1984, pages 180–1.

(c) Additional pay, based on twice-yearly personal performance appraisal.
(d) Performance pay: productivity of the whole organization, determined monthly.
(e) Function pay, paid according to each employee's qualifications, job ability and job performance, and allowing for that individual's growth within his/her job during the year.

On such a basis the future criteria for moving from one job-related skill level, with its appropriate pay, to another would be geared to increasing job knowledge and job flexibility, (reflecting the ability to work on additional tasks), attending particular courses, or acquiring new knowledge (such as electronics). Employees would be expected to consult with their manager in deciding whether to try for the next skill level. This system also provides the opportunity for employees to move out of their existing occupational grouping, resulting in pay progression, personal career development and increased labour flexibility throughout the organization.

Performance-related and variable pay arrangements have been much discussed in recent years, and already in practice the most fundamental tenet of all – the pay relationship between boss and subordinate – has been overturned: for example, the much-publicized high-performing computer salespeople who earn more than their managers and directors. Performance-related pay has come into fashion at a time when profits are on a rising trend, and the real test will come when and if businesses turn in poor results. At that stage, unless some form of penalties is imposed, bonuses will be seen as just another 'norm'.

The adoption of such schemes also has important implications for an organization's external relationships, particularly with its shareholders, as the rationale for performance-related pay comes under increasing scrutiny from financial analysts and journalists. Shareholders, including employee shareholders, will increasingly demand information about the size of the bonus element in pay awards and the basis on which it is calculated.

It is important to design a reward package which is consistent with the goals and culture of an organization. It is also important that its employees appreciate that there is a link between their performance, their remuneration and the aims and performance of the organization. Relevant measures to enable managers and employees to judge performance should be assessed regularly. For those employers and executives who manage remuneration appropriately, the potential returns in business performance and individual reward are far-reaching; in this competitive world, creative remuneration packages can give an advantage to both the organization and to the individuals working for it.

In the final count, if remuneration systems are to be a positive influence rather than a negative and disruptive force, the most important task will be to try to get as much agreement as possible about their aims and to reduce the amount of misunderstanding which tends to surround them. To achieve these fundamental objectives, increased employee involvement both in the initial shaping of the pay structure and in devising its objectives is likely to be helpful. Through involvement at the start there is a much greater chance that the pay system will lead to the release of employee potential and cooperation rather than effort being misspent on how to beat it. At a time of rapid change and searches for increased efficiency and competitiveness, as well as desire for a higher quality of working life, such positive responses will be at a premium if both organizations and the people working in them are to survive, grow and prosper.

Further reading

ACAS, Introduction to Payment Systems, London, 1981.
Progressive Payment Systems, D. Grayson; Work Research Unit, WRU Occasional Paper No. 28, 1984.
Reward Management, a handbook of salary administration, Michael Armstrong and Helen Murlis (2nd edition, IPM, 1991).

14

The framework of industrial relations

The study of *industrial relations* may generally be defined as being
concerned with the ways in which working groups, both formal and
informal, behave and interact. More specifically, it describes the
efforts aimed at securing cooperation between management and trade
unions at the workplace so that the most efficient methods of
production may be achieved. All too often, however, these efforts must
be viewed negatively – as means of overcoming conflict between
'authority' and worker groups. Mistrust, rooted in the industrial
history of Great Britain, particularly the inter-war years of economic
depression, is still very much at the back of workers' minds, associating
the words 'progress and change' with 'insecurity of employment'.
Tradition plays a prominent part both in the principles and structure
of industrial relations, neither of which have developed much during
the twentieth century (indeed, to say that they have stood the test of
time is a common defence against any attacks). The trouble is that
today we are beset with fundamental economic problems, such as the
fight against inflation and the need to increase productivity, finding
solutions to which is hampered by the institutional rigidity of the
system.

Traditional structure

Industrial relations are governed by a multitude of collective agreements, statutory orders about wages and working conditions, arbi-

tration awards, management decisions, trade union regulations, court rulings which have established precedents, social conventions, and custom and usage – all referring to the employment of labour. Trade unions, employers' federations, individual private firms, and public authorities take part in making these arrangements, which often vary within the same industry from one part of the country to another. Such is the basic complexity of the subject.

The Trade Union Amendment Act 1867 contains one definition of trade unions which is still accepted today:

> A trade union is any combination, whether temporary or permanent, for regulating the relations between workmen and masters, or between workmen and workmen, or between masters and masters, or for imposing restrictive conditions on the conduct of any trade or business.

This was amended by the Trade Union Act 1913, which provided that the above objects, together with the provision of benefits to members, must be the principal objects of a combination.

The Trade Union and Labour Relations Act 1974 defines a trade union as an organization which consists of workers whose principal purposes include the regulation of relations between those workers and employers or employers' associations.

The overall purpose of a trade union is to bring together workers' aspirations into an effective force, and any appreciation of trade union attitudes must accept that these aspirations are different from management's. They may be summarized into four aims:

1 Efficiency in production must be realized with the minimum human cost; in particular, essential changes should result in the least possible threat to security of employment.
2 Constant improvement in working conditions – the *raison d'être* of the trade union movement. This covers claims for higher wages, shorter hours, guaranteed earnings, holiday arrangements and pay, improved environment, regard for seniority in promotion and at times of redundancy, and an overall policy of full employment. Adequate grievance procedures and provisions for arbitration over disputes are further safeguards.
3 The development of internal strength, better to achieve all the other objectives. Unions constantly strive to increase their membership, and hence their power, provide leadership to unorganized groups, point the way to further improvements in conditions and worker benefits, and are ever critical of the actions of government authorities and employers which affect the labour force of the country.
4 In doing so, unions seek full recognition as the exclusive agents of

employees who come within their respective purview. Thus they encourage workers to regard themselves collectively, rather than as individuals: rules of conduct and conditions of employment are established for all, with no special terms for individuals.

At the end of 1990 there were 335 trade unions in Great Britain, of which nearly half had less than 1000 members each, accounting for only 0.3 per cent of all trade union membership; on the other hand, the twenty-three unions each with over 100,000 members accounted for 80 per cent of total membership. The tendency for the number of unions to fall, through amalgamation, continues: 596 unions in 1964, 501 in 1975, and 373 in 1985. The total membership of trade unions has also decreased in recent years: from a peak membership in 1979 of 13,289,000 to 9.9 million in 1990.*

There are basically three main types of trade union, although very few fit exactly into one or other of the categories (it would almost be true to say that there are as many categories as there are unions):

1 The *craft union* which seeks to unite all workers of a particular craft, trade, occupation, or grade of skill, irrespective of the industry in which they happen to be working.
2 The *industrial union*, which seeks to unite all workers engaged in a particular industry, irrespective of their craft, trade, occupation, or grade of skill.
3 The *general union* which seeks to unite workers of every industry and occupation who are not catered for by either of the other two categories. Normally associated with general unions are unskilled or semi-skilled workers in industries where long-established craft unions recruit the skilled people, for example, engineering and building; workers of all grades of skill in new or recently organized industries with no tradition of craft or industrial unions; groups of workers in isolated pockets of their industry who are not catered for in either craft or industrial unions.

Such then is the pattern into which unions have grown over the years, spreading out along the lines of development which seemed appropriate and convenient at the time and in whatever direction was necessary to protect the interests of their members.

Craft unions are the oldest type of worker organizations (having developed from the medieval guilds). In addition to their concern with wages and conditions of employment, they are very conscious of the status of their craft and take a close interest in apprenticeship and other training schemes. They often have a strong element of the

---

*A full analysis appears in the *Employment Gazette*, April 1992.

benevolent society about them, and their high rates of contributions enable them to pay generous benefits. Craft unions have tended to grow in two ways: the days of the small unions are passing and development has often involved the amalgamation of unions of related crafts; or, in industries where their members comprise a large proportion of those employed, they have enrolled workers of lower grades of skill.

There are no *industrial unions* in the full sense of being without opposition in their own industry and organizing every grade of worker, including salaried staff, in that industry. Generally accepted as two good examples, however, are the National Union of Mineworkers and the National Union of Railway, Maritime and Transport Workers. The former evolved as local coalfield unions came together, but there are some groups of maintenance workers who remain outside the NUM. The NURMTW started out deliberately intending to become an industrial union by the amalgamation of several small unions of manual workers in the railway industry, but its efforts so far have always been frustrated by two occupational unions, the Associated Society of Locomotive Engineers and Firemen, and the Transport Salaried Staffs' Association; also, in railway workshops skilled people are often organized by the appropriate engineering unions. On the other hand, some industrial unions have expanded in such diverse directions that there is little to differentiate between them and general unions. The Union of Shop, Distributive and Allied Workers, for instance, was originally concerned with the business of distribution, but now includes van people, clerks, and workers in a variety of manufacturing industries and consumer services like laundries and catering.

No clear line of distinction can be drawn between industrial and *general unions*. Best known among the latter are the Transport and General Workers' Union and the General, Municipal, Boilermakers and Allied Trades Union (GMB). Both are among the giants of the trade union movement and were formed by amalgamations in 1921. They organize unskilled and semi-skilled workers in a wide range of industries and occupations, and in some cases they have absorbed craft unions. Without having precise spheres of influence, in general the TGWU covers roads, transport, and docks, while the GMB organizes manual workers in municipal concerns, gas, water, and electricity, and has recently merged with the former boilermakers engineering union. The situation becomes even more complex with the further diversification of some of the large conglomerate* unions:

*The merger of NALGO, NUPE and COHSE in 1993 produced a new union with 1.4 million members.

r example, the Electrical, Electronic, Telecommunication and lumbing Union absorbed into membership both the Association of ritish Professional Divers and the National Association of Senior robation Officers!

In addition, there are a large number of staff and professional ssociations, some with a horizontal structure covering many different ndustries, such as the Clerical and Administrative Workers' Union, here a variety of non-manual workers within a wide range of ndustry are members, and others with a closed membership like the ational Union of Teachers. The picture is further complicated by uch bodies as the Civil Service and insurance unions, the structures f which are so complex that they are impossible to classify. The rowth of these 'white-collar' unions and staff associations has been phenomenon of the 1960s, and can, therefore, be traced to more iodern aspirations − particularly as regards employees' needs) combat the increasing impersonality of their environment and emoteness of senior management. Staff want greater influence over ie decisions that affect their working lives, and, to this end, they vant their representatives involved in decision-taking and answerable) them.

The basic unit of most trade unions is the *local branch* or lodge which lects its own officers and discusses matters affecting its members' iterests (see Figure 25). Purely domestic matters are normally decided n the spot; issues of wider importance are sent forward to the union's istrict or national centres. Branches vary in size from a handful to iousands of members, although the average in craft union branches is bout 100. Each branch usually has a secretary and a small number of ther officials; they are voluntary and undertake their duties in ddition to their normal employment, receiving very little if anything y way of payment.

In many industries union membership is also organized on the job, here the lead is taken by *shop stewards*. Their range of duties varies in ractice: they may do nothing more than collect weekly dues; at the ther extreme, they may try to obtain higher rates of pay or to settle rievances by negotiating directly with management. They may be esponsible for union recruitment, contacting newcomers to the ictory, and also detecting any encroachment upon recognized work- ig conditions. Shop stewards of different unions within the same rganization may be linked by a *stewards' committee*, and may also sit on int committees representing management and workers.

On a district or regional basis, trade union branches may appoint epresentatives to local *trades councils* to consider questions of common iterest to trade unionism in that area. Most of these councils are based eographically on a county or group of counties. One of their

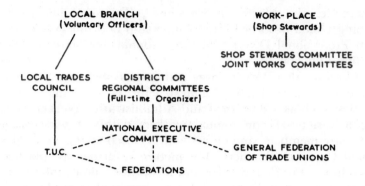

Figure 25   Trade union structure

important functions is to act as channels of communication betwee
local unions and the Trades Union Congress (TUC), which lacks an
local organization of its own; with national executives of trade union
they are the only bodies which can contact the TUC direct. Althoug
membership of local trades councils is voluntary, the advantages t
union branches are obvious: apart from offering a voice in high place
trades councils play a prominent part in the education and training c
local union officials, and are usually represented on local employmer
committees and other joint bodies in which the interests of the workin
community are involved.

The members of a union's local branches elect delegates to represer
them on district and national committees of the union, and particu
larly at the union's *national conference* when policy and any alterations t
rules are decided. Most unions have some kind of *regional organizatic*
with full-time paid organizers, either elected by members or appointe
by the national executive committee, and the bigger unions also hav
networks of regional committees or councils which often have gre
influence on behalf of their members in their area.

The central organizations of the larger unions follow the sam
general structural pattern. Each controls its own funds and has a hea
office with full-time staff. A permanent body of officials, including
general secretary, is responsible to a *national executive committee* of the union
which may be part-time or full-time, and is usually elected at th
national conference of branch delegates. The executive committe
plays a major part in the running of the union, carrying out the polic
decisions of the delegates between conferences and preparing report
which, together with resolutions submitted by the branches, form th
basis of conference agenda. The general secretary is normally a full
time paid official, in most cases elected by a vote of all members, bu

sometimes by the delegate conference. General secretaries normally take part in all important union meetings, in negotiations with employers, and are usually among each union's delegates to the annual Trades Union Congress. Most unions also have a *president* (again full-time or part-time) who is usually of comparable importance to the general secretary.

The distinction between craft and industrial unions is further complicated by the fact that in a number of industries *federations of trade unions* have been formed to enable collective bargaining to take place on an industry-wide basis. The number of trade unions affiliated to such federations is large, and several trade unions are members of more than one federation. Some of these decide policy and take action on behalf of their particular unions: for example, the Confederation of Shipbuilding and Engineering Unions and the National Federation of Building Trade Operatives; others act purely in a consultative or coordinating manner. In national negotiations workers may therefore be represented by more than one body, but although the authority of federations over constituent unions varies, ultimate power as regards action about disputes always rests with the individual union.

Yet another part of the total structure is the *General Federation of Trade Unions*, established in 1899 by the TUC as a central body which today, in practice, mainly takes responsibility for financing trade union mutual-aid services. Any of the fifty-six member unions of this federation can draw upon a central fund to supplement its resources in the event of a strike or lock-out. The federation also provides research, and statistical and educational services of the type which large unions can afford from their own resources.

Most of the large and important trade unions are affiliated to the *Trades Union Congress*, which caters for a total membership of over eleven million workers. The official functions of the TUC are:

1 To do anything to promote the interests of all or any of its affiliated organizations.
2 Generally to improve the economic and social conditions of workers in all parts of the world and to render them assistance whenever necessary.
3 To affiliate to or subscribe to or assist in other organizations having objectives similar to those of the Congress.
4 To assist in the complete organization of all workers eligible for membership to its affiliated organizations, and (subject to its rules) to settle disputes between the members of such organizations and their employers or between such organizations and their members or between the organizations themselves.

In furthering these objectives the TUC operates in the context of a comprehensive political and social programme, including nationalization, the extension of social services, adequate participation of workers in the management of public services, a maximum working week and minimum wage for workers in all industries, cash benefits and training for the unemployed, industrial health and welfare services, full educational facilities, adequate housing, and adequate pensions.

Annually in September, delegates from affiliated unions meet to settle future policy and elect a *General Council* to implement decisions taken at the Congress. The duties of the General Council are to coordinate industrial action of trade unions, to promote legislation affecting labour, to foster common action on general conditions of employment including wages, to settle differences between affiliated unions, and generally to seek in every practical manner to strengthen the trade union movement. Government usually consults the General Council before deciding policies or taking action on any matter affecting the nation's labour force.

But although the scope of these duties is very wide, the TUC's executive powers over the individual unions affiliated to it are limited. Its resolutions cannot bind any trade union, which remains completely autonomous. The General Council will never intervene in any dispute, unless requested by the affiliated unions involved, so long as there is any prospect of a settlement being achieved through the traditional methods of negotiation. If a deadlock is reached, and particularly if this affects workers in other industries, then the Council may take the initiative in trying to effect a settlement.

Another important function of the General Council is to apply the *Bridlington Agreement* which states the general principles necessary to ensure smooth working relations between unions. Under this agreement the Council may investigate disputes between unions, usually relating to demarcation of work or competition in the same industry to attract members. In the last resort, any union which does not accept the decision of the General Council in such a dispute may be excluded from membership to the TUC.

The General Council consists of thirty-seven members elected by the whole Congress, representing nineteen trade categories on a proportionate basis. The TUC has a permanent headquarters and its staff come under the supervision of the general secretary. It maintains a liaison with government departments, employers' organizations, and many other bodies. It has five group committees, each covering a number of related industries, and also a number of standing committees dealing with problems of organization, economic affairs, education, and international issues. It represents employees on the ACAS.

The TUC plays an active part in international trade union activity, through its affiliation to the International Confederation of Free Trade Unions and the European Trade Union confederation. It also nominates the British workers' delegation to the annual International Labour Conference.

More and more important economic decisions are being taken internationally by worldwide corporations. It has been estimated that as much as 25 per cent of British industry is now owned by American firms, and entry into the European Economic Community is another recent event. Trade unions are clearly becoming conscious of the implications in this development, such as employers wielding new economic weapons – switching investment between countries, for example, or even placing orders elsewhere if one area is faced with industrial strife.

International trade unionism thus sees the need to develop beyond its past 'fraternal' phase. Typical of the action already taken are attempts by unions to regulate relationships with the Bowater and Michelin groups. Representatives of the unions concerned hold periodic meetings in Geneva, where they exchange information about the companies' profitability and how much members should hold out for in their respective countries when they negotiate with these firms. Thus they work out common objectives and seek to get better terms than if each were to negotiate separately.

Employers' organizations

Employers' organizations, like trade unions, have grown in an entirely haphazard manner; possibly more so, since there are some 1600 of them. They fall into three main groups:

1 Those which deal with questions of labour relations and negotiate with trade unions to settle conditions of employment and avoid disputes.
2 Those which deal with these purposes and also deal with trading and professional questions.
3 Those which deal only with trading matters.

Just as their functions vary so do their structures, although for purposes of settling working conditions most employers are organized upon an industry basis, both locally and nationally. Most of the major industries in the country have local or regional organizations, combined into national federations. But, like their counterparts in the trade union movement, these federations have very limited executive authority over their individual members, especially as regards wages and working conditions. The activities of many employers' federations are very comprehensive in safeguarding the interests of their members, providing them with advice and assistance on a wide range of problems, and undertaking the organization of training courses for management.

A survey of members of employers' associations was carried out by the Donovan Commission, which listed many benefits accruing: collective action and uniform decisions; technical information; advice on trade union matters; representation and liaison with government bodies and trade unions; advice on wage rates; advice on pricing policies; information and advice on government and local authority regulations; advice on training schemes and on holiday arrangements. Some associations also provide management consultancy services and assistance with work study and productivity bargaining.

Representing employers of some 70 per cent of the working population engaged in private industry throughout the country, the *Confederation of British Industry* is the employers' equivalent of the TUC. Its aim is to secure the cooperation of employers' national federations in dealing with all industrial relations questions affecting employers and their workers. A General Purposes Committee takes executive action and there are many other standing committees corresponding to those of the TUC. There are regional associations in several parts of the country, either where most activities are centred (for example, shipbuilding on the Clyde and in Belfast) or sectional bodies dealing with the manufacture of particular products within an industry.

Disputes machinery

The machinery for the settlement of disputes (Figure 26) involves negotiation in the first place, and in some industries there is a chain of reference upwards from local disputes to national level.

This procedure for settling disputes may lead to state intervention: the parties involved may ask for this voluntarily, or it may take place compulsorily. The Secretary of State for Employment himself is obliged under certain circumstances to offer his assistance, particularly when he feels the national interest is at stake, to prevent and settle disputes. In the first place, conciliation officers may try to effect a settlement at any stage of a dispute by bringing the parties together and informing public opinion of the facts behind it. The Minister may also order an enquiry in one of two forms. Where the public interest is

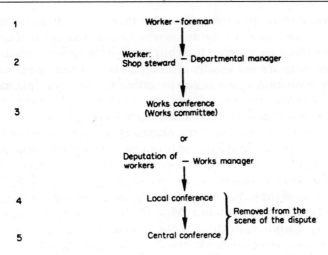

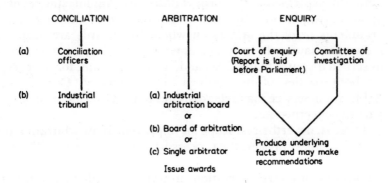

Figure 26   Settlement of disputes

seriously involved, the Minister may set up a Court of Enquiry which has formidable powers and can compel witnesses to attend and give evidence under oath; it lays a report before Parliament and may make recommendations from which a reasonable settlement of the dispute can be expected. This form of impartial public examination has often been successful in the past. Under the Conciliation Act 1896, the Minister may also appoint a Committee of Investigation which is normally employed where the national interest is not so closely involved. Its procedure is less flexible and its report is not laid before Parliament. Finally, arbitration may be tried, with the consent of both parties, when all other means of settling a dispute have failed. Both parties must agree to such action, for there is no means under the Conciliation Act 1896, or the Industrial Courts Act 1919, of compelling an unwilling party to go to arbitration. Arbitration awards under both these Acts are not legally binding on the parties concerned but, since they arise from a joint desire to settle a dispute by arbitration, the question of enforcement rarely occurs in practice. Once awards have been acted upon, they form part of a normal contract of employment.

The Secretary of State may refer cases for arbitration to the Central Arbitration Committee (CAC) or to one or more persons appointed by himself. Most cases are dealt with by the former, which is a permanent and independent tribunal free of any form of governmental control. The members of the CAC comprise independent persons and representatives of employers and unions. Most of the cases that it has dealt with since its establishment in 1919 (as the Industrial Court) have related to wage increases, hours of work, and holidays with pay. It may also be asked by the Secretary of State to give advice to him on questions which, in his opinion, ought to be referred to the CAC. Its awards are normally expressed in the form of decisions with full statements of the opposing arguments, but without discussion of the merits of those arguments or of the factors on which the awards are based. Many industries have voluntary agreements providing for the reference of unsettled disputes to the CAC and, most important, for the acceptance by both parties of its findings. The Advisory, Conciliation and Arbitration Service may refer disputes to the CAC for arbitration if the parties concerned agree.

There is, nevertheless, scope for improvement in arbitration through the CAC, for at present the process has two weaknesses. The fact that no reasons for awards are given is certainly no help to either trade unions or employers' federations in trying to settle their future policy. Second, the CAC had no resources to pursue any enquiries or research they might like to make into the background of claims presented to them.

No one would regard arbitration as a panacea for all industrial relations problems. In no way is it a substitute for collective bargaining; but it is a logical extension of existing processes, and there is much to be said in favour of arbitration being written in to all organizational policy statements on industrial relations as the final step in negotiations. Arbitration is especially suited to the settlement of disputes of right, demanding the interpretation of existing written agreements or contracts. These must be distinguished from disputes of interest, for example where a company's ability to pay or comparability with similar workers elsewhere is in question. Most managers, supervisors, and shop stewards alike probably require further training in this area to ensure that they fully understand the aims and processes of arbitration. Finally, a practical issue: it is vital to ensure that the act of arbitration works speedily and without external pressures of any kind.

Actually, the procedure described above for the engineering industry is one of only a few cases where anything more than the most general rules are laid down for settling disputes. Even where procedures are most closely defined, they are often applied in a very flexible manner. Both sides normally realize the need to allow for settlements that reflect variations in local circumstances, and accept that any dispute may take a course which does not strictly follow procedure. After all, precise procedures cannot of themselves be expected to solve industrial problems; in view of the rapidity of technological development, conflict is almost inevitable and indeed may help to clarify the situation and speed the way for any necessary changes.

Two developments in industrial relations practice which have caught the attention of the media during the 1980s are no-strike agreements and pendulum arbitration. The former are comprehensive single union agreements which have been designed to gain flexibility in working practices in such ways as to make strikes 'unnecessary'. At the core of many of these agreements is pendulum (or final offer) arbitration. This is a simple, elegant and, at least superficially, attractive method of impasse resolution in which arbitrators are constrained to choose what they judge to be the more reasonable final offer of either party. The arbitrator has no freedom to split the difference, nor compromise nor fashion the award. Supporters of this concept claim that it encourages the *negotiators* to compromise and that, as a result, negotiations rarely end in a strike or lock-out or, indeed, the intervention of the arbitrator.

The problems faced by the Donovan Commission

Trade unions, which were granted a privileged legal position early in the twentieth century when they were very weak compared with employers, have now become extremely powerful. In turn, society has come to question this position, believing that unions should suit their policies and actions to the national interest, and that the welfare of the majority of the community should not be sacrificed to the sectional interests of a few. It was in this context that the Royal Commission on Trade Unions and Employers' Associations was appointed in 1965, to examine these specific problems:

1 The role of trade unions and employers' associations in accelerating the social and economic advance of the nation.
2 Relations between management and employees.
3 The role of trade unions in promoting the interests of members, and the comparable role of employers' associations.
4 The law affecting the activities of trade unions and employers' associations.

These problems had manifested themselves over the years in the following ways:

Demarcation disputes, between workers and workers, rather than with their employers.
Unofficial strikes, which accounted for the large majority of working days lost.
Union power over individual members, including the withdrawal of a union card, thus depriving a person of his/her livelihood. The intimidation of individual workers, especially during unofficial strikes, was another common abuse of power.
The closed shop, where union power was exercised over workers who were not members of the union at all.

In its Report, the Donovan Commission distinguished between two systems:* the formal system employed in the official institutions, and the informal system created by the actual behaviour of trade unions and employers. Industry-wide collective agreements, which are supposed to settle pay, hours of work, and other conditions, form the keystone of the formal system; but the informal system, or what really happens in practice, is often at odds with the formal. Over the past thirty years there has been a decline in the extent to which industry-wide agreements determine actual pay, and today local plant bargaining is usually much more important.

In summary, it was found that the existing system of industrial relations had many shortcomings: the tendency for extreme decentralization and self-government to degenerate into indecision and anarchy; the propensity to breed inefficiency; and the reluctance to accept change – all these are characteristics that become more damaging as they develop, as the rate of technical progress increases, and as the need for economic growth becomes more urgent.

The changing economic situation of the 1980s and 1990s – deep into recession, eventual signs of recovery – has called into question

Royal Commission on Trade Unions and Employers Associations 1965–68 (Cmnd 3623, HMSO), Chapter 3.

the continuing relevance of the Donovan Report, twenty-five years on. For instance, the Report's analysis rested centrally on the pluralistic ethic of industrial relations, that management must accept the presence of fundamentally differing interests in the workplace, acknowledge the consequent restraints, and be prepared to negotiate accordingly. The unitary frame of reference on the other hand, implies but one source of authority and one focus of loyalty, relying on the workforce as a whole to follow a common objective as a healthy functioning team.

The irony of the period since Donovan reported is that the era of greatest change and innovation in workplace practice and behaviour was the 1980s when managers were able to get closest to the unitary style. In the printing and newspaper industries, for example, the most far-reaching changes were successfully imposed upon employees with the minimum of negotiation. Today the buzzword is the 'decollectivization'* of industrial relations.

On the other hand, trades unions' own efforts to develop their strength, especially through mergers to form new powerful conglomerates, may mean that they will be well placed to re-assert themselves as economic recovery succeeds recession. In which case, to what extent will the Donovan analysis fit the new phase? In fact, 'basic Donovan' seems to have stood the test of time and, indeed become institutionalized by legislation. The dichotomy between the formal system of industrial relations at national level and actual behaviour within organizations may have disappeared; but there are indications that it has merely been transferred to this lower level, so that there always will be an informal system, to set against the formal, in local factories, workshops, stores and offices. The reality seems to be that we will always have to live with an imperfect formula for industrial relations because in the last resort these depend on relationships rather than written procedures.

Labour legislation in perspective

Dating back well over a century, the mass of labour legislation requires some form of framework to place it all into perspective. One categorization† distinguishes between:

---

*'The Donovan Analysis: does it still hold good?', Ewart Wooldridge, *Personnel Management*, June 1989, page 42.
†See *Labour and the Law*, O. Kahn-Freund (Stevens, 1972), and 'Some Comments on Current Labour Law', T. O'Sullivan in *Personnel Review*, Vol. 7, No. 1, 1978, pages 5–13.

(a) Auxiliary law, which provides support for the industrial relations system, creating institutions and procedures and allowing them to operate.
(b) Regulative law, giving rights to individual workers within the employment relationship.
(c) Restrictive law, which lays down what is and what is not allowed when conducting collective bargaining or any associated trade disputes.
(d) Participative law, aimed at integrating workers and their unions more closely into the commercial, social, and political operation of their organizations.

The early history of such legislation clearly concerns auxiliary law, and judicial interpretations of it which tended to create case law which was restrictive in nature. The early 1960s saw the emergence of regulative law and the creation of individual rights not usually covered by collective bargaining. This was followed by more restrictive law, culminating in the Industrial Relations Act 1971, which in turn was rolled back by new legislation, avowedly auxiliary in nature – TULRA 1974 and 1976 and EPA 1975 – all of which is completely lacking in restrictive law.

These changes reflect swings in the political pendulum, of course, and one obvious conclusion is that trade unions seem to be successful in opposing restrictive law and interventionist thrusts in labour law generally. Nevertheless, the Conservative Government, which was returned to power in 1979, quickly proposed changes which amount to the introduction of restrictive legislation affecting the closed shop, picketing, and ballots of union members before strike decisions. Since that time reforms of employment and trade union law have been aimed at obtaining a better balance of power between trades unions and employers and between trades unions and their own members. All this has played a key role in transforming British industrial relations. The Government believes that the Employment Acts of 1980, 1982, 1988 and 1990 and the Trade Union Act of 1984 have helped to make union leaders more accountable to their members and to promote an acceptance of the rule of law in industrial relations. Thus, in 1991, industrial disputes were recorded at their lowest level for more than a century.

The previous statutory recognition procedure was repealed in 1980, leaving employers free to decide whether or not they wish to recognize a particular union or unions for collective bargaining purposes. The law now makes a trade union responsible if industrial action is called for or organized by any of its officials. So, if a trade union acts unlawfully, for example, by calling for industrial action without a proper secret ballot of members, legal action can be taken against the union itself. The law also means that if a union defies a court order, for example an order to withdraw an unlawful call for industrial action, it can be held to be in contempt of court. Severe penalties can be imposed in such circumstances, including sequestration of the union's assets.

Prior to the 1980 the organization of almost any form of industrial action was protected by 'statutory immunities'. The legislation reforms since then have restricted the scope of such immunities in a number of ways, so that to have their benefit, the organization of industrial action must now:

- Be in contemplation or furtherance of a trade dispute between workers and their own employer.
- Not involve workers who have no dispute with their own employers ('secondary' or 'sympathetic' action).
- Not be done to establish or maintain a union-only labour agreement ('the closed shop').
- Not involve unlawful picketing.
- Not be done in support of any employee dismissed while taking unofficial industrial action.

Before calling for industrial action, a trade union must first obtain the support of its members in a properly-conducted secret ballot. Moreover, trade union members have the right to restrain their union from calling on them and other members to take action unless a ballot has supported the action.

All individuals have the right under the law not to be dismissed or refused employment because they are not or will not become trade union members. Anyone wishing to complain on these grounds may do so to an industrial tribunal. Other rights include: a statutory remedy for workers who have been unjustly disciplined by their union; inspection of their union's accounting records; and the right to have subscription deductions from their pay stopped if they leave the union. A Commissioner for the Rights of Trade Union Members has been appointed by the Government to ensure that members need not be disadvantaged in bringing legal proceeding against their union to enforce rights and duties. The Trade Union and Labour Relations (Consolidation) Act 1992 brought together much existing legislation, including measures concerning: the legal status of trade unions; the rights of trade union members (including rights to vote in the election of union leaders); organizing, or taking part in, industrial action or picketing; protection of employees and workers against closed shop practices; collective bargaining; and procedure for handling redundancies.

Further steps along the road of reforms were announced in the

Green Paper, *Industrial Relations in the 1990s,* and further legislation may be expected along these lines:

- Provision that seven days notice should be given before strikes and other industrial action.
- A right for members of the public to seek injunctions to halt unlawful industrial action affecting public services.
- The right for employees to join the union of their choice.
- The right to a postal ballot on union mergers.
- A proposal that collective agreements should have the status of contracts binding upon both parties unless they include specific provisions making them unenforceable.
- New powers for the Certification Officer to investigate alleged mismanagement of union finances.

Since the second half of the 1970s the European Community has exerted growing pressure on the UK to align its domestic employment laws more closely with EC legislative requirements; often against the will of our government which generally sought to block proposals (except those on health and safety). Most recently, as the 1992 unification project approached reality, the Single Europe Act strengthened the original Treaty of Rome's social policy dimension, although at the same time plans to harmonize employment law throughout the Community were modified; particular emphasis was placed on flexibility, with member-states being left with considerable discretion as to how European legislation should be applied within their own boundaries.

The 'social charter' (The Community Charter of the Fundamental Social Rights of Workers) is a proposal for a European platform of social but primarily employment rights. Together with proposals for economic and monetary union, the social charter became the focus of discussion about the future direction of the EC, the most controversial aspect being the concern of different member-states as to whether the competitiveness of their national economies would be helped or hindered by measures based on the charter. In the context of increased competition and economic restructuring after 1992, most concern was felt over the possibilities of businesses relocating their operations in those countries where labour market conditions and legislation are to their advantage: such 'social dumping' would tend to exert downward pressure on labour standards in the more advanced countries.

The British Government, on the other hand, opposed the charter on the grounds that it might jeopardize the deregulatory approach to the labour market which was seen as a key element in boosting competitiveness, creating jobs and attracting international investment.

Other less-developed member-states' support for the social charter has also been cool for fear of its impact on labour costs in their domestic economies. The final version of the charter sought to accommodate Britain's objections, but statutory intervention may still be necessary with regard to some of the twelve employment rights affected:

1 The free movement of workers within the EC.
2 'Fair remuneration' for employment.
3 The improvement and approximation of conditions of employment.
4 Social security.
5 Freedom of association and collective bargaining.
6 Vocational training.
7 Equal treatment for men and women.
8 Information, consultation and participation arrangements.
9 Health and safety at the workplace.
10 Young people.
11 Retired people.
12 Disabled people.

Despite the inevitable compromises reached during the evolution of the social charter and the procedural or constitutional pitfalls involved, the political impetus is such that EC law is certain to have considerable influence on British industrial relations during the 1990s — especially as regards the participation issue, the definition of maximum working hours, and a typical contract of employment.

In some areas collective bargaining strategies are already developing a European dimension — big companies, in particular, closely follow the sorts of settlements reached by their rivals with their workforces throughout Europe. In business terms European employers generally favour economic and monetary union: the existing systems show how much simpler and less uncertain life would be with a single currency, with savings on transaction costs and producers knowing both what they will have to pay for supplies and what they will receive for their goods in the months ahead. After all, what is the point of removing barriers and opening up markets by 1992 if governments can continue to change competitive conditions by allowing their respective currencies' exchange rates to fluctuate?

Second, European legislation will have the effect of bringing management and labour sides closer together. Although the British Government and many employers resist compulsion in these matters, the principle that workers should have rights to information and consultation, as set out in the European Company Statute, will certainly not be dropped. Such rights will be exercisable in future through board-room representation, through separately established works councils or in other ways agreed jointly between the organization and its workers.

Third, it can be argued that a European Monetary Union (EMU) will not be realizable nor sustainable unless collective bargaining does become European in scope. It will happen in practice partly as a result of pressures from workers and their unions agitating to remove differences in wages and salaries paid for similar jobs in different countries. Demands will be made to close any gaps, and if employers maintain that productivity levels are different, then workers and unions will call for any investment necessary to make up that difference. Such will be the approach to future negotiations; in fact, there is already some evidence* of the use of 'European performance comparisons', covering a widening range of issues, by both employers and unions in the formulation of their strategies.

Institutions

One way of further comprehending the scope of current legislation and its application is to look at the roles of the institutions which now exist to assist in the smooth running of industrial relations in this country.

(a) Advisory, Conciliation and Arbitration Service (ACAS)

This is headed by a ten-man council appointed by the Secretary of State for Employment, and consists of a chairperson and nine other members, three appointed after consultation with the CBI and three after consultation with the TUC. The service has the duty of offering advice, conciliation, and mediation in both private and public sectors, where this is considered likely to be of assistance. Having regard to the procedural agreements already existing in an industry or area of employment, the service does not normally seek to intervene, unless and until there has been a failure to obtain a settlement within those procedures.

Conciliation is undertaken by the full-time professional staff of the service, although outside people may be called in as mediators if it is thought fit. At the joint request of the parties in dispute, single arbitrators or boards of arbitration may be appointed to determine

---

*'Collecting Bargaining in the New Europe', Peter Coldrick, *Personnel Management*, October 1990, page 61.

differences on agreed terms of reference. A panel of people experienced in industrial relations has been set up for this purpose.

The 'A' stands for 'advisory', signifying that the organization has been given the statutory duty to provide a free advice service on industrial relations matters. In fact this takes up about 40 per cent of total staff time: dealing with requirements for basic information; responding to some enquiries by paying short visits to the employers concerned; and 'in-depth' assistance with projects, surveys, joint working parties and extended training exercises.

The extent of the ACAS's services can be found in statistics about its workload in 1990. Its assistance was sought in 1260 disputes and there were some 200 other requests to provide arbitration. It handled over 418,000 enquiries on all aspects of industrial relations and employment policies received from employers, managers, trade unions, employee representatives and individuals. Specialist staff made nearly 7000 advisory visits. There were over 52,000 conciliation cases during the year, relating to unfair dismissals and complaints under the equal pay, sex discrimination and race relations legislation. The Work Research Unit furthered its aims of encouraging industry and commerce to adopt measures that can lead to improvements in the quality of working life and so to improvements in economic performance.

(b) Industrial Tribunals

Originally set up in 1964, these tribunals exist to adjudicate on matters arising from the Contracts of Employment Act 1963, the Industrial Training Act 1964, the Redundancy Payments Act 1965, and the Equal Pay Act 1970. They sit in regional centres, and also deal with individual cases and complaints under the Trade Union and Labour Relations Acts and the Race Relations Act 1976; they have powers to award compensation and make orders determining the rights of individuals or organizations. Their procedures are informal, and they are required to offer opportunities for conciliation between the parties before hearing a case.

(c) Central Arbitration Committee

This is the old Industrial Court, given a new name, and as such continues to deal with claims under equal pay legislation, for example. In addition, the ACAS refers to it for arbitration claims by registered trade unions when an employer has failed to disclose information to them or has not complied with a requirement to negotiate with them. Disputes may also be referred for arbitration, if the parties concerned agree.

(d) Certification Officer

The registration of trade unions is intended to ensure that, in order to benefit from the rights and privileges originally established by the Industrial Relations Act, trade union rules comply with statutory minimum standards. These standards, which also apply to employers' associations, refer to the constitutions, management, links with members, property, and the financial arrangements of all registered organizations. The Certification Officers' tasks are to check on these rules, ensure that they are observed in practice, and to vet the administration of unions and employers' associations so as to safeguard the public interest, and protect the rights of members and those seeking membership. He can investigate complaints against registered organizations, and may take unresolved cases to the ACAS for adjudication. He is responsible for certifying the independence of trade unions under the Employment Protection Act 1975.

(e) Employment Appeal Tribunal

This body hears appeals from the decisions of industrial tribunals on points of law (they previously went to the High Court). It also hears appeals from the decisions of the Certification Officer.

ACAS Codes of Practice

Some sections in the 1972 Code of Industrial Relations Practice have been superseded by ACAS codes on disciplinary procedures, on the disclosure of information to trade unions for collective bargaining purposes, and on time off for trade union duties. But the 1972 Code is still important because of the significance of the remaining sections on responsibilities, employment policies, and communication and consultation.

The provisions of the Code on disciplinary procedures as set out in Chapter 6, page 117, and the guidelines of the other two Codes are relevant to the issues that have just been considered in this chapter.

Disclosure of information

This Code was prepared following the Employment Protection Act 1975, which placed obligations on employers to disclose such information which it would be for good industrial relations to disclose. The Code lists examples of information which can be relevant in certain bargaining circumstances; these include:

(a) Pay and benefits: job evaluation systems, grading criteria, fringe benefits, total pay bill.
(b) Conditions of service: training, promotion, redeployment, equal opportunities, health, safety and welfare matters.
(c) Manpower: labour force organization, turnover, absenteeism, manning standards, planned changes in work methods.
(d) Performance: productivity and efficiency data, savings made from increased productivity, returns on investments.
(e) Financial: cost structures, profit and loss, allocation of profits, loans, and liabilities.

At the same time it is appreciated that some information could cause substantial injury to an employer if disclosed; for example, cost information on individual products, detailed analyses of proposed investments, marketing policies, and tender prices.

Unions are urged to take a responsible attitude to requests for information, making them well in advance and coordinating their requests with other unions. It is important too that their representatives are sufficiently well trained to understand and use the information effectively. Employers are advised to be open and helpful and meet requests as soon as possible. A refusal should be explained and be capable of substantiation. Negotiators should try to arrive at a joint understanding on such matters as the information likely to be required and the way it should be presented.

The Code imposes no legal obligation on an employer to discuss any specific item of information, but if a request is refused, a union may complain to the Central Arbitration Committee, which may ask ACAS to conciliate before hearing the complaint itself. The Code is admissible in any proceedings before the Committee; if the Committee upholds the complaint, it may make an enforceable award on terms and conditions of employment for the employees concerned.

Time off for trade union duties

This Code has to cover a wide variety of circumstances and problems: employers have to cope with exigencies of production and safety requirements, for example; and the trade unions have to overcome communication difficulties arising from shift work, part-time work, scattered workplaces, and members' domestic commitments. It is therefore essential that local agreements be made on arrangements for enabling time off in ways appropriate to particular situations. But even if formal agreement cannot be reached, this should not preclude the granting of release.

The Code is based on the realization that, in addition to his/her work as an employee, a trade union official may have important duties concerned with industrial relations, and if they are to be performed properly the official should be permitted reasonable paid time off during working hours. Relevant duties include:

(a) Collective bargaining with the appropriate level of management.
(b) Informing constituents about negotiations or consultations with management.
(c) Meeting with other shop stewards or union officials on matters that are concerned with industrial relations between his/her employer and any associated employers and their employees.
(d) Interviews with and on behalf of constituents on grievance and disciplinary matters concerning them and their employer.
(e) Appearing on behalf of constituents before an outside official body such as an industrial tribunal.
(f) Explanations to new employees whom he/she will represent of the role of the union in the workplace and industrial relations structure.

The Code advocates training in relevant subjects: any shop steward who has duties concerning industrial relations should be permitted reasonable time off for initial basic training, and for training sessions where there have been changes in the structure or topics of negotiation at the workplace or legislative changes affecting industrial relations.

The Code also points out that to operate effectively and democratically, trade unions need active participation in certain union activities; reasonable time off during working hours is therefore recommended for taking part, as representatives, in meetings of the official policy-making bodies of the union such as the Executive Committee or annual Conference or representing the union on external bodies such as the committees of ITBs. The ACAS also advocates time off for voting in union elections and for meetings of members during working hours where there is an urgent matter to be discussed.

In order that officers perform their duties efficiently and communicate effectively with members and colleagues, management should make available facilities like accommodation for meetings, access to a telephone, notice board, and the use of office facilities.

Union officials must be prepared to accept certain obligations in all this. They should bear in mind management responsibilities for maintaining production and services to customers, and for making the operational arrangements for the time off. Officials should therefore give as much notice as possible of their need for time off, and management and union should seek to agree arrangements for other employees to cover the work of officials or members taking time off. Where such union meetings in work time are deemed necessary, the two sides should agree on a time that minimizes the effects on production or service, for example towards the end of the shift or just before or after a meal break.

The Code also deals with industrial action. Time off should be approved, it says, to use agreed procedures to resolve problems constructively and avoid industrial action. Such arrangements are particularly needed where communication and cooperation between management and unions are in danger of breaking down.

Further reading

Contemporary British Industrial Relations, S. Kessler and F. Bayliss (Macmillan 1992).
Employment Disputes and the Third Party, Sir Pat Lowry (Macmillan, 1990).
Modern Employment Law, 6th edition, Michael Whincup (Heinemann, 1988).

15
Labour relations at the workplace

No general framework of industrial relations can of itself create the harmony and trust between management and workers in individual organizations necessary to develop the spirit of cooperation so essential for achieving success in business. Responsibility for establishing good relations rests with both management and workers, but there can be no doubt that the initiative must be taken by the former. Confidence must be earned over years of consistent dealing with day-to-day personnel problems, in a manner which reflects management's attitudes towards the basic need of individual employees for a satisfactory working environment in its fullest sense.

Maintaining contact and spreading understanding between management and workers is the purpose of communications in industry. Slowly it has come to be realized that improvements in efficiency, leading to increased productivity, depend in large measure on the cooperation of workers, and that this can only be obtained if they are told of and comprehend management's aims and plans. The achievement of effective communications is the subject of the next chapter: the point to be made clear here is that experience shows that the most important factor in communications is the quality of relationships within the organization between management, supervisors, and worker groups.

Industrial relations in Britain have changed considerably in recent years, mainly due to the impact of the recession, new labour law and the effect of new technology on the structure of industry, work patterns and employee relations. There can be no doubt that the power of the unions has declined as a result, with such obvious indications as high unemployment, falling union membership and dropping union density.

A 'new trade unionism' is emerging, with a design which embraces single union recognition, flexibility, single status, consultation forums and pendulum arbitration; not to mention some managements' willingness to surrender privileges relating to involvement in companies' affairs when these need to be traded off in order to reach strike-free deals. Other challenges are presented to trade unions by the sweeping changes in the ways people work and their attitudes towards unions. At the most basic level a clear and growing majority of British workers no longer belong to a trade union – the proportion in TUC-affiliated unions is now below 40 per cent. Britain's unions have failed to crack the growing high-tech industries and have been slipping back in their traditional base of manufacturing. More and more employers, especially those setting up for the first time, do not see the need for unions and do not recognize them. All this against a background of changes in the composition of the workforce, which in themselves make fresh demands on unions to adapt, and the fact that the pace of technological advance (and the impact which this has on unions) seems unlikely to diminish.

The decline of multi-employer bargaining with trade unions and the decentralization of collective bargaining within organizations have been important developments in recent years: the teaching profession, the water industry, electricity after privatization, and British steel are significant examples. It is generally believed that these trends will encourage lower rates of wage inflation, greater labour market flexibility and (eventually) higher levels of employment.

In the event, the distribution of bargaining power between the parties may continue to be the deciding factor between centralization and decentralization of negotiations. Nevertheless, decentralization does appear to be gaining ground in situations which concern:

- A multi-product company.
- Relatively unstable markets.
- A multi-divisional structure.
- Decentralized functions.
- A preference for negotiating with shop stewards.
- Plans to relate pay more closely to performance.

A decentralized format clearly allows organizations to respond with greater sensitivity to market changes. It also allows for the possibility of moving to single-union agreements at decentralized autonomous factories or units. At the same time, the substantially enlarged roles of both line managers and local shop stewards have to be recognized.

Shop stewards

Key figures in labour relations at any workplace are shop stewards. Their emergence can be traced to the remoteness of union branch and district officers whose concern for all workers in their areas means that they can devote comparatively little time or effort to any single establishment. The strength of the shop steward movement has always been based on the argument that rank-and-file union members must act for themselves in their own local interests, even if this means taking unofficial action with unofficial leaders.

Typical of the constitutional powers that have been granted to shop stewards are the conditions set out in the 1922 agreement between the Engineering and Allied Employers' Federation and the engineering trade unions, which established a procedure for the ventilation of grievances and for dealing with questions raised at the workplace by shop stewards. The agreement permitted workers who were members of trade unions employed in federated establishments to appoint shop stewards to act on their behalf. The names of these stewards were to be intimated officially to management on election by the trade union concerned. Shop stewards were to be subject to the control of the trade unions they represented and could act only in accordance with agreements signed by the employers and unions. The employers, for their part, agreed that shop stewards should be accorded facilities for dealing with questions raised in their departments, including time to carry out their duties in connection with works committees and power to visit other departments of the establishment while doing so. Both employers and shop stewards were forbidden to enter into arrangements contrary to any agreement between the employers' federation or local association and the trade unions.

Shop stewards are the main link between the members of a trade union working in a particular department and the full-time local officials of that union. Although their election normally must be confirmed by the branch or district officers of the union, they are not themselves officials of the union. But they are accepted by their employer as the union's accredited representative and spokesperson, providing a recognized point of contact, especially in large firms where employee representation on works committees may be confined to shop stewards. They assist in settling complaints and disputes between workers and management at workshop level, and may also take part in such technical matters as rate-fixing on piecework operations where it is desirable to take workers' points of view into account. In big organizations it is usual for shop stewards to have their own committee under the chairmanship of the most senior steward, called the *convener*.

As regards their union, shop stewards' chief functions are to recruit new members, to maintain membership, and in some cases to collect dues. Through union branch meetings they may assist in formulating policy, and are then responsible for reporting back and explaining that policy to the members they represent. Conversely, they report to the union about wages and conditions of employment in their firm. They may also play an important part in the initial stages of claims in respect of industrial injuries incurred by any of their members.

It is an important prerogative of shop stewards in most establishments that they have direct access to management. Although it is unusual for them to take part in any national machinery of negotiations for their industry, there is an increasing movement towards local negotiations for the adjustment of central agreements, and stewards play an obvious part in these; in fact they often take the initiative in presenting claims to management for local increases on negotiated rates. But the role of shop stewards in the settlement of disputes, including those relating to demarcation of work, manning of machines, and redundancy, is generally limited to the stage at which those disputes, having failed to reach settlement at workshop level, pass into the hands of full-time union officials at branch or district level. In recent years, judging by the incidence of unofficial strikes, there has in fact been a marked increase in the number of disputes dealt with entirely by shop stewards. These usually relate to demands about working arrangements, rules, or discipline; the amount of work considered reasonable for a given wage; changes in working methods and the use of labour; and the treatment of individuals by supervisors and departmental managers.

Discussing all these subjects with management places shop stewards in the van of the movement towards industrial democracy, aimed at integrating managerial authority with the rights of individual employees. The onset of higher levels of unemployment also increases shop steward activity as they fight to preserve security of employment and stability of earnings. They also demand the right to participate with management in reaching decisions that affect their well-being.

Authority to call a strike on their own initiative is rarely given to shop stewards by their unions. Nevertheless, by reason of the influence which their activities give them at the place of work, they sometimes do call workers out on strike without the permission of their union officials and sometimes in breach of agreements. But since the unions concerned have not sanctioned this 'unofficial' action, the workers involved do not receive any strike pay.

This analysis of the place of the shop steward in the local structure is echoed in the advice on good policy given in the Code of Industrial Relations (CIR) Practice, which in turn was supplemented by a CIR report on the facilities that should be afforded to stop stewards.

In the first place, it is suggested that trade unions need to clarify the stewards' functions and responsibilities – election arrangements, the issue of union credentials, the observation of agreements, how to handle grievances, communication with members – all matters that could be dealt with in a more standardized way, and hence more efficiently. Employers should also review their present attitudes towards shop stewards. Although the latter are now generally recognized as making a valuable contribution in the field of industrial relations, it should be management which takes the initiative, and which sets the tone of the relationship by actively seeking their help.

The functions of shop stewards that are of joint concern should be jointly reviewed, especially as regards the facilities necessary to carry them out. In trying to apply industry-wide agreements, it must be recognized that the key areas are usually at company or unit level. Management and unions, therefore, need to decide on constituencies, the number of stewards to be appointed, the range of their duties, and the facilities needed for them to perform effectively.

The growing significance of plant bargaining is relevant here, of course, for it is likely to develop further as processes become ever more specialized and capital-intensive industries strive to retain their skilled labour. A major consequence is the shift of power and authority on the shop floor from union executives to the shop stewards. Productivity bargaining, which cuts through the complexity of wage agreements, job redefinition, shiftwork, and overtime payments, has added to this local power. Shop stewards, whose original tasks were largely limited to recruiting members and collecting subscriptions, now find themselves negotiating local agreements, explaining their nature to the workers they represent, and even supervising the way they operate.

Many trade unions undertake their own educational activities, and as long ago as 1948 the General Council of the TUC urged unions to consider the training of shop stewards in such subjects as the elements of production and costing as well as industrial relations. The growth of the use of work study in industry also stimulated this type of training, which has since been taken up by technical colleges and universities. Some progressive employers, when introducing work study practices into their organizations, arrange for shop stewards to train in the technique so that union members might have greater confidence in it. Since 1951 the TUC has run full-time courses in production and management for shop stewards and members of joint production committees; their main purpose is to assist workshop representatives who act on behalf of unions in negotiations and joint consultation to increase their competence by acquiring knowledge of the terminology, principles, and elementary techniques of management. The subjects studied include industrial efficiency, works management, work study, wage systems, costing, company finance and accounts, and problems of productivity. The more progressive trade union leaders thus seem convinced of the need for wider training of their future officials, but many unions still do little or nothing in this direction. A further interesting development is the decision of several Industrial Training Boards (initially shipbuilding, construction, and water supply) to make grants to employers who release their shop stewards for approved training courses. So employers who do not believe in training trade union representatives in the firm's time in future may be indirectly subsidizing those who do. Again, the Code of Industrial Relations Practice urges management and trade unions to review the type of training most appropriate for the stewards' needs, and to take all reasonable steps to ensure that stewards receive this training.

Each union should also take care to see that its own shop stewards are adequately informed about its policies, organization, and the agreements to which it is a party. Management, too, should ensure that stewards are well informed about its objectives and employment policies.

Workshop rule

Some industries appear to be much more prone to friction between workers and management than others, and there often seems to be a hard core of firms within each industry which have continuous trouble over workshop regulations. Since other comparable organizations have much less trouble, the only conclusion must be that it is not only collective agreements and union rules which lead to workshop friction, but also worker–management relations in each individual establishment. These relations are intimately connected with the operation of workshop rules which are usually out of reach both of union control and national agreement, but are very much the concern of the shop steward. It is most important to appreciate this 'separation', because it is not a fact that is advertised by either unions or employers' associations. Officials who are ultimately responsible for maintaining union authority and agreements no doubt feel that their position would be weakened if they were to acknowledge that a considerable part of shop steward activity was beyond their control. It is, nevertheless, one way of describing the 'unofficial system' identified by the Donovan Commission.

In addition to union rules and legislation (such as the HASAWA) a wide variety of domestic rules apply in each workplace. There are agreed rules about procedure and conditions of work which supplement those made in district and national agreements between unions and management; these may be written or simply based on custom and practice. Then there are works rules laid down by management as part of workers' contracts of employment; these must be written, but often overlap into works custom. Finally, there are workgroup rules established by workers on the job, usually dealing with such matters as the pace and sharing of work. Many of these rules are made unilaterally by workers or management until challenged by the other; they normally then form the basis of negotiation and, once settled, both sides are obliged to see that they are kept. Some managers feel that the existence of shop stewards makes rule-making and enforcement easier, others believe the opposite. It is obvious, however, that a system which includes worker representatives is more democratic than one which relies exclusively on management decisions.

An element of self-government is also reflected in decisions on two broad groups of topics: those matters in national agreements which are left to be settled locally, and matters that are essentially domestic to the establishment itself, such as complaints about the canteen or the settlement of holidays. In either case the calling of meetings to discuss problems, together with informal discussion between stewards and workers, constitutes a type of self-government in the workplace. The implications of this for trade unions are of the utmost importance. If low attendance at branch meetings makes the self-government of trade unions difficult, and if workshop groups, in themselves largely self-governing, become the active focus of membership participation, the possibility of strain between workshop, branch, and outside officials increases. At the moment this apparent gap is bridged successfully because shop stewards often form the core of branch membership attending meetings in any case, and union officials themselves usually take great trouble to maintain close contact with the shop stewards in their areas.

A large proportion of shop stewards accept the need to play a responsible part in maintaining works discipline, one reason being that discipline is in the general interest. It can be argued therefore that management should never try to weaken the hold of stewards over their members but rather provide them with opportunities for strengthening their confidence. The existence of agreed rules between workers and management on the factory floor gives responsibilities to both sides, but trade union members are often unable to see the practical limits to stewards' militancy. They feel that if they act in a 'constitutional' manner they may become a part of the management team, and this is one of the main reasons why some unions are opposed to giving formal powers to shop stewards. In practice, however, 'constitutional' stewards often achieve better results than their more militant colleagues, as there is a great deal to be said for not pressing opposition to its ultimate limits. Stewards are obviously unable to change their management and they are wise to recognize that successful negotiation includes the ability to save the other side's face, so that a working relationship profitable to both sides can be continued.

Thus an accurate analysis of the roles of shop stewards seems very difficult, closely involved as they are with their unions, the policies and behaviour of local managers, and the collective agreements, traditions, and organizational problems of the industry in which they work. It is an over-simplification to regard them merely as subordinate trade union officers carrying out instructions or applying national agreements within their local spheres. Indeed, operating in such a variety of different situations, shop stewards need considerable latitude if they are to represent workers effectively, and it therefore seems almost impossible to subject them to detailed control by their unions. Union leaders themselves are faced with a dilemma, knowing that stewards' activities at the workplace are essential, yet ever aware of the threat they pose to the cohesiveness of union policy and standards of discipline. Since stewards cannot be rigidly controlled, can they not at least be more strongly influenced to accept the objectives and priorities laid down by their union's leadership? To a large extent each union must find its own solution to this problem, mainly by improving communications with its ordinary members and their workplace representatives. The TUC could also help by trying to give a much clearer sense of direction to the shop steward movement as a whole.

A number of reviews of workplace industrial relations reveal an ever-widening range of issues and matters of concern, varying in type, size and complexity. These were well illustrated in a survey* of 2041 establishments, covering both private and public industries and services, carried out by the Social Services branch of the Department of Employment, which paints a comprehensive and fascinating picture of the contemporary industrial relations scene, including the following major points:

(a) Recognition and membership

67 per cent of the establishments surveyed recognized trade unions as representing some employees at the place of work, so nearly one-third

*Workplace Industrial Relations, Neil Millward, Employment Gazette, July 1983.

did not. Altogether 66 per cent of manual workers were union members and 46 per cent of non-manual workers were. Levels of trade union membership and recognition followed similar patterns, both being generally greater in the public sector. In the private sector, in fact, over a third of establishments had no trade union members, while nearly another third had union membership densities of 90 per cent or more because of the closed shop. The size of establishments is strongly associated with the extent of recognition. So is (inversely) the proportion of women employed; the higher that proportion, the less likely is a union to be recognized and the lower the membership density. In nearly three-quarters of establishments where manual workers are recognized, there are written agreements relating to the primary manual negotiating group, usually brought about as a result of discussion and agreement, although in a small number of cases industrial action had been threatened or the ACAS had been called in to help.

(b) Shop stewards

In three-quarters of the establishments where manual unions are recognized, one or more shop stewards had been appointed; in just over a half there were senior stewards or conveners, and in 5 per cent of cases one or more of those senior stewards spent all or nearly all of their work time on trade union matters. Full-time conveners are rare in establishments with less than 500 employees, but most of those with over 2000 had them. Just over a quarter of stewards had received training during the previous year, mostly organized by the unions themselves, but taking place at the initiative of management in many cases. A relatively high use of the time-off provisions of the Employment Protection Act occurs, and the training is regarded as very useful by both stewards and management. Substantial majorities of senior stewards have access to office facilities provided by management.

(c) Multi-unionism

Multi-unionism is widespread in Britain: nearly a half of the establishments surveyed had two or more manual trade unions with members in the workplace. In many cases, however, these unions combine for negotiating purposes, so that managers have to deal with only one bargaining unit in practice. Manual and non-manual workers are almost always represented by different unions and have separate negotiating arrangements with management.

(d) The closed shop

The survey revealed that, overall, nearly a half (44 per cent) of all the manual workers encompassed normally had to be trade union members in order to keep their jobs, but that the closed shop was much less common among non-manual workers. At the same time, it was clear that substantially more establishments have very high levels of manual trade union membership than are reported as having a comprehensive manual closed shop. The institution of the closed shop grew substantially over the twenty years up to 1980, and analysis shows four major sources of variation in its incidence: ownership (largely public versus private sector), the size of the establishment, the size of the organization of which the establishment is part, and the composition of the workforce – i.e., the same factors which distinguish between establishments which recognize trade unions and those which do not. 8 per cent of manual workers are in pre-entry closed shops, compared with 44 per cent of all manual workers who are in some form of closed shop. Virtually all non-manual workers in closed shops are covered by post-entry arrangements. Where post-entry closed shops operate, workers are normally expected to join the union concerned within a month of starting work. Closed shops are generally supported by agreements, in written form, between management and unions. The arrangements often contain a provision for some workers to be excluded from the requirement to be members of trade unions, commonly on grounds of religious belief, and less frequently for reasons of conscience or non-membership of a union prior to the closed shop agreement.

The check-off (systems of deducting trade union subscriptions from pay packets) is even more widespread than the closed shop, affecting three-quarters or more of the establishments surveyed. The check-off is almost universal in nationalized industries and public corporations and very common in national and local government and larger businesses in the private sector.

(e) Trade union branches

Typically trade unionists belong to branches with between 200 and 2000 members: the smallest of these are based at workplaces; somewhat larger are the 'single-employer' branches, where membership is drawn from more than one establishment; and 'multi-employer' branches are generally the largest. Workplace branches usually meet less than once every two months, whereas multi-employer branches meet more often than once a month. Nevertheless the former type has the best attended meetings, with 20-30 per cent of members turning up, compared with only 5 per cent in multi-employer branches. It is, of course, well-known that shop stewards attend branch meetings much more frequently than ordinary members.

(f) Appointment of workplace representatives

The commonest method of electing shop stewards and other lay representatives is by show of hands at a meeting. Ballots are used in only a small minority of cases. Periodic re-elections usually occur once a year. In only a half of all cases is there ever more than one candidate for a shop steward election.

(g) Management organization

In the 2041 establishments surveyed it was found that fewer than a half of the managers who dealt with industrial relations matters in those establishments spent the major part of their time on such work, and only about a quarter of them were employed as personnel or industrial relations managers. Of the latter, one-third had a formal qualification relevant to such work. Taking all management respondents together, it appears that education and training for industrial relations personnel work consist largely of on-the-job training and training that is specific to the organization in which people are employed.

In two-thirds of commercial organizations there is someone at board level who has responsibility for personnel or industrial relations matters. There is a considerable amount of consultation on industrial relations problems – managers looking outside their own organizations to that end, and consulting employers' associations, personnel managers in other places and trade union officers, in that order.

(h) Consultative committees

There was clearly a considerable growth of such bodies during the 1970s – 37 per cent of the establishments surveyed reported their existence.

Establishment size, organization size and public ownership are the main characteristics associated with the presence of consultative committees, establishment size being particularly significant. Nearly a half of these committees meet at least monthly, and in the vast majority of cases senior managers attend regularly. The most important matters which they discuss concern production issues, employment, pay and working conditions. It is clear that where consultative machinery and collective bargaining machinery exist together, there is usually some overlap in the issues with which they deal.

Other channels for employee representation on specific issues exist
n a substantial proportion of establishments: these include health and
safety committees (37 per cent), job evaluation committees (10 per
cent) and various types of individual representation.

(i) *Disclosure of information*

Given three principal topics – pay and conditions of service, manpower requirements and the financial position of the organization –
the survey revealed that the amount of information communicated to
the workforce on each topic came in that order, although it is also
significant that worker representatives rate the amount of information
they receive on the three topics a good deal lower than managers rate
the amount they give. Not surprisingly, the higher the assessment of
the amount of information, the more useful is that information
regarded as being. There is also a strong relationship between high
amounts of information received from management and a favourable
assessment of that establishment's industrial relations. In only a very
small proportion of establishments is it necessary for disclosure of
information to be requested under the provisions of the Employment
Protection Act 1975.

(j) *Industrial relations procedures*

The most common types of industrial relations procedures are for
dealing with discipline and dismissals (found in 83 per cent of
establishments) and individual grievances (80 per cent); procedures
for dealing with collective disputes over pay and conditions are
substantially less common. The presence of each of the three types of
procedure is strongly related to the degree of trade union organization
at the workplace.

Formal disciplinary procedures have become much more common,
and more standardized and universal in their application, since the
early 1970s, largely as a result of the impact of unfair dismissal
legislation. When procedures at establishment level do not lead to the
resolution of an issue over discipline there is frequently provision
within them to invoke an external procedure or go to a higher level in
the organization. The body or person most commonly specified is
higher level management, although the ACAS is also frequently
mentioned. Such provisions are by no means unused; in 13 per cent of
establishments a body or person outside the organization had been
brought in during the previous year to help settle a disciplinary
dispute. Even relatively formal procedures are used flexibly and trade
union officials are often brought in by management before the final

stages of a formal procedure are reached. Managers are very much more likely than worker representatives to be satisfied with the working of the disciplinary procedures at their workplace. The main reason usually given for dissatisfaction, where it exists, is the length and complexity of the procedure and this is true of both managers and worker representatives.

In both the public and private sectors, pay and conditions procedures, where they exist, are almost as likely to be written down as disciplinary procedures. Overall 62 per cent of the establishments surveyed have negotiating procedures, i.e., written procedures for dealing with collective pay and conditions disputes. There is provision for third-party intervention rather more frequently for pay and conditions procedures than for disciplinary procedures. The specified third party also varies between the two types of procedure: the ACAS and joint union/management bodies are more frequently mentioned in negotiating procedures. However, there is more use of trade union officials, and employers' associations also feature more prominently in practice than is provided for in the procedure. Most disputes about pay and conditions are dealt with under the formal procedure and dissatisfaction with pay and conditions procedures is uncommon.

(k) Bargaining over non-pay issues

A surprisingly large range of issues is subject to joint regulation: for example, issues concerning physical working conditions, the redeployment of labour within the establishment, manning levels, redundancy, major changes in production methods, recruitment, pensions, the length of the working week and holiday entitlements.

(l) Industrial action

The survey provided some interesting information about various forms of industrial action and the types of establishment affected. In broad terms, manual workers are more likely to take strike action, whereas non-manual workers are more likely to take non-strike action; in the latter case, overtime bans are the most frequent form. There is a strong relationship between the occurrence of every type of industrial action and the number of workers at the establishment, and both strike and non-strike industrial action are clearly related to union membership density. Recognition and the presence of representatives increase the likelihood of an establishment being affected by industrial action. The proportion of the workforce which is male and the proportion which is full-time are both strongly associated with industrial action, as are the levels of pay bargaining: there is much greater likelihood of manual workers taking strike action where they negotiated their pay at establishment level and where substantial numbers are paid by results.

(m) Picketing

A relatively recent large-scale form of industrial action is that of picketing workplaces. In the previous year about an eighth of the establishments surveyed had been picketed, the proportion being over a half for those with over 1000 employees. Primary picketing, in connection with a dispute at the establishment in question, is almost never connected with non-strike industrial action. On this basis, about one-third of strikes involve picketing nowadays. Strikes are more likely to involve picketing the longer they go on and the greater the proportion of the workforce involved. Widespread strikes are less often subject to primary picketing than purely local strikes; and employees striking for the first time are less likely to set pickets than 'experienced' strikers. Establishment-based shop stewards or local union officials are the most common organizers of picketing, although the 'identity' of some pickets is sometimes disputed – including allegations that a minority of pickets are not members of the establishment's workforce. Picketing generally has the effect of preventing goods or services entering or leaving the establishment or of preventing some of the establishment's employees from entering the premises.

Joint consultation

Works committees

Works committees date from a recommendation of the Whitley Committee set up in 1916 to investigate means of securing a permanent improvement in relations between employers and workers. In addition to proposals affecting industrial relations at national level, it was suggested that works committees representing both managers and workers should be set up in individual establishments, in the hope of giving employees a wider interest in, and greater responsibility for, the conditions in which their work was performed. As long ago as 1919 a Ministry of Labour industrial report listed the following as suitable functions for works committees:

1 The issue and revision of works rules.
2 Questions of discipline and conduct as between management and workpeople (for example, sickness, malingering, and bad timekeeping).

3 Terms of engagement of workpeople.
4 Arranging lectures on the technical and social aspects of the industry.
5 Training of apprentices and young people.
6 Suggestions for improvements in methods and organization of work.

It has long been government policy to encourage rather than to compel private industry to discuss its problems with labour. This policy has been generally followed in the case of the *nationalized industries* with the exception of the coal industry which has a statutory obligation to set up joint consultative machinery. Section 46 of the Coal Industry Nationalization Act 1946 reads:

> It shall be the duty of the [National Coal] Board to enter into consultation with organizations appearing to them to represent substantial proportions of the persons in the employment of the Board, or of any class of such persons, as to the Board's concluding with those organizations agreements providing for the establishment of joint machinery for
>   (a) the settlement by negotiation of terms and conditions of employment, with provision for reference to arbitration in default of such settlement in such cases as may be determined by or under the agreements; and
>   (b) consultation on
>   (i) questions relating to the safety, health or welfare of such persons;
>   (ii) the organization and conduct of the operations in which such persons are employed and other matters of mutual interest to the Board and such persons arising out of the exercise and performance of the Board of their functions.

There are many basic difficulties to be overcome in making joint consultation work effectively. Trade unionists tend to object to joint machinery when non-unionists become members of the committees concerned. (In practice, methods of selecting representatives vary considerably; in most cases there is a secret ballot of all workers, but in many firms representatives are elected or appointed by the local union branches.) Then there is the historical mistrust of management by so many trade unionists who feel they have nothing to gain from discussing improved methods: that it is not their concern to make suggestions which may result in higher profits for shareholders, and that ideas for new processes might mean working themselves out of their jobs. For their part, employers in the past have objected to joint consultation on the grounds that trade unionists are not primarily loyal to their firms and therefore may not be trusted with much of the information that is necessary for joint committees to function efficiently. Worker representatives have been charged with using joint committees to debate political matters and to re-open questions that have already been settled at a higher level of district or national negotiation. Many managers see in joint consultation a surrender of their prerogatives to direct and control. They are often unable to perceive that, by consulting the workpeople in the same way as they would consult their supervisory staff, they are not in the least lessening their own responsibility for the final action decided upon. Managers who take employees into their confidence, far from losing their prerogatives, may secure intelligent support for decisions because there is a better understanding of the motives and considerations underlying them. When managers use consultative methods enthusiastically and without reservation, they are as a rule met with a corresponding attitude. Suspicion breeds suspicion, however, and apathy indifference.

While managers bring to joint consultative meetings facts and figures and a broad view of the plan to be followed, workers can also bring something of value to the table. They are familiar with processes and materials, and by reason of long practical experience they know the limitations of each. No one is more aware than they of the causes of waste, both of time and materials, or why work is rejected on inspection. While the manager is versed in the effects of these deficiencies, the worker is often best qualified to speak as to their causes.

Complaints that joint consultation is a waste of time seem to arise mainly in organizations where relations are bad. ('Management gets the shop stewards and union representatives it deserves.') Once again much depends on top management initiative and on the attitude of the chief executive, in particular. Many organizatons are still paternalistic in outlook, very willing to consider employee welfare services, but they refuse to allow any important policy or production matters to be discussed at works committee meetings, so that many of the charges of abuse of joint consultation made against workers can often be traced back to earlier management attitudes. A policy of ensuring discussion at every level of the organization is the best way in which confidence and mutual respect between management and employees can be built. This requires management to take the initiative in fulfilling the need of each individual employee for satisfactory working conditions in every respect.

Despite its rather chequered history, and doubts expressed about the benefits for the effort involved, the principle of joint consultation was actively encouraged in the Code of Industrial Relations Practice:*

*Published after the Industrial Relations Act 1971.

'Consultation means jointly examining and discussing problems of concern to both management and employees. It involves seeking mutually acceptable solutions through a genuine exchange of views and information . . . Consultation about operational and other day-to-day matters is necessary in all establishments whatever their size. Establishments with more than 250 employees should have systematic arrangements for management and employee representatives to meet regularly.'

The content and objectives of joint consultation within any organization are subject to four broad influences: management or employer philosophy and strategy as regards employee relations; employee and trade union strength and organization at the level at which consultation takes place; the nature of trust between the two parties; and the degree to which the external environment (notably the product market) creates unity or division between the parties. All these factors interact and can change over time, thus producing the dynamics of joint consultation in practice.

Historically there has been a progression from the traditional approach of management seeking the views of employees (through their representatives) prior to taking decisions to what may be termed advanced joint consultation in which the aim is to promote industrial democracy at work, when distinctions between consultation and negotiation become blurred. In such situations it is possible to recognize six components* of joint consultation in practice:

1 Published *objectives*, which tend to refer to mutual benefits in terms of greater efficiency and enhanced employee commitment.

2 Although consultation is usually about matters of common interest, the actual *subjects* discussed may vary from the trivial (tea, towels and toilets) to production problems, personnel assessment systems, even investment decisions.

3 The *processes* involved in consultation may also vary greatly: for example, the flow of information may be predominantly upward, focusing on the contribution of employees, utilizing their shop-floor experience, to improvements in the quality of decisions; if it is downward, it is assumed to aim at encouraging a common awareness of economic and financial factors bearing on the performance of the organization; two-way flow of information usually indicates the use of joint consultative machinery to structure each side's expectations prior to bargaining.

---

*'Joint Consultation in Practice', by Mick Marchington; Chapter 16 in *Personnel Management in Britain*, edited Keith Sisson (Blackwell, 1989).

4 The *powers* of a consultative mechanism may be stated explicitly or deliberately left ill-defined: there is often reference to what may *not* be discussed and consultation generally does not involve taking decisions.

5 The *parties* to consultation may vary: employers may be represented or led by line or personnel management, while the employees' side may consist of manual or staff workers, alone or in combination, or may even include some senior managers; representation may be by union or department.

6 The *character* of consultation may be radically different depending on the presence of unions within the workplace and the degree to which contentious issues are channelled through separate negotiating committees.

ACAS's recent survey* of joint consultation produced the following details on subject-matter discussed:

Table 7 Matters discussed on local consultative committees
Percentage of local committees

	Matters which are among the three most time consuming	Matters which receive discussion
Working conditions	32	89
Quality	31	87
Pay	27	57
Output	26	82
Welfare	26	75
Safety	20	72
Working methods	18	78
Financial results	15	66
Changes in staff levels	10	67
New equipment	10	83
Training	8	78

The survey, which included other methods of consultation, such as quality circles and joint working parties, and a range of communications techniques (briefing groups, suggestion schemes, seminars, company magazines) presented clear evidence that new developments in employee consultation were under way:

Consultation and Communication: the 1990 ACAS Survey, Occasional Paper 49, ACAS 1991.

- Managers consult their employees on a wider range of issues than in the past and in a wide variety of ways.
- Traditional joint consultative committees now meet more often and discuss important issues including ways of improving output and product quality.
- Joint working parties of managers and workers meet to assess future change in as many as two-fifths of workplaces; they often plan improvements in production methods, employee relations policies and training.
- Trade unions are playing a positive role, and recent increases in consultation have tended to augment rather than replace existing collective bargaining.

Single union agreements

The growth of foreign investment in British industry, particularly in the computer-based high-tech product sector, has been accompanied by the successful negotiation of a considerable number of single-union agreements. The industrial relations policies involved in such agreements* centre around four main elements: deciding on union recognition or non-unionism, the selection of the most appropriate union, the fundamental principles of the agreement, and the content of the agreement, particularly the clauses on operational commitments and the preclusion of industrial action.

In such situations the alternatives to single union agreements are a multiplicity of unions or no unions at all. Where management seeks flexibility and single status within the labour force (as is common in new production units) multi-unionism seems likely sooner or later to erode the achievement of these objectives. The contrasting alternative, having no unions, may raise such antagonism, especially in regions where there are strong traditions of trade union membership, as to become counter-productive. From the unions' point of view, the prize to be gained from a single union agreement is the creation of new jobs and new union recruits, often in areas of high unemployment. Management, in turn, are interested in finding which union's approach to relations between managers and employees and between the organization and unions is most compatible with the personnel philosophy and policies for the new unit.

*An excellent case study, based on Pirelli General's new factory in South Wales, can be read in *Personnel Management*, June and July 1989 issues.

The basic aim of any agreement obviously must be to make provisions to ensure the operational and commercial success of the unit to the mutual benefit of the organization and its employees and to bind and commit the signatories to this aim. These general provisions must, of course, be linked to the particular form of work structuring in operation within that organization, which in turn must be part of a personnel management strategy designed explicitly to meet the requirements of making the products and the technology and markets involved.

A number of principles are fundamental to the functioning of any single union agreement:

- Employee commitment to and identification with the achievement of the unit's operational objectives.
- Single trade union recognition and single staff status to include common conditions of employment and an integrated salary structure.
- Acceptance of industrial and employee relations, policies and attitudes which foster employee cooperation, communication and involvement, and preclude industrial action.

The agreement itself should cover such detail as: operational objectives and arrangements; single union recognition and representation; a procedure for the resolution of differences and disputes; a joint management−union negotiating committee for determining the salaries of both blue-collar and white-collar staff in the unit; procedures for handling employee complaints and discipline, with appeals facilities; a range of communication and consultation channels; and comprehensive terms and conditions of employment. The critical clauses are perhaps those which spell out the procedures (and the reasons for them) for the resolution of all disputes and the preclusion of any form of strike or industrial action by either party, along these lines:

'The organization and the trade union fully recognize that any form of industrial action taken by either party would be totally alien to the spirit and intent of this agreement and a denial of its basic principles and objectives. Furthermore, it is recognized by both parties that such industrial action would only result in unnecessary financial losses to both the unit and its individual employees and thereby damage its longer-term interests. Accordingly, both the company and the trade union agree and commit themselves not to take, support or allow any form of industrial action in any circumstances and, to give effect to this commitment, bind themselves to follow strictly the procedures and provisions of the agreement.'

To give effect to these undertakings, comprehensive and interrelated procedures must be specifically designed to resolve peacefully any disputes or complaints which may arise. If all else fails the parties (or if they are unable to agree, the ACAS) should appoint an independent arbitrator to resolve the matter by means of compulsory and binding arbitration.

A good practical example of a single union agreement is that between Nissan Motor Manufacturing and the Amalgamated Union of Engineering Workers (AUEW) at the new plant at Washington in the north of England.

Under this agreement the engineering workers' union became the only union recognized by the employer in a deal which cut right across traditional multi-union activities and job demarcations, and established working flexibilities previously unknown in the motor industry. At the new factory Nissan now has only two categories of job description – technical and manufacturing – and maintenance repair tasks are allowed to be carried out by the production workers involved in any production line breakdown. This flexibility also covers future technological changes and does away with the need to re-negotiate every time a new work process is introduced.

The philosophy which lies behind the agreement emphasizes teamwork and the crucial role of the foreman in team-building. It is standard practice for the foreman to meet the workforce for a few minutes at the start of each shift, and for the talk at these meetings to be more about quality than schedules. To this end the Nissan agreement has built in the demand that all workers should be at their place of work before the start of the shift: involvement is the keyword – clocking-in has been abolished and the company is not out to punish lateness.

Next to the importance placed upon teamwork was Nissan's demand for flexibility (abandonment of traditional job descriptions and demarcations) and the implementation of common terms of employment. By fostering team spirit Japanese employers ensure that it is in their employees' own interests to be concerned with quality, getting the job right and keeping the working environment clean and tidy. Assembly line workers are also allowed to handle their own minor maintenance jobs and they assist maintenance personnel whenever they have to be brought in to deal with bigger tasks.

The AUEW was picked as the 'single union' not because the final agreement was better for Nissan with them than it would have been with other possible unions, but because it was the one that the company thought the majority of employees would be most willing to join. In the single-union shop the AUEW represents not only production workers up to senior engineer level but also clerical staff.

Although the agreement has been dubbed a 'no-strike agreement', this is not strictly accurate since it cannot actually prevent workers from striking. There are, however, strong constraints against strike action built into the procedures for discussing pay and manning levels.

Disputes will be settled initially through a works council made up of representatives of management and employees which can act both as a consultative and a negotiating body. Where disputes are not settled in-house they can be referred to the ACAS who will first attempt to resolve them by conciliation and then, if necessary, by referring the issue to binding 'pendulum' arbitration, where the arbitrator must decide in favour of one side or the other. (It is argued that pendulum arbitration encourages both sides to make more reasonable claims and offers so that there is less distance between their initial positions.)

Conclusion

Industrial relations troubles occur most frequently in three types of industries: those which deal in perishable goods – docks, markets, transport; those where processes are long and complicated – engineering; and those where trading conditions fluctuate widely – building, car manufacturing. In the first, management fear stoppages much more than in most industries, and this plays into the hands of militant worker representatives. In engineering and other complex industries, there is a greater than usual need for coordination and expert negotiation by management with worker representatives who know where and when best to exert their strength. As for the last, much of the trouble could be removed if management succeeded in forecasting labour requirements more accurately, thus avoiding periods of labour shortage followed by redundancies.

Solving industrial relations problems at the workplace therefore demands a variety of approaches:

Increasing joint consultation

This means more worker participation in management. Such an increase would inevitably mean greater delegation of authority over worker discipline, and many managers would probably be willing to concede this if worker representatives agreed to cooperate more in raising productivity. Not that the idea is without opposition, for both supervisors and union branch officials see such a move whittling away some of their own methods of control. Nevertheless, consultation helps to ensure that management will lead as well as command.

The very word 'participation' has taken on greater significance, particularly in the context of European concern for industrial democracy; for this has appeared as much more important in some member-states than it has yet in Britain. Participation in an enterprise must take three distinct forms: for those who work in it, it must first involve direct material advantages from the results obtained; second it must mean that they are kept informed of developments in the enterprise on which their fate depends; third, it means that their practical proposals are taken into account. The IPM has suggested a Code of Practice on employee involvement and participation to encourage employers, employees and unions to develop appropriate policies and methods and to define standards of communication and consultation against which progress can be judged.

The Government carried out applied research surveys in 1985–6 to assess the effects of the requirements for companies to include statements in their annual reports on the extent of their employee involvement arrangements. The Employment Act 1982 requires that these should be aimed at:

(a) Providing employees systematically with information on matters of concern to them as employees.
(b) Consulting employees or their representatives on a regular basis so that the views of employees can be taken into account in making decisions likely to affect their interests.
(c) Encouraging involvement of employees in the company's performance through an employee's share scheme.
(d) Achieving a common awareness on the part of all employees of the financial and economic factors affecting the performance of the company.

The results showed that over half of the company reports surveyed referred specifically to at least three of these four categories. Fewer than 7 per cent of the reports failed to make any reference to employee involvement, and most of those were from smaller business where communications tend to be more direct, personal and informal.

Better training

The better training of everyone involved in labour relations will in the long term help to remove the opposition of supervisors and union officials just mentioned. There can be no doubt that managers, supervisors, union officials, and shop stewards alike would benefit from fuller training in the techniques of industrial relations, negotiating skills, and joint consultation.

Publicity for good practice

One method for improving standards throughout the country is to devise a means of examining and publicizing instances of good or bad industrial relations. Best done by neutral investigators, the position of the ACAS seems apposite here, since the preparation of its annual report would provide an excellent opportunity to publish the results.

Management leadership

This emerges as the most important factor in improving industrial relations at the workplace, for the initiative must come from management in any drive for cooperation. It is management's responsibility to keep production flowing, to deal with any threats to efficiency, and, above all, not to allow awkward problems to degenerate into crises and disorders. It is vital that managers and supervisors understand that in fulfilling this responsibility they must do everything possible to harness the abilities of their labour force with their own to create an effective team. Leadership of the quality demanded can itself cause resentment among workers and fellow-employers. It needs strength of character, courage, and integrity to maintain, and only rarely at present can there be found industrial leaders who work in anticipation of claims, who spot potential grievances, and are prepared to take constructive action to prevent them actually materializing.

Not that too naïve a view should be taken of methods to secure industrial peace. In reality a constant conflict takes place between labour and management (regulated to an increasing extent by the state) over sharing power and dividing income. This conflict centres around eternal issues of individual freedom, the desire for economic progress and improved standards of living, and resistance to change by vested interests – problems that people have always struggled with all over the world. Clearly there are no permanent solutions to these eternal issues, so that the practice of industrial relations becomes a matter of effecting minor adjustments from time to time in order to secure a balance between the contenders for power.

Future trends

What of the future of workplace relations? A range of surveys* has shown that the general population has not lost its allegiance to trade

*'Industrial Conflict: will the giant awake?', Paul Edwards *Personnel Management*, September 1991, page 28.

unionism or collectivism, nor has the 'them and us' atmosphere been eliminated. The break-up of some large bureaucratic organizations has exposed managers and workers alike to the pressures of the market, with much recent debate turning on a contrast between a deep change in attitudes and a more pragmatic, temporary acceptance of the economic situation. A greater awareness of the pressures may lead to a feeling that industrial action of any sort cannot be afforded, but this is not to say that tensions between management and workers have been dissolved. Strikes have declined because of changes in the political and economic climate (fewer days lost in 1991 than for over a century), and the restructuring of workplaces has resulted in old-style confrontations becoming less common. However, more demanding systems of work are creating new pressures; for example, rising accident rates correlate with the drive for improvements in productivity and have to be set alongside the decline in strikes.

The immediate prospect is for the recession to continue to put a brake on militancy. But as the recession eases, business-cycle pressures may build up in the reverse direction. Within the workplace, exposure to market forces does not simply mean that all forms of responding to pressures are accepted — it can also destabilize industrial relations as old assumptions have to be reworked. Decentralization may encourage this by giving local representatives more issues to bargain over compared with previous situations which were dealt with through higher-level agreements. For trade unions there is an opportunity here, in that there is a range of issues, covering work speed, absenteeism policy, appraisal, promotion, health and safety, all of which can generate discontent in workers' minds. Unions need to find a way to tap into this realm. For personnel managers, the workplace may become less manageable than it was in the 1980s as new groups are subjected to the rationalizations that have long applied to manual workers and as new issues arise.

Further Reading

Effective Negotiations, Alan Fowler (IPM, 1986).
Strike Free, Phillip Bassett (Macmillan, 1986).
Workplace Industrial Relations in Britain, W. W. Daniel and Neil Millward (Heinemann, 1984).
Industrial Tribunals, Roger Greenhalgh (IPM, 1992).

16
Communications

The process of communicating

In management terms, the word *communications* describes the process of conveying messages (facts, ideas, attitudes, opinions) from one person to another so that they are understood. The key-word in this definition is 'understood', and many organizations would profit by giving more attention to this simple fact rather than trying to develop increasingly sophisticated systems of communications that add confusion to complexity. Most people in senior managerial posts spend the majority of their time communicating with other staff, and for this reason alone the need for efficiency in this aspect of their work is clear. Management activity has previously been analysed in Chapter 11, and the relevance of effective communications to this analysis can be explained in parallel terms:

Management activity	*Importance of Communications*
1 Setting objectives	(a) Information required from clients, potential customers, suppliers, competitors, local and national government.
	(b) Internal information required, e.g. labour turnover and scrap rates.
2 Planning use of resources	Information required about these resources (labour, money, equipment, accommodation, time, and ideas), their availability, quality, and advice on how best to use them.

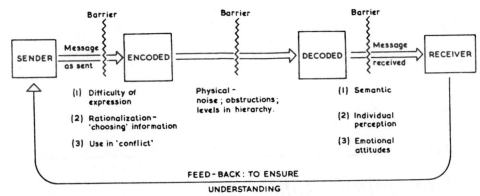

Figure 28   Model of the process of communication

3 Taking Action	Giving instructions; devising procedures.
4 Measuring results	Understanding of the standards set – quantity, quality, costs, time taken.
5 Corrective action	Giving revised instructions where necessary.

The passing of a message from the mind of its sender to the mind of the receiver may seem a straightforward affair. The fact that it is not so in practice is the reason why communications pose perennial problems in all business organizations. A model of the process will serve to illustrate the nature of the barriers which must be overcome if communications are to be successful (Figure 28).

Apart from human frailty, such as forgetfulness, there are five barriers:

Ability to express meaning

This is obviously essential to the understanding of any communication. It is a difficulty keenly felt by many first-time supervisors, promoted to such positions because of their outstanding technical skills, but who sometimes lack a sound background education and hence the ability to express themselves clearly either verbally or in writing.

Rationalization

Rationalization is the selection of information passed on, so as to enhance the position of its originator. Thus he/she feels important, as being the only person in a group who knows everything about a situation. Or if an atmosphere of conflict exists where relationships are bad between certain sections of an organization, information can be used virtually as a weapon, being conveyed or withheld as the advantage of either party dictates (cf. Stephen Potter's concept of 'one-up-manship').

Physical barriers

Any obstruction, noise, or discomfort on the part of the receiver (workroom too hot or too cold, for example) will increase the likelihood of a message being conveyed inaccurately. The number of levels through which a message has to pass from top management down to the shop floor also forms a series of physical barriers, as each level has an unfortunate tendency to cut off a piece of the message or embellish it in some way before passing it on.

Semantic barriers

These refer to the difficulty the receiver has in understanding a message. This is the obverse of supervisors' difficulty in expressing themselves and is obviously a great problem in those industries and public services which employ large numbers of immigrant workers. Just as lecturers must try to pitch their talk at what they believe to be the level of comprehension of their audience, so supervisors must give instructions or make requests in simple words which their subordinates, whose educational background may leave much to be desired, can understand.

The perception or emotional state of the receiver

The receiver's likely reaction should always be taken into account by the sender. For example, departmental heads may want subordinates to deal with an emergency which crops up late in the day: they may ask them to do so in a manner intended to convey their confidence that these particular workers are the best people to deal efficiently with the crisis. But, at that moment, subordinates may have a variety of reasons for wanting to get home early, so that their reaction may be bitter, silently accusing their bosses of dodging difficult problems and passing the 'dirty work' on to them.

All these barriers complicate the seemingly simple task of passing messages between people. The important point to grasp is that, if a communication system is to be efficient, it must include a feedback mechanism whereby senders can check that they have succeeded in overcoming the barriers. In small businesses this is comparatively easy, because most communications take place face to face between individuals and understanding can be checked immediately. The problem is much greater in large firms where individuals may not have such close contacts: communications become more and more impersonal, and verbal exchanges are replaced by circular letters or papers pinned on notice boards. Some organizations have appointed executives charged with the special responsibility of ensuring that communications flow smoothly by 'auditing' the system continuously, removing bottlenecks (caused, for example, by a departmental head's absence), and generally effecting improvements.

What to communicate

Shared information is one of the key factors in the morale of an organization and hence in its efficiency. Obviously everything cannot be communicated to everybody all the time – no other work would get done. What should be communicated will largely be determined in practice by the direction of the communication. This may be downwards in the form of policy or instructions from senior staff to subordinates; or upwards, as reactions to communications received or as control information supplied to senior staff; or horizontal, as part of the normal business procedure of keeping staff 'in the picture'.

Management's aim in practice should be to communicate downwards all relevant information that will enable employees to give their best to their jobs. This will include:

1 Information about the job itself – its importance, its duties and responsibilities, its relation to other jobs, and the relations of the person doing it to other staff and the general public; the aim of the job and how it fits in with the work of the organization, accepted standards of performance, cost consciousness and the need for economy; accident prevention; and reasons for changes being made in the job.

2 Information about conditions of employment – calculation of wages or salary, sick pay, superannuation, length of notice, holiday arrangements, welfare and social amenities; promotion opportunities, provision for further training; the employer's attitude towards membership of trade unions and professional organizations, staff complaints procedure; and suggestion schemes.

3 Information necessary for staff to carry out their work – manage-

ment plans and policy, objectives and targets to be reached, day-to-day instructions, and the quantity and quality of production expected.

On this subject, the Code of Industrial Relations Practice advises management regularly to provide employees with information about:

1 The performance and plans of their organizations.
2 Organizational and management changes that affect employees.

All managers, including supervisors, should regard it as one of their principal duties to explain organizational policies and intentions to their subordinates; they must, of course, themselves be supplied with the right information to be able to do so.

Basically, the upward flow of communications from staff to their superiors supplies information for management control purposes. As already mentioned, there must be feedback of reaction to instructions or plans, so that top management can be sure that these have been understood; indeed, depending on the nature of this reaction, original ideas and concepts may need to be modified before finally being put into effect. Other communications received by management will include a constant flow of data, statistics, and reports, all giving information necessary for decision-making; and subordinates will submit requests from time to time as well as putting forward suggestions to improve efficiency.

Horizontal communications take place between units and departments within a business, with the basic aim of keeping all staff informed generally of what is going on. No industrial organization is likely to expand unless its staff are fully aware of each other's efforts, achievements, and problems; for example, unless horizontal communications are good, there is the risk that two research sections in different parts of an organization may be duplicating each other's work. Apart from such tangible factors, the development of a good corporate spirit upon which morale and productivity greatly depend can be attributed to the effectiveness of this type of communication.

How to communicate

The principles of good communications are simplicity itself – so much so that they are commonly taken for granted, which inevitably means that they are neglected in practice. Communications will be effective when the barriers in Figure 28 are overcome – by trying to see things from the receivers' point of view and taking account of their feelings and levels of perception. Conciseness, clarity, and concentration on reactions are other precepts that appear easier to preach than perform. It is essential to provide for two-way flow, or feedback, so that questions can be answered and difficulties resolved. The system of communications itself must be well understood throughout the organization and consistently applied so that all staff have confidence in it.

In most business organizations, three main methods of communication are used:

1 Managers talk to supervisors and employees.
2 Written material is used – circular letters, papers put on notice boards, newssheets, and house journals.
3 Information is given to, and news exchanged with, employee representatives at formal meetings of joint consultative bodies.

The first method of face-to-face contact is widely practised, of course. Speech has all the advantages of direct two-way communications. It enables the mood, attitude, and responses of the receivers, whether individuals or groups, to be taken into account, and gives some guarantee of understanding by allowing questions to be asked and alternative courses of action to be discussed – all of which provides managers with clear-cut opportunities to exercise effective leadership.

There are disadvantages, however. No matter how much care is taken, some risk of varying interpretation of the communication by different people still remains. Spoken communications can also be very time-consuming; apart from the problem of securing full attendance at meetings, it takes much longer to communicate in this way or by seeing people individually than sending out a written memorandum. Then there are many organizational problems, too, which inhibit the effectiveness of verbal communication. In large complex units there may be several levels of supervision and many specialist departments away from the main flow of information; shift working adds to the difficulty since some senior staff and supervisors may not see each other for days at a stretch. All these complications contribute to the dangers of inaccuracy and misunderstanding: details tend to get lost as information is passed orally from one grade or section to another. The position of foremen is often tricky in complex organizations. They seem to be best placed to convey information between management and workers; but to their embarrassment, fuller and more prompt information is often given to workers by their union representatives. It is difficult to decide the right course of action in such situations. If information reaches the shop floor direct from supervisors, workers may feel that management is acting in an arbitrary manner; if it comes from the union, it shows that there has been full consultation, but supervisors may feel aggrieved. One solution lies in having staff and foremen representatives as part of the arrangements for joint consultation.

A communication in writing, on the other hand, usually means that the tone and choice of words can be carefully considered and checked with colleagues or supervisors before being sent out, thus providing less scope for ambiguity or misinterpretation. Obviously, too, a permanent record exists of what has been communicated. The disadvantages are that since contact is impersonal, there is no opportunity for questions or discussion; indeed, there can be no guarantee that the communication has even been read, let alone understood. The effectiveness of written material therefore depends largely on whether it can command attention; a well-known illustration of this precept is the practice of some firms of chalking urgent messages on a wall facing, or on the floor immediately inside, the factory entrance where it must be seen.

In reality both verbal and written methods of communication are used. Verbal are usually considered more suitable for complex or controversial subjects, which may be discussed first and then confirmed in writing, and written for transmitting routine information which staff need and expect. Visual communications must also be mentioned: films and slides are used extensively for training purposes, of course, and they can also be applied as aids to solving such management problems as the introduction of work study or new production processes.

Reference has already been made in Chapter 10 to the use of a *works handbook* in induction training, providing newcomers with essential information. The contents may well start with a brief history of the organization, notes about its links with the neighbourhood, and a description of its products. It should include full information on terms and conditions of employment, with notes for the guidance of employees in specified circumstances, such as sickness, accident, and change of address; what to do when they wish to purchase some of the company's products; what to do if they are absent or desire leave of absence; where they may and may not smoke (and why); what to do if they come in contact with an infectious disease; and all the other information essential to the smooth running of a business organization. If the company has working agreements with particular trade unions, the terms of these agreements could be included in the handbook, and the new employee be given information about how to join the appropriate union.

It is essential that there should be strict control over a company's *notice boards*. They must be positioned so as to be readily accessible, but not so as to cause traffic congestion by crowds of employees trying to read the notices at the same time. Using a standard pattern, size, and colour for all notice boards will help to make them familiar; those placed out of doors probably need to be locked and protected by a glass cover. All notices should be posted and taken down by the central department controlling the boards (usually the personnel department); the notices should be dated and handed in to this department, with a copy for filing. No notice should be allowed to outlive its usefulness, being taken down immediately after it has served its purpose.

Many organizations publish a regular *newssheet* giving information about their activities, past, present, and future, of a technical, financial, and social nature. This kind of internal publicity is invaluable for passing on authentic information which employees should know, and greatly helps to prevent the circulation of wild rumours, thus removing the necessity of the traditional 'grapevine'. As far as the costs of newssheets are concerned, some firms make a nominal charge for them, mainly on grounds that anything free is little appreciated, while other firms prefer to give them away; this is possibly a subject on which the opinion of worker representatives might be sought at the outset. The method of distribution varies: in this country they are usually handed around within the organization, but in the USA some firms go to the expense of posting their newssheets to employees' homes, seeking in this way to gain the moral support of their families.

The publication of *house journals* or *magazines* is an extension of the use of newssheets, the difference usually being in the length of time between publications. Newssheets are issued frequently, full of news and urgent in their appeal; magazines are more leisurely in tempo and are more concerned with long-term policy. A house journal is often printed with an eye to outside publicity for the company, in which case it is likely to be edited by the company's publicity department and be a charge upon advertising costs. Nevertheless, it may still be of social significance in fostering a deeper understanding of the working of the organization as a whole and of the problems of staff in other departments. Reactions among employees are generally favourable, but it is evident that a modicum of entertainment and humour is essential for a successful publication. Most editors experience difficulty in obtaining articles from staff, and the organization of a group of unofficial and keen news reporters throughout the firm is very desirable. Although house journals vary considerably in both content and presentation, several definite principles emerge: clarity, brevity, and honesty in presentation of official information must be keynotes, and regularity of publication is also of prime importance. Staff appreciate information regarding future plans and, above all, explanations of actions or delays which, at times, with insufficient details available, are very hard for them to understand or accept: a great impact on morale can be made in this way.

Of course, some workers will always tend to dismiss all this written material as propaganda, and there can be little doubt that newssheets and house journals alike are of limited value unless supported by as much personal contact between top management and the shop floor as possible. In the same way as an organization's advertising costs are sometimes challenged, so it is virtually impossible to measure the return obtained from the considerable sums of money often spent on these publications. The effectiveness of their role in any communications system can only be demonstrated negatively – by ceasing publication, and assessing their value in this way.

It is unfortunately true that some house journals are started for the wrong reasons, often merely as status symbols to impress the shareholders or satisfy the vanity of the board of directors. It is also true that some senior executives look on the value of these journals purely as a means of reporting social events, and not for any serious or important company purpose. But explaining costs, a new pension scheme, a department's closure – these are ideal and vital subjects for house journal treatment, and journals clearly do have a value in providing background information on complex subjects (for example, circulating new agreements among managers, supervisors, and worker representatives prior to discussing their implementation). The question for those who doubt the house journal's role as a serious medium for communications is – how else can top management effectively keep in touch with several thousand employees?

For some years the Industrial Society has advocated the system of *briefing groups* as a simple but effective means of communication. These are groups who meet their immediate superiors regularly to hear and discuss proposals and decisions that affect their jobs or conditions of work. The organization of the groups depends on the number of levels involved and the working arrangements, but their membership should not exceed twenty. Thus, with two levels in a management hierarchy, information can be quickly disseminated among 400 employees; with three levels, this rises to 8000. That is to say, directors and senior managers brief heads of departments, who in turn brief groups of supervisors, who then brief their subordinate staff.

The formula for successful *joint consultation* has already been described in Chapter 15. To work effectively as channels of communication, joint committee meetings must be held regularly, with formal agenda and arrangements for the fullest possible distribution of minutes. There are always very real problems associated with worker representatives reporting back to their constituencies – problems arising from the number of employees represented, shift working, and lack of ability on the part of representatives. Where decisions taken after consultation are felt to be unpalatable, worker representatives find themselves placed in a position of stress, in that they are being asked to do management's job in conveying information to shop-floor workers. Some of these problems are being overcome by giving worker representatives proper training in their duties. In any event, it can be argued that only a minority of employees take any active sustained interest in joint consultative discussions of policies and plans; nevertheless, the knowledge that information is available for the asking, and will be discussed with worker representatives, greatly helps to establish an atmosphere of confidence throughout an organization.

Sweden provides an excellent example of the way good communications help to achieve harmony between management and workers (albeit in their favourable circumstances of having a much smaller working population and industrial trade unionism). Works councils were established by an agreement signed in 1946 which stated two purposes:

1 Setting up a scheme for regular contact between management and workers, as one means of improving productivity.
2 Meeting workers' demands for better insight into the management of the organization for which they worked.

These purposes are founded on a general recognition of the desirability of workers understanding the importance of their own jobs against the background of the organization as a whole.

It should be clearly understood that these main methods of communication – through management, by means of written material, and through joint consultation – are not alternatives to each other: rather they are complementary. In fact, there can be no standard pattern or one correct system of communications. The methods used must be those which match up to the peculiar circumstances of each organization, the way work is carried out within it, and the quality of relationships between all its staff. An organization is structured in its own particular way to enable it to carry out its business in the most efficient manner, having regard to the morale of its employees. If the emphasis is placed on vertical communications, work may be done quickly, but comparatively few staff will know what is going on around them; they will derive much more personal satisfaction from a situation where horizontal communications are stressed so that staff throughout the organization are informed and consulted about plans and policies. Good communications will bring about good relations between staff, but these will not then bring about efficiency defined exclusively in terms of achieving speedy results. In most organizations a balance has to be struck between such efficiency and employees' morale.

Even the generalization that communications should always be two-way must be questioned, despite the fact that it is democratic and makes for greater staff satisfaction. There are significant qualifications. Two-way communication is best when accuracy is essential and when a situation is changing, but it is time-consuming; when routines are well understood and speed of response is all important, then one-way communication may be more effective. Personnel specialists asked to advise top management about communications should therefore not waste their time looking for the ideal answer; rather, they must try to predict the outcome of the various methods available, and decide which offers the greatest advantages in balancing efficiency against staff morale.

The communications system of every organization is linked closely with many other aspects of its management. For example, good communications must be backed by sound personnel policies and the mutual confidence between management and employees that only the application of these policies can build over the years. Efficient communications also will increase the satisfaction people get from their jobs. This is particularly important in the case of supervisors, whose jobs tend to become diluted by the incursions of experts; a conscious effort needs to be made to enlarge jobs by building variety, responsibility, and opportunities for individual judgment and initiative into them. Where this has been successfully achieved, a high degree of cooperation and enthusiasm on the part of employees has resulted.

A method of analysing how effectively companies are communicating with their employees has been devised by the CBI with its communication audit programme, which also embraces consultation processes, quality circles and the operation of share ownership schemes – in short, a company's total effort to secure employee involvement. Audits are based on individual interviews or group discussions with a representative sample of employees (usually about 10 per cent); the exercise normally is conducted in two stages: the first based upon employees up to but not including supervisors; the second managers and supervisors – hence splitting and assessing the views of the 'consumers' of information from those of the 'providers'.

Wide-ranging conclusions were reached as a result of the first series of audits conducted by the CBI. One feature in common to nearly all the organizations concerned was a measure of inconsistency of approach adopted within each organization to communication. Whatever the reasons for this – for example, lack of strategic decisions on communications or the machinery (such as briefing groups) not running smoothly – it reveals a serious situation, for it usually means that the 'grapevine' still flourishes and that management has lost the initiative in the communications process.

Averaging the responses to communications audits in ten different companies* produced results which are worth studying by the management of any organization which is concerned about the quality of communications with its workforce.

Table 8

Employee attitudes: responses to. CBI
questionnaire in audited companies

	Disagree total %	Agree total %
I am generally well informed about things here.	51	49
The reasons for management decisions are explained at the time	65	35
The company keeps me well enough informed about its business performance	53	47
There is good two-way communication here. Management talks and listens.	61	39
The information that management gives us is generally reliable.	24	76
I know how well we are doing in my department at the moment.	33	67
I know how well we are doing in other departments here at the moment	76	24

There were some recurring findings in these audits which should cause concern. Even when briefings are given, communications may not be two-way: questions which cannot be answered immediately may not be subsequently dealt with; sometimes briefers are unwilling to raise questions with their own superiors in case it reflects badly on them. Hence the reasons why the majority of employees did not feel that management decisions were clearly explained. Apathy towards consultative committees is commonplace because feedback from representatives to their constituents is often inadequate – 'we never see the minutes of meetings'. Too much reliance is generally placed on the written word, and there was a strong desire among employees for more face-to-face communication.

Sometimes certain media are overloaded or the wrong medium is

*Table taken from 'Checking on Employee Involvement: the CBI Communication Audit', R. Thomas and S. McAdam, *Employment Gazette*, October 1986, pages 423–6.

used, especially when efforts are made to promulgate information company-wide. Recently developed techniques, such as videos and employee reports, may be well-intentioned, but they must be put to the acid test – 'what do employees get out of them?'.

The overall credibility of management information appeared to be quite high. But employees tended to be suspicious when information was given intermittently: 'They're only interested in telling us what they want us to know'. The message is that communication is a continuous process, and employees should be informed about business performance in bad times as well as good: employee interest cannot simply be turned on and off.

Information will fail to have much effect if management actions are inconsistent with it – company purchasing policies running counter to messages about cost containment is a well-known example. Where profit-sharing and share ownership schemes are operated, a substantial number of employees are likely to find them confusing: for most companies, achieving a widespread understanding of such schemes is a long, hard slog. Finally, 'walking the floor', and talking to employees, on the part of senior managers is generally valued, provided they are not seen only when there are problems.

The art of persuasion

Staff problems often pose difficult situations where a full appreciation of communications techniques can decide a course of events. How does one explain to an employee who has been passed over for promotion why a job has been given to someone with far fewer years' service? How can a sophisticated training scheme be introduced into an organization whose senior executives have all 'come up the hard way'? How can one's boss be persuaded to take a different course of action from that which he/she has set his/her heart on?

These things can be done by communicating effectively: by presenting a case that is irrefutable. The construction of such a case demands careful thought along these lines:

1 First convince yourself and clarify your objectives. Make sure you are aware of all the facts. You may not necessarily use all these facts but remember why you discard any of them.
2 Learn the views of others in controversial matters and what is desired and what is not. Try to anticipate any awkward questions.
3 Your preparation must be thorough and your ideas realistic. Present your case in terms of what the other person wants and can

understand. Practise your approach, adapting it to the type of person you are dealing with. If possible, 'lobby' or convince key people of your goals.

4 Always present your ideas in a way that enables any one of your audience to change his/her mind without loss of prestige. Establish common ground at the outset so that you start with agreement. Avoid as much argument as possible and direct criticism to existing weakness showing how improvements can be achieved.

5 Do not force your ideas on to the other person nor make him/her feel he/she is being obliged to accept a proposal against his/her better judgment. Let him/her be satisfied completely.

6 Finally, you should be ready to follow up with supplementary facts and figures once initial agreement has been established and policy is being planned in detail.

Measuring success in communicating

A successful communications system will only be achieved if top management are determined that it shall be so. They must set good examples themselves, clearly expect others to follow them, and check from time to time that there are no bottlenecks. The personnel department can provide the necessary help here. One simple method is by questioning – for example, why someone is doing a particular job or why a change has been made: if explanations are inaccurate, of if the person does not know, the personnel officer should take the matter up with the employee's supervisor. When major changes have been introduced, it is good practice for the works committee to discuss how the communication aspect has been handled and if it could be improved. Projects can be devised for management trainees to examine the communications network: a senior executive could provide examples of recent decisions and the trainee would then follow these through. To whom did managers talk? When? How? How did the next level of staff hear? When? How? Such investigations will show not only if a decision becomes lost, but when and why. Finally, written surveys can be used. Staff may be asked to complete a questionnaire about a recent decision showing if they were informed through their supervisor, by the company newssheet, whether they read it on a notice board, were told by a representative, or heard a rumour. Another method is the attitude survey where employees are asked (anonymously) what they know of their firm's policies and what their attitudes are to conditions, supervisors, managers, and their own jobs.

General attitudes towards communications in industry have been well summed up in *People at Work* (page 5):

The management of nearly all the firms visited believed that good communications would give employees a better understanding of their work and of factors, such as the state of order books, which might affect it. They also believed that good communications would help employees to work intelligently and efficiently and to accept the need for change when it arose. Most management also held that there was value in letting employees know what was going on in the firm generally and that in the absence of facts, rumours, often unfounded, would take their place. Most managements also were anxious to know what employees thought about the firm and the way it was run, so that they could take this into account in shaping their plans and policies. For their part, employees felt that they should have clear and definite information on matters necessary for carrying out their jobs; also that they should be given full information about their terms and conditions of employment. Employees also attached importance to arrangements for raising and discussing with the management matters affecting their jobs and working conditions, and also the general running of the firm.

If there is such a thing as an 'art of communicating', it surely lies not so much in giving information as persuading people to listen. What matters is not what is said or its tone, but how it is *heard*; and what is heard is judged against the accumulated experience, favourable and fearful, of each individual and working group throughout the organization. Thus the key factor in communications emerges as *confidence in management*, built up over years of fair dealing, so that what is heard is believed.

Further reading

Effective Employee Communications, M. Bland and P. Jackson, (Kogan Page, 1990).
People at Work – A Report on Communications in Industry (HMSO, 1963).
The Manager's Responsibility for Communications, Notes for Managers No. 2 (Industrial Society, 1979).

17
Problems of morale

Definition of morale

The state of *morale* in any business organization can be judged by the degree of willingness its employees show towards their work. Basically, as with so many other aspects of industrial efficiency, much depends on the quality of the initial selection of staff, particularly for senior posts. But satisfaction at work is the principal factor in high morale, which means that pay must represent a fair reward, the duties of the job must hold employees' interest, and, above all, they must enjoy the social contacts established at their workplace. No matter how well paid and interesting jobs are, if the people performing them do not get on well together and respect each other's abilities, then morale will be adversely affected. In the last resort every organization is a sum of individuals whose morale depends on their mutual adjustment. If this is satisfactory, then an integrated work community develops into which newcomers will be readily accepted and will quickly acquire the prevailing good corporate spirit.

One of the main functions of every manager and supervisor controlling other staff is to create and maintain a level of morale which evokes their full cooperation in obtaining maximum operational efficiency throughout the organization. There may well be certain influences which are outside the individual manager's control; company policy, the industry's history of labour relations, and economic conditions in the firm's locality may all have a bearing. Nevertheless, managers can have more effect in determining morale in their departments than any other factor, and should be expected to show a measure of social skill in creating an effective team spirit among their subordinates.

The links between morale and other aspects of personnel management are strong. Most departmental heads ensure for themselves that staff selected are suited to the jobs available. Some have the opportunity to influence the wage and salary structure of their organizations or departments in ways calculated to keep morale high. Communications are also important, for employees' interest cannot be roused unless they know what is going on; knowledge can therefore be used as an incentive to stimulate effort and as a means of inculcating pride in achievements. Employees should fully understand both their own part in the life of their firm and the firm's purpose in the community as a whole; they should be made to feel that they are playing an essential role in achieving that purpose. Good managers will take pains to ensure that subordinates have these attitudes. To do so, they must develop the ability to deal effectively with social relations between their staff, as well as showing technical and administrative skills. In short, they must be leaders of people, and if they are good leaders they may even be able to obtain a response from their team which prevails over external factors beyond their personal control which may tend to lower morale.

Discipline

Optimum performance in any organization depends on the willingness with which workers carry out the instructions of their supervisors and managers and the way they conform to the rules of conduct established to aid the successful attainment of the organization's objectives. If unreasonable rules are imposed, great damage may be done to morale. No matter how much value people place on their independence, in the work situation they look to their supervisors to lead them, and as long as they get what they consider to be a proper lead they accept the concept of discipline. This is, in effect, *self-discipline*, resulting from positive and intelligent leadership and the willing cooperation of subordinates within a framework of policies, procedures, and rules which controls the organization as a whole. Thus it is wrong to conceive of discipline as something restrictive which is imposed by force or threats of punishment: it can only be maintained by self-respecting workers who follow leaders in whom they have confidence.

Where this is so, there need be only the minimum of rules about conduct, safety, and efficiency, making clear to all employees and new recruits the responsibilities they have towards each other. Once a work group is fully aware of the standard of discipline required by its supervisor, it quickly becomes a matter of tradition, and the members of the group will themselves insist on its acceptance by newcomers: 'We don't do things like that here' is the common cautionary phrase. Any breach of discipline or disobedience of rules is usually attributed to thoughtlessness or deliberate intent, but are these the right reasons? For, in reality, few workers would ever be so undisciplined as to refuse to carry out a superior's orders, provided the actions demanded are reasonable. Once again the importance of communications emerges here, for the words with which instructions are issued must make sense to workers, having regard to their training and experience.

It is sound policy to have as few rules as possible, for their proliferation breeds contempt for the very concept of discipline; in such a situation, often very little effort is made to enforce the more unpopular rules, thus undermining management's authority. In any case, breaches of disciplinary rules may be tolerated to some extent in practice, as illustrated by this simple diagram of the *Line of DisciplinE*:

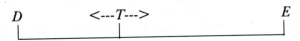

$$D \qquad\qquad <\text{---}T\text{---}> \qquad\qquad\qquad\qquad E$$

D represents the absolute enforcement of a rule, where no breaches are tolerated (matches forbidden in a coal-mine). E represents the situation where there is complete non-enforcement (for example, an office rule against receiving phone-calls). The line DE is thus the maximum possible range of toleration, although in practice it is rarely as great as this. A point T lies somewhere between D and E, and the degree of tolerance is DT for most rules. Thus if a couple of people were loitering at an exit waiting to clock off, their supervisors might think they had special reasons for wanting to leave promptly, and do nothing about it; if three or four people were there, they might wonder if they should do something, but decide not to; if five or more people were concerned, however, they definitely would take disciplinary action. In this case, T represents five, where the point of toleration is crossed.

Tension arises between management and workers when they disagree about where point T appears on the Line of DisciplinE. This is frequently the case, for instance, with no-smoking rules. There is one story of a worker who was using an oxyacetylene burner near some flammable gas tanks and was suspended because he was smoking. The farcical nature of the rigid imposition of a no-smoking rule in this case caused his fellow-workers to strike for his reinstatement. Finding, for each disciplinary rule, a point T on which management, supervisors, and workers agree is a matter of compromise which follows recognition of the causes of conflict and the discussion of remedies. This is often done with a no-smoking rule by specifying certain areas within the workplace where smoking is permitted.

One cause of tension which can have an impact on staff morale is the disagreement that sometimes arises about the range of toleration of indiscipline between senior managers who do not directly control labour and first-line supervisors who do. Top management may be prepared to put up with some degree of disorder, as long as production targets are reached; similarly they may decide to turn a blind eye to such things as bad time-keeping or absenteeism during periods of acute labour shortage. Disciplinary policy in these circumstances tends to be one of expediency, with supervisors being placed in the difficult position of having to vary point *T* from time to time to meet the demands of production.

Supervisors, for their part, want to see order maintained and no large-scale breaking of rules allowed, especially in big departments where the situation could rapidly get out of hand. Of course, there must be some allowance made for people's needs as human beings: this means the strict enforcement of medical and safety rules on one hand, but a much more permissive view taken of such things as chatting, provided it does not go too far, on the other. Finally, toleration cannot be permitted to exceed the point where the status and prestige of managers and supervisors are jeopardized.

Most supervisors do not seem to consider it necessary to have direct disciplinary authority over workers, as long as they can rely on the powers of their managerial superiors: that is, they must have confidence in the consistency of management policy, know that management will back them up in their relations with subordinates, and be assured that workers fully realize that their supervisors have effective powers in the last resort. Supervisors normally have all the authority they need to deal with minor infringements, but when considering sanctions for more serious offences, prior consultation with senior management has two advantages: it avoids the risk of decisions being reversed at a later stage and helps to develop the supervisor's resources of personality and leadership. These benefits will only be gained, however, if there is a consistent management policy about discipline throughout the organization.

The quality of working life

The report *On the Quality of Working Life** presents the conclusions of a government-sponsored enquiry into this area of staff management.

*Report for the Department of Employment, N. A. B. Wilson: Manpower Papers No. 7 (HMSO, 1973).

The themes of efficiency and satisfaction at work, and the links between them, are explored to see how it might be possible to plan for the better use of human resources with improved productivity and work satisfaction. The report also examines the influence of the environment and technology on the quality of life at work and how people's expectations from work have developed in recent years. In fact, this approach reveals that a number of modern methods of working cause stress, including: forced, uniform pacing, especially when the pace is high; repetitiveness and short-term cycles leading to monotony; triviality and meaninglessness at work; large, impersonal structures of organization, working arrangements and relations; and objectives which seem distant and unreal to the worker. Small wonder that, in reaction to such stresses, problems of absence, labour wastage, and under-utilization emerge.

In trying to counter these problems, the report takes the view that the largest single factor in job motivation is that people will work hard when they feel that in some sense they are working for themselves. The aim must be to increase job satisfaction by providing scope for development and autonomy, while maintaining productivity at the same time. This can be achieved, first, by giving people the opportunity and encouragement to be less passive, more versatile and more self-directed towards defined objectives; and second, by making all desirable work behaviour obviously rewarding by a combination of inherent and extrinsic incentives.

One positive outcome of the report was the creation in 1974 of the Work Research Unit of the Department of Employment, with the objective of promoting work systems which improve the quality of working life. This was pursued in practice mainly through the Job Satisfaction Research Programme,* concerned with the technology of change processes, evaluating the effects of changes on employees' lives, and examining new forms of work organization. More precisely the programme described:

(a) The process of change, the way it is managed by people in the organization, the conditions necessary for success, and the contribution of external and internal change agents.
(b) The content of changes and their effects on individual attitudes, on behaviour at work, and on the organization's output and operating methods.
(c) The costs and benefits, including those which are difficult to

*An excellent case analysis is presented in 'The Civil Service Road to Job Satisfaction', Alan Hodgson, *Personnel Management*, October 1985, pages 54–7. It includes a detailed statement of the job satisfaction process.

quantify, that accrue to individuals and to the organization as a result of change.

Looking back over their years of experience, many people now in senior management posts suspect that the recent years of super-specialization in business activities have gone too far in de-skilling jobs and diluting supervisory responsibilities, with subsequent adverse effects on employee satisfaction. Some organizations have consciously tried to reverse this trend through the processes of job rotation, job enlargement, and job enrichment. Behavioural scientists affirm that most employees are capable of more than routine repetitive tasks, the tedium and predictability of which, however, can be countered by building greater variety into them and allowing discretion as regards the time or order of their completion.

Job rotation, which has already been mentioned under training, relieves monotony, enables employees to acquire new skills, and increases flexibility in the staffing of departments. *Job enlargement* seeks to increase satisfaction by adding new tasks to existing work in order to make it more interesting or challenging. *Job enrichment* concentrates on responsibilities, allowing more discretion over such matters as quality control and the choice of working methods; in this way the fragmentation of tasks comprising individual jobs is reduced and there is much more scope for employees to identify themselves with what is going on around them. A much greater feeling of unification of purpose is thus achieved. Results of all three approaches have been very encouraging and higher degrees of cooperation and enthusiasm have been acknowledged particularly when employees have been allowed to participate in planning their work, and have shared in setting personal objectives.

The borderlines between such concepts as 'job enrichment', 'participation', 'involvement', and 'consultation' can never be exactly defined, for they all centre on attitudes of mind and managerial style, rather than formal techniques. They all share the same basic belief that people will give of their best when they understand the purpose of their work activity and the factors influencing it, and when they feel they are making a useful contribution towards organizing it. Two case-studies must suffice as evidence of the results of applying this theory in practice.

The ICI fibres factory at Gloucester is now a participative management classic. The workload on each different type of machine varied widely according to the type of yarn being manufactured; it was therefore thought that a computer would be the best means of arranging the necessarily very complex work plan for the machines. But the constants on which the computer program was based were the performances of a standard person and a standard machine; it could not make allowances for such things as unplanned maintenance problems, nor could it appreciate that, by making voluntary alterations in their working patterns, the operatives had considerable scope to improve the efficient running of their machines. In fact they proved to management that they could make better decisions on how to adjust the work plan to meet day-by-day events than the computer could. The simple procedure now is for the work flow to be scheduled in pencil on a long roll of paper, with much rubbing out and dove-tailing by the time that everyone involved has made a contribution to the best solution. The main virtue of the case lies surely not in the triumphant reaction to the impersonal computer, but because the development took place without any directives from ICI 'top brass' – enlightened local managers saw the opportunity to encourage their operatives to use their own knowledge and ideas. This untapped reservoir of experience and common sense must surely exist in all organizations where the planning function is carried on remote from the men and machines actually producing the goods.

The participation of employees in effecting necessary changes in working practices or conditions can boost their morale: and certainly the opposite is likely to be true if changes are simply imposed upon them from above. The relevance of such considerations to the contemporary industrial scene, into which the introduction of new technology is so important, is particularly strong. Electronic processing data by computers has been closely followed by microelectronic integrated circuits which can cram the processing power of a major computer on to very small devices at a very low cost. This has made it possible to consider the modification of any product or process involving elements of measurements or control, or data processing, storage and recall.

All too often, when technological changes of this nature have been undertaken, the following comments* have resulted:

On the process of change: training staff for new tasks has been too little and too late; communication with staff about the changes was insufficient; the process was attempted too quickly.

On the content of changes: original investment decisions were made with inadequate data and too optimistic forecasts of savings; there was little attempt to set up a team to manage the changes – they were just expected to happen; focus was largely on technical aspects leaving problems affecting work organization and individuals to be dealt with

*'Technological changes and the context of jobs', G. C. White, *Employment Gazette*, August 1983.

later, after irrevocable decisions had been taken about the 'best' technical solution.

There are alternative ways in which organizations and unions representing their employees can deal with the choice and installation of new technology. Specialist staff may be used to test and introduce it into the production system, at the same time advising on possible changes in departmental boundaries. All this is then put into effect by management edict, with retraining, new rates of pay and hours of work being negotiated. (It has been known for new processes to be set up on greenfield sites to avoid having to deal with vested interests, resistant attitudes and other human problems.) A more consultative strategy may be adopted, with an outline plan developed by senior managers, then a detailed specification worked up, during which consultations take place with all interested parties to canvass opinions where there are options for which acceptability by employees is important.

A third strategy is much more participative: in exploring the systematic effects of a proposed technological change, a plan for its introduction is developed by all those in the organization likely to be affected. In practice this means that as much as possible should be left for those who do the work to decide for themselves. This participative style for the management of change has been found to have a number of advantages:

1 It affords opportunity to learn in the organization, to live with the new technology, and how to cope with change as part of the way the organization normally functions.
2 It involves people as participants rather than recipients of change; it results in better quality outcomes both for the organization from a commercial viewpoint and for individual employees.
3 The process of 'selling' the new technology, of getting acquainted with it and its effects is not a separate issue but an integral aspect of the change.
4 It helps to identify those matters about which negotiations between the management and employee representatives are needed and agreement must be reached before implementation.

This approach has led to the technique of *autonomous working groups*, in many respects more powerful than job rotation, enlargement or enrichment because of its potential for developing employee skills as well as contributing to the quality of working life. A workgroup is allocated an overall task and given discretion over how the work is to be done; it is 'self-regulating' and works without direct supervision. *High performance work design systems* take this concept even further, into the field of complex, expensive technology, rapidly-changing products and markets, and technical and organizational innovation.

High performance work design encourages manufacturing flexibility, output quality and the effective use of expensive assets. The problems which it addresses are technical and strategic rather than operational, and it thus offers a package encompassing corporate goals, product and process innovations, management style and the management of change itself. It can be argued that organizations need to pay more attention to such matters if they are to remain competitive in world markets which are becoming increasingly volatile.

A pioneering case study* concerns the computer manufacturing plant of the Digital Equipment Corporation in Ayr, Scotland. Here management undertook a high-performance work design approach to change its products as the European market developed. It established autonomous groups, each of about a dozen members, with full 'front-to-back' responsibility for product assembly and test, fault-finding and problem-solving, and some equipment maintenance. The group members used flexitime without clocks and effectively policed their own team discipline. Individual members were encouraged to develop a range of skills and to help others develop their capabilities on the job. Management had to adapt to a supportive style in their relationships with these groups, which initially had team leaders whose job was to encourage group autonomy and then withdraw. The need for patience and the ability to stand back and let the groups reach their own decisions became new management skills.

Consideration of the quality of working life (QWL), then, is about making jobs fulfilling and worth doing well. It is also an approach to organizational effectiveness in general, based on harnessing the talents of employees. This comment on the work of Dutch Landen, head of OD at General Motors, sums it up:

> He espoused QWL, not as a means to higher productivity or lower absenteeism, grievance loads and scrappage, but instead as the right and decent way to manage with the highly educated workforce of the late twentieth century. At the same time, his department's meticulous research on QWL impacts on such measures provided ammunition to show even the most hard-hearted authoritarian managers QWL represents a better way to manage. Those who have ears to hear and eyes to see have heard, seen and been convinced. Those who have not, have not been able to believe despite study upon study showing the same findings: humane treatment of workers makes sound business sense.

*Reported in detail an article by David Buchanan in *Personnel Management*, May 1987, pages 40–3.

'Teleworking' − technology-aided home-based work − has become a focus of interest in recent years, especially since the Henley Centre for Forecasting predicted that as many as four million people could become teleworkers by the mid-1990s. Such forecasts must be viewed carefully, however, in the light of many previous 'fashionable' innovations, for example, job enrichment, job rotation, consultative leadership, styles and telephone conferencing − none of which, in reality have gained very widespread use. The most likely direction of future developments is not full-time full-scale networking but the steady adaption of new technology to organizational needs involving a growth of multi-locational contracts. Put into perspective, teleworking may become a growing element in some managers' jobs and is very likely to be adopted more widely as an alternative career-break for women professionals, in order to retain them as core employees.

Current examples of teleworking include:

(a) Rank Xerox UK − some seventy middle or senior managers in marketing, finance, personnel, management services and corporate affairs, established as freelance new technology home-workers. Each individual forms a limited company and for up to three years, until full independence is established, is cushioned by a contract with Rank Xerox for up to half its expected turnover. The parent company also helps with microelectronic and other equipment plus counselling on 'small business' skills.

(b) ICL contract programming service was started as a career-break scheme to permit women with scarce computer skills to continue to serve the company part-time. Its homeworkers each had an average of fifteen years on-site experience before joining the scheme and enjoy similar benefits to on-site staff, although most work part-time and are hourly-paid.

(c) The DTI remote works unit, a scheme which has European Social Fund backing for equipment and consultancy; ninety-five work units were created involving disabled people linked by modem and telephone to their employing organizations.

The major problem with teleworking is that it requires a basic change to a more open style of management control. There needs to be a shift from managing input (working methods) to managing output (judgement by results). The freeing of work from traditional locational and time restraints poses problems which many supervisors at all levels find it difficult to come to terms with: in particular, they often wish to continue to control hours of work rather than grant autonomy to homeworkers over their time and thus fully exploit the potential flexibility of telecommuting.

Teleworkers themselves need not only technical skills and knowledge but also psychological preparation – the inculcation of values and strategies facilitating the ability to self-start, to use 'small business' skills and cope with isolation, and this must be an on-going process. Attitudinal changes are necessary on both sides. Home-based workers typically experience personal anxiety and time-management problems involving the separation of work from domestic pressures; they frequently consider their large-firm clients to be mistrustful and some feel the need to hire office space so as to appear 'professional'.

Success in introducing teleworker schemes, then, particularly among high-status staff, requires careful preparation, training and resourcing, and progress is likely to be rather slower than publicists of the concept suggest. Home-based satellites may not be the cheap or easy option that is often claimed: above all, good communications channels, regular meetings and other ways of preventing isolation from the organization's culture are of paramount importance*.

Dealing with individual staff problems

From time to time every supervisor and manager has to tackle problems posed by individual subordinates, usually of a personal, domestic, or disciplinary nature. Help may be sought from the personnel department, but it is important to observe correct procedure: a problem should always be dealt with by an employee's immediate superior initially. With personal matters, which employees wish to discuss only with a senior manager or someone in the personnel department, they should nevertheless speak to their foremen first, to make the necessary arrangements.

Having to deal with individual problems in human relations is a part of the job which seems to cause great concern, being raised time and time again on training and development courses by supervisory and managerial staff of all levels. They are most conscious that the delicacy of many of these situations inevitably produces an atmosphere of embarrassment, which in turn often results in a problem being handled clumsily, leaving both superior and subordinate dissatisfied at the outcome. The basic difficulty, of course, is that at this point in time the relationship between them is entirely different from their

---

*A checklist of ten points for consideration by personnel managers when introducing teleworking is featured in 'Home Truths About Teleworking', John and Celia Stanworth, *Personnel Management*, November 1989, page 48.

normal day-to-day working contact which is rarely founded on close personal feeling.

Experienced personnel managers find that the best way of dealing with these situations is for managers deliberately to detach themselves and 'cold-bloodedly' apply a set procedure for solving them. One such procedure that has successfully stood the test of time is taught on TWI courses for supervisors. It consists of the following steps:

Getting facts

Obtain all possible facts about the individual. Note the rules and customs affected by the problem. Note the possible effect of the problem upon other people. Talk with appropriate people and get their opinions and feelings.

Weighing facts

Fit them together and consider how they may relate one to another. Consider gaps and contradictions. Seek further facts if necessary.

Determine an objective

Decide what you wish to accomplish by considering the effect you want on the individual, the staff, and the work of the section. What would be a really satisfactory situation?

Deciding upon the action to be taken

Determine possible alternative actions. Consider which of these will best conform to the practices and policies of the organization. Which will have the best effect on the individual, the staff, and on the work of the section? Which is most likely to achieve the objective?

Taking action

Consider who is the best person to take the action and who should help in the matter. Decide if seniors should be consulted. Determine the best timing for the action.

Checking results

Decide the timing and frequency of the follow-up. Watch for changes in attitudes, relations, and the output of work. This problem may lead to others.

The most important part of this procedure is *determining an objective*. Supervisors and managers appreciate the need to collect all the relevant facts, but so often then go straight on to consider what action to take, without pausing to decide exactly what they are trying to achieve: thus the advantages of various courses of action become muddled together and a confused solution emerges. If, instead, a clear objective is first defined, each alternative course of action can be considered in the light of its likelihood of realizing that objective.

To take a simple example, if good employees are frequently late because of inconvenient buses, two objectives are open: either to do everything possible to retain their services, because they are good at their job; or to dismiss them, because they persistently break a disciplinary rule. But only if their superiors clearly decide on one of these objectives (once all the facts have been gathered about where the workers live, bus times, alternative transport, their duties on arrival) are they likely to take direct action to solve the problem, without dithering or postponing the outcome.

Absenteeism

There are various signs of low morale in an organization – poor production methods, numerous complaints about quality, lax discipline, bad time-keeping, and high rates of absenteeism and labour turnover. From the point of view of the personnel manager, perhaps the latter two are the most significant.

Working time lost through strikes and restrictive practices makes sensational headlines for the press, while absenteeism rarely rates a mention. Yet it is many times the problem of strikes: in recent years rarely have more than 10 million working days per annum been lost through strikes; yet nearly 300 million working days are being lost each year through absenteeism. This amounts to about twelve days a year for each employee – an obvious figure to concentrate on in trying to increase productivity.

Absenteeism falls into three main categories, based on the reasons which cause it: illness, when medical certificates are usually demanded after three days, and frequent absences of up to three days are regarded with suspicion; permitted leave, which the firm knows about beforehand; and voluntary absenteeism, usually for personal reasons which may not be revealed in detail, or sickness may be feigned. Identifying and dealing successfully with this last category are fundamentally management problems. Progress in solving it will not be achieved by public pronouncements at national leval about malingering, but only by detailed effort by local managers. Their problems are not helped by the seeming inability or unwillingness of anyone to define the degree of illness that justifies staying away from work. Every general practitioner is placed in the peculiar quandary of never being able to prove that patients are not sick or in pain if they insist that they are; and no doctors will take the legal risk of sending someone back to work even when they strongly suspect them of malingering. Doctors, in effect, refuse to do what they regard as really the manager's job.

There can be no doubt of the significance of absenteeism to management. It means idle machines, the reorganization of production, reduced output, increased costs, and extra strain upon those employees who do turn up for work. In fact, where production depends basically on a spirit of cooperation and teamwork, workers should always be impressed with the problems caused by absenteeism, in the hope that this may have some impact on their social conscience when contemplating staying away.

The personnel manager is concerned, too, about the way absenteeism reflects morale, especially the extent to which high absence rates in particular departments may indicate bad management there. It means work for the personnel department in other ways as well: records must be kept, enquiries and interviews held, and there may be subsequent labour turnover if people are dismissed for persistent absence from work. Periodic reports must be prepared, including statistics showing time lost through absence as a percentage of total working hours, so that top management can consider whether any general action or changes in personnel policy are needed.

Three major factors are consistently associated with the level of absenteeism:

1 Personal, which are controllable to a certain extent through the organization's selection policy: thus age, sex, the length of journeys to and from work, length of service, and family responsibilities are all relevant.
2 Organizational, which are very much under the direct control of local management: for example, the heaviness or unpleasantness of jobs, the stress involved, shiftworking and the amount of overtime, income levels, and employee morale generally.
3 External: factors such as local levels of unemployment, which are largely outside the control of individual organizations.

Responsibility for the control of absenteeism should rest squarely on the shoulders of supervisors: they are most closely involved in the problems arising, know the individuals concerned best, and can assess the truth or otherwise of reasons given for absence. But this immediate authority must be supported from above by a clear personnel policy on absenteeism, which can be strengthened if initially agreed with the unions. Such a policy must be made known throughout the organization; it should obviously lay down that good attendance is required, and should clearly set out the procedure to be followed in the event of absence. Above all, it must be applied consistently.

The well-established fact that absence rates are highest in large units gives another clue to help in tackling the problem. The crucial point is that in small organizations the boss can keep in personal touch with all employees and can see them when they come back to work from sick leave; he/she can also arrange for them to be visited if they are away for long. Achieving such close personal contact in large organizations involves willingness by top management to delegate authority.

A contemporary illustration is provided by a three-tiered approach developed by the personnel division of the London Borough of Lewisham* based on involvement at the strategic and departmental levels as well as that of individual line managers and supervisors. At the strategic level councillors and chief officers set corporate targets. The personnel division has a module in its computerized personnel system for monitoring absenteeism and prepares bi-annual reports comparing absence levels among different departments and categories of staff as well as the incidence of long-term and short-term absenteeism.

The personnel division also publishes guidelines to help managers control absenteeism or, expressed more positively, to improve attendance. They detail procedures to follow in cases of absence: as soon as employees phone in sick, for example, the line managers or supervisor must find out 'in a discrete and sympathetic manner', how long they are likely to be away and what is wrong with them. Managers are also expected to have a private word with individuals after *every* absence, regardless of its length: this is not a heavy-handed approach (as originally feared by union representatives) but simply intended to show staff that their absence has been noticed. Under a rolling review procedure, managers must hold a more in-depth counselling session with any employee who has three or more periods off work within three months. The purpose here is to spot problems early on,

Personnel Management Plus, February 1992, page 16.

offer advice, or refer individuals for professional help. If this fails to reduce persistent absenteeism, managers can then activate a disciplinary procedure.

The personnel division also has important roles in making new employees aware of the council's rules and procedures for absence, and providing line managers and supervisors with a training programme (1000 managers dealt with in four months) in the knowledge and counselling skills they need to ensure high levels of attendance. Senior managers are coached in setting targets and drawing up action plans for their departments.

A handbook, frank in its approach, is also used to help participants explore the causes for absence and to suggest ways of reducing it. No longer is it accepted that if an absentee produces a doctor's note, there is nothing for anyone else to do: managers must not believe unquestioningly everything they are told — at some point they need to ask why, preferably sooner rather than later, albeit in a sympathetic way. Linked to all this is the provision of a full occupational health service to the council by the local King's College Hospital.

Excellent results were reported when the scheme had been running for two years: sickness levels had dropped by 30 per cent, which represented increased productivity of £1.5 million annually, and showed encouraging progress towards the council's target of a 3 per cent absence rate by the end of March 1993.

Since absenteeism is a disciplinary matter, affecting both efficiency of production and the well-being of employees remaining at work, a strong case can be made for the creation of joint absentee committees to investigate all cases of seemingly unjustified absence, with the main objective of directing moral censure against absenteeism. Many firms practise methods of rewarding workers with good attendance records, bestowing upon them a certain status and prestige. Others set themselves the specific target of reducing absenteeism throughout the working week to its level on pay-day (invariably the day of lowest absence).

Employers must carry out their own research to identify the precise nature of their absenteeism problems. Statistical analyses should lead on to an assessment of people's predisposition to stay away: working conditions may then be investigated as well as the quality of supervision in the departments affected. Finally, positive efforts must be directed at developing human satisfaction at work. Genuine team spirit must be inculcated among groups, largely by training supervisors to deal with human relations problems properly; if this could only be achieved, the pressure from members of the team exerted on those who tend to 'dodge the column' would be far greater than management would ever dare to impose.

Labour turnover

Labour turnover is the term used to describe the movement of workers into and out of the employment of an organization. To enable the problems involved and their causes to be seen in proper perspective, an index of labour movement has been devised, expressing the total number of workers replaced as a percentage of the average number of employees during a year:

$$\text{net labour turnover} = \frac{\text{total replacements}}{\text{average working force}} \times 100$$

$$\text{or } T = \frac{100R}{W}$$

Since some separations are unavoidable (married women leaving to have babies), or in some cases desirable (employees may be encouraged to leave to get advancement their present firm cannot offer), the formula may be adjusted to take these factors into account, in which case:

$$T = \frac{100(R - U)}{W} \text{ where } U = \text{unavoidable separations}$$

An annual calculation is considered the best, since shorter periods may contain particular unusual influences; sometimes, however, quarterly indices are produced when it is felt that they may indicate seasonal trends.

There is, however, one great weakness about this method of calculation, since it obscures the extent of the stable element of the labour force. For example, a labour turnover index of 33.3 per cent could mean either of two things: if a different third of employees left each year, none of the original employees would be left after three years; but if labour turnover affected a particular third of jobs, the holders of which constantly left after only one year's service, then two-thirds of the original employees would still remain after three years. These two situations differ markedly in the degree to which the labour force consists of experienced workers; so an index of labour stability also needs to be calculated at the same time as that of turnover. Two such indices are:

$$\text{skill dilution index} = \frac{\text{no. with over 1 year's service now}}{\text{total employed now}} \times 100$$

and

$$\text{skill wastage index} = \frac{\text{no. with over 1 year's service now}}{\text{total employed 1 year ago}} \times 100$$

(These assume a worker to be experienced after one year, but the actual period may be adjusted as necessary.)

Returning to the traditional method of calculating labour turnover and the criticism that it takes no account of the length of service of those leaving, an alternative measure of an employer's ability to retain labour is to calculate the *half-life period* – the time taken for a group of new recruits to be reduced, by separations, to one-half of its original size. This concept is easy to understand and compute, yet readily provides a means of comparing different firms and different batches of entrants.

Labour stability and turnover are relative terms: employers do not want to lose too many of their staff, but equally a low turnover can adversely affect promotion prospects for able younger employees and reduce opportunities of injecting new ideas from outside. Turnover statistics should therefore be compared with figures of other employers, available from such sources as the *Employment Gazette*, employers' federations, the Institute of Personnel Management, and the Industrial Society.

There can be no doubt about the unfavourable effects that employees leaving have on the minds of those remaining, undermining morale and interest, and lowering efficiency. Considerable costs have to be faced in replacing the leavers and training their successors, and there are also the hidden costs of lessened effectiveness throughout the organization. Excessive turnover is a bad thing socially too, low morale being reflected by the unsatisfactory relations that exist between management and workers: it shows that management has not established the links that bind individuals to their working groups. Workers who leave soon after starting jobs because they do not feel at home demonstrate how management has failed to carry out one of it main functions, that of influencing workers' behaviour towards cooperation. Just as it has been said of the army, 'There are no bad soldiers, only bad officers', so industry can be accused – 'There are no bad workers, only bad managers.' Every disgruntled employee is a source of ill-will towards the firm he/she leaves and is likely to damage its reputation.

The costs of replacing staff vary, of course, with the seniority of appointments and the amount of advertising involved. But with even the lowest-graded jobs, costs probably exceed £50 per replacement. First, there are administrative recruitment costs associated with advertising, interviewing, medical examinations, and processing the necessary paperwork. Further expense is incurred while the newcomer is relatively inefficient during the early weeks of a job, which is also a time when accidents, damage to equipment, and wastage of materials are more likely to happen. Training costs must be added – induction, and the time of supervisors and other staff devoted to job instruction. During the time that vacancies exist, capital equipment is probably standing idle. And, finally, there are the intangible costs of lower staff morale and frustration for supervisors when there is a continuous movement of employees in and out of jobs.

Any study of the causes of this turnover that leads to constructive action will therefore be an attack on threatened instability among workers still remaining and a means of pin-pointing where management is lacking. The measurement of labour turnover must first be supplemented by knowledge of the reasons why employees leave. *Exit interviews* are the most commonly used technique, aimed at determining the real cause of leaving as opposed to the stated reason. This is a procedure that requires the most tactful application, for human motives are complicated and it is very difficult to achieve the desired standard of accuracy. Sympathetic and sensitive interviewers can obtain a great deal of useful information, however, which will have a direct bearing on their firm's personnel policies and practices, and hence their employment situations, as well as retaining leavers' goodwill. The occasion should not be used to try to persuade an individual to withdraw his/her resignation. The interview must be held in private and the person interviewed assured that it will be treated confidentially. If it proves impossible to interview an employee who has resigned, a questionnaire may be sent to him/her after he/she has left.

Separations fall into three main categories: voluntary, which are potentially avoidable; those due to management action; and involuntary separations which are unavoidable. Employees who leave of their own accord do so usually because they dislike the job, its pay and conditions, or the people they work with; personal welfare matters, such as poor transport or accommodation difficulties, may also be involved. Whichever of these reasons is appropriate, the leavers think they will be able to do better elsewhere. Employees dismissed by management leave for reasons of unsuitability (inefficiency, incompatibility); breaches of disciplinary rules (insubordination, persistent lateness, or absenteeism, for example); or redundancy due to trade recession or reorganization. All these reasons are capable of a certain amount of management control. Within limits, jobs can be made more attractive and pay and conditions improved; better selection methods will reduce the number of unsuitable employees and proper induction will help recruits settle into existing workgroups; and there are techniques designed to improve such matters as time-keeping, staff health and welfare, and the quality of supervision. Only trade recessions are beyond management control, but even then there are many ways by which the effects of redundancy can be minimized. Above all, management must treat employees as individuals, keep them informed of matters likely to affect their working lives, and try continuously to imbue them with the idea of cooperation for a common purpose. All this effort on the part of management is necessary if employees are to identify themselves with the organization and if morale is to be maintained at a high level.

Viewed positively, all this amounts to the management of retention (rather than turnover) by reinforcing the 'right' reasons for staying – a combination of job satisfaction and environmental reasons which themselves relate to the organization's goals. In contrast, the 'wrong' reasons for staying are those which are beneficial to neither employee nor the organization. Ultimately, rightness and wrongness, whatever their specific meanings to individuals, will require the provision of a work environment that is broadly compatible with employees' personal goals and their values in working and living. Managers must realize that 'the average worker' does not exist, and develop personnel policies and practices which are responsive to the disparate values of employees. Only then will it be possible to develop strategies aimed at retaining employees; if an organization reinforces the right reasons for staying and abstains from reinforcing the wrong reasons, its turnover – as distinct from turnover rate – might be more satisfactory.

Mergers and takeovers

Obviously there are many similarities between labour turnover and redundancy situations and what happens to the morale of staff when they become involved in mergers and takeovers. In fact, there may be no personnel problems at all if the amalgamation of two organizations is purely a financial arrangement and both carry on trading as before. On the other hand, staff fears are likely to be great where takeover efforts become a struggle, which is eventually lost, against the advice of the board of the firm taken over. Many mergers take place when trading conditions are at a low ebb and it is hoped to revive matters by creating a more efficient operating unit: but inevitably this means streamlining the two organizations, centralizing administration and services, closing departments, and making considerable numbers of employees redundant. The application of a carefully prepared redundancy policy, as discussed in Chapter 6, is therefore one essential in such a situation.

In the first place, the maintenance of morale is a public relations exercise: policies (humane) and procedures for the period of amalgamation should be fully explained to everyone concerned in both organizations, trade union representatives consulted, and relevant local bodies (job centres, press, and local authorities) informed. It is often the case that the firm taken over is smaller and less efficient than its new parent organization. Its employees will be very conscious of their inferiority, and if their morale is allowed to deteriorate so that good employees leave, some of the anticipated benefits of the merger will be lost to the new organization. The only way of forestalling this problem is for top management deliberately to demonstrate the same attitude towards all staff and to bring conditions of service throughout the new organization into parity. Unified rates of pay and fringe benefits, and common facilities for trade union representation are among the essential requirements if charges of prejudice against the taken-over staff are to be avoided. Where individuals are likely to suffer financial hardship as a result of the amalgamation, personal arrangements should be devised to cushion the blow over a period of time.

Again, a comprehensive programme must be worked out, if possible, for the mixing of staff of the previously separate firms: visits perhaps to start with, then job rotation for short periods throughout the new organization, and sharing in training courses and discussion groups – all building up to full integration. Above all, the employees of the taken-over firm must not be allowed to feel that they have lost promotion opportunities.

Traumatic as the initial impact may be, the economic facts may very well be that a firm caught up in a merger or takeover is in reality being presented with the prospect of a more prosperous future than it had before. This in itself can present hope of a challenge that can be stimulating to morale. It is unfortunate that, financial speculators being as they are, merger negotiations often have to be cloaked in secrecy. For the evil reputation which mergers and takeovers have developed is due entirely to their impact on individual employees in the organizations affected; most of their fears could be readily dispelled if they were given the maximum amount of information early on, and they would then be able to view the immediate future with much more confidence.

The amount and nature of the information given out during a change in control forms the most important single factor in reducing anxiety. Statements that people have nothing to fear, or that jobs will remain secure, and that there will be no major changes in work patterns, are *not*, by themselves, reassuring or convincing. Employees will be reasured more by precise knowledge of the direction that affairs are taking than by general expressions of benevolence. Equally important, notice of the changes to be expected should be given as soon as possible, for nothing causes more unrest than continuing uncertainty.

Further reading

The Human Implications of Mergers and Takeovers, P. F. Barrett (IPM, 1973).
The Missing Workforce — Managing Absenteeism, Andrew Sergeant (IPM, 1989).
People at Work (The Volvo Experience), P. G. Gyllenhammer (Addison-Wesley, 1977).
Relocation — a practical guide, Sue Shortland (IPM, 1990).

18

Working conditions, welfare and status

Physical environment

The physical surroundings in which people are employed have an obvious effect on the amount of work that can be produced. They also have a psychological impact on workers, considerably influencing their attitudes towards their jobs. Thus it has been alleged that as much as 30 per cent of all absence from work is caused by illness stemming from anxiety neuroses which develop as reactions to the type and conditions of work. This is the essence of the practice of occupational medicine – how far a patient's condition can be attributed to his or her work. (This is discussed in more detail in Chapter 19.)

Good housekeeping

The concept of *good housekeeping*, in the sense of insisting on cleanliness and tidiness of working areas, is as important in industry as anywhere else. The environment in even the dirtiest and most unpleasant industries should be made as amenable as possible by providing good lighting, using bright colours to cheer the appearance of depressing buildings, and by covering wet surfaces with impervious materials. Considerations of comfort should also take into account the temperature, ventilation, humidity and spaciousness of workshops. In offices, too, much can be done to ensure high physical standards by proper maintenance: floors polished and windows washed regularly are examples. Providing the best furniture and equipment the organization can afford will benefit morale: first-class executive and clerical staff deserve good desks and chairs and equipment to use. Order and system in a firm's activities are generally appreciated by employees of all grades, and management should never permit any departure from the highest standards of good housekeeping.

Fatigue

One of the first investigations carried out by research workers* in industrial psychology was concerned with the question of *fatigue*, which can always be identified by reference to a firm's production curve throughout the day. Where it presents a problem, obvious remedial measures include the reduction of working hours and the use of refreshment breaks during the day. Time and motion studies can help to evolve easier methods of work, particularly by devising mechanical aids to alleviate the drudgery of heavy jobs. Much depends, too, on the quality of managers and supervisors: on their ability to adjust the speed of production lines so as to obtain optimum performance from their subordinates, and on their handling of human relationships so as to avoid the emotional strains that cause nervous fatigue.

Noise

Most people find that certain types of *noise* 'get on their nerves' and are a great source of annoyance when they are trying to focus their attention firmly on some task. Continuous, meaningless, loud noise is usually accepted by workers as part of the working situation, but noise which has meaning, especially if it is elusive, like partly heard conversation, can be very distracting. Sharp, intermittent noises (those which make people jump) cause strain, as does human speech which is only just distinguishable above the background noise level. The learning of new jobs, especially if they involve mental effort, can easily be upset by unfamiliar sounds. Thus noise imposes upon the senses of workers, competing with what is relevant to their jobs; it may be meaningless, but it is insistent, and the workers affected have to turn their attention to it from time to time to make sure that it is meaningless. The constant shifting of attention has been called 'mental blinking', during which significant events may go unnoticed or be misinterpreted. Since distractions of this nature inevitably have

*There was an Industrial Fatigue Research Board during the First World War.

adverse effects on production, noise is an aspect of the physical environment that management cannot afford to neglect. Positive measures may include isolating the offending machines or processes, installing silent mechanical parts, and lining walls and ceilings with sound-absorbing materials.

Monotony and boredom

The *monotony and boredom* that arise from repetitive work also have physical effects, although different individuals will not have the same feelings about their jobs. Monotony and boredom are products of people's minds, but it is generally accepted that the more intelligent a person is, the more bored he/she will become with repetitive tasks. So the fact that a process is repetitive does not necessarily mean that the operator concerned will find it boring; there are monotonous aspects in almost all jobs, especially those associated with mass production in many factory industries, but many operatives get considerable satisfaction from 'long runs' with no interruptions to their work, particularly when their piecerates are good. The problem must therefore be viewed in the right perspective, and its basic solution lies in the initial selection of workers whose employment history shows a record of adjustment to routine work or who possess 'knitting-minds'.

There are a variety of palliatives for jobs that are entirely repetitive. Operatives can be trained to perform several different tasks and then alternate between them. They can change their positions from time to time, for instance by fetching their own materials for processing. Even their outlook can be changed occasionally by rearranging the workroom if possible. Rest pauses provide obvious breaks in routine, but these must be properly planned to avoid production losses likely when workers make up their own reasons for pausing. Music-while-you-work and chatting are usually permitted within reason. Work study specialists are interested in this problem, of course, and it is noticeable that several of the remedies suggested serve as reminders to them that the task of obtaining the greatest output in the quickest time must take the human factor fully into account. Other positive measures to relieve boredom include attempts to stimulate workers' interest through proper induction, so that they understand how their jobs fit into the overall scheme, and by invoking a feeling of competition through the regular display of production records.

Ergonomics

The study of all aspects of the working environment and its effects on workers' productive capacities, and the application of anatomical, physiological, and psychological knowledge to the problems arising therefrom, is known as *ergonomics*. Its emphasis is on fitting the job to the person, and it has been the subject of a great deal of research work during and since the war. Studies have included taking measurements of averages and ranges of the population at large, and determining the maximum force that can be applied by arms and legs in different positions – both of which have influenced the design of vehicles, many types of mechanical apparatus, and the optimum heights for seats and workbenches. Maximum working periods under arduous or very hot conditons have been calculated and better results obtained through various experiments with rest, refreshment, and shielding from heat sources.

As modern machinery and equipment improve, however, so the psychologist comes more into this field. No longer is the concern so much with relieving workers of heavy work as with their problems as receivers of communications – taking in data, ordering it, perceiving its importance, and doing something about it. People can only absorb a certain amount of information or carry out a given amount of activity in a set period of time: it is important to try to measure these perceptual limitations if performance is to be improved, otherwise instructions may be presented to operatives in a manner which makes unreasonable demands on their powers of understanding. Control indicators on highly mechanized equipment have been investigated too, leading, for example, to the development of methods (for equipment that seldom fails) whereby sound signals first attract an operative's attention to dials which display more detailed information about something that has gone wrong.

These are examples of how applying the principles of ergonomics can overcome problems where exacting or confusing equipment is in use, making work easier, safer, and less likely to be disrupted by sudden crises. All this can help personnel managers in advising on working situations which cause strain and dissatisfaction among workers, as well as guiding design engineers in their work on machines and equipment that take into account the limitations of the human beings who have to operate them.

Hours of work

Most civilized concepts of the length of the *hours of work* accept that the demands made on workers should make allowance for their needs as human beings taking part in other spheres of personal and community life. During the past century the number of hours in the standard working week has been progressively reduced from 60 to 40. Actual hours worked have also fallen, but not by as much; in 1978 these averaged 43.6 hours a week, with but little reduction since.

In fact, overtime has become an established feature in the lives of a substantial proportion of all workers, especially people in their 30s with growing families. Contrary to popular myth, high overtime workers have relatively low sickness and absenteeism records, for clearly pay is their major motive. Low basic rates provide the main stimulus, but highly skilled workers will also do overtime in order to preserve their differentials. Another constraint can be found in the fact that, quite apart from compulsory overtime worked in some public services, in many firms, particularly construction and engineering, production schedules and manpower levels are planned, and contracts accepted, on the assumption that regular overtime will be worked. Yet most managements will maintain that they regard overtime as voluntary, while accepting many reasons why they might wish it to be worked. These include the need to maintain plant; the demands of the type of service provided, for example, transport; to meet emergencies or occasional peaks in demand; and because it is cheaper than recruiting extra labour. Less impressive reasons are those of increasing workers' pay and meeting normal demand for products or services – yet both are frequently encountered.

A wide variety of factors – legal, social, domestic, male or female, young or old – influence the number of hours worked. To take two examples: the married woman's desire to augment her family's income may well be satisfied by a part-time job only; while the need to study or the desire for leisure may curtail the hours worked by a young man, although marriage and a family may then change his preference to one for immediate cash return from overtime. Levels of income determine that labourers generally work longer hours than craftsmen and technicians, and manual workers longer than clerical and administrative staff: one result of this, of course, is the effect it has on wage structures of narrowing the gap between skilled and unskilled workers. Methods of payment have a bearing too: time-workers have little opportunity to make extra money apart from overtime, whereas pieceworkers can always earn more from extra effort during normal hours. People with family responsibilities tend to work longest; the trouble is that for some of them overtime becomes virtually an addiction, a self-sustaining activity usually devoted to acquiring more and more luxury goods. The value to production of the very long hours worked by this minority is very doubtful, since they almost certainly involve a lower average effort over the total hours worked, so that the input–output ratio in fact moves adversely in terms of labour costs.

Employers seem traditionally opposed to any reduction in the length of working hours, and this is reflected in the current controversy over the EC proposal to legislate for a 48-hour maximum working week. Premium payments for overtime were originally developed, in part, to induce workers to continue beyond the limits of the ever-contracting standard week, while trade unions saw the premiums as penalties which would persuade employers to take on more people rather than work existing employees for longer hours. The facts are inescapable, however, that when overtime is worked, or if hours are reduced while weekly pay packets stay the same, unit production costs must rise unless there is an equivalent rise in output.

A reduction in the actual as well as standard working week may not mean that everyone will work fewer hours than at present – they may well find supplementary part-time jobs elsewhere. Even those workers who do not take an additional job are available to do more household chores, thus giving more married women the opportunity to work. A shorter working week is not the only way in which greater leisure could be secured: longer weekends and more holidays are both possible developments. There is a growing demand for four weeks' annual holiday and it seems fairly certain that this will be conceded generally within the next few years. British workers lag behind their Continental counterparts both as regards annual leave and the number of paid public holidays.

Most factors with a contracting influence on working hours are growing; in particular, the proportion of the total labour force which tends to work shorter hours – skilled workers, married women, professional staff – is continually increasing. Economic factors including income, productivity, the balance of payments situation, and the net effect of all these influences on the supply of manpower, are difficult to assess. There may very well be a fall in the total man-hours worked in the years ahead, so that the aim must be to use the hours which are worked more efficiently. Much will depend on the rapidity of the changes and how well management can adjust its activities to cope with them.

In current conditions with high unemployment levels, some hope has been placed on reductions in working hours as one means of creating additional jobs. However, surveys carried out in 1981 and 1982, shortly after a national engineering industry agreement on shorter hours had been implemented, produced conclusions that reductions in working time may not lead to increased employment, and that increased productivity and, to a lesser extent, increased overtime are commonly adopted methods of compensating for such reductions. In fact, the results of these surveys confirmed previous studies which indicated that productivity offsets were one of the main ways by which employers avoid the costs of shorter working time, and thus constituted an important reason why reductions in hours are not usually followed by the recruitment of additional workers. Indeed there is some evidence of employment actually being reduced as a means of obtaining some of the productivity increases needed to make up for reductions in working time. Thus the conclusion of the surveys was that, on balance, shorter hours lead to higher labour costs, because increases in productivity tend not fully to offset the reduction in working hours and because of additional overtime.

A review of basic hours of work carried out in 1986 by the association Professional Personnel Consultants concluded that one in three manual workers and one in five white-collar workers are now working a four-and-a-half-day week. But there has been almost no movement towards a four-day week and, looking ahead for five years, the survey reports that the number of organizations planning further reductions in working hours is negligible.

Throughout European industry as a whole, two trends can be detected during the 1980s. One is towards a continuing reduction of working time. The other is that, because of increased world trade and the economic recession, there is more and more emphasis on maintaining and improving the edge of international competitiveness. Many organizations are thus looking for ways of linking the reduction of working time to demands made on them by the market for better prices and higher quality of products.

In the light of this situation it is surprising to find little or no cost-benefit analysis of different patterns of working. Personnel managers should be prepared to play their part in this aspect of pre-planning as well as advising on the implementation of subsequent changes. Many decisions to reduce working hours have been taken without adequate research into the economics of the exercise. Obviously it is no simple forecasting job – factors affecting and affected by changes in working time are extremely complex, including the nature of the business, the staff, plant, equipment and buildings, and the way the personnel management function is organized. Nevertheless, more calculations do need to be made in advance, and there needs to be more monitoring of experiments. More thought needs to be given to the organizational development aspects – with the personnel management role primarily that of coordinating the processing of changes, so that the most appropriate methods of working can be selected and implemented effectively.

Another development is the annual hours contract* – one which enables the employer to vary the number of hours worked in a defined period within the context of the standard working hours for the year as

*'Annual Hours: an idea whose time has come', Phillip Lynch, *Personnel Management*, November 1985, pages 46–50.

a whole. It can be used in a number of ways: for example, the length of the working day can be varied – up to say nine hours a day in the period of peak demand. Extra hours worked in the high period can be compensated by shorter days in the slack period, or by aggregating the hours to blocks of time off ('shift-free' days). A review conducted by the Industrial Society in 1986 showed that nearly 150 British companies had introduced or were contemplating annual hours systems. Those already working on this basis reported the benefits as being reduction in overtime, lower labour costs, reduced absenteeism, greater flexibility and increased productivity. But there are disadvantages, too: a disinclination to work 'pay-back' hours, difficulty in organizing shift-cover, complexity of shift rotas and problems in scheduling holidays. (Thirteen of the firms' surveys stated emphatically that they met no pit-falls at all and that the concept had been of great benefit.)

Flexibility also extends to other forms of contract. The maximum–minimum contract pre-defines the range of hours that an employee may be required to work. Then there are contracts that provide for work to be undertaken *at* home, others for work to be undertaken *from* home. (Rank Xerox, in their well-known net working concept, linked homeworking to self-employment.) There are opportunities for increasing the use of part-time contracts and job sharing. The latter offers particular advantages to the employer if the arrangements include specific references to the need to cover for any absence of the job-sharing partner; and job-sharers also form an experienced pool of labour for switching to full-time work if required. Self-employment contracts clearly provide for considerable flexibility since contracts are entered into to meet particular requirements and can be renewed or not, depending on business needs.

Thus there is a range of techniques which enables organizations flexibly to alter basic working hours to meet the need to accommodate volume variability. It is claimed* that such flexibility of tasks, initiatives in working time and alternative forms of contract can all provide scope for improving the cost effectiveness of operations in both the public and private sectors – with advantages for employees, too, including greater job satisfaction and the possibility of longer consecutive blocks of time off.

Not that the concept of the flexible firm is without controversy, and it has been argued that the development of temporary and part-time work, self-employment, subcontracting, freelancing and home-working cannot be explained by any deliberate attempts to create an employment periphery. In fact, much of the expansion of irregular,

---

*'Trends in the Flexible Workforce', Catherine Hakin, *Employment Gazette*, November 1987, pages 549–59.

and hence insecure, work can be attributed to sectoral shifts in the structure of employment, by cost-cutting measures and by rationalization – a variety of managerial measures, but hardly a recognizable strategy with developments consciously designed to achieve functional flexibility or to offer employment security to a 'core'.

Indeed, a major effect of viewing flexibility as a panacea (undefined) is to legitimize casualization by creating an insecure, untrained workforce (but one which management needs do nothing about). Yet research* suggests that the expansion of a casual, poorly trained and cheap employment 'periphery' is the last thing needed to improve Britain's productivity record and competitiveness.

Having in mind 'the demographic time-bomb of the 1990s', and the skills shortages inherent in this, jobshare schemes are one way of helping employers to attract and retain staff. When first practised a decade or so ago, jobsharing was largely negotiated on an *ad hoc* basis between individual employees and their employers, but the trend more recently has been towards employer-led schemes: Boots, BT, the British Council and the Civil Service have well-established programmes, and some fifty-six local authorities† have declared formal jobsharing policies and employ over 2000 jobsharers. Many of these policies form part of integrated equal opportunities strategies aimed at encouraging women to return to work after maternity leave and helping people with disabilities.

The benefits of job sharing most mentioned by employers are that two people bring with them two sets of skills and experience, and can also offer increased flexibility. Fears about higher labour costs have been generally disproved: extra administrative costs are minimal and, indeed, there can be savings in national insurance costs. Where extra costs are incurred in training, these can be compensated for by higher productivity, lower absenteeism and lower staff turnover.

Factors in the success of jobsharing schemes have proved to be:

- A formal policy stating in principle which jobs are open to sharing.
- Full consultation between management and trade unions.
- Clear guidelines to ensure consistent implementation from an early stage.
- Training on jobsharing for line and senior managers to encourage positive attitudes.
- Record keeping and regular monitoring of schemes to assess commitment, success, impact and progress.

*'The flexible firm: a model in search of reality', Anna Pollert (University of Warwick, 1987).
†*Employment Gazette*, November 1989, page 579.

Shifts

The numbers of workers employed on *shifts* continue to rise and there may be a further increase in the near future. Overhead costs are spread over a longer production day in this way; but overtime is not necessarily eliminated, and double-shift and Sunday premiums are commonly found in practice. Capital equipment and labour can be used more efficiently in shifts, although their introduction will not be readily achieved if workers' net wages are reduced through loss of overtime. The appeal of shiftworking then, like most other changes in conditions, will largely depend on how attractive it is made to workers financially.

When shifts are first contemplated in a discontinuous process where employment has previously been day work, the double-day system (say, 6 a.m.–2 p.m.; 2 p.m.–10 p.m.) probably offers the greatest advantages to all concerned – for management because the second shift is the one which alleviates fixed charges most; for employees because the physical and social difficulties are much less than when nightwork is involved. Of course, there should be the fullest consultation and discussions before any system is actually implemented.

The main problem about working a three-shift system is the 'unnatural' aspect of nightwork. Some difficulties are physiological (body-temperature rhythms, digestive disturbances, inability to sleep during the day), but the real unpopularity of continuous shiftworking is due to the social disturbances caused. In particular, complaints are directed at the 'dead fortnight', when afternoon and night-shifts virtually preclude any normal evening social life. In order to overcome these problems, the Continental, or 3–2–2, system is coming more and more into use, and is already firmly established in the chemical and iron and steel industries. It entails more frequent changes than the

Table 9

	Weeks			
	1	*2*	*3*	*4*
Monday	6–2	—	10–6	2–10
Tuesday	6–2	—	10–6	2–10
Wednesday	2–10	6–2	—	10–6
Thursday	2–10	6–2	—	10–6
Friday	10–6	2–10	6–2	—
Saturday	10–6	12–10	6–12	—
Sunday	—	10–6	2–10	6–2

Average weekly hours 42

traditional pattern, with the result that employees concerned can take part in normal social activities at least two or three times *every* week. The rotation of shifts over a four-week cycle is three mornings, two afternoons, two nights, three rest days, two mornings, two afternoons, three nights, and two rest days, as shown in Table 9.

The two notable features of this arrangement of hours are that it gets away entirely from the 'dead fortnight' and that there is a 24-hour break between each selection of the 3−2−2 shifts. On the debit side, there are the possible difficulties a family may have initially in following the system, and the fact that there are no entirely free weekends (although the different Saturday hours partly help to overcome this).

Good reports have come from industrial organizations using the system: ICI operate it in two of their factories, and a survey of 5000 employees showed an 86 per cent response in its favour. Shorter and more frequent spells on each shift were found to be less tiring and the variety was more enjoyable. Employees said that they seemed to have more time off, and obviously opportunities were much better for social and family life. Senior staff, for their part, found it much easier to keep in touch with shiftworkers and supervisors.

Enlightened management might well take the view, in any case, that because shiftworking is inherently unpopular, the system of operation should be decided by those involved, as long as productive efficiency is not adversely affected. This should leave scope for administrative ingenuity to meet the personal convenience of employees whenever possible as regards the frequency of shift changes, starting and finishing times, and when the rest days occur.

The potential costs and benefits of shiftwork have long continued to be a topic for political debate, and there is a large body of opinion which favours legislation on that subject. But although much is known about the medical, psychological, and social consequences of shift-work, there has been little analysis of the economic effects of modifying shiftwork patterns. If there are important benefits in terms of cost savings and job creation in an economy prone to under-investment, then economists would appear to be adopting a stance that is diametrically opposed to the rest of the social sciences.*

Economists have also suggested† that organizations should do more by way of cost-benefit analysis of the effects of shiftwork, especially as regards formal costing. This might well result in an increase in the amount of shiftwork and a reduction in the levels of overtime. The

*'Proposed Changes in the Extent and Nature of Shift Working', Bosworth and Dawkins, *Personnel Review*, vol. 4 no. 7, 1978, pages 32–5.
†National Economic Development Office, *Multiple Shiftwork* (HMSO, 1970).

benefits of shiftwork, accruing from capital saving by obtaining a higher amount of output from a given stock of capital and by the more intensive use of capital enabling it to be 'written-off' more quickly, have not yet been fully realized. There has been too much reliance in recent years on overtime as a means of increasing capital utilization, although this may be relatively expensive because of the size of overtime premia.

The adverse effects of shiftworking are potentially widespread, including a drain on the health service and higher rates of marital breakdown. But in addition to these medical and social factors, implications for the level of employment should also be taken into account. If organizations elected to use a relatively small single-shift labour force without higher levels of investment to compensate, the result might be substantial levels of unemployment. While state unemployment relief might thus require large sums, quite small subsidies encouraging shiftwork could alter those organizations' decisions in favour of shiftwork, and there could be important social gains in that case.

Any legal reforms concerning shiftwork will need to be precise in their proposals, simply because there is such a multitude of different patterns and systems of work, some admittedly involving high social costs, but others, such as double-day working, with very little. Perhaps the most significant pointer to likely legislation is the European Commission Report, *The Problems of Shift-working*, of 1977 which proposed:

(a) To reduce the extent of shiftworking by placing more constraints on decisions about such forms of work at plant level and ensuring a thorough examination of all the issues at the point of decision.
(b) To improve the conditions under which shiftwork is carried out so as to reduce its negative effects.

In specific terms, first, all shiftworkers above a certain age or with a certain length of service on shifts should have the right to return to normal day work. Second, there should be a reduction in the length of the working week, longer rest periods and earlier retirement for shiftworkers. To some extent, by way of comparison, some of these proposals have already been incorporated into legislation in France.

Flexitime

Flexible working hours represent an approach to attendance at work which, within limits set by management, enables individual employees to vary their hours day by day and, to that extent, come and go as they please. Several advantages are claimed for such systems, many of which have now been put into practice, largely in commercial and government offices employing clerical workers. Flexible working hours operate best when individual workers are responsible for activities which do not require the presence of others. In most industrial jobs, certainly on production lines, this is rarely possible.

Morale is improved by allowing staff to arrange their days to fit their particular needs and leisure pursuits and to make the best use of available transport; the stresses and strains on individuals can thus be reduced with consequent benefits to their health and efficiency. The pioneering schemes have demonstrated that absenteeism is reduced because there are no longer fears associated with being late for work, and the temptation to take the odd day off is also reduced. Very important is the encouragement to married women to work by being able to adjust their hours to the demands of running a home.

The major management constraint quite obviously is so to control the scheme that neither general efficiency nor service to customers suffer in any way. This means that most offices have a 'core time', commonly 10.00 a.m. to 4 p.m. when all staff are expected to be present – the flexibility lying in actual starting and finishing times. Flexible hours permit employees to work more or less hours in a working day than is normal, but over a period of say three weeks or a month, the full contracted hours must be worked. A rule must therefore be agreed about how many 'credits' or 'debits' of hours any employee may carry forward and for how long. Hours may be worked so that the occasional day or half-day may be taken, although management has to control this so as to prevent inefficiency due to periods of under-staffing. It is also necessary that time off should not lead to regular four or four and a half day working weeks.

The practical considerations involved in operating a flexitime scheme were well illustrated in a report* of no fewer than 180 flexitime schemes operating throughout the Ministry of Defence, with a general conclusion that the fears and misunderstandings that might have impeded the progress of flexitime had long since given way to confidence in its working and to an appreciation of its benefits to both staff and management. Flexible working hours (FWH) were shown to bring a realism into attendance arrangements and to succeed in controlling what for years, particularly in large urban areas, has always tended to be uncontrollable. It makes 'honest folk' of those who, whatever their nominal attendance system, are unable to sustain a regular pattern of attendance from day to day because of the realities of modern life: peak-hour travel, transport delays, traffic jams, strikes,

---

*'Flexible Working Hours in the Ministry of Defence', L. Muddeman, *Management Services in Government*, February 1979, page 39.

even the demands of domestic life in our modern complex society, all militate against precise, consistent starting times. FWH not only brings order into this disorder; within limits that are clearly defined and acceptable to management, it gives staff a new facility deliberately to vary arrival and departure times for personal reasons, and to do so with candour and dignity. This recognition of the stresses of modern life and of the needs of the individual, subject to the overriding obligation to complete the prescribed number of hours of the accounting period and be present in core times, sets FWH ahead of any other system of attendance.

Evidence from these 180 schemes clearly shows that flexibility in attendance helps management both in coping with an irregular pressure of work and in facilitating a reduction in overtime working. For the individual it can provide an opportunity to benefit from the quiet hours of the day when work is less subject to the interruption of the telephone and visitors. Efficiency improves as absenteeism, in the form of lateness, unauthorized early departure, or protracted lunch breaks, disappears. More perhaps than any other system FWH is self-policing, because the obligation to build up hours by the end of the accounting period rests inescapably and directly on the employee.

In the early days of FWH at the Ministry of Defence some staff murmured against the strict time-keeping system – due largely to a misconception of the object of time recording, which was not to record arrival and departure times for the management, but to record total hours as they accumulate and enable staff to see how these compare with the target hours.

In the end, however, it must be recognized that amid all the arguments for and against, what matters most is the spirit in which management and staff approach FWH. The written schemes within the MOD therefore usually contain the statement: 'The introduction of FWH allows you greater freedom but places greater responsibility on you as well. To make it work, you will find that you will have to give and take with your colleagues.' This is the heart of the matter – a plea for fairness and good sense in producing and working the scheme because FWH, like any agreement, will not work if designed to be exploited.

Welfare

The important thing about employee benefits and welfare services is that they should spring from the right motives, otherwise management and worker attitudes towards them might clash. If management regard them as paternalistic acts of benevolence, preening themselves as good employers with their workers' interests at heart, they may very well be surprised by a reaction alleging fraud. For employees often feel that the costs of welfare provisions are used as a cheap excuse for refusing claims for better working conditions, and that amenities provided unilaterally could be withdrawn at any time without breach of agreement. The view is often expressed — 'Cut out the welfare, and give us the cash in our wages'.

Welfare policy must therefore be based on sound principles:

1 Management should never obtrude into the private lives of employees through welfare schemes (thus avoiding accusations of paternalism).
2 Amenities should be provided only when desired by employees. The sincerity of this desire may be judged by their willingness to administer the activities, clubs, and benefits themselves.
3 The amenities provided should be beneficial in the long run to both management and employees (thus avoiding charges of bribery or extravagance).

Practice in the provision and administration of welfare facilities varies enormously between different organizations, as does the extent

Figure 29

to which their personnel departments become directly involved. Broadly speaking, however, the following seven services and amenities are normally considered to fall within the welfare sphere:

Canteens

These may be controlled directly by the firm or organized through outside caterers. In most cases the prices of meals are subsidized, apprentices getting very cheap meals, while senior executives pay near the economic price. Food can be a constant source of complaints, of course, and joint consultative committees are usually formed to deal with them and help the canteen manager with constructive suggestions. Outside working hours canteen buildings are often used for other social purposes and may be licensed as clubs.

Accommodation

Any large organization which recruits professional and technical staff from a distance will find it necessary to assist them in finding accommodation for their families. Help may take many forms, ranging from maintaining lists of approved lodgings or running hostels for single people, to advancing loans for house purchase. Many firms own houses and flats which they rent to employees and some have special arrangements with local authorities concerning council housing for key workers. Obviously the whole question of providing such assistance needs the most careful control, especially as regards the legal position of employees who leave a firm while still receiving its help with accommodation.

Transport

Linked with the housing problem is that of travelling to work. Hence again practice varies widely: firms may own or hire fleets of coaches or lorries, provide senior staff with cars or car allowances, and will certainly make representations to local bus companies to arrange services convenient for their employees. In any given area there is a committee which advises the transport authority on local problems: personnel managers must ensure that their organization's views are heard in that committee.

Sickness benefits

The importance of firms' private benefit arrangements has been progressively reduced by state provision, culminating in the National Insurance Act 1966. As far as firms' own sickness arrangements are concerned, a notable recent development is the tendency for the distinction made between payments during absence to 'staff' and 'workers' to disappear.

A new statutory sick pay scheme (SSP) was introduced in 1982,* in part to resolve GPs' complaints that the attention they had to give to the 'cough and cold brigade' took up valuable time which would be better spent in treating really ill patients. The scheme requires that people who are ill for between four and seven days fill out their own sickness benefit claim form stating that they are ill and unfit for work, and sign it themselves. Doctors no longer have to provide sick notes for the first week of an illness, but will issue them after the first week.

This self-certification system removes the usual requirement for a doctor's statement in support of a claim for sickness, or other state incapacity benefit.

From the personnel manager's point of view, any self-certificating scheme must be founded on clear policies and good communications, controls and records. Detail must be right in several respects: absence control procedure; notification; record keeping; disciplinary procedure; managers' and supervisors' roles; the role of the organization's occupational health service; the format and content of the organization's own self-certificate; statement of sickness policy and procedure in conditions of service; consultation and arrangements with unions and the organization's insurance company.

The self-certification form needs to include full identification of the employee in the form of name, pay/clock number, department, period of absence covering inclusive dates, nature of illness, signature of employee and the date signed; declaration as to accuracy including a reminder that a false statement is a breach of disciplinary rules; and a question as to whether a doctor was consulted, with his/her name and address. Most employers operating self-certification require the certificate to be countersigned; some insist that the form be completed in the presence of the countersignatory, believing, for example, that filling in the form in the presence of a supervisor reduces the number of incorrect or fraudulent certificates.

Adequate records are needed to identify patterns and incidence of absence affecting individuals, groups or particular times, and these will assist in the sound administration of the sick-pay scheme.

*Consolidated, with some amendments to detail, by the Social Security Act 1985.

Obviously the records must be accurate, as they may be used to determine entitlement, challenge statements, or even spot ailments which may be alleviated by action within the organization's occupational health service.

Pension schemes

Most large organizations now operate their own superannuation arrangements for professional and technical staff and many have schemes that include all their workers. These may have some value in attracting and retaining the steadier type of employee, although there is the contrary argument that a person's reluctance to lose pension rights is the wrong motive for staying with an otherwise unsatisfactory employer. An organization's own pension scheme may be contributory or non-contributory, and may be administered by its own trust or through an insurance company.

Here again state provision has caught up with some private arrangements, as a result of the Graduated Pension Scheme which was introduced under the National Insurance Act 1959 to supplement retirement pensions. The scheme applies to all workers whose employers are not contracted-out on grounds that they already guarantee comparable benefits under their own occupational pension schemes (at present, private schemes cover more than one-third of the working population, including half of the men). The level of employees' earnings now affects both the rate of their pension contributions while working and their retirement pensions. No contributions are paid by employers who contract out, normally done when they have their own 'generous' contributory schemes.

Long-service awards

These are most commonly given at the conventional 'coming-of-age', twenty-one years' work with the organization, although further awards are often given for greater service. They can be of considerable motivational importance to those eligible, and the administration involved needs to be carried out carefully. When firms have traded only for twenty to thirty years, for example, or when they have expanded rapidly during that period, early staff records may be scanty or non-existent, and the welfare officer may have to undertake a considerable amount of 'detective work' among older employees to verify claims to awards. Obviously certain rules will have to apply to any long-service scheme: those relating to broken periods of service over the years are always crucial to the equitable treatment of employees when deciding on awards.

Social activities

These may range from an informal Christmas party or summer outing to the provision of a sports and social club with a large full-time staff to run it. Facilities on this scale are often the subject of controversy; certainly, extravagant provisions can never be justified while employees' more fundamental needs for improved working conditions or security of employment may be neglected. Nevertheless it is very useful to have social facilities where employees and their families can meet, especially in remote locations of small towns where little other entertainment is available in any case. Even when full-time administrative staff are provided, each section or activity should be allowed reasonable autonomy, within the social club's rules and subject to the firm's overall financial control, of course.

Personal problems

Employees should first notify their immediate superior if they want help with a personal or domestic problem, but may ask to see or be referred to someone in the personnel department. All its staff should be prepared to help directly with problems if employees approach them as individuals: this is preferable to passing a person with worries on to a colleague unless absolutely necessary.

A variety of counselling services provided by 'outside agencies' are also available: in recent times these have made notable contributions on personal matters, occupational guidance, redundancy problems, stress, midlife crises and career conflicts, for example. Two brief case studies provide illustrations. In 1985 British Airways launched 'Crewcare' – a 24 hours counselling service for all its cabin staff, operated by fifteen cabin crew members who were given training in counselling and who operate on a rota. The counsellors are available to help with personal crises and stress and can also give information on how to obtain specialist advice where necessary. The team is supported by a professional counsellor who acts as a consultant and counselling supervisor.

A general characteristic of such counselling services is that they are insulated from the management structure, in order to preclude any possibility of 'leaks' back to an individual employee's manager or the personnel department, i.e. the professionals operate outside the usual hierarchical framework. This functional separation is essential to create the atmosphere of trust and confidentiality without which staff would be unwilling to use the service. It also helps in tackling issues which the 'client' may not want aired in the workplace, e.g. highly sensitive problems of office politics which could not normally be taken to the line manager (who, on occasion, may be a major factor in the problem).

In this context the term 'counselling' must be precisely defined as 'helping people explore problems so that they can decide what to do about them'. Hence it is different from giving advice: counsellors are *not* in the business of analysing, diagnosing and offering expert solutions — their aim is to help clients find their own solutions, since these will be more valid, appropriate and workable than anything another person can suggest.

Perhaps the best-known recent example of an in-house counselling service is that of the Post Office.* Counsellors are now part of the workforce, with the specific remit of overcoming stress. Not only are its occupational health nurses trained in counselling but managers, too, are given an appreciation of counselling skills and how to recognize different stress agents within the organization. The letter sent by way of introduction to employees explains the nature of the service:

Dear Colleague,
I am writing to introduce myself as the new specialist counsellor for the Post Office in all businesses in the X and Y postal district areas. My name is. . . .
　You will already know of the practical help with personal problems that you can receive from the welfare service, or from the occupational health service if the problem is affecting your health. These services will continue to offer guidance and assistance as at present but some personal problems can be pretty complicated and deep rooted and I will be working alongside welfare officers, doctors and nurses to help you with them. Through my appointment the Post Office is widening your choice as to the kind of help which best suits your particular needs in dealing with any personal difficulties which you may have.
　WHAT IS COUNSELLING? Specialist counselling is an additional personal service introduced to help people who are in distress or under stress to learn to cope with a problem for themselves and to grow as people through being able to do so. It takes time. Most of us can benefit from such help at some time in our lives and the problems do not necessarily have to be big ones — simply big enough to be causing us personal difficulties which we cannot effectively resolve on

*'A Post Office Initiative to Stamp Out Stress', G. Sadu, C. Cooper and T. Allison, *Personnel Management*, August 1989, page 40.

our own. It takes courage to tackle your own problems and if you do, you will be given encouragement and support in doing so. Often the hardest part is taking the first step — asking for help.

WHAT KIND OF PROBLEMS CAN I HELP WITH? The list is endless — any kind of personal problem or crisis. My aim is to help anyone who is stressed or in distress, whatever the reason — particularly where the problem is having an effect on health or work performance, or relationships either at work or at home.

If you think I can help you, or you are at all unsure, give me a ring and we can have a short conversation on the phone to see if I can help. If you want the call to remain anonymous, I will not insist on you telling me who you are.

WHAT WILL I DO? Initially I will listen and encourage you to talk about whatever is bothering you. I will not pressure you — you will lead the way. Sometimes simply talking a problem through in this way is of real help.

Secondly, I will do my best to help you to find a way through your difficulty. If we cannot come up with a solution together I will try to put you in touch with other people inside or outside the Post Office who may be able to offer exactly the support you need.

Can I also point out that our discussions will be in complete confidence. Unless you give me permission I will never reveal who you are, what we have talked about, or even that you have been to see me.

HOW CAN YOU GET IN TOUCH WITH ME?

• Either give me a ring and make an appointment or give me a ring and have a telephone conversation. The number is Postline.... When I am not available, a telephone answering service is in operation and your call will always be returned. If you don't want to ring — drop me a short note suggesting how I might contact you. My address is Box Y, Post Office HQ, Any town.

• If you would rather not come direct to me you can approach your local welfare officer, nursing adviser, supervisor, manager or union representative. They can discuss the best way of helping you with your problem and can arrange an appointment for you if you decide to talk to me about it.

Above all — please do not think you will be wasting my time. I am here to help you to the best of my ability.

Sincerely....

Staff benefits — practical example

A good example of a contemporary approach to a staff benefits package is provided by a case study* of Warrington District General Hospital. Its Staff Acquisition and Retention (STAR) initiative is financed by the hospital's League of Friends and other trust funds, and encompass the following:

- A chiropody service, with a chiropodist offering two sessions a week.
- An optician's service, again two sessions a week, providing staff with free eye tests and prescriptions once a year, and a discount on prescriptions made up.
- A well person's clinic, open to all staff (some 380 of whom made use of it in the first year).
- A staff shop: stock includes frozen convenience foods and household goods (prices lower than high street retailers); staff may use the internal phone system to place orders.
- A nursery, taking up to fifty children, whose parents may visit them during their breaks; this service is run by an outside contractor, using hospital premises, and staff are charged a commercial rate.
- A paternity leave scheme, giving up to six days 'compassionate' leave.

Although recruitment poses few problems in the Warrington area, the fact remains that during the first year of STAR, staff turnover fell from 7.8 per cent to 3.5 per cent.

Staff–worker status

For many years efforts have been made to narrow the differences between 'staff' and 'workers'. The Institute of Personnel Management's Golden Jubilee statement of personnel policies declared support of the progressive removal of distinctions in security of employment and conditions of work, including fringe benefits, for different categories of employee, and more recently the Code of Industrial Relations Practice made the same point.

Fundamentally the distinctions are akin to those drawn between social classes. One group of employees work comparatively short hours and are trusted to carry out a reasonable amount of work during that time; and there is a larger group who normally work longer hours and are generally not trusted by their employers, the work being much

*'A Healthy Approach to Staff Benefits', Anat Arkin, *Personnel Management Plus*, September 1990, page 18.

more closely supervised and paid for in ratio to the hours spent in the workplace or the effort expended. There is no escaping the fact that this mistrust in turn causes a lack of confidence in management by employees – a general situation which is wholly unhelpful to labour relations.

Practical distinctions are commonly seen between security of employment, the amount of notice due, promotion opportunities, length of holidays, and generosity of sickness pay. It is commonplace to hear that a skilled craftsman with twenty years' experience in a firm works forty hours a week, has pay deducted if he is a few minutes late for work, draws only his National Insurance benefit when sick, and has three weeks' holiday a year. His teenage daughter, employed in the same firm's typing pool for twenty days, works thirty-five hours a week, loses no pay if late nor if she is away ill, and is entitled to four weeks' holiday. The historical distinction is that between 'office' and 'works', but several factors have served to blur this: the rapid increase in numbers of professional, technical, and clerical staffs compared with production workers; the fact that so many women are employed in these groups (whose better conditions are envied by men); above all, the growing together of the interests of professional and technical staff and skilled operatives on the one hand, as opposed to office staff on the other. All these factors help 'workers' over the barriers that previously existed.

Recent reported attempts to make progress with this problem seem to be inspired by different motives on the part of management. In some cases, equality of conditions is aimed at in order to retain labour by building up loyalty towards the employer; in others, concessions have been made virtually as part of the process of productivity bargaining. The approach of most organizations seems to be aimed at tackling equality of status step by step, either dealing with one aspect at a time or progressively granting improved status to certain types of staff according to their length of service, degree of responsibility, or general reliability.*

One symbol of staff–worker distinction that regularly comes under attack is the clocking-in system. There is no clearer indication of mistrust of workpeople than this insistence on a record of the times they arrive and depart (irrespective of how much work they do while

---

*A contempary case study, the introduction of single status within Tioxide UK Ltd (which gained an IPM/*Daily Telegraph* Award for Excellence in Personnel Management), is reported in 'Single Status as the Key to Flexibility', Gerald Kennedy, *Personnel Management*, February 1988, pages 51–3.

A more detailed case, a historic account of the harmonization of terms and conditions of employment in Hall Brothers (Whitefield) Ltd, can be found in the *Employment Gazette*, February 1988, pages 94–101.

there). More faith must be placed in the responsibility of individuals by management, and indeed in the ability of supervisors to control the time-keeping and attendance of their subordinates. Apart from these emotional aspects of management and worker views on the subject, clocking-in is also administratively expensive. The experience of firms who have abandoned it is that their confidence has been fully justified by results; there has been no deterioration in employees' time-keeping, and new documentation for wages purposes was speedily evolved.

Many practical difficulties have to be overcome. Fixing annual salaries for workers accustomed to overtime pay, piece-rates, and production bonuses requires the most careful negotiations. Workers will reject offers which amount to less than their previous total earnings inclusive of overtime and other premium payments. If the offers are too high, on the other hand, management will be faced with greater costs unless increases in productivity are obtained at the same time. Professional and clerical workers inevitably react defensively to some extent, seeking to preserve their past privileges. This may lead to greater interest being taken in white-collar unions, the bargaining strength of which will grow, possibly straining staff relationships with management. On the financial side, wage agreements may have to be renegotiated to take into account the staff concept of pay increases based on length of service: although this may cut down on labour turnover, it means substituting incremental rises for the present practice of frequent (often annual) wage claims.

It is not easy to change employment conditions which have their origins in the dim past of industrial history, are largely based on the privilege of superior social class, and are resented for that very reason by the majority of workers. Traditional trappings of status are irrelevant in our contemporary economic circumstances, but getting rid of them calls for the closest cooperation between managers and trade union representatives, encouraged by the strength of public opinion, and stimulated by advice on good practice which is available from government departments. There can be no doubt that success in this sphere would materially contribute to improving workers' attitudes to the whole social structure of industry.

There is, of course, nothing new in the notion that harmonized terms and conditions of employment can provide the basis of the social justice needed for good industrial relations. Unfortunately, probably because costs get more emphasis than business benefits, harmonization is often seen as a desirable long-term objective rather than as a subject of specific action programmes. There is, for example, a significant cost entailed in providing a common pension scheme.

Given the opportunity of starting a new business, most employers would now wish to offer single-status terms of employment – but established organizations find it very difficult to break from tradition and history. Yet the benefits which harmonization can bring in terms of greater commitment, flexibility, productivity and quality are becoming clearer and will demand more attention and investment. Workforces are smaller, and status differences which have been accepted in the past are now more conspicuous; if they are no longer perceived as being relevant to the business, they will become obstacles to cooperation and teamwork.

The harmonization case study of Johnson and Johnson Ltd* revealed a number of lessons:

First, we should keep organization structure, skills and resources, payment and benefit systems and terms of employment under constant review to ensure they are always relevant and that they support the objectives of the business. Next that programmes involving changes of this kind need to be 'shared' with all employees, becoming part of company culture only when they are 'owned' by everyone. There is a lesson here for personnel departments which hold on to the ball too long and do not involve other managers at all levels early enough.

Future success will be with companies which are highly focused by technology and market expertise, which are able to adapt rapidly to changes in markets and technology. Such companies will have an overwhelming emphasis on coordination and the fullest identification of their people with the overall business purpose. They will be the companies which secure opportunities for business and individual growth and development. There will be no room in them for differences and divisions which consume energies and are unrelated to the work to be done – no room for what Eric Hammond has called 'industrial apartheid'.

Further reading

The Best of Both Worlds: a Guide for Employers, Department of Employment, 1991.
Flexible Patterns of Work, edited C. Curson (IPM, 1986).
Managing Change: the organization of work (CBI, 1985).
The Skilled Helper: a systematic approach to effective helping, Gerard Egan (Brooks/Cole, 3rd edition, 1989).

*'Harmonization: the benefits and the lessons', Terry Mullins, *Personnel Management*, March 1986, pages 38–41.

19

Health and safety

To a large extent the health and safety of workers has been controlled by legislation, notably the Factories Act 1961; the Offices, Shops, and Railway Premises Act 1963; the Employment Medical Advisory Service Act 1972; and the Health and Safety at Work Act 1974. The important thing is that most employers accept these as enforcing only minimum conditions and are concerned to improve on them wherever possible.

The Health and Safety at Work Act (HASAWA) 1974

Based on the work of the Robens Committee on Health and Safety at Work,* the aims of the Act are: to secure the health, safety, and welfare of people at work; to protect others than those at work against risks to health and safety; to control the keeping and use of explosive or highly flammable or otherwise dangerous substances, and to prevent the unlawful acquisition, possession and use of such substances; and to control the emission into the atmosphere of noxious or offensive substances from premises.

Section 2 of the Act goes on to state that it is the duty of employers to ensure, so far as is reasonably practicable, the health, safety, and welfare at work of all their employees. The matters to which that duty extends include in particular:

*Cmnd. 5034 (HMSO, 1972).

(a) The provision and maintenance of plant and systems of work that are safe and without risk to health.
(b) Arrangements for ensuring safety and absence of risks to health in connection with the use, handling, storage, and transport of articles and substances.
(c) The provision of such information, instruction, training, and supervision as is necessary to ensure the health and safety at work of employees.
(d) The maintenance of any place of work under the employer's control in a condition that is safe and without risks to health, and the provision and maintenance of safe means of access to and egress from it.
(e) The provision and maintenance of a working environment for employees that is safe, without risks to health, and adequate as regards facilities and arrangements for their welfare at work.

It is also the duty of employers to prepare a written statement of their general policy with respect to the health and safety at work of their employees and the organization and arrangements for the time being in force for carrying out that policy, and to bring this statement and any revision of it to the notice of all their employees.

Employees also have duties to members of the public, and must conduct their undertakings in such a way as to ensure, so far as is reasonably practicable, that those who are not in their employment who may be affected thereby are not exposed to risks to their health and safety. At the same time it shall be the duty of employees while at work to take reasonable care of the health and safety of themselves and of other persons who may be affected by their acts or omissions at work; and as regards any duty or requirement imposed on their employer or any other person by the relevant statutory provisions, to cooperate with them so far as is necessary to enable that duty or requirement to be complied with. No person shall intentionally or recklessly interfere with or misuse anything provided in the interest of health, safety, or welfare in pursuance of any of the relevant statutory provisions.

All employers are required to produce a policy statement on health and safety, which, to be effective, needs to incorporate the following elements:*

1 A written statement of the basic objectives, which is supplemented by more detailed rules and procedures to cater for specific hazards.

*HM Chief Inspector of Factories, Annual Report 1973.

2 Definitions of both the duties and the extent of responsibility at specified line management levels for safety and health, with identification made at the highest level of an individual with overall responsibility.

3 Definition of the function of the safety officer (if one exists) and his/her relationship to line management.

4 Monitoring of safety performance and publishing of information about the performance.

5 An analysis of hazards to be undertaken subsequent to an inspection of the workplace; such analysis to identify unsafe work methods and unsafe work situations.

6 An information system which will be sufficient to produce an identification of needs and can be used as an indicator of the effectiveness of the policy. The amount of detail required by such a system will depend on these needs, bearing in mind that the cost of obtaining the information should be realistically related to hoped-for benefit.

7 Training programmes for all management levels including that of the supervisor.

8 Commitment to consultation for safety and to a positive form of worker involvement. It is not, however, sufficient to publish a policy, however comprehensive it may be, unless the policy is translated into effective actions at all levels within the organization. Success, in terms of an acknowledged and continuing commitment at all management levels, is more likely where the policy is underwritten by the main board. They need also to make adequate financial provision for carrying the policy into effect. The requirement to monitor performance at a high level in the organization is of particular importance.

A set of rules and procedures may thus be summarized as:

1 *The organization for safety* – allocation of responsibilities within management; definition of the scope and function of the safety officer (where he/she exists) and his/her relationship to line management, a commitment to joint consultation and worker involvement.

2 *Hazard control* – standards for plant and machinery, housekeeping, handling, floors and floor surfaces, protective clothing, fire, flammable and explosive substances.

3 *Health* – including welfare, noise, toxic and corrosive substances, dusts and vapours.

4 *Procedures* – designed to meet objective standards through plant inspection, safe operating procedures, plant safety rules, accident

investigation and analysis, safety audit, self-inspection to identify hazards; control and monitoring of performance.

5 *Safety training* – basic commitment to provide high standards of safety training for operators, supervisors, and line management.

A primary aim of any policy ought to be the involvement and motivation of the workforce. This is best achieved through a demonstrated commitment and concern on the part of management. In this context first-line supervision is of primary importance and more recognition ought to be given to its role. This means that particular attention should be paid to training in hazard identification and to the support of first-line supervision in actions needed and taken. The needs of workers relate to protective equipment and devices, to training relative to their jobs and the hazards involved and to job descriptions. The importance of their contribution can be stressed in terms of reporting of defects, in inspection and audit of the workplace, and in the correct use of rules and procedures relating to safe systems of work.

The HASAWA provides for the appointment of safety representatives and committees, and a code of practice came into effect in October 1979 setting out regulations and guidance notes for both. Safety representatives, with prescribed functions, may be appointed from among employees at a workplace by recognized independent trade unions. They are allowed time off work with pay to carry out their duties. If any two safety representatives ask, in writing, for a safety committee, an employer, after specified consultations, would have to establish one within three months.

The code lays great emphasis on the advisability of using existing representatives and joint consultative machinery, although obviously it would be necessary to guard against the possibility of using safety as a bargaining lever in negotiations over pay and other conditions of service. It is calculated that about 150,000 safety representatives have now been appointed, and a great continuous task is that of training them to carry out their duties properly; this is being tackled mainly by the TUC. Of course, the effectiveness of safety representatives will to a large extent be governed by the response of management: they must give a positive lead by example and by their dealings with representatives and safety committees.

The terms of reference of safety committees usually include: the promotion of cooperation between management and staff in instigating, developing, and carrying out measures to ensure the health and safety at work of all employees; and to act as a focus for staff participation in the prevention of accidents and avoidance of industrial disease. Within such objectives certain specific functions may be defined, including:

(a) Consideration of the circumstances of individual accidents and cases of notifiable diseases; and the study of accident statistics and trends, so that reports can be made to management on unsafe and unhealthy conditions and practices, together with recommendations for corrective action.

(b) Examination of safety audit reports on a similar basis.

(c) Consideration of reports and factual information provided by inspectors of the enforcing authority appointed under the HASAWA.

(d) Consideration of reports which safety representatives may wish to submit.

(e) Assistance in the development of safety rules and safe systems of work.

(f) Periodic inspections of the workplace, its plant, equipment, and amenities.

(g) A watch on the effectiveness of the safety content of staff training.

(h) A watch on the adequacy of safety and health communication and publicity in the unit(s) for which the committee is responsible.

(i) The provision of a link with the appropriate inspectorates of the enforcing authority.

A Health and Safety Commission and Executive has been set up to administer the legislation. The Commission, with a chairperson and up to nine members appointed after consultation with employer organizations, trade unions, and local authorities, has major research, educational, and advisory responsibilities. It also undertakes the continuing job of preparing proposals for revising, updating, and extending the statutory provisions on health and safety at work and for issuing approved codes of practice. The Executive was formed initially by transferring the existing government inspectorates covering factories, mines and quarries, explosives, nuclear installations, and alkali works. It has the power to enforce statutory requirements on safety and health. Local authorities have also been given certain enforcement powers. In particular, inspectors now have powers to issue improvement and prohibition notices, which would enable them to require practical improvements to be made within a specified time or require preventative measures immediately without first having to obtain a court order.

The HASAWA is an enabling Act in addition to and only partly replacing previous legislation. The greater part of those Acts, in particular the Factories Act and the Offices, Shops and Railway Premises Act (main provisions included below), remains in force but repeal, amendment, revision, and updating will continue as necessary, over a period of years. Meantime it must be generally recognized that the 1974 Act has established the most comprehensive system of law ever, covering not only the health and safety of *all* (for the first time) people at work, but also the general public who may be affected by the activities of people at work.

The retirement of the chairman of the Health and Safety Commission in 1984 provided an opportunity for an overview of achievement during the nine-year period for which he had held office. Two notable statistics emerged: a 30 per cent reduction in the annual number of people killed at work and a general reduction in lost-time accidents; but, in case these improvements tended to breed complacency, there still had been 16 million working days lost because of accidents during the period.

The economic recession has undoubtedly had the effect of reducing spending on safety measures because of competitive and financial pressures, and some safety representatives reported finding resources from management to be much scarcer. There is something of a feeling abroad that many workers are only too pleased to have jobs, which inevitably means that working safely is not given such a major priority as it was before.

Although it may be impossible to eliminate all accidents, the present totals could be slashed by better work systems, management methods and procedures. The best results are achieved where employers and workers together put their backs into it. The way forward may be for safety representatives and managers to pick out the improvements which need to be made, arrange them in an order of priority, and agree a tentative timetable for completing each item.

The Factories Act 1961

The main sections of the Act refer to health, safety, and welfare of workers, as follows:

Health

Daily removal of dirt and refuse and a weekly cleaning of floors is required, as is the periodical cleansing, painting, or lime-washing of walls, ceilings, and partitions. The amount of space allowed for every person employed is a minimum of 12 cubic metres. The temperature of workshops where a substantial amount of work is done sitting must not be less than 16°C and standards may be laid down for efficient ventilation and lighting. All floors liable to be wet must be efficiently drained. The provision of suitable and sufficient sanitary accommodation is obligatory. Persons employed in rooms where poisonous substances or fumes are in use must have facilities to take their meals elsewhere in the factory. Other regulations relate to work in underground rooms, lifting excessive weights, employment involving lead processes, and the notification of industrial poisoning or diseases.

Safety

Accidents causing loss of life or disablement of a worker for more than three days must be reported to the health and safety inspector; certain dangerous occurrences must also be reported, even though no injury results. Several sections of the Act relate to the safeguarding of engines, prime movers, transmission machinery, and dangerous parts of other machinery. These requirements are most stringent: not only is the occupier of a factory required to fence such machinery securely but the person who sells or hires out any machinery not complying with the Act is liable to penalties. Hoists and lifts must be of adequate strength and construction, must be properly maintained, and examined every six months; similar regulations apply to all forms of lifting tackle – chains, ropes, and cranes. Every factory must have a certificate from the local fire authority to the effect that its buildings have reasonable means of escape: workrooms must be arranged so that there is a free passageway to the escape doors. Exits must never be locked when employees are in a workroom, and in all factories employing more than twenty people effective steps must be taken to ensure that they know the means of escape and the routine to be followed in case of fire.

Welfare

Provision of drinking water and washing and cloakroom facilities are compulsory. All employees, male and female, must be provided with seats if their jobs allow opportunities for sitting without detriment to their work. Every factory must have a first-aid box or cupboard of the prescribed standard, with increased provision for every 150 persons employed.

The above are the main requirements of the Act. There are many other provisions relating to the protection of employees' eyes, limitations on hours of work of women and young persons, and provision for 'out-workers' and piecework. The factory occupier must keep a General Register, in which data are recorded showing that the prescribed requirements of the Act are being observed (for example, particulars of young persons employed, accidents, and industrial diseases). HM Inspectors have power to inspect every part of the factory by day and night; they may ask for registers and certificates, question any person in the factory, and may take samples for analysis. The officers of local authorities and fire services have similar powers in carrying out their duties under the Act. It is a sensible measure for personnel managers to arrange that these visiting officials should always be received and conducted about the premises by the same member of their staff, thus ensuring that any action which may be necessary as a result of these visits will be consistent.

The most significant item of legislation since the 1974 Act was the Control of Substances Hazardous to Health (COSHH) Regulations which came into effect in October 1989. These regulations require employers to:

- Assess the risks to people's health caused by workplace exposure to hazardous substances, and decide what precautions are necessary (the assessment should be recorded).
- Prevent such exposures or, where this is not reasonably practicable, implement control measures.
- Ensure that control measures are used and that equipment is properly maintained and procedures observed.
- Where necessary, monitor atmospheric contaminants and keep records (for thirty years) of the measurements obtained.
- In certain cases, carry out and record health surveillance.
- Inform, instruct and train employees about risk and the precautions to be taken.

As well as being aware of these regulations, personnel managers are also responsible for disciplining employees who fail to fulfil their duties under the regulations, for example, by refusing to attend for health screening or not wearing personal protective equipment.

Recent additional requirements take the form of European Directives, which add six new sets of regulations, effective from January 1993, covering: general health and safety management; work equipment safety; workplace conditions; manual handling of loads; personal protective equipment; and display screen equipment.

The Offices, Shops, and Railway Premises Act 1963

The purpose of this Act was virtually to extend the requirements of the Factories Act to offices and shops, where some 7.5 million people are employed. Its main provisions are:

1 Suitable and sufficient sanitary conveniences and washing facilities must be provided and properly maintained, with effective lighting and ventilation.

2 Stairs and gangways must be of sound construction, provided with handrails, and be kept free from obstruction.

3 Drinking water must be provided and means for drinking it.

4 Arrangements must be made to hang up outdoor and working clothes and also to dry them.

5 Seats must be provided for employees who normally can sit at their work. In shops at least one seat must be provided for every three employees.

6 If employees in shops eat meals on the premises, suitable facilities must be provided.

7 No one under 18 may clean any machinery if this exposes him or her to risk of injury from moving parts. No untrained person may work at certain machines except under supervision.

8 No one may be required to lift a heavy load likely to injure him.

9 A first-aid box or cupboard must be provided. Where more than 150 people are employed, a trained first-aider must be available.

10 A room in which people work must not be so overcrowded as to cause risk of injury to health; account must be taken not only of the number of people in the room but also the space occupied by furniture, fittings, and machinery.

11 Workrooms must be of such a size that there are 4 square metres of floor space or 12 cubic metres of capacity for each person.

12 A reasonable temperature must be maintained in rooms where people are employed other than for short periods. Where work does not involve severe physical effort, a 'reasonable' temperature is specified as not less than 16°C after the first hour. Thermometers must be provided to enable employees to check temperatures.

13 The Act also covers fire precautions and means of escape, and the notification of accidents at work.

Occupational health services

The principles of occupational health emanate from the answers to three questions:

1 Has a patient's illness been caused by his/her job?

2 Will his/her work retard his/her recovery?

3 Does his/her disability affect his/her capacity to do the job (for example, can a bronchitic be sent back to a dusty job, or should a manager who has been mentally ill return to a job where he/she controls other people)?

The tasks that can be carried out by the staff of an occupational health service include:

1 Assisting in placing applicants in suitable jobs: this involves initial research to find out the health requirements of different types of work.
2 Intelligent medical surveillance; following up suspicions of hazards; looking at special problems (for example, older workers); examining employees, who are well at the time, to try to detect any early symptoms of illness.
3 Treatment services, which in themselves can provide a great deal of information about hazards to health: sophisticated statistical analysis should reveal where and why hazards are occurring.
4 Regular inspection of the working environment.
5 Involvement in the planning stages of new buildings, to prevent known hazards being built into them.

The successful fulfilment of these tasks should in itself justify the expenses of the staff salaries, accommodation, and equipment of such a service. There will be tangible gains in terms of time saved as a result of quick treatment and through diagnosing of illnesses and industrial diseases at their early stages. But there will be other intangible benefits as well, in the effect on staff morale through knowing that medical treatment is immediately available, the preventive work carried out, the preliminary screening of potential employees, the planned rehabilitation of those returning to work after injuries or long illness, and the control exercised over the environment. The latter covers the elimination both of physical hazards and those which cause mental stress provoking psychosomatic illness and neurotic symptoms. The extent of services provided in practice varies with the size of the organization, and ranges from the minimum first-aid boxes prescribed by legislation to superbly equipped medical centres with full-time doctors and nurses in attendance. A specialist medical officer is rare in firms with less than 5000 employees, however: small firms tend to employ part-time medical officers, often with a group of firms sharing the same doctor. Where a firm has a surgery of its own, a State Registered Nurse with specialist training in industrial nursing is usually in charge, and at least one nurse will be present during all shift hours.

Clearly advice on the detailed application of legislative requirements falls within the province of medical officers, and much of their work will be closely linked with that of the personnel department. They will be concerned with the employment of disabled people, which is obligatory for firms working on government contracts. They will make periodic inspections of canteen facilities. They may consider eating habits; for example, trying to find the number of workers who arrive without having breakfast, and so advise on canteen opening hours. They will review accident figures, consider their causes, and make recommendations accordingly; and their prestige should play an important part in safety education. Their opinion will be sought on such difficult personnel problems as terminating the employment of people with prolonged illnesses, and on policy matters such as whether employees with colds should be encouraged to stay home to avoid infecting their fellows.

With so many close ties, it is vital that the correct relationship should be established between personnel officers and medical officers. In functional matters medical officers play their own part in securing the efficiency of their firm by maintaining the 'happiness' of workers, and in this they are members of the management team (rather than having the solitary role of the GP in the community). They should consult with personnel officers so that the coordination of personnel policy is made effective, but in professional matters they must have direct access to the highest level of authority, the board of directors. It is probably best in these circumstances that copies of all their proposals affecting employees should also be sent to the personnel department. It is essential to remember, however, that all dealings between doctor and patient, whatever the situation, are confidential, and this principle must always be respected. Over a period of time the works medical officer is generally able to establish a comprehensive medical history of every employee. This record is also confidential and may not be mentioned in other than general terms to the employer, unless the state of an employee's health demands some specific action (for instance, an employer may not place persons known to be suffering from certain communicable diseases next to other employees, or it may be necessary to transfer an employee from one job to another owing to some disability). Besides individual medical histories, the medical officer may also keep group records for statistical purposes.

A great deal of research work is being done both by individual doctors and by industrial health services,* such as the famous pioneering venture at Slough. The emphasis is usually on preventive medicine: for example, trying to find links between anxiety neuroses, pressure of work and noise, the effect of hours of work on illness, or the ways epidemics spread in a workplace. Such a wide range of activities smacks of the larger organizations, but there are cases of quite small

---

*A modern example of a large-scale occupational health scheme is presented in *Personnel Management*, October 1987, pages 68–71. Dr Gwilym Hughes sets out British Telecom's programmes, with coverage of policy, problem drinking, drugs, violence, AIDS and heart disease.

employers obtaining excellent results from combining resources to provide health facilities.

The benefits of occupational health facilities seem obvious, yet it is not a subject that is without controversy. Criticisms are sometimes heard about the lack of uniformity in the activities of industrial doctors and the fact that some of them have little or no specialist training. The value of routine medical examinations, upon which the practice of occupational medicine is largely based, has been questioned, too. But typical of the nature of the controversy was this statement* made at the 1966 annual conference of the Institute of Personnel Management: 'I am convinced that if a personnel manager attempts to solve a placement problem without a medical report on his file, he is working with his eyes bandaged and his ears plugged.'

The mental health of employees has grown in the concern of occupational health services in recent years. Dr Ann Fingret, chief medical officer of the BBC, has explained the Corporation's approach thus:†

> To establish a mental health policy in a culture such as the BBC's, it is necessary to accept the 'tablets of stone' about the working environment: this is, that there is an unshakeable belief that high pressure, long hours and total commitment are essential to produce programmes of excellence and that there is always a striving for perfection within severe time and financial constraints.
>
> Our approach, therefore, has been to increase self-knowledge, to raise employees' awareness of danger signs within themselves and in others, to provide information on substance abuse, and to provide and explain methods of relaxation. Areas can be pin-pointed in which at any time groups of individuals may perceive themselves to be stressed – that is, having pressures beyond their coping abilities. For such groups we have run seminars on the recognition of stress, its relevance to illness and the management of stressful situations.
>
> The Corporation has also encouraged staff to take part in workshops on stress management organized outside the BBC by professional trainers. These courses have had two parallel learning lines: one concerned with personality and time management and the other with relaxation and exercise. A survey of those who had attended the courses had shown that many of them had achieved significant changes in lifestyle.
>
> Our policy has been to try to teach individuals to know their own personality strengths and weaknesses, to know the options that are available in any change situations and to formulate possible responses to

*Dr W. Marshall, Group Medical Officer, Baker Perkins Holdings Ltd, in his talk on 'Physical and Mental Health Problems at Work'.

†*Personnel Management*, October 1987, pages 70–1.

recognize stress-inducing situations and to deal with them using the various possibilities around time management, relaxation and exercise. These are simple messages, but their relevance still seems largely unknown or unacknowledged.

Stress at work

Links between work demands and many physical and mental illnesses have been clearly demonstrated, and a main focus of concern among personnel managers has become how to help people cope with the consequences of stress and avoid its more serious effects. Perhaps less attention has so far been given to those aspects of work which give rise to stress.

In many surveys, the most anxiety-provoking 'stressors' centre not on tasks or the content of jobs but on people's relationships with others. These have several manifestations:

1 Supervisors and managers whose style is routinely suspicious, punitive and coercive.
2 Work rules which are unnecessary or inflexible or arbitrary.
3 Ignoring or disregarding the commitment and potential of employees as sources of ideas and information for improving operations.

Aspects of work which are now recognized as being common sources of stress are: the physical and interpersonal environment; overload, ambiguity and conflict of tasks, objectives and roles; responsibility for others; management style; personnel and employment policies; job and task design and the extent of the job holder's control and discretion over them.

There are many factors at work which are contingent on, even if they do not entirely and exclusively cause, stress. The ways in which they affect people and the ways in which people interpret such experiences are complex. From this diversity and complexity emerges a strategy which uses several complementary techniques for detecting changes in the level of stress and a mix of approaches for tackling it:

1 Identify sources of work stress.
2 Include organizational and job design in production planning.
3 Include job holders in planning changes affecting their work.
4 Increase awareness of work aspects likely to cause stress.
5 Improve management and supervisory skills.
6 Examine and rectify ambiguity and conflict of objectives.

7 Provide opportunities for employees to improve coping skills and get help.

The overall objective of this aspect of personnel management is not just to avoid the consequences of stress and injury to individuals but to provide opportunities for positive well-being and development to improve organizational effectiveness.

Suggestions for preventive and remedial action include the following:

1 New or re-designed work systems should be examined for opportunities and options to design jobs that are better suited to those already in the organization.

2 Seminars on the problems – to encourage managers to watch for signs of stress, to ensure that their styles of management do not exacerbate it, and, when making changes, to examine the implications for people's jobs and the way changes are brought about.

3 Examine the rewards, promotion and other personnel systems to see whether they offer conflicting or incompatible incentives to employees.

4 Include in the appraisal system opportunity for career counselling, which should, if possible, be independent of line management; this provides a way of anticipating and preventing phenomena like 'burn-out' or mid-career crisis.

5 Give people information about the future as soon as it is known and help them to handle it.

6 Increase individual options and control over tasks – ask, 'Do we need to have a rule about this?' 'Does everyone need to be treated in the same way?'

7 Social support derived from colleagues at work is known to have direct effect in reducing work stress – hence implications for the organization of teams and membership of working groups.

Transition and change for individuals and organizations are particularly stressful periods, and more attention should be paid to their repercussions on staff and employees. It is possible to suggest several specific actions* which, on their own or in combination, may help to reduce the pressures on individuals and make managing the process of organizational change more satisfactory:

1 Do not change everything at once – leave a stable and secure basis from which new arrangements can be explored, in particular, leave work teams together if they are working well.

---

*'Work design, organisational change and stress', Geoff White, *Employment Gazette*, November 1985, page 434.

2 Ensure that there is adequate and direct feedback about new methods; this helps learning and encourages rapid adjustment.

3 Give sufficient time for rehearsing and learning through experience, especially when alternatives and options need to be tried out.

4 Involvement of people in the process of change pays off in adding important data, gives people some degree of control over their own work, and an awareness and ownership of the new arrangements. Their involvement must not be illusory, trivial, irrelevant or superficial. It must be seen as an integral and legitimate part of their job which is reflected in the rewards system.

5 A step-wise, incremental sequence of changes, giving adequate time for acclimatization is worthwhile, with identifiable achievements signalled and publicized.

6 Planning and feasibility testing should be as close to the users as possible.

7 Project teams set up to implement changes, and particularly their leaders, should have adequate time and resources and should not be expected to carry out the task on top of an existing full operational load.

8 Conflict and resistance are likely to be reduced if an open exploratory style is adopted encouraging collaboration and seeking help, looking at the causes of mistakes rather than who to blame for them, looking at how work is actually done rather than the procedures originally laid down.

9 Some aspects of the process of change might specifically address the reduction of conflict and overload on people. Stress will arise if people are overloaded or have conflicting work objectives: it is not necessarily that they have too many decisions to make, but face too many constraints and pressures.

10 Finally, enhance opportunities at every level to exercise judgment, enhance feelings of competence, ability to cope, use skills and make decisions.

Attention to the design of work and its organization contributes not only to the well-being of individual employees but to the effectiveness of the organization for which they work. Detecting and directly attacking the work pressures that induce stress is not only considerate and humane, but helps towards the more effective use of human resources in the pursuit of business objectives to which they contribute.

The Employment Medical Advisory Service

Formed from the old factory doctor system which had grown piecemeal for over a hundred years, the Employment Medical Advisory

Service (EMAS) was created by an Act of 1972 and was subsequently incorporated into the Health and Safety Executive formed under the HASAWA 1974.

EMAS is headed by a director of medical services, with a national organization comprising nine senior employment medical advisers (EMAs) responsible for Scotland, Wales, and seven English regions, controlling a field force of 140 doctors (EMAs) and employment nursing advisers (ENAs). It is also responsible for the work of EMAS nurses in skill centres and employment rehabilitation centres. The head office staff include specialists in occupational toxicology, mental health, respiratory diseases, research, and the medical aspects of rehabilitation for employment.

Any employed or self-employed worker, trade union representative, or employer can look to EMAS for help with an occupational problem. Its two main functions are to help to prevent ill-health caused by work, and to advise people with health problems about the type of work which suits them or which they should avoid. In practice EMAS is responsible for:

(a) Advice to the inspectorate and other policy divisions of the Health and Safety Executive (HSE) on occupational health aspects of health and safety regulations and codes of practice.
(b) The regular medical examination of persons working with processes known to be hazardous; and other investigations and surveys of workers in relation to their work.
(c) Advice on the occupational health aspects of poisonous substances, immunological disorders, physical hazards, noise, vibrations, radiation, dust, and mental stress.
(d) Occupational health research, including commissioning studies from the Medical Research Council and cooperating in studies mounted by industry.
(e) Advice on providing occupational, medical, nursing, and first-aid services.
(f) Advice on medical aspects of rehabilitation for employment and of training for and placing in jobs, principally to the DE, Training Commission and careers service.

As for powers to investigate possible health problems, EMAs and ENAs have the same authority as health and safety inspectors, notably the right of entry into premises. An EMA may also cause employers to permit medical examination of workpeople they deem at risk.

Looking back over the first ten years of activity, the director of medical services claimed in 1984 that there had been four main developments in occupational health practice since the EMAS was established: the integration of the various disciplines involved and the increasing participation of non-medical scientists; the development and growth of the specialisms of occupational hygiene and occupational health nursing; the recognition of the need for increased professionalism and therefore more specialized training in the field; and the acknowledgment of the need for a partnership between professional government advisers and those in industry or academic life.

In practical terms, reports on the investigations carried out by EMAS field staff show that the preponderant hazard investigated was exposure to chemicals, which reflects the general unease about the health hazards of working with little-known substances; the second largest category was that of exposure to dust and fumes and related respiratory problems.

An Occupational Health Advisory Committee (replacing the Medical Advisory Committee) was set up by the Health and Safety Commission in 1987. Members include health professionals and representatives from the CBI and TUC. The objective is to make progress in controlling illnesses associated with work; at the time of the Committee's creation some 50 per cent of the working population had no access to occupational health services. The Committee's projects include guidance on job placement and rehabilitation, a review of occupational disease reporting under health and safety regulations, and guidance on mental health at work.

Among other bodies interested in occupational health is the *Work Research Unit*, which monitors a number of research projects sponsored by the DE through the Medical Research Council. The main focus of these projects is stress at work, following up initial concern expressed by the TUC about the potential ill effects of paced assembly line work, particularly in vehicle manufacture. Some kinds of work are thought to have undesirable consequences for workers, resulting in a high incidence of physical and mental symptoms of ill-health. It is further recognized that these symptoms may only represent a fraction of the total problem and that stress may have adverse consequences for the social and domestic life of employees. The investigations of the WRU are therefore based on the brief that knowledge of the effects of work and career on an individual's general life-style, family, leisure, and health will increase understanding of these relationships and help to influence satisfactory employment policies and practices in industrial firms and the community at large.

Safety of workers

The size and nature of the problems associated with safety at work are shown by the following statistics: there are over 400 people killed at work every year and a grim total of more than 12,000 seriously injured; during 1982, the Factory Inspectorate made some 190,000 inspections and took more than 1200 prosecutions for various breaches of safety legislation.

The personnel manager's function in the prevention of accidents is basically to reinforce and coordinate the efforts of the safety and medical officers. These should reflect concern for both the individuals who suffer accidents and their effect on the reputation, efficiency, and morale of the organization as a whole (indeed, it is not unknown for strikes to be called to obtain better safety precautions). Detailed activities include:

1 Ensuring that dangerous machinery is properly guarded, that there are adequate fire exits, and that all the other legal requirements are observed.
2 Atmospheric conditions, temperature, and humidity: the important factor here is that anything which makes workers feel uncomfortable attracts their attention to themselves and away from their work, thus making accidents more likely.
3 Lighting: more accidents occur in artificial light than in daylight; uniform lighting is also important, since accidents often occur when people leave well-illuminated workplaces and pass into dimly lighted surrounding areas.
4 Speed of production: the speed of machinery running throughout the day should be closely controlled in relation to the increasing fatigue of the machine-minders; on the other hand, too frequent changes in speed may affect workers' coordination and expose them more often to danger points.
5 Personal conditions arising, for example, from the immaturity and dash of young people or the inexperience of workers taking on new tasks; these considerations underline the importance of adequate training, no matter how simple the process is.

Particular attention needs to be paid to the fencing of dangerous machinery. Why is it that, despite all the educational effort and the publicity given to the huge annual toll of deaths and injuries, some employers still in effect get away with non-observance of the Factories Act? The simple truth seems to be that so few employers or machinery manufacturers fully appreciate what the law demands. The two most relevant judgments are: 'A machine is dangerous if . . . in the ordinary course of human affairs danger may reasonably be anticipated from its use unfenced, not only to the prudent, alert and skilled operative intent upon his task, but also the careless, inattentive worker whose inadvertent or indolent conduct may expose him to risk of injury or death from the unguarded part.'* 'The duty to fence securely is an absolute one. The duty is not to be qualified by such words as "so far as practicable" or "so long as it can be fenced consistently with its being used for the purpose for which it was intended", and if the result of a machine being securely fenced is that it does not remain commercially practicable or mechanically possible, that does not affect the obligation.'† In the eyes of the law, then, the plea that a machine cannot be effectively guarded is unacceptable, as is the excuse that productivity or profits would be reduced if guards were to cover it properly.

The personnel manager must investigate all aspects of any accident: its nature; its cause, which is usually attributable to some fault in equipment, working arrangements, or negligence on the part of a worker; and its effect. Statistics of accidents are usually recorded for this last purpose, showing their frequency rate measured in terms of the number of accidents causing loss of time per 100,000 working hours, and the severity rate, the actual number of working hours lost per 100,000 hours.

Carrying out these duties demands the closest liaison with specialist staff throughout the organization; with maintenance engineers to ensure the guarding of machinery and testing for safety of all new equipment; with designers, method engineers, and work study staff, to insist on safe working methods and, if necessary, the sacrifice of speed for the sake of safety. As the company may be sued at common law for damages resulting from negligence which causes accidents, personnel managers must also keep in close touch with their legal advisers, to instruct them on any technical matters arising out of such actions, and to produce for their information all relevant records and reports. They must also see that the employer's obligations under the National Insurance (Industrial Injuries) Act 1946 are fulfilled, and that those who are injured at work know how to make the necessary claims, confirmed by their departmental records.

Prevention is better than cure, and the basic necessity is to try to develop a responsible frame of mind on the part of all employees. The largest organizations usually appoint full-time safety officers, and even small firms make an executive responsible for safety as part of his/her duties. The safety officer is usually backed up by the appointment of a safety committee, and there is no doubt that this represents one of the best examples of joint consultation in practice. Under the chairmanship of the safety officer, representatives of management, supervsiors and workers meet together to discuss ideas aimed at improving safety,

*Mitchell *v.* North British Rubber Co. Ltd.
†John Summers and Sons Ltd *v.* Frost.

studying reports of accidents that have occurred and making surveys of their place of work to ensure that safety precautions are being carried out.

Some interesting psychological research has been carried out in industry on the question of *accident proneness* – a phrase which applies to that small minority of people who seem to be more susceptible to accidents than their fellows. It is possible to discover who some of these accident-prone people are: for example, there are tests for skilled workers which call for rapid and accurate coordination of hand and eye, intelligence, and mechanical aptitude. The results indicate that those who fail the tests have a higher accident rate than those who pass them. On the other hand, there is a body of opinion which believes that the concept of accident proneness may be accepted too readily, since no one has yet succeeded in pin-pointing an accident-prone group and, by excluding that group, modifying the accident rate. Furthermore the intricacies of tasks, the experience of workers, and the conditions under which they work can make it virtually impossible to establish valid comparisons. Another explanation, then, is that individuals may have 'accident spells' related to impaired health or domestic stress.

Considerable help in accident prevention is available from outside the organization, particularly from the Royal Society for the Prevention of Accidents (RoSPA) which plays a leading role in tackling the problem, by gathering statistics, through publicity, and safety education. The Society continually strives to improve its activities; it has appointed seven Regional Industrial Safety Organizers to stimulate the growth of safety consciousness and the development of company policies within their areas. The CBI and TUC have also shown their willingness to help by collaborating in arranging a series of joint conferences on industrial safety; and there is a national body, the Industrial Safety Advisory Council, made up of representatives of the CBI, TUC, RoSPA, the nationalized industries, and the British Insurance Association, which gives consideration to research and joint consultation on safety.

The form of safety organization adopted by a firm must be the one best suited to its particular circumstances. It must be properly conceived, with clear objectives, and must have the backing of the power of the boardroom. But the fact that accident figures remain so high, despite technical and scientific advances, clearly emphasizes the human factor which is fundamental to the problem. Future research therefore might well concentrate on ways in which employee behaviour patterns in the workplace contribute to accidents. 'It must be driven home repeatedly that factories and building sites are not playgrounds for the irresponsible, but working places which require the exercise of discipline – especially self-discipline and self-restraint – in the potentially dangerous environment which they create.'* A continuous process of education must go on, sponsored by the board of directors, the personnel manager, the medical officer, and the safety officer and his/her committee; all organs of joint consultation must be encouraged to make worthwhile suggestions and offer constructive criticism on the subject. The combination of all these efforts, applied in a sustained manner, will greatly help, but the ultimate solution to the whole tragic problem of accidents will only be achieved when every employee conscientiously accepts personal responsibility for working safely.

Nowadays, at one level, health and safety at work means noise levels, eye strain from VDU screens, the effects of statutory sick pay, the latest research on accidents, and the impact of trade union safety representatives. But it also has macro aspects at national and corporate levels. Of late, government policy has been restrictive: as part of public expenditure cuts the Health and Safety Executive has been pruned; and the Government has also shown its disapproval of any legislative proposals which impose what might be considered to be unreasonable cost burdens on industry.

The Royal Society, by publishing a report† on risk assessment – that is, ill-health or accident prediction, as opposed to the more traditional prevention of recurrence after the event – has given the management of health and safety an academic cachet which it previously lacked. But although this report made a useful contribution to consideration of the problems of risk decision-making, based on cost-benefit models, this should not be allowed more emphasis than traditional health and safety day-by-day problems at the workplace.

A central tenet of the HSWA is that all organizations should publish written statements of their policies for health and safety and explain the arrangements in force for implementing them. Yet there is a body of research which shows that the documents published by many organizations fall significantly short of the guidelines prepared by the Health and Safety Executive. A major survey carried out by the Plastics Processing ITB in 1982 of 121 firms in that industry showed how easy it is to declare a policy commitment to safety, but how difficult to translate the good intentions into a coherent procedural reality; for example, 55 per cent of the policies made no mention at all of the need to ensure that new machinery was safe and without health risks at the time of purchase: the implication is that most firms choose to ignore the dangers of new equipment.

There is an argument in favour of creating a new safety management specialism of risk appraisal, appreciating that it is a multi-disciplinary

*From the 1967 report of HM Chief Inspector of Factories.
†'Risk Assessment – a study group report', The Royal Society, 1983.

subject calling for training in depth across the board and combining a large number of traditional aspects around some of which barriers exist at present. Risk assessment so far has reflected public concern in that it has dealt mainly with the prospect of major hazards (nuclear disaster, storage of dangerous gases and substances). It embraces a range of sophisticated and elegant procedures for calculating risks: to bring these down to the more mundane level of the dangers existing in normal workplaces, the methodology needs to be simplified – to be **understandable by line managers and local safety officers – and the training of practitioners needs to be improved dramatically.**

Many work-related accidents appear superficially to be caused by carelessness or incompetence on the part of the workers involved. In reality, they are frequently the outcome of wider organizational failings: an HSE analysis* of 1000 fatal accidents found that the vast majority could have been avoided by taking reasonably practicable precautions (in other words, by employers and employees fulfilling their statutory duties under the HSAWA). Of particular note was the conclusion that management failures were the primary cause of more than 60 per cent of those accidents, while the corresponding figure for employees was just 12 per cent. The most common underlying causes of fatal accident were declared to be the provision of inadequate training and supervision and the use of unsafe methods of work.

The value of accident statistics as measures of safety performance should not be overestimated: they are, after all essentially figures about failure, recording events which should not have happened. Also they are only partial measures: research has shown that for every major injury accident there are ten property damage incidents and twenty near misses; a low level of actual accidents does not therefore mean that all is well with safety. To evaluate safety performance more fully, the collection and analysis of accident statistics needs to be supplemented by some more direct assessment of how far an organization is succeeding in controlling and eliminating work-related hazards.

Audit systems (some marketed commercially by consultants) provide a means of doing this, and are now seen by the HSE as an essential ingredient in any successful safety policy. Audits are essentially intended to fulfil two objectives: to provide an assessment of how far behaviour at the workplace conforms with safety rules and procedures, and thus to provide information on the adequacy of those rules and procedures. Some schemes, focus solely on the 'hardware' aspects of accident prevention, such as machine guarding, use

---

*Monitoring Safety, HSE Occasional Paper 9 (HMSO, 1985).

of protective clothing and equipment and exhaust ventilation; others follow the approach favoured by the HSE and also cover such 'soft ware' elements as safe systems of work, instruction, training and supervision. Important decisions need to be taken over the use to be made of audit results, including the identity of those to whom reports are to be submitted, the feedback that should be provided to line managers, and who is to be responsible for initiating and checking any follow-up action.

Organizations frequently make very impressive statements about their commitment to health and safety at work, often stressing its importance equally with other areas of management activity. However, few follow such statements through by taking health and safety into account when appraising the performances of managers — yet in the absence of such accountability, policy statements on health and safety are likely to incorporate a good deal of wishful thinking. The lack of appraisal in this area signals to managers that health and safety do not, in practice, merit the same priority as more general commercial and operational matters.

Further reading

Economics of Health and Safety, Jeremy Heywood, *Employment Gazette*, January 1985.
Health and Safety at Work (Robens Committee), Cmnd. 5034 (HMSO, 1972).

20

Administering the personnel function

Structure

The structure of personnel departments varies greatly from industry to industry and among different organizations within the same industry. In saying that a 'typical' structure is represented by Figure 30, it is nevertheless a hypothetical model, and probably no single department exists anywhere exactly along these lines.

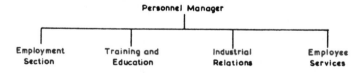

Figure 30

In charge of the function will be a *personnel manager*, supervising and coordinating the work of the department, probably dealing himself/ herself with senior staff problems, and controlling the personnel policies and manpower planning of the organization as a whole. There is considerable divergence of opinion as to whether the head of a personnel department should be a member of the board of directors; the overall importance of his/her role must be balanced against the fact that it is advisory in nature, whereas the position of a director is near the ultimate in executive authority.

One interesting piece of research* reported that in 1984 the position was that in 43 per cent of organizations surveyed there was specialist personnel management representation on the board. The larger the organization, the more likely was there to be such representation: in organizations with less than 500 employees only 8 per cent had such specialists on the board; 501–2000, 40 per cent; 2001–10,000, 49 per cent; and over 10,000, 70 per cent.

The *employment section* is normally the largest: it involves the 'bread-and-butter' work of recruitment, transfers, promotion, and dismissal of employees, control over working conditions, and personnel records. The executive in charge would probably deputize for the personnel manager, and in a large organization might supervise a subdepartment of the type shown in Figure 31. The staff of this section might well form a hierarchy, which would then represent a channel of promotion. Newcomers entering personnel management could profitably start as assistants in the records department or job review section; as they acquire experience, they could be given some interviewing to do until ready for promotion. The employment officer would therefore be a senior executive, in charge of personnel officers responsible for executive and male operatives recruitment, a lady recruitment officer for female operatives, and assistants in charge of records and job reviews.

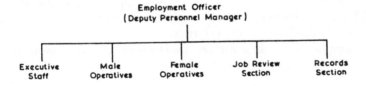

Figure 31

Another senior executive would control the *training and education section*, responsible for everything in this field from apprenticeships to the development of managers. In fact, where the range is so wide, and especially when an organization runs its own internal courses, a number of training officers will be required; these may well be people seconded from line management for a year or two. An experienced 'diplomat' would be the executive looking after the organization's *industrial relations* interests, in direct contact with worker representatives and local trade union officials. The scope of *employee services* might also be such as to warrant a number of staff subordinate to a senior

Personnel Management, December 1986, page 35.

welfare officer: for example, the safety officer, the domestic supervisor in charge of cleaning services, the canteen staff, and the secretary of the social club. The number of assistant personnel officers employed in each of these main sections would depend on the size of the organization, the amount of work to be done, and on the firm's attitude towards executive succession. There would also be an establishment of clerical staff (for records), secretaries, and typists.

The structure and range of activities of the personnel function in an actual major enterprise is well illustrated by the organization chart given as Figure 32.

Personnel functions may be organized in the manner indicated in Figure 32 in a variety of settings. For instance, there are very large companies, among *The Times'* top 100, which have managers at the centre responsible for a number of the 'critical functions' of operating management as well as for strategic management. They tend to have corporate personnel departments (for example, Ford and Sainsbury) because personnel management is one of these 'critical functions' and there is a need for a standard approach without which the company would find it difficult to meet some of its business objectives. On the other hand, those companies with multi-business activities, and corresponding multi-divisional organization structures do not need large, centralized corporate personnel departments. Were such departments to interfere in the day-to-day operating management of subsidiary companies, it would negate the very principle of local managers being judged by performance.

To complicate the issue further, there are great variations in how the corporate or multi-divisional split works in practice. There is a spectrum covering the extent to which decisions on personnel and industrial relations policies are fully centralized, decentralized under constraint or totally devolved to operating units. The majority of large organizations claim to have one overall policy towards the management of their employees. This may be true in the field of communication, participation and involvement, but a crucial difference exists in the degree of enforcement between organizations with centralized and decentralized bargaining. The former tend to instruct operational units, whereas the latter give varying degrees of discretion. Similar differences are revealed when looking at a range of personnel and industrial relations decisions and are fundamentally associated with the business strategy and structure of the enterprise, especially the extent of financial decentralization and product diversification.

An IPM survey* of twenty-eight organizations carried out in 1984

Personnel Management, January 1985, page 17.

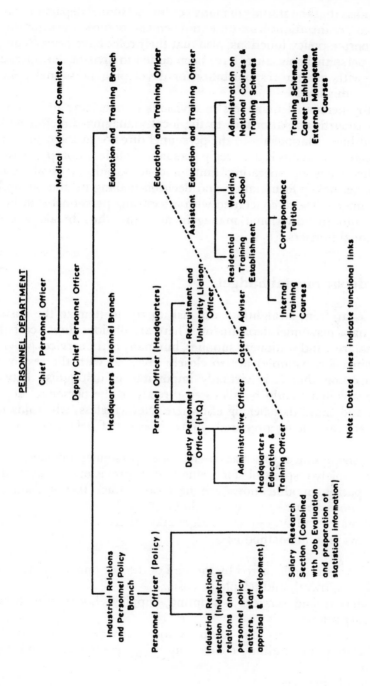

PERSONNEL DEPARTMENT

Chief Personnel Officer

Deputy Chief Personnel Officer

Medical Advisory Committee

Industrial Relations and Personnel Policy Branch

Headquarters Personnel Branch

Education and Training Branch

Personnel Officer (Policy)

Personnel Officer (Headquarters)

Education and Training Officer

Education and Training Officer

Industrial Relations section (Industrial relations and personnel policy matters, staff appraisal & development)

Salary Research Section (Combined with Job Evaluation and preparation of statistical information)

Deputy Personnel Officer (H.Q.)

Recruitment and University Liaison Officer

Catering Adviser

Assistant Education and Training Officer

Administration on National Courses & Training Schemes

Administrative Officer

Headquarters Education & Training Officer

Residential Training Establishment

Welding School

Correspondence Tuition

Training Schemes. Career Exhibitions. External Management Courses

Internal Training Courses

Note: Dotted lines indicate functional links

Figure 32

concluded that the staffing of many central personnel departments has fallen as organizations have decentralized and reduced the significance of corporate policy functions; also that their roles have been changed. More personnel specialists have been added to divisions or operating units, with greater responsibility for developing personnel policies given to this level.

Many personnel managers in divisions of operating units have a direct reporting relationship to the local managing director, with a 'dotted line' relationship to the personnel director at the centre. The rationale behind this is to develop personnel policies appropriate to the specific needs of operating units and to avoid an escalation of personnel policy formulation and decision-making up the hierarchy. This process is also concerned with integrating personnel staff in the units into the divisional management team, thus breaking down functional barriers.

The departmental budget

It is a far from straightforward task to try to itemize the costs of running a personnel department. There are obvious direct costs like staff salaries and stationery supplies, but many of the services provided (training, for example) are so closely involved with the rest of the organization that it is virtually impossible to distinguish between charges which should be allocated directly to the personnel department and those that belong elsewhere. Nevertheless, when financial estimates are being prepared, some measure of definition must be agreed between senior executives so that a clear-cut budget can be established. Once this has been done, personnel managers then become solely responsible for seeing that its provisions are kept. If, as time passes, modifications are necessary, then they should give instructions about how they should be effected.

Estimates and subsequent budget allocations can be subdivided in many ways. One method is:

1 Expenses to be incurred by the staff of the personnel department – salaries, travel, and telephone costs.
2 Materials and services – printing, supplies, books, membership subscriptions.
3 Resources to carry out company-wide activities – students' fees, education and training courses, meetings, conferences, and literature.
4 Consultancy fees.
5 Overheads, such as office rentals, heating, and lighting.

The actual categories of expenditure might be – basic staff costs (wages, stationery); education and training services; health provisions; canteen services; social activities; and other welfare amenities.

Although details of expenditure will be prepared and checked by accounts department staff and auditors, the personnel manager must be given copies of the figures produced in order to control deviations, and actual expenditure must be compared month by month with the original budget to guard against over- or under-spending and the possibility of fraud. All staff in the personnel department must be impressed with the fact that the budget is exactly what it means, and that there will be no additional funds allocated to the department during the budgetary period nor further expenses entertained. Proper recognition of this is an essential part of sound management.

Proving the personnel department earns its salt

In the public services, the pressure to demonstrate 'value for money' has concentrated on an examination of manning levels and this has inevitably required the personnel manager to take a major role in identifying possible over-staffing and in taking any resultant corrective action. In the private sector, cost-cutting programmes often focus on the rather arbitrary distinction between 'direct' and 'indirect' staff and on cutting the latter to reduce the weight of overhead charges on the direct costs of labour and materials.

But personnel departments are themselves subject to similar scrutiny. How do personnel managers show that, on a cost-benefit analysis, their departments have a higher value than their costs? Can personnel activities be expressed in a financially quantified input/output formula? If not, what should the basis of the value-for-money judgment be?

In answering questions of this kind, it is essential to be clear as to whether effectiveness or efficiency is being assessed – or both. Effectiveness is concerned with meeting objectives, efficiency with the use of resources in doing so. The objectives of recruitment, for example, are to secure the requisite number of new employees of the required standard of skill or ability at the required times. A recruitment function is effective if it meets these aims, but it may not be efficient – i.e., its *per capita* recruitment costs may be much higher than necessary.

There are many cost indices in the personnel field which assist in monitoring and assessing efficiency. Examples are:

(a) Cost per accident or per man-day lost caused by accident and total accident costs.

(b) Similar costs for sickness and absenteeism.
(c) *Per capita* recruitment costs.
(d) *Per capita* training costs (internal and external).
(e) Labour turnover costs – *per capita* and total.
(f) Administrative costs of servicing a joint consultative committee system.

The value of producing such costing information lies not so much with the actual level of cost in a particular accounting period, but with trends. Are unit costs for a particular function rising or falling? Is this justified by changes in demand? Or by results?

Help from outside organizations

To be fully effective, personnel managers must not only know their jobs, but they must also use every available method of persuading people throughout the organization to act on their advice; influence brought to bear from outside often may tip the scales in their favour. In any event, many firms are too small to employ personnel specialists and therefore must look outside for guidance with their labour problems. Such help may come from a variety of bodies, including several government departments, and may range from management consultants, who offer advisory services on every aspect of personnel work from recruitment to welfare, to professional associations and voluntary bodies.

Department of Employment services

In 1990 the Employment Service (ES) took on Agency status, and with it the future of some 35,000 staff then working for it throughout the country. Agency status is about providing better service for customers and achieving greater value for money for the taxpayer. A series of objectives relating to the placement of unemployed people, especially in innercity areas, and improving the accuracy of benefit payments have been defined. In the light of these, one major task of the new Agency became the integration of unemployment benefit offices and job centres into a unified 'one-stop shop' employment service – so that the previous 2000 UBOs and job centres will be rationalized into less than 1200 offices, each able to offer a full range of job-seeker and benefit services from initial assessment of clients through job advice counselling, training opportunities and return-to-work programmes. The move in a sense turns the wheel of history full circle back to the days of the early Labour Exchanges.

The first point of contact in every job centre is a self-service job information section. This is supported by an advisory service manned by a new professional corps of employment advisers – people for whom the DE has devised special training programmes to develop staff with the right blend of skill and sensitivity, of maturity and knowledge of the market, and of discretion and judgment to be able to offer the maximum possible help to the ever-varying multitude of job seekers and employers.

The occupational guidance service is also being developed, with additional specialist training for the staff concerned. It is intended for the benefit of adults who may either be compelled to take up new types of employment or who may wish to change not simply to a new job but to work of a different kind. The service tries to help about 50,000 people a year, most of whom are under 25: many are students seeking their first jobs; about 20 per cent are people who are being compelled to change their occupation; about 30 per cent of all clients are women, a number of whom are returning to employment after some years away. The potential for extending this service was shown by an experiment in South Wales, when a special publicity campaign led to an increase of more than one-third in the number of applications for interviews.

The gathering of labour market intelligence by the DE should be of particular value to personnel managers (who would otherwise have to do this for themselves). Systemic collation, interpretation, and dissemination of the information are necessary, of course, but early experiments gave clear indications that the service will be able to make a material contribution to the reading of labour market trends and needs, and to the development of programmes to meet them.

Improved methods of communications within the widespread network of the DE is at the heart of all its efforts, particularly the use of computer facilities. A facsimile transmission system exists to link offices in the major conurbations, thus enabling the rapid exchange of information about job vacancies and the faster matching of job seekers to jobs. In London, a computer-based job bank carries details of 15,000 jobs at a time, with plans for employment advisers to have terminals which will give them immediate access to the computer. If this works successfully, then the idea will be extended nationally, and during the 1990s on-line job matching could be as radical a breakthrough as the initial job centre programme in helping to provide better services for more people.

The work of 364 *Local Employment Committees* must also be mentioned here. They are the main advisory bodies attached to employment offices, securing for the Minister the full benefit of local knowledge on industrial problems, and bringing the offices into close contact with local employers and with workers. The members of the committees are appointed for five years and are equally representative of employer and worker interests.

The Careers Advisory Service is administered throughout the country by local education authorities. This service gives advice and vocational guidance to young people on their choice of work and the training necessary for it, helps them to find suitable jobs, and keeps in touch during their early years of employment. Employers are also helped to fill their vacancies for young workers.

Training

The range of D of E training activities is dealt with in Chapter 10.

Rehabilitation

Free courses are offered at twenty-five Employment Rehabilitation Centres to help people gradually readjust themselves to working conditions, with expert vocational guidance about suitable jobs.

Safety, health and welfare

The Department is responsible for the administration and enforcement of appropriate legislation by Inspectors of the Health and Safety Executive in factories, offices, and shops. The Industrial Health and Safety Centre in Horseferry Road, London, displays safety, health, and welfare methods and appliances used in factories.

Publications

These include the monthly *Employment Gazette*, quarterly *Statistics on Incomes, Prices, Employment and Production*, and a variety of pamphlets on current labour legislation, accident prevention, and careers.

Management consultants

The obvious occasions to use management consultants are when specific major problems need to be examined but the organization concerned does not possess the skills or resources to do so for itself, or when its own experts are divided on the best course of action. Assignments need to be clearly defined and time limits set, so that the consultants are kept fully occupied and the best value is obtained for their fees. The terms of reference should require a specific estimate of the likely effects of any recommendations being implemented. It usually eases the consultant's investigations and his/her relationships with the organization's staff if worker representatives or local union officials are consulted beforehand about the reasons for bringing him/her in, and if one person is nominated as his/her main point of contact, introducing him/her to people and making sure he/she is properly briefed.

Which consultant to choose? The BIM's Management Consulting Services Information Bureau and the Management Consultants' Association supply appropriate lists. Having sought their advice, an organization must then approach perhaps two or three different consultants and try to assess which is likely to offer the best service in tackling its particular problems.

Professional associations and voluntary organizations

There are several professional associations and voluntary organizations* concerned with various aspects of personnel and welfare work.

The Institute of Personnel Management

The mission of the Institute of Personnel Management (IPM) is to be the professional body for all those responsible for the optimum use of human resources to the mutual benefit of the enterprise, each person and the community at large. Its strategic aim is to position the IPM as the leading organization in the UK and Republic of Ireland for the development of human resource management and the dissemination of information on this, attracting into membership personnel practitioners and others involved in these areas of management and being consulted by government and national organizations.

To achieve this strategic aim the IPM takes those actions necessary to establish and project the profession and the Institute's status and authority. Specifically it:

- Sets, maintains and promulgates standards and ethics in professional conduct and effective practice.
- Instigates and evaluates research to update the information resource and to develop the profession.
- Communicates with members, government and other national organizations and the community.
- Provides opportunities for members and others to exchange information and ideas for the benefit of the profession.

*The addresses of those mentioned here are given in Appendix 1, page 455.

- Promotes systems to educate and train for personnel work and for the continuous development of its members.
- Provides a range of services to members to help them maintain and improve their professional performance.
- Plays a part in the rest of Europe and the worldwide community.

Looking at appointments advertisements as a whole reveals a growing emphasis on the demand for personnel officers to be properly trained and qualified. The IPM is itself an examining body: students may prepare themselves for its qualifications at some forty colleges throughout the country or by correspondence courses. In addition, fourteen universities and colleges run their own full-time diploma courses in personnel management, most of which last a year.

A European Association for Personnel Management was founded in 1963, of which IPM and twelve other West European associations of personnel management are members. The EAPM holds an international conference every two years, selecting different venues in Europe.

The Industrial Society

The Articles of Association of the Industrial Society state that it consists of persons interested in 'promoting the industry and commerce of the UK, in particular by improving management and industrial relations'. In fact its membership comprises over 16,000 organizations which include companies, nationalized industries, government departments, local authorities, employers' associations, and trade unions. The practical problems that the Society is concerned with are mainly the development of good leadership by managers and supervisors in works and offices, better management–trade union relations, the evolution of conditions of employment appropriate to the requirements of modern jobs, adequate communications, and the development of young employees to play a full role in today's changing industries. Some of its activities are very similar to those of the IPM, although in some cases on a rather larger scale. The Society provides a comprehensive advisory service for its members, including special surveys and reviews of conditions of employment; this is supported by an information service which deals with legal and general enquiries. A wide variety of short conferences and training courses are held in different parts of the country, and in-company training facilities for supervisors are offered to members who lack the resources or experience necessary to set up their own programmes. It, too, issues a journal and publishes booklets on current management problems, and gives specialist advice to firms who publish their own house journals. The more technical aspects of its work cover a catering advisory service and the production of sound-filmstrips mainly intended for training purposes. Finally, a special department exists to meet the needs of developing countries overseas: this includes a tutorial system for experienced men and women in personnel management and industrial relations, and running courses on management and supervision for overseas technical trainees completing their studies in Britain.

The British Institute of Management

The British Institute of Management (BIM), as its name implies, has wider interests in the field of management than just the personnel function, but this nevertheless plays a significant part in its activities. Its claim is to be a national clearing house for information on management policies, practices, and techniques, and on management development, including education and training. Over 13,000 member organizations support its activities, and there are some 45,000 individual members organized into seven regions and about fifty branches throughout the country. As with the two previous organizations, the BIM offers conferences and training courses, a library and information service, seminar and study group arrangements, and its own publications – books, pamphlets, the journal *Management Today*, and a quarterly series of management abstracts. Unique features of its work are the Management Consulting Services Information Bureau and the exchange of facilities with management organizations overseas.

Other bodies

The Tavistock Institute of Human Relations investigates and advises on problems of relations and morale within industry. It is concerned with the study of human relations in conditions of well-being, conflict or breakdown in the family, the work group, the community and the larger organization; disciplines range from social science to organizational development.

The British Association for Commercial and Industrial Education arranges meetings, courses, and conferences, and publishes a monthly journal and a wide range of booklets, with the aim of encouraging educational and training work in industrial and commercial undertakings.

The Royal Society for the Prevention of Accidents deals with industrial accidents, supplies posters, films, and leaflets, runs training courses for safety officers, and gives advice to firms and other enquirers.

The Institute of Manpower Studies, based at the University of Sussex, is an independent national centre of knowledge and practical experience in manpower management, the operation of labour markets, employment policy, training policy, youth training and skills analysis.

The Human Resource Development Partnership was created in 1989 to bring together the IPM, the IS, the BIM, the Employment Department and several other kindred organizations, in order to use their combined skills and experience to influence and raise the level of debate and action on HRD in the UK and to help develop a people culture which supports the development needs of both organizations and the people within them, to their mutual benefit. The Partnership's mission statement relates to the processes of HRD, emphasizing: making change possible and managing it effectively; developing trainer expertise; promoting the fullest involvement of people in their work; group and team working; self-development and continuous development; and communications at work.

Reception and security

Reception and security are two aspects of administration which are often allied and come within the purview of the personnel department.

First impressions strike deep, and efficient and courteous reception arrangements do nothing but good, enhancing an organization's reputation and ensuring goodwill. It is wrong therefore to assume that anyone can do this work, that a reception desk can be manned by somebody who is not busy elsewhere at the moment or by an unsupervised business trainee as part of his/her learning to deal with the public. Reception work requires special skills which can only be exercised by a pleasant-mannered person, mature, experienced, of some seniority, and who has been properly trained. In a large organization it is a task which demands undivided attention, and no other work should be undertaken during periods on duty; any incidental pressures, or indeed fatigue towards the end of the day, result in enquiries or the arrival of visitors being treated as interruptions, and the consequent resentment is painfully obvious to the visitor.

The mechanics of good reception lie in giving prior notice to the reception staff of the names, expected times of arrival, and intended destinations of all visitors and new arrivals. This does not apply only to those expected by the personnel department but should be a standing rule for all departments. Where security is important, visitors should not only be checked in by receptionists, but also checked out again when they leave.

As far as security of property is concerned, joint disciplinary action against stealing has already been mentioned in Chapter 15. No one, manager and worker alike, feels comfortable knowing that a thief is on the prowl, and a works committee may very well be able to take effective action. On the other hand, some workers feel that an employer is 'fair game', and things left lying about are taken. Quite clearly this is illegal. Employees are entitled only to what their employers have agreed to give them; if they have been told to help themselves to stationery or samples, then they are free to accept this offer. But such goods are employers' property, and employees have a right to them only as servants, entirely confined to the arrangement made with them.

Does an employer have the right to search a worker suspected of stealing? Search an individual unjustly and he/she becomes an enemy. It is better to invite all staff, or the section affected, to turn out their pockets and handbags. If they agree, all is well; if they refuse, there is nothing that can be done. The best advice is not to try to detain or search anyone unless there is no alternative: call in the police to do this.

Many organizations employ security staff. The numbers, type, and duties of these vary considerably – commissionaires, gatemen, night patrolmen, with duties ranging from controlling traffic to the prevention of pilfering; often they have a direct link with the local police. It is a mistake to employ any but able-bodied gate police or watchmen in an organization where the pilferage risk is high and where security is important; the old-fashioned pensioner type of night-watchman is a bad risk. Security measures are often publicized on notice boards and by giving special instruction to employees. Losses due to carelessness or negligence should result in punishment. Few firms have any systematic approach to this or impose fixed scales of fines. Demotions may be used for some offenders, with suspension for more serious cases, and dismissal as the ultimate sanction.

The Official Secrets Acts 1911 and 1920 provide heavy penalties for unauthorized use of uniforms, falsification of reports, forgery or alteration of official documents, impersonation of official persons, or for passing secret documents or information to unauthorized persons. All visitors to government offices, departments, and factories may be asked to sign a declaration which sets out the main provisions of this legislation.

The records section

An efficient records system is fundamental to producing the control information essential for effective personnel management. The boast of some senior staff that they know all about their subordinates is no substitute for this (and they should have better things to occupy their minds anyhow). In large organizations, the sheer volume of work involved in maintaining staff records and keeping them up to date is staggering, and demands that three sound principles must be applied in deciding what records of individuals and statistics for management should be kept:

1 The utmost simplicity in methods of recording information and in the design of any forms used.
2 The preservation of only absolutely necessary information: records are pointless unless they serve a useful purpose.
3 The avoidance of duplication, especially when considering needs for cross-reference.

The basic personal record is founded upon the application form, which is filed as the first document in each individual's folder. It is followed by his/her interview notes; as well as copies of correspondence between the company and the employee, the folder will come to hold such documents as his/her follow-up reports, time-keeping record, and notes of promotions or transfers. On its cover will be listed quick-reference personal data and brief information about his/her movements and progress within the organization.

There are many records systems marketed by firms specializing in this activity, designed to meet the general requirements of the average industrial and commercial organization; in addition, numerous records sections devise procedures and print forms to suit their own peculiarities. There is thus a great divergence of practice – some use a simple card-index system, some keep personal documents in index envelopes, some keep them in folders; most organizations have computer installations which can be used for tabulations for the personnel department. No matter which system is used, it needs to be reviewed from time to time (at least once every five years) and the personnel manager must keep abreast of new developments and systems, for example by attending the annual Business Efficiency Exhibition.

From these personal records statistical information can be collated which will be useful both to the personnel department and to line management as records of control. Thus the personnel manager should be able to submit periodic statements to the chief executive about manning and labour turnover, time-keeping, absenteeism, education and training, health, and accidents. The following minimum information about employees is essential for statistical analysis:

1 Basic data – age, sex, address, domestic responsibilities (tax code number provides this), date of joining, occupation, rate of pay; a record of previous jobs may also be an advantage.
2 Absence data – length of absence, date of last absence, shiftwork or overtime, if changes of job are frequent, job at time of last absence.
3 Sickness and injury data – diagnosis, whether self-inflicted, whether contagious, whether treatment continuing, whether change of occupation desirable.
4 Labour turnover data – date of leaving, reason, whether job performance had been satisfactory or not.

The personnel department is usually called on to provide weekly or monthly returns showing the numbers employed in each department and departmental costs of wages and salaries. It should also be possible to produce at short notice statements about the composition of the labour force, by age groups, by sex, and by length of service. Statistics must be prepared to show the relation between the actual and estimated labour strength in the various departments; line managers will want to know the proportions of skilled and unskilled labour employed, and how much of the labour force is termed directly or indirectly productive, for the calculation of prime and overhead costs.

Every departmental head is personally responsible for controlling the time-keeping and absence of the people working in his section. The personnel department, however, will keep a record of individual performance in this respect and will also collate this into departmental and factory summaries, giving an overall picture of time lost and an analysis of the known reasons for lateness or absence, from which management action can be recommended about supervisory training, or representations made to the local bus company, for example. The training officer will keep records of employees' educational progress, and these too can be collated as factual evidence available when manpower and staff development programmes are being prepared. The medical section is responsible for statistics on general health matters affecting the organization, including analyses of industrial diseases and accidents. Health records of individuals may be maintained separately, but since records department staff are always impressed with the confidentiality of the documents they handle, there is no real excuse for duplication. Medical statistics can be very revealing to the industrial doctor, who can associate problems with the working environment in ways that would never occur to scattered GPs each examining one or two patients from the same workplace.

Outside organizations, such as the British Institute of Management, the Royal Society for the Prevention of Accidents, the Department of

Employment, and government departments which place contracts with private firms frequently call for statistical information relating to labour strength. Since many of these returns are demanded regularly, the personnel department should familiarize itself with the forms in which they are required and design its tabulation methods accordingly.

The deficiencies of present records systems are largely due to non-observance of the three principles which should govern procedures. Sizeable sums of money are spent on systems that are not fully effective and, in particular, lack the simplicity which enables management control information to be produced quickly. It is very rare for any organization to prepare a single record which contains all the details likely to be needed, so that any new demand which calls for a thorough survey of personnel records may entail the vast task of gathering information from several different sources. In such cases, the natural tendency is to say that the information is not available, so that the problem which led to the request may then be tackled purely by guesswork.

The difficulties posed by some systems are such that the accuracy of the more intricate calculations must be very suspect, especially when the work is done by junior clerks aiming for 'a quiet life'. This also applies to requests for statistical information from outside bodies and government departments – if this is not readily available in the form specified, a records department is very likely to guess rather than impose hours of work on its clerical staff calculating accurate answers. Part of the trouble is that different definitions are used for standard terms, which makes comparisons between different organizations very difficult: for example, has labour turnover been adjusted to account for unavoidable separations, or do figures of lost time include employees with prolonged sickness absence?

In the light of these potential deficiences, any efforts that may be made to improve personnel records will largely depend on the importance which management attaches to the information that records can provide. For example, when vacancies exceed applicants, selection procedures may become nominal; but an analysis of training costs for newcomers who soon leave sometimes shows that it is more economic to work shorthanded with a stable and experienced labour force and to select more carefully to this end. Adequate and accessible records enable many complex problems of management to be investigated without delay.

Use of computers

The relevance of the computer to personnel records work is obvious, for its initial use in most organizations is the mechanical handling of vast quantities of simple paper work, such as wage and salary calculation and keeping employee records up-to-date. But it can also process data, selecting, storing, analysing, and presenting the information required by management. In this last respect, the most efficient method of functioning is to programme the computer on the 'exception' principle, so that information is only brought to management's attention when it deviates from what is normal or expected. This in turn, of course, depends on management's ability to define its needs (allegedly the greatest cause of the inefficient use of computers). The computer can also be used to check and control processes, and this has possible applications to the manpower planning activities of the personnel department. A logical extension of this use is in simulating future conditions so that decisions can be taken about changes to be effected deliberately by management (reducing working hours, new types of wage structure, for example).

The 1985 'Computers in Personnel' survey* revealed that of nearly 400 organizations which took part, 73 per cent had computerized personnel information systems (CPIS), in part reflecting growth in the use of microcomputers as opposed to mainframe hardware and the availability of CPIS packages which contain word processing modules.

The Oracle package† is a very good example of CPIS systems, the scope of which, in terms of the number of data fields which can be held, is more than sufficient for any application. The facility exists for users to create their own data fields against any individual's records, grouped by a classification of use (for example, educational record). Full history of such details can be maintained, and the security facilities offered on the system are good.

The array of applications which come with the package are impressive: they include full person information, position information including full job descriptions, budget information, organizational hierarchies, recruitment processing, absence control, skills analysis linked to training and management development, and (despite initial tremors caused by the Data Protection Act) performance appraisal information.

One of the most important features of any CPIS is the quality and ease of use of the inquiry language. Oracle uses 'SQL' developed as

*Personnel Management, September 1985, pages 49−50; updated annually − see September 1986, page 55 and September 1987, pages 51−2.
†Consulting the Oracle, C. Richards−Carpenter, Personnel Management, November 1990, page 85.

a rational database enquiry system by IBM, and this is now arguably the industry's standard application. Another important feature of the Oracle system is the potential to set it up on so many different computers: they can be combinations of mainframe, mini- or micro-machines with a choice of many operating systems.

Another example of developments in computer software power being applied to personnel management is the advanced 'Sussex' manpower planning package.* Claimed to set the standard for man-power packages for years to come, it is menu-driven and is designed to be used by line managers as well as personnel practitioners. 'Sussex' helps both policy options to be evaluated and informed recommendations to be made. It can be used on a standard micro-computer, it has colour spread sheet-style screens for data entry, and output options including built-in colour graphics and easily understood tables.

The Data Protection Act

All computerized personnel records systems fall within the scope of the Data Protection Act and must comply with its provisions. These apply to any organization holding personal data about individuals: regist-ration with the Data Protection Registrar is required, explaining why the data are held, broadly categorize what data, and outline how they are obtained and to whom they may be disclosed.

The Act sets out eight principles on which the protection of data is based, specifying that information must:

1 Be obtained and processed fairly and lawfully.
2 Be held only for one or more specified and lawful purposes.
3 Not be used or disclosed in any manner incompatible with these purposes.
4 Be relevant and not be excessive for these purposes.
5 Be accurate and be kept up to date where necessary.
6 Not be kept for longer than is necessary.
7 Be disclosed on request to the person concerned at reasonable intervals.
8 Be kept secure against unauthorized access, alteration, destruction, disclosure or accidental loss.

---

*Demonstrated by the Institute of Manpower Studies (University of Sussex) at the CIP 1991 Exhibition.

For their part, employees have a range of rights in respect to the information which is kept about them. The most important of these are – rights of access to personal data; rights to compensation for inaccurate data and for loss or destruction of unauthorized disclosure of data; and rights to apply for correction or erasure of data.

Further reading

Computers and Personnel Systems: a practical guide, Alistair Evans (2nd edition, IPM, 1991).

The IPM Code on Employment Data (IPM 1988).

'Personnel Records Systems', Fact Sheet 2, *Personnel Management*, February 1988.

21

Human asset accounting

Starting from the premise that if personnel managers are to be really effective, they must have a means for measuring the resources for which they are primarily responsible, techniques of human asset accounting have been developed to record and present information about the value of an organization's employee resources which should prove of great value for managerial control and decision-making purposes.

The people employed by an organization are among its most valuable assets, and yet their value does not appear in statements of its financial position. The death of an outstanding company leader may cause an immediate fall in that company's quotation on the Stock Exchange; key staff caught up in a takeover may decide to leave an organization, having a potentially profound effect on its performance: such are examples of the real value of people – yet there is no way of telling from the usual type of accounting information whether the human assets of an organization are increasing or decreasing in value, whether they are being used effectively, or whether a satisfactory return is being obtained on them.

Conventional accounting procedures treat expenditure on building up human assets as revenue expenditure, writing off costs of recruiting, training, and developing staff against the income of the period in which it is incurred. But are such costs revenue expenditure or are they really capital expenditure? If the latter, a proportion should be charged against the income of all periods receiving benefit from this expenditure, and this could have a significant impact on an organization's income statement and balance sheet. Furthermore, management's attitudes to such expenditures might well alter if such costs were not borne out of current income, but were looked at as contributing to the building of assets which will produce benefits for some time to come. This means accounting for staff in the same way as machines – as assets on the balance sheet, the costs of which are written off against profits year by year; if any machine becomes obsolete before the end of its anticipated useful life, its remaining book value is written off as a loss, thus reducing the company's profits. Viewing investments in obtaining and developing staff in the same way requires that the amount of cost not yet written off should be carried forward in accounting statements as an asset. A change of this nature in the treatment of expenditure on staff would have a marked effect on an organization's measurement of costs and income in any period and on its declared financial position at any particular point in time.

But the concept of human asset accounting is one thing – gaining its acceptance by existing managers is another. The difficulties of isolating and measuring the costs of human resources are formidable: so much accountancy is influenced by conventions which have stood from time immemorial; the need to capitalize human costs has not been as great in the past as in present conditions; and it is difficult to forecast the time period over which benefits will be received from expenditure on human assets. It is also true to say that managements of most firms do not think of their staff as assets in the same way as other property of the firm. 'Human assets' are not owned in a legal sense, and many people regard it as degrading to subject human beings to a monetary value in the same way as a piece of machinery. Yet it is the human resources which use the other assets of an organization to produce goods or render services: the other assets take on value because of their potential when combined with human assets. Thus a human asset accounting system would create information to show the investment made in staff and the financial effects of changes taking place in the human assets during defined periods of time.

Techniques

Although there are two major approaches, at least two other variations must be included in describing the methods so far proposed for human asset accounting. The Institute for Social Research at Michigan and its Human Resource Accounting Association have developed a technique which attempts to identify those costs which an organization expends in improving the performance of its labour force in the long term: these include recruitment, training, and development costs. A variation can be seen in the case of Texas Instruments, who examine replacement costs for groups of people which take account of learning time on a job and the individual's salary during that time. The Institutes of Cost and Management Accountants and of Personnel Management have put forward a joint concept in Britain – of calculating the asset value of people by first computing a multiplier based on the price:earnings ratio and applying it to the total remuneration of the company. Finally, the concept of added value is sometimes used, an approach where the training cost attributable to an individual over his/her expected working life is examined and related to his/her improvements in performance.

Rensis Likert and William Pyle are the names most closely linked with the Michigan initiative in seeking a method to include a figure for people in company accounts, which represents the investments made to acquire and train people to expected levels of effectiveness in their respective occupations, less the amortization of this investment based upon expected tenure.[*] This is not the same as the idea, repugnant to so many people, of trying to put a cash value on individual employees: rather, the concept is one of developing methods for measuring an organization's investment in its staff and the rate at which those particular inputs are more productive than others. This approach relies on the historical cost of acquisition and development to give a present cost of replacement. It is thus primarily a method of monitoring how managers are utilizing their human resources over time; linking human asset accounting with conventionally measured business results will enable better insights on preferred management strategies of allocating, maintaining, and utilizing human resources. As a negative example of such strategy (but which serves to highlight the importance of including human assets in an accountancy system) Likert[†] makes the point that certain managerial styles have the effect of liquidating human assets while producing short-term increases in profit. Conventional accounting reports an increase in profit, but the deterioration in the attitudes and motivation of employees and the increases in labour turnover, followed by costs of hiring and training replacements, result in reduced profits in the long run.

This American system requires a series of accounts to be opened for each manager, covering: recruitment outlay and acquisition costs; familiarization; formal and informal training; and development costs. Included in these accounts as investments in human assets should be all outlays which have an expected value extending beyond the current

[*]Annual Report of the R. G. Barry Corporation, 1970.
[†]*The Human Organisation, Its Management and Value*, R. Likert (McGraw-Hill, 1967).

accounting period (usually one year). Thus the costs involved in recruiting and inducting a new manager are amortized over the whole working life of that person with the organization; outlays on his/her training and development are amortized over shorter periods of time. In this way what may be called the 'opening value' of a new employee is increased by further enhancing expenditure and decreased by amortization and wastage, for example, which diminish his/her asset value.

This approach has recently been further developed by the use of replacement cost methods. Historical costs, as already set out, are converted to current values in the same way that some companies provide for amortization on plant by estimating the cost of replacing each item with something similar at the end of its useful life.

The method developed jointly by the IPM and ICMA* has the primary objective of placing some value on the human resource so that it can be included in normal credit/debit transactions. It would thus be useful in describing the total asset situation, for share evaluation and takeover purposes. It is concerned with total remuneration, together with a multiplier derived from the price:earnings ratio of that company.

This multiplier method is based on the assumption that there is no direct relationship between costs incurred on individuals and their value to an organization at a particular point in time. It is argued that there are many factors of motivation, attitude, and working environment which affect a person's value to the organization and which can only be expressed in subjective terms. Hence the valuation method must itself be capable of representing these subjective factors in a financially quantifiable form. This is achieved by the use of a multiplier which, when related to pay, can be used to weigh the value of different grades of staff within a total value for the organization.

Practical applications

The main benefit which must be claimed from this sort of analysis lies in the need to calculate the return on all investments. Unless it is made clear that expenditure on training and development offers long-run benefits and increases the profit-earning capacity of a company, it may be regarded as an expenditure the firm can only afford when profits are at a high level and may be dispensed with as soon as profits turn downwards.

Human Asset Accounting, W. J. Giles and D. F. Robinson (IPM and ICMA, 1972).

As an example of the wider implications of human asset accounting, the problem of redundancies* may be considered. Present calculations concern the amount of compensation which will be incurred as a charge against the revenue of the company. In addition, personnel managers and trade unions are greatly concerned about the social and personal impact of redundancy decisions. In terms of human asset accounting, redundancies represent the scrapping by one user of a valuable resource and its transfer into a community pool from which it can be withdrawn and put to work by another. The unqualified factors in this process are: the real efficiency of the existing use of the resource; the cost to the community of retraining the redundant person; and the comparative cost of retention and retaining within the present user organization.

The efficiency of the use of human assets could be demonstrated by recalculating returns on capital to include this element in addition to conventionally measured assets. Clearly, if a company is relatively unprofitable and overstaffed this will only highlight a known deficiency. None the less the existence of a valuation and the need for an acquiring company to show how it intends to utilize the assets would represent a considerable advance. Equally, an awareness of the value and return on human assets should create a real incentive for management to be more efficient. It could well forestall situations in which human assets are scrapped as part of a programme of stripping more tangible assets. It should also help management to decide on what is fair compensation in individual cases. Also, if the current and potential asset values of employees threatened with redundancy could be related to the retraining and unemployment costs which will fall on the community, more rational decisions could be taken within government on supportive policy.

Accountancy and personnel management

Predictably, the novelty of this whole concept has led to criticisms, both from personnel managers and accountants. The concept itself has been challenged, and pointed questions asked about practical applications and the suggested measurements of asset values.† Nevertheless, although the techniques may call for refinement, the underlying philosophy is undoubtedly coming to be more widely accepted. In

*'Progression Human Asset Accounting', D. Robinson, *Personnel Management*, March 1973.
†'Human Resource Accounting − a critical comment', J. A. Cannon, *Personnel Review*, Summer 1974, pages 14–20.

summary this may be restated thus: the employees of an organization are a valuable resource and it is important to know how valuable. They have great potentialities if properly trained, organized, and motivated: the effects of the programmes designed to realize these potentialities must therefore be properly evaluated.

Personnel policy objectives can be stated in the language of key business ratios, such as:

1 Sales value per employee.
2 Profit per employee.
3 Added value per employee.
4 Costs per employee.

or by expressing employment costs as a percentage of sales value, profit or added value. There are a number of advantages in using such quantifiable measures, not least that the business objectives become 'sold' as part of the personnel policies. The discipline of examining training objectives, for example in terms of sales value or added value, brings out what can be assessed and raises the useful question – why is this training programme being proposed, if it cannot be related to the business?

This sort of analysis provides a realistic assessment of what part personnel management can play in the achievement of wider business goals. The model ensures that personnel specialists integrate their activities closely with top management and that they serve a strategic purpose by using their professional techniques, like all other managers, to spot business opportunities which contribute to profit objectives.

The closer and growing contacts between accountants and personnel specialists have been an interesting phenomenon in recent years. One example is an attempt to develop a cost-effective approach* to industrial safety and health at work. Expenditure on reducing industrial risks could be distributed more efficiently, and measures to improve safety and health standards at work should be related to their efficiency in reducing human and material costs: this is the concept underlying the approach.

In the past, prevention costs have been generally ignored in discussions on the costs of accidents. Setting up a safety programme imposes a financial cost on an enterprise and contributes nothing directly to output. At whatever level the prevention cost is fixed, it is likely that some accident risk will remain. If the prevention programme is increased at additional cost, the risk level should fall, and

*Research paper for the Robens Committee, T. Craig Sinclair, Science Policy Research Unit, University of Sussex (HMSO, 1972).

with it the cost of accidents. Therefore an economic optimum can be determined, and a relationship worked out between cost and risk for a particular industry or firm to provide a quantitative means of assessing priorities. Areas can be selected which will give the greatest return in terms of accident cost reduction for a given outlay, and in this way management can be provided with guidelines for framing policy.

As a practical example, Sinclair's analysis shows that while the risk of death in agriculture is ten times that in pharmaceuticals and equal to the risk in steel-handling, the expenditure on accident prevention in agriculture is less than 2 per cent of that in pharmaceuticals and less than 10 per cent of that in steel-handling.

Methods must be evolved to produce this sort of information about human assets readily, otherwise the administrative inconvenience involved will detract from acceptance. Once this has been done, the whole concept will become more attractive: the very idea that employees are a resource which is valuable and must therefore be utilized as such, rather than being an unmeasurable factor of production, is potentially a major step forward in the efficient management of organizations.

Further reading

Cost Effective Personnel Decisions, J. A. Cannon (IPM, 1979).

22

Auditing the personnel management function

In the ultimate, the success of any business organization, private or public, comes as the result of the efforts of its employees effectively aimed at attaining the desired objectives. The nature of its achievements is a direct reflection of the abilities of everyone involved, from the board of directors to the lowest-graded worker. In assessing its own efficiency, management must consider this factor of the *quality* of employees above all, as well as the organizational structure within which they will work. No business can rise above the capacities of its staff; unless ratings of individual abilities are positive for the majority of employees, then it is unlikely to be successful or to develop in the future. The organization itself must function smoothly, too; even the best staff cannot work efficiently unless their responsibilities are clearly defined and there is an effective structure for the various levels of its hierarchy. The necessary information is clearly available within every business, and it should be used to carry out regular, objective assessments of individual abilities and organizational efficiency, which in turn should lead to action to correct defects and improve performance.

The purpose of this final chapter is, in effect, to summarize the main points made throughout the book by presenting a checklist which will enable personnel managers to *audit* the activities of their particular department, methodically reviewing their whole range by reference to acknowledged good practices. The continuing theme to be kept in mind during this process is that every aspect of personnel management has an impact in two ways: one on business efficiency and the other on the individual employees involved. Both must be taken into account in assessing the success of the personnel management function.

Techniques for managing total labour resources

Yes/No   Action

1 Has the organization a *manpower plan*? In detail, is the following information readily available:
   (a) An organization chart?
   (b) Precise job descriptions for all posts shown on the organization chart?
   (c) An estimate of future labour requirements for five years ahead?
   (d) A training and development programme, designed to meet the estimated labour requirements?
   (e) A recruitment programme, designed to fill anticipated gaps?
   (f) A genuine assessment of the impact on these detailed plans of such imponderables as technical advance, sociological changes, and other local, national, or industry-wide factors?
   (g) A procedure for keeping the manpower plan under constant review, so that it is flexible above all else?
2 Has the organization *personnel policies* which are written, published, and fully understood by all employees?
3 Do the staff of the personnel department adhere to a *recruitment procedure* based on:
   (a) Receipt of a full job requisition from the departmental head?
   (b) A full analysis of the job, if this is not already available?
   (c) Familiarity with all local sources of labour supply: above all, friendly, personal contact with the job centre manager, careers advisory officer, and careers masters in schools and colleges?
   (d) Continuous check on the response, cost, and effectiveness of staff advertising?
   (e) Adequate training of all recruitment officers in the techniques of dealing with applications, taking up references, and interviewing candidates?
   (f) The use of selection tests and group selection methods where appropriate?

Yes/No   *Action*

(g) The fullest preparation of members beforehand, when panel interviews are arranged?

(h) Follow-up of successful candidates to validate the selection techniques used?

4 Are the problems associated with *transferring* employees dealt with realistically throughout the organization?

(a) Are supervisors impressed with the need to spot signs of trouble which may eventually lead to transfer requests?

(b) Do managers have a positive attitude towards transfers, recognizing that some changes are inevitable if an organization is to grow?

5 Does a clearly defined policy and procedure for *promotion* exist within the organization?

Have these matters been resolved:

(a) Seniority or merit as the basis for promotion?

(b) The extent to which senior appointments shall be filled internally or by recruitment from outside?

(c) Providing members of promotion boards with full job descriptions, and their training in selection and assessment techniques?

6 Is there a *dismissal procedure* which is fully understood by management and employees?

Does this allow individuals the right to state their case personally?

And does it allow the right to appeal against dismissal decisions?

Has a redundancy policy been prepared, in consultation with worker representatives, so that it is available should the need ever arise?

In the event, does the policy provide for everything possible to be done to minimize the number of redundancies and to help those affected to find other jobs?

7 In striving to obtain optimum use of available labour, is special attention given to the problems of employing:

(a) Married women?

(b) Older people?

(c) Disabled workers?

(d) Imigrant workers?

Have senior management agreed a code of 'affirmative action' in applying the Race Relations Act?

8 Is *training* viewed positively throughout the organization as the best means of increasing the productivity of all grades of staff?

(a) Are training needs assessed effectively in the first place, priorities settled, and standards defined?

Yes/No   *Action*

(b) Is a development programme then established for each individual likely to benefit from further training?

(c) Does the organization provide its own training officers by withdrawing executives from line management for short periods?

(d) Are those responsible for training and job instruction properly qualified in the relevant techniques?

(e) Have the advantages of using separate job instruction areas been fully evaluated, as opposed to the 'understudy' method?

(f) Do line managers fully accept the fundamental importance of training-on-the-job, as opposed to sending subordinates on infrequent external courses?

(g) Nevertheless, is the best use made of all the training facilities provided outside the organization?

(h) Are employees who return from outside courses positively encouraged to apply the techniques learned and to develop new ideas?

(i) Are relationships with neighbouring organizations such that a 'training circuit' can be arranged?

(j) Are results of all training efforts followed up and evaluated?

(k) Is full advantage taken of the range of opportunities presented by the Training Agency?

9 Do *rates of pay* allow for any flexibility within the limits imposed by collective agreements, legislation, and government policy?

10 Is management prepared to face up to the realities of getting rid of *restrictive practices* through *productivity bargains*?

11 Does management take the *initiative* in improving working conditions and in developing better methods of wage negotiation?

Is it feasible to boost morale by a programme of regular changes in the working environment?

12 Has the organization a clearly defined attitude towards *trade union membership* of its employees?

13 Is management practice such as to encourage *shop stewards* to act in a constitutional manner?

Does management help in ensuring that shop stewards are adequately trained for their tasks as worker representatives?

14 Is *joint consultation* practised positively, as a method of obtaining employees' views on problems and proposed changes before final decisions are taken?

(a) Do senior staff take the lead in encouraging joint consultation?

(b) Are important items included on joint committee agenda?

Yes/No   *Action*

15 Are the barriers to effective *communications* fully understood throughout the organization?

Do the job descriptions for managers and supervisors make clear their responsibilities for communications?

Is the concept of a feedback mechanism emphasized as a means of ensuring that communications are understood?

(a) Are notice boards efficiently controlled?

(b) Does the organization publish a house journal or newssheet?

(c) Are employees issued with a handbook containing information about the organizations's structure, policies, working conditions and the rules of conduct?

Is any one executive charged with ensuring that the communications system throughout the organization functions efficiently?

16 Are checks made to ensure that a *consistent disciplinary policy* is applied by all managers and supervisors?

17 Is *labour turnover* accurately recorded, and constructive use made of the information thus provided?

Are exit interviews arranged with leavers, and followed up by management action on any deficiencies revealed?

18 Are *welfare services* provided for the right motives?

Are social activities largely administered by the employees taking part in them?

19 Are there differences in the way '*staff*' and '*workers*' are treated in the organization?

Is anything being done to remove these differences?

20 Does the organization's provision for the *health* of employees exceed the minima laid down by statute?

Are occupational medical services provided?

21 Are continuous efforts made to impress on all employees that *accidents* will only be prevented when they accept responsibility as individuals for working safely?

22 Is optimum use made of *outside organizations* and the various types of help they can offer in solving personnel problems?

23 Is the personnel records system able to produce whatever management control information is required quickly and accurately?

Getting the best from individuals

24 Are individuals provided with precise *job descriptions*?

25 Are they properly *inducted* into the organization when they start?

Especially school-leavers?

26 Are *standards* of job performance clearly laid down?

27 Is there a regular formal *assessment* of how well these performance standards are being realized?

28 Are managers kept aware of research findings about the behaviour of individuals at work and the ways they function in groups?

    (a) Is the organization willing to participate directly in research work in this field?

    (b) Do managers know how to promote *job satisfaction* and remove the *frustrations* which individuals experience at work?

    (c) Are managers and supervisors readily accessible to their subordinates?

29 Are the principles of *participative management* encouraged within the organization?

    In particular:

    (a) Do staff agree *targets* with their superiors for improved performance?

    (b) Is special attention given to *enlarging the jobs* of individuals, and is the application of this concept discussed with them by superiors?

    (c) During performance reviews, do staff help to identify *organizational shortcomings* which hinder progress?

    (d) Does the organization run a *suggestions scheme* to encourage individuals' ideas on increasing productivity?

30 Is *joint consultation* practised in ways which allow problems to be dealt with by those employees whose working lives are directly affected?

    (a) Initially to share in deciding the rules and regulations governing the behaviour of individuals in the workplace?

    (b) To sit in judgment on any breaches of these rules?

    (c) To try to exercise some measure of control over absenteeism?

    (d) To share in the continuous campaign for safe working throughout the organization?

31 Are the techniques of *job evaluation* and *merit-rating* used to reward the efforts and talents of individuals?

32 Are employees interviewed by their departmental heads when they return to work after *absence*?

    Are they visited by someone from the organization during periods of absence which last longer than three days?

33 Is special attention given to the *conditions* in which individuals work (e.g. environment, types of work, hours)?

34 Could the social problems of *shift working* be overcome by adopting a Continental system of shifts?

35 Have supervisors and managers been trained in an effective procedure for dealing with *individual staff problems*?

Much of what has been advocated above as being good personnel management practice has now been incorporated in the provisions of the TULRA 1974 and 1976, EPA 1975, the EP (Consolidation) Act 1978, and the codes of practice issued by ACAS following all this legislation. Some aspects of the Employment Acts of 1980, 1982 and 1988 and the Trade Union Act 1984 and the Trade Union and Labour Relations (Consolidation) Act 1992 must also be taken into account. It may therefore be said that there is now an 'official view' of good personnel management practice, at least in part, which may be audited in the following manner:

Yes/No   Action

1 Is it clear which managers are responsible for *recruitment?*
Are they aware of each individual's rights under current legislation?
Do they ensure that each job applicant is informed of his/her rights to belong to a trade union?
Do they keep a written record of the reasons for rejecting unsuccessful applicants?

2 Do *contracts of employment* provide written notice to all employees of periods of notice?
Do they provide full details of holiday entitlements?
Do they give each employee in writing the name (or job title) of the person with whom grievances can be raised, and also outline subsequent steps in the formal grievance procedure?

3 Are specific managers designated with authority to *dismiss* employees?
Are they aware of what constitutes fair dismissal?
Does dismissal procedure encompass the following stages:
(a) Oral warning?
(b) Written warning?
(c) Opportunity for an employee to state his/her case, and to be accompanied by his/her trade union representative?
(d) Right of appeal to a higher level of management?
Are written records of all dismissals kept for at least a year?

4 Do all your organization's procedural and substantive *agreements* comply with the terms of the Act?
Do they match up to the recommendations of the ACAS code of practice?

5 Are your organization's policies as regards union *recognition* and the *representation* of manual, white-collar, and managerial staffs settled and clear?

6 Do all voluntary recognition agreements specify precisely the categories of employees they cover? (Great help in the

Yes/No   Action

future in forming bargaining units and in avoiding inter-union competition for members.)

7 Are all employees issued with an *annual statement* of the organization's activities?

Does the information provided conform with Stock Exchange rules?

Do you ensure that your own managers receive this information beforehand?

8 Have you reviewed all existing procedures for the settlement of disputes in the light of the relevant Codes (adherence to which will be important evidence in unfair practices hearings)?

9 Have you established which union representatives with whom you deal have the *authority to call strikes?*

10 Are your *works' rules* of conduct up to date, and do they comply with the requirements of the Act?

11 Are you aware of the facilities available to help settle disputes?

The tasks of the personnel manager have already been described as basically those of advising on the planning necessary to make optimum use of total available labour resources and how to derive most benefit from each individual's abilities. If all the criteria listed above are accepted as good practice, then the job of the personnel manager is obviously a difficult one. It will involve hard work, some tedium (preparing precise job descriptions, for example), and a measure of embarrassment and discomfort when dealing with individual personal problems or tough negotiations with worker representatives. The fact remains that these difficulties cannot be shirked for the sake of 'a quiet life' – they must be tackled, and successfully at that, if personnel management is to become increasingly respected as an honourable profession.

Cost effectiveness and the personnel function

In considering objectives and the implementation of new personnel management projects, ideas, and actions designed to achieve them, current economic conditions ever more insistently require that the principles of cost effectiveness and productivity are taken into account. This, too, like the audit approach, can best be done by following a recognized procedure in a disciplined manner:

1 The proposed activities must be closely defined, in discrete packages, specifying objectives, employees likely to be affected, and probable time-table.
2 Any legal requirements associated with such activities should be identified, and must be given high priority.
3 The feasibility of activities must be assessed in terms of:
   (a) The necessary skills required for implementation already being available within the organization.
   (b) Ease of implementation: the extent to which the proposed activities are likely to be acceptable to line managers.
   (c) The net economic benefits: i.e. the cost effectiveness of each activity.
   (d) The economic risks: can the organization afford not to undertake the proposed activities?

Clearly, a crucial feature concerning implementation is the willingness of line management to cooperate, since attitudes, organizational structure and policies, and managerial styles will all probably be involved – and they are all difficult to change. Equally important is the estimation of potential benefits and cost, and hence a calculation of the financial impact of the proposed activities. Quantifiable data should be used wherever possible, and pilot studies will often produce the best evidence in this respect. Target benefits may also be suggested, derived from a preliminary estimate of results to which the personnel managers are prepared to commit themselves. Intangible benefits, for example, effects on morale or staff development, should also be included.

Finally when the feasibility of all activities has been assessed in this manner it should be possible to rank the proposals in priority order, according to legal requirements and economic benefits, allocate required resources, and then proceed with implementation. Complete management control must then be exercised by means of a continuous monitoring and evaluation process.

On to the year 2000

A brief review of 'futuristic' literature points to expectations among senior managers and personnel specialists of great opportunities for business growth and personal development of employees. Those organizations which are poised to make the most of such opportunities possess the following characteristics:

1 Objectives which focus on achieving ever increasing quality and effectiveness throughout the whole chain of the customer satisfaction process.

2 Targeted on long-term shared goals and values.
3 Implementing strategies and plans which have been developed participatively.
4 Organized in structures combining decentralized decision-making and effective coordination and cooperation.
5 Reinforced by extensive networks of alliances with suppliers, distributors and partners.
6 Developing managers who are both leaders and coaches.
7 In which the full potential of all staff – their imagination, creativity, intelligence and enthusiasm – is mobilized, realized and recognized.

A major lesson of history (repeatedly obvious since the Second World War, yet still not learned) is the need for higher rates of investment in the modernization of plant and equipment and in education and training. Too often in the recent past full order books have resulted in attention being devoted only to immediate production needs, consequently leading to complacency; whereas our industrial rivals, especially in Germany and Japan, have continuously emphasized research, improvement and change.

Key personnel management issues which must be faced over the next decade or so certainly include: the development of higher staff retention rates; the need to improve organizational career structures for scientists and engineers to aid both recruitment into those professions and to stop people moving from them for more money and prospects abroad or in other specialisms; the development of a philosophy of continuous change; improvement in the degree of collaboration between specialists in business, emphasizing the values of working as teams; above all, the urgent need to tackle the issue of education and training – in particular, more investment and extension of the time allowed for education and training offered to our young people before and after they start work.

Further Reading

Work 2000 – the future for industry, John and Celia Stanworth (Paul Chapman Publishing, 1991).

Appendix 1
Addresses of organizations

1 The Institute of Personnel Management, IPM House, Camp Road, Wimbledon, London, SW19 4UW.
2 The Industrial Society, Robert Hyde House, 48 Bryanston Square, London, W1H 8AH.
3 The British Institute of Management, Management House, Parker Street, London, WC2B 5PT.
4 The British Association for Commercial and Industrial Education, 35 Harbour Exchange Square, off Marsh Wall, London E14 9GE.
5 The Royal Society for the Prevention of Accidents, Industrial Safety Division, 52 Grosvenor Gardens, London, SW1.
6 The Tavistock Institute of Human Relations, Tavistock Centre, Belsize Lane, London, NW3.
7 Institute of Manpower Studies, Mantell Building, University of Sussex, Falmer, Brighton, BN1 9 RF.

Appendix 2
Human relations in Japan

Comparative studies take many varied forms, from individual personnel officers visiting each other's departments to large scale international study tours. Their practical value is that participants almost
invariably return to their own bases with some new useful ideas which
will improve the practice of personnel management within their own
organizations.

The point can perhaps best be made with an example – an account
of the findings of a small study tour* which went to Japan to
investigate, *inter alia*, how Japanese firms achieved their much-vaunted
employees' commitment towards running their organizations efficiently. In fact, the way that Japanese managers handled human
relations made a striking impact on their British visitors, who
concluded that, whereas in the UK 'personnel policy' normally is
aimed at either the minimization of problems from the workforce or
organizational controls and mechanisms in respect of terms and
conditions of employment, in Japan it is a positive policy for the
maximization of the individual employee's commitment and contribution to the good of the organization. The higher the level of individual
commitment, the more secure the employees – enlightened self-
interest.

Japanese lessons must be understood, however, in the context of
Japanese culture, in which the values of harmony, loyalty and respect

---

*Reported in the *Employment Gazette*, August 1983, page 371.

for hierarchy stand out particularly and provide for a very disciplined and organized society. Equally it is apparent that the rights of individuals are subordinated to the collective good of groups and of society as a whole. The need for consensus as opposed to conflict is fundamental.

The structure of employment must also be grasped in order to appreciate the efficiency/human relations equilibrium achievement. Companies have two categories of employee: regular workers (70–75 per cent of the total labour force) and part-timers (25–30 per cent). The regulars are taken on from high school or university, are given life-long employment, and are members of the labour unions. Female workers leave when they get married as a matter of custom. Part-timers will normally be employed on short contracts, will therefore have no life-time employment, will receive inferior conditions of employment including wages, will not belong to labour unions, and will be given the most menial tasks to perform.

The significance of this structure lies in the flexibility it offers when business conditions require reductions in the size of the direct labour force. This can be done successfully, without impairing life-time employment for regular workers, principally through product diversification. Such success has been the answer to many problems, yet equally the safety valves of being able to dispose of part-time labour readily and having significant guaranteed natural wastage of young female regular workers, as well as being able to dispose of labour-intensive sub-contractors, also provide opportunities for the companies to maintain true life-time employment for regular workers.

It must also be appreciated that Japanese labour unions have different objectives from British trade unions. Britain has a structure of national unions which have members in a multitude of industries. In Japan the labour unions are organized on company lines, with some coordination at national level. The objectives of the unions are to encourage the growth and stability of the companies and from that growth to ensure the security and prosperity of their members. Thus they regard of fundamental importance that the companies remain prosperous and efficient. While their philosophies do not rule out industrial action, such action is incompatible with their normal thinking. Regular consultations take place at local level and include sales, profits, production schedules and overtime requirements. New technology is sometimes included, although this is considered unnecessary in other companies as it could have no impact on the security of regular workers' jobs.

Most of the organizations visited had written and public statements of personnel policy. Backed up by reinforcing techniques and slogans, induction training, departmental job rotation, counselling, personal development, individual commitments to quality/productivity/effort recorded in the personnel department or in writing in front of the worker concerned – the overall impact was one of enormously impressive coordinated common commitment to the strength and growth of the organization.

Supportive to this fundamental orientation of 'personnel policy', a number of practices were noted:

(a) Safety: very low accident figures, with safety receiving consider-able propaganda support and inculcated as an individual respon-sibility through induction, action groups and campaigns. The strong onus is on individual responsibility for safety.

(b) Job organization: rotation is used in many organizations for personal development. No distinction is recognized between mechanical and electrical crafts. A difference is drawn between normal and sophisticated maintenance, but the aim is to progress normal maintenance staff through training to the level of sophisti-cated maintenance staff.

(c) Discipline: all the organizations worked to clear rulebooks; they expected and received very high level of compliance with rules. Discipline is not enforced by stringent supervision but rather by group pressures and self-discipline.

(d) The labour force takes responsibility for their immediate physical environment, keeping it clean, organized and tidy. The cumulat-ive effect is one of efficiency and a work-conducive environment. Protective clothing is commonly worn, even shoes for indoor use to keep the floors clean and tidy.

(e) Sporting facilities: consistent with developing a young, hard-working and company-orientated workforce, extensive sporting and social facilities were provided by the companies to ensure fit bodies and full occupation of spare time.

(f) Suggestion schemes: these are frequently found in Japan, of large size but usually with low rewards. The Japanese firm, Sharp, claimed that they had received 15,000 suggestions in the previous year. Provision of suggestions by employees is expected and seen as part of their commitment to the betterment of the company.

(g) Quality circles: with different names and with different emphases, quality circles, involving all employees and operating out of hours, were in evidence in most factories in Japan.

From a visit such as this a number of suggestions emerged which might very well benefit the practice of personnel management in Britain:

1 Employee commitment was seen as being as important as the quality of designs or equipment to the success and growth of the organization. To this end a number of factors require attention if real unity of purpose is to be achieved:
   (a) The elimination of artificial status barriers.
   (b) The development of an approach to work organization which allows for employees to undertake meaningful roles and make a positive contribution to the success of the organization.
   (c) The introduction of an approach to management development which allows for managerial resources to be developed in a broad and rounded fashion in-house to cater for the organization's immediate and long-term managerial needs.
   (d) Improvements in two-way communications about the organization's performance, policies and future.
   (e) Greater individual responsibility for work, quality and environment.
   (f) Major improvements in the standard of housekeeping in factories.
2 Training efforts must be increased to develop skilled craftsmen into multi-skilled craftsmen and sophisticated machinery technicians; to develop committed young employees prepared to make their careers within the organization; to develop new skills for new roles in the face of rapid technological change; to achieve significantly higher levels of individual safety consciousness; and to develop sound labour relations based on formal industrial relations training.
3 At all the factories visited in Japan the delegation were enormously impressed by the standards of reception they received: all sites had attractive product displays, guests were clearly expected, greeted on arrival, and all in all an impression of welcome was clearly conveyed.

However, the overall conclusion must be that the lessons to be learnt from Japan cannot be reduced to mere techniques to be taught on training courses and subsequently applied in a mechanistic manner. What is really required is a change in the managerial process as a whole to reflect the Japanese experience. A key point is that the work must be planned and organized properly, involving those who do the work. The aim must be for everyone to work 'smarter' and more effectively, rather than just with greater effort. Then the need to recognize and develop employees as assets is very apparent. This includes treating training and development activities as investments rather than as costs, drawing upon employees' talents and ideas, and involving them fully in their work and the decisions affecting them at work.

Specifically, employee relationships as a whole should be revised to ensure that they reflect teamwork, a sense of common purpose, greater identification of areas of agreement, fewer and less significant status differences between employees, greater reward for experience, loyalty and merit, and recognition of the non-economic as well as the economic needs of employees. Improving everyone's quality of working life is not inconsistent with applying these lessons, but is rather an essential element in devising new methods for success.

Index